The Family, Society,
and the Individual

The Family, Society, and the Individual

SEVENTH EDITION

WILLIAM M. KEPHART
The University of Pennsylvania

DAVOR JEDLICKA
The University of Texas at Tyler

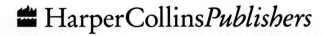 HarperCollins*Publishers*

Sponsoring Editor: Alan McClare
Project Editor: Ellen MacElree
Art Direction: Lucy Krikorian
Cover Coordinator: Lucy Krikorian
Cover Design: CIRCA 86, Inc.
Cover Photo: Terry Farmer/Tony Stone Worldwide
Photo Research: Mira Schachne
Production Assistant: Linda Murray

The Family, Society, and the Individual, Seventh Edition

Library of Congress Cataloging-in-Publication Data
Kephart, William M.
    The family, society, and the individual / William M. Kephart and
Davor Jedlicka. — 7th ed.
        p.   cm.
    Includes bibliographies and indexes.
    ISBN 0-06-043287-X
    1. Family.   2. Family—History.   3. Family—Cross-cultural
studies.   4. Family—United States.   5. Mate selection—United
States.   I. Jedlicka, Davor.   II. Title.
HQ503.K46   1991
306.85—dc20   90-43374
                                               CIP

90   91   92   93   9 8 7 6 5 4 3 2 1

Contents in Brief

Contents in Detail

PART *FOUR*
MARITAL INTERACTION AND THE FAMILY LIFE COURSE   239

PART *FIVE*
THE FAMILY AND SOCIAL CHANGE 319

Preface

The human family has many dimensions and many variations and is studied by a number of academic disciplines, including anthropology, communication, home economics, nursing, psychology, religion, social work, and sociology. *The Family, Society, and the Individual,* Seventh Edition, while primarily sociological, is also interdisciplinary. We take a broad liberal arts approach and draw from the findings of all areas of family research.

The Family, Society, and the Individual has been used at over 1000 colleges and universities during its first six editions because students and faculty have liked it. They appreciate its clear writing style, frequent use of meaningful examples, and broad topical coverage that reflects the latest findings from the many areas of the family field.

This edition of *The Family, Society, and the Individual* contains a variety of fresh material reflecting changes in the family, the society, and the academic disciplines that study them. The roles of women, attitudes toward the unmarried and the divorced, sexual attitudes and behavior, and the significance of stepparents are undergoing important changes—and the changes are, by all signs, ongoing. A new chapter, "Pregnancy and Parenthood without Marriage," introduces interesting research on single mothers and fathers and their children. The chapter on family functions has been enlarged, with new emphasis placed on the expanding health care function of maturing families.

The widely acclaimed chapter on Black Americans has been updated and expanded with improved coverage of black family strengths. The sections on mate selection, always among the favorites with undergraduates, have been rewritten to reflect the latest research. And the chapter on the Old Order Amish has also been completely revised: as you will see, major changes are underfoot in Amishland!

Thorough updating of this edition reflects the impressive developments in family research. The challenge has been to incorporate the various changes without impairing the flow and readability of the book. These have always been hallmarks of *The Family, Society, and the Individual,* and we are confident that they remain so.

The Family, Society, and the Individual has been immeasurably strengthened by the comments and suggestions of a number of interested persons—both users and nonusers of the text. Special thanks, in this regard, are due to: Lois Bryant, University of Missouri (Columbia); Terry A. Dean, Rose State College (Midwest City, OK); Stan Davis, Monroe Community College (Monroe, MI); Mark G. Eckel, McHenry County College (Crystal Lake, IL); Carol Mosher, Jefferson Community College (Louisville, KY); Barbara Risman, North Carolina State University; Glenn W. Samuelson, West Chester University (West Chester, PA); Marios Stephanides, Spalding University (Louisville, KY); and Gipson Wells, Mississippi State University.

William Kephart
Davor Jedlicka

ONE

Cultural and Historical Setting

Chapter
1

Introduction: Perspectives on the Family

The basic purpose of any society is to sustain itself over a long period of time. To do so each generation must (1) produce enough children to maintain a satisfactory population level and (2) raise the children so that they willingly participate in the social and institutional life of the society. Although utopian and futuristic views often portray a world where both of these tasks are accomplished without the family, it is the family—our oldest institution—that continues to sustain societies and perpetuate cultures.

Their universality suggests that all families have certain functions in common. Yet family organization varies substantially from one society to another, and also within the same society. In the United States, for example, family characteristics vary according to social class, religion, ethnic background, and historical experience.

In the study of preliterate societies, emphasis is often placed on the roles of husband and wife and the socialization of children. In our own highly industrialized society, however, it is also important to study the links between the family and the social forces that act upon it.

What these forces are, and how they relate to the family, has been the subject of much debate—within the framework of both theory and research.

And while the debate is by no means settled, we will focus on those aspects that seem to be of interest both to family theorists and to undergraduates.

THE INDIVIDUAL-SOCIETAL PERSPECTIVE

One of the difficulties in formulating a theoretical perspective on the family is that the aims and desires of the individual sometimes conflict with the goals of society. One example is the number of children needed for replacement. Demographers call this number *replacement-level fertility*. When individuals decide that it is not in their interest to have two or three children, the population of that society will eventually start to decline. In fact, fertility in at least eleven European countries has remained below replacement level for several years.[1] Theoretically, these countries could eventually become extinct.

In the past, parents' need for their children as old age security helped to motivate people to have a number of children, but today in many countries children no longer fill that function. Instead, couples tend to be motivated by the emotional satisfaction of parenthood. Yet that motivation may not be as strong as the former economic dependence on children. As a result, society and the individual find themselves at cross-purposes regarding the optimum number of children.

Individuals' aims and desires also can conflict with the goals of society when laws and regulations that serve society's best interests restrict the freedom of some individuals or groups. Unrestricted freedom as regards mate selection, sexual behavior, marriage, and divorce would benefit some individuals, but for society as a whole it is quite possible that chaos would result.

For example, it might seem at first glance that if a husband and a wife are unhappy and want a divorce, they should be entitled to one. Why is it necessary for the law to spell out certain grounds? After all, if the couple are unhappy, whose concern is it but their own? It might be that the best interests of this particular man and woman would be served by waiving all legal proceedings and permitting them to go their separate ways. A moment's reflection, however, will reveal some fallacies in such a procedure.

For one thing, if it were recognized and accepted that couples could dissolve their marriages at will, the whole process of mate selection might lose much of its significance. What is the need to exercise caution and wisdom in selecting a marriage partner if one's mate can be discarded for any reason whatever? And if a second marriage proves to be less rewarding than anticipated, why not try for a third?

---

[1]Lincoln H. Day, "Numerical Declines and Older Age Structures in European Populations: An Alternative Perspective," *Family Planning Perspectives*, May–June 1988, 139–43.

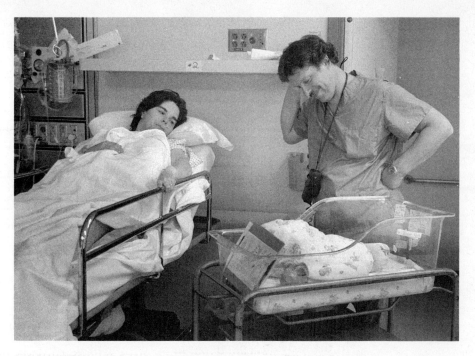

Each generation must produce enough children to maintain a satisfactory population level. (© *Palmer, The Picture Cube*)

Under such a system, who would provide for the support of children born of these unsuccessful marriages? How would the rules of inheritance operate? What would prevent couples from separating for the most trivial of reasons? Would it be possible to uphold the monogamous form of marriage, or would the matrimonial institution as we know it be in grave danger?

Suppose, on the other hand, that in order to preserve the institution of marriage, laws were passed stipulating that no one would be permitted to marry unless he or she could pass rigid physical examinations and intelligence tests and that a couple, once married, would be required to stay married and produce children in accordance with a quota set by the state. An institutionalized system of this kind also would invite social chaos. What would happen to the sexual and familial needs of all those who failed the qualifying examinations? How could individual desires with respect to the number of children be reconciled with official quotas?

Theoretically, when society establishes institutional bonds so tight as to ignore the individual's needs, the social fabric weakens under its own tension. Conversely, when the institutional bonds are loosened to the point where individual desires are indulged at the expense of society, institutional breakdown may also occur. Social institutions are most effective as stabilizing forces when they reconcile the needs of society with those of the individual.

THE FAMILY FUNCTIONS

In 1934, William F. Ogburn contended that the American family had lost many of its traditional functions to other agencies, such as the school, the church, and the state.[2] His report fueled the debate about societal encroachment on family functions. On one side of the debate are those who agree with Ogburn that the family functions are disappearing, or decreasing in importance, and that the family is weakening. On the other side are those who believe that the family today is as strong as ever. The middle view is that family functions are adjusting to social change. As society becomes more complex and more demanding, the family may rely more strongly on societal support. Therefore, social institutions today share in performing traditional family functions. Let us examine this proposition in greater detail.

The Economic Function

In the early days of our country, the American family was an economically producing unit. The first settlers built their own homes, constructed their own furniture, raised their own food, and made many of their own clothes. Mother, father, sons, and daughters all cooperated in the necessary economic endeavors. Hareven notes that

> as long as the household functioned as a workshop as well as a family home, there was no clear separation between family life and work life. Even though preindustrial families contained large numbers of children, women invested relatively less time in motherhood than their successors in the 19th century and in our time did and still do. The integration of family and work allowed for an intensive sharing of labor between husbands and wives and between parents and children that would not exist in industrial society.[3]

Gradually, however, with the rise of factories and power machinery, the manufacture of both hard and soft goods passed from the home. Most families no longer raised their own food, but bought it. Today there is a minimum of home baking, and what little baking there is tends to be of the instant-mix variety. Practically all clothing, bedding, and furnishings now

---

[2]William F. Ogburn and Clark Tibbitts, "The Family and Its Functions," *Report of the President's Research Committee on Social Trends in the United States* (New York: McGraw-Hill, 1934), 661–708.

[3]Tamara K. Hareven, "American Families in Transition: Historical Perspective Change," in Arlene S. Skolnick and Jerome H. Skolnick, eds., *Family in Transition* (Boston: Little, Brown, 1986), 43.

Table 1.1 POVERTY FOR NONFARM AMERICAN
FAMILIES, 1987

Size of unit	Poverty level	Minimum income needed for an additional person
1 person	$ 5,779	$1619
2 persons	7,397	1659
3 persons	9,056	2555
4 persons	11,611	2126
5 persons	13,737	1772
6 persons	15,509	2140
7 persons	17,649	1866
8 persons	19,515	3590

Source: U.S. Bureau of the Census, *Statistical Abstract of the United States: 1989* (Washington, DC, 1989), 420.

are bought, and such activities as cooking, cleaning, and laundering can be provided by suppliers outside the home.

These changes, as might be expected, have had a marked effect on American domestic life. The family no longer produces anything as an economic unit. Since the passage of compulsory-school legislation and child-labor laws, children have become economic liabilities instead of assets. It is hardly surprising, then, that some family textbooks today make no mention of the economic function, while others refer to it only as a historical fact. Yet it is a serious mistake to conclude that the modern family has no economic function. The economic function of the family may not be obvious, but it exists. Think, for example, of the family as the means of increasing economic security by virtue of its living arrangement. If family members take responsibility for cooking, cleaning, nursing, and other household services, the difference between what it would cost to have these services performed by someone outside the family and the cost of obtaining these services from family members contributes to economic security.

Consider also the familiar argument that "two can live more cheaply than one." Usually the rent for two persons is not double the rent for a person living alone. Similarly, just about as much heat energy is needed to prepare one meal as two. As much energy is needed to heat or cool a home for one resident as for two. In fact, living together is so efficient that some individuals could remove themselves from poverty through marriage or cohabitation, as the figures in Table 1.1 show.

According to these figures, a person living alone needs at least $5779 to live on the edge of poverty. If two people with poverty-level incomes live together, however, their combined income will be above the poverty line. In 1989, the poverty level for two people living together began officially at $6493, whereas two combined individual poverty-level incomes exceed

Home entertainment can help a family share common interests. (© *Lewin. The Image Bank*)

$11,000. This extra monetary advantage could make a difference in how well parents fulfill their obligation to raise and educate their children.

The Socialization and Education of Children

Learning begins as soon as a child is born, but learning does not take place in a vacuum. The child learns from adults, usually by observing and listening to the parents. Children also learn indirectly through daily interaction with parents and others around them. Through this process, known as *socialization*, a child learns the necessary language, customs, and skills. If socialization goes well, a child is likely to develop a positive orientation toward others and toward self.

A subcategory of socialization is the educational function of the family. In colonial America education was much more likely to be a family function than it is today. Children were likely to follow their parents' footsteps; hence the educational process was largely vocational. In later periods some schooling was available, but the terms were short and for the greater part of the year the children were at home, working.

As society became more complex, formal education seemed to take over that function from the family. Only recently have research findings revealed that the family remains essential not only in socializing but also in educat-

Parents are their children's first and most influential teachers. (© *Crews, Stock, Boston*)

ing the young. A recent report by the U.S. Department of Education found the role of the family to be as important as ever, as summarized in these words:

> Parents are their children's first and most influential teachers. What parents do to help their children learn is more important to academic success than how well off the family is. Parents should create a "curriculum of the home" through daily conversations, household routines, attention to school matters, and affectionate concern for their children's progress.[4]

Because sociologists have not yet learned the extent to which socioeconomic forces influence the family's ability to provide educational services, much controversy surrounds these findings. Obviously, parents with superior education and a higher income can provide much more at home than parents with poor education and a lower income. On the other hand, the children of Indochinese refugees, most of whom came to the United States "without money, with no or little knowledge of English, and few if any marketable skills," are among the most successful students in high schools and

[4]William J. Bennett, "The Role of the Family in the Nurture and Protection of the Young," *American Psychologist*, March 1987, 246.

colleges across America. Their success is said to depend on their families' values of "hard work, educational achievement, and family cohesiveness."[5]

togetherness

The Health Function

In recent years much has been learned about the importance of family cohesiveness in maintaining good health and recovering from illness. A strong, nurturing family seems to be good for both mental and physical health. Even traumatic injury may be easier to overcome when there is a family at home.[6]

Perhaps more than any other profession, nursing historically has recognized the family as "the unit of care."[7] Whall notes that from the beginning of nursing as a profession, Florence Nightingale worked with the wives and children to heal the wounded soldiers. Over the years this emphasis shifted from family-centered care to strictly individual care, but today some of the old traditions are being revived, especially during the treatment of mental illness.[8]

One reason for this revival is that families already are absorbing a major share of care for even the most seriously ill patients.[9] For example, most schizophrenic individuals in this country live with their families, where the environment seems to retard rather than promote relapse. In general, families of psychiatric patients have a positive influence on recovery rates.

Marriage in general tends to improve life chances, especially for men. Swan reports that "single men suffer a mortality rate nearly double that of married men and triple that of single women"[10] In his review of the literature, the same author cites even more convincing findings:

> Divorced men between the age of thirty-five and sixty-four have a mortality rate three times as high as divorced women and two and a half times as high as married men. Divorced men die at a rate one third higher even than single men. These figures for widowed men are only slightly lower than for divorced men.[11]

---

[5]Ibid., 247.

[6]Ellen J. MacKinzie et al., "Factors Influencing Return to Work Following Hospitalization for Traumatic Injury," *American Journal of Public Health,* March 1987, 329–34.

[7]Ann L. Whall, "The Family as the Unit of Care in Nursing: A Historical Overview," *Public Health Nursing,* vol. 3, no. 4, 1986, 240–49.

[8]David Spiegel and Terry Wissler, "Using Family Consultation as Psychiatric Aftercare for Schizophrenic Patients," *Hospital and Community Psychiatry,* October 1987, 1096–99. See also Nick Kates and Jan Hastie, "The Family and Schizophrenia: Recovery and Adaptation," *International Journal of Mental Health,* vol. 15, no. 4, 1987, 70–79.

[9]Spiegel and Wissler, 1099.

[10]George Steven Swan, "The Political Economy of American Family Policy, 1945–85," *Population and Development Review,* December 1986, 744.

[11]Swan, 744.

Marriage seems to prolong lives, especially men's lives. If suicide rates are a measure of mental disorder, married women also seem to fare better than the unmarried. In general, changes in marriage and divorce rates in our society can have a profound effect on the mental health of the American people.

OUR PRESENT FAMILY SYSTEM: WEAKNESSES AND STRENGTHS

On the one hand, the American family is reported as a weak institution, with most of its traditional functions taken over by other institutions. On the other hand, the family is still called "the backbone of the nation." Let us examine both riders of the argument.

Weaknesses

Those who view American family life as weak point to the consistently high divorce rates through the 1980s. More than one million divorces took place each year; more than half involved at least one child under eighteen years of age.[12] More than one million children have been involved in divorce each year since 1972. The chances of a child's parents being involved in a divorce are three times greater today than in 1950.

Divorce is a legal severance of marriage, but it is by no means the only index of marital disruption. Many persons who cannot afford the cost of a formal divorce desert their spouses or separate informally. Other couples persist in living together even though their marriages bring more sorrow than happiness. This category includes both spouse abuse and child abuse.

Of more than passing concern is the number of single teenage girls who become mothers. Each year, more than 10,000 girls have babies before their fifteenth birthday.[13] Another 26,000 become mothers before their sixteenth birthday. Most of these girls must raise their children without the child's father.

Some observers believe that our lax marriage and divorce laws have contributed to family disorganization, and it must be admitted that these laws and their implementation leave much to be desired. Americans are permitted to marry at extremely young ages. In several states, young people may wed at age fourteen, or even thirteen.[14] Moreover, our marriage laws

---

[12]National Center for Health Statistics, "Advance Report of Final Divorce Statistics, 1986," *Monthly Vital Statistics Report,* vol. 36, no. 8, December 1987. "Annual Summary of Births, Marriages, Divorces, and Deaths: United States, 1988," *Monthly Vital Statistics Reports,* vol. 37, no. 13, July 1989.

[13]National Center for Health Statistics, "Advance Report of Final Natality Statistics, 1986," *Monthly Vital Statistics,* vol. 37, no. 3, July 1988.

[14]*The World Almanac and Book of Facts 1989* (New York: Newspaper Enterprise Association, 1988).

are so constituted that if a couple are underage in the state where they reside, there is nothing to prevent them from crossing state lines and marrying in a jurisdiction with a lower age requirement.

Our divorce laws have been in a state of flux, leaving many litigants confused. Although procedures assigning fault have given way to the no-fault system, many states have some combination of fault and no-fault grounds. In some states the legal grounds seem to be little more than convenient catchalls for all kinds of marital squabbles. If the couple wish to expedite matters and to travel to one of the "quickie" divorce states, such as Nevada, there is no real legal impediment.

Finally, a number of social commentators have pointed with alarm to the increase in obscenity, pornography, and nonmarital sexual behavior. The mass media, it is contended, have been inundated with tasteless, gratuitous violence and sex. The movies in particular seem to have forfeited their claim to being an art form and have lost most of their adult audience.

Some observers believe that such an atmosphere undermines the very structure of marriage to the detriment of the children, the family, and society. One popular writer summarizes this view in these words:

> Because family life has been so badly damaged over the past several generations, many millions of children have been denied the best kind of mothering and fathering and family life. As a consequence our society is filled with millions of adults who cannot make family life succeed; hence, the high divorce rate, the high illegitimacy rate, the large number of people who live together in various kinds of arrangements short of marriage and so on.[15]

This is rather a pessimistic view, at least according to the critics. Little wonder, they say, that public opinion polls support the belief that the American family is indeed in trouble.

Strengths

Supporters of the American family system maintain that the rising divorce rate is merely an indication of increased freedom to dissolve unpleasant relationships. They also contend that most Americans do not approve of such things as pornography and extramarital sex, and certainly most Americans abhor wife and child abuse. In fact, in the 1980s sociologists tended to see strengths in areas where few saw them a decade ago. Not only is divorce seen as a possible solution for problems, but stepfamilies are described more in terms of strengths than of weaknesses.

Much of this change in views is based on improved knowledge through research. A recent study showed that stepchildren have no more problems than other children, popular belief to the contrary. If additional research

---

[15]Harold M. Voth, *Families: The Future of America* (Chicago: Regnery Gateway, 1984), 57.

confirms these findings, we can expect children's socialization to proceed successfully even after divorce and remarriage.[16]

Recent research also has shown that the family health-care function is an important strength. Social and medical scientists working together have found that prevention of illness, effective treatment, and speedy recovery are influenced significantly by the family. The family function in health care goes beyond the nurturing role for ill members. It seems that the very knowledge that one is cared for in times of crisis because of love and not because of duty has a therapeutic value in itself.[17]

Perhaps people have sensed all along that ours is still a family-centered society because the strengths of the family still outweigh the weaknesses. The fact that over 90 percent of both sexes continue to marry suggests that marriage still has much to offer. Even when marriages fail, a full 80 percent of all divorced persons remarry.[18] This high percentage is even more remarkable when it is realized that many persons do not remarry only because of a lack of opportunity.

Let us mention finally the position of women and children in our society. Until fairly recently, wives were expected to be subservient to their husbands. Denied the opportunity to work outside the home, forbidden by law to vote or to hold public office, deprived of formal education, limited in their legal rights, women traditionally were relegated to second-class citizenship. In some societies this state of affairs continues. In our society, however, inequalities between the sexes have been greatly reduced.

Children, too, have been accorded legal and educational rights. Free public education, child-labor laws, juvenile courts, social and athletic programs, and counseling services now are taken for granted. The most important change, however, has been in connection with the attitude toward children. Today there is a sincere conviction that the formative years are crucial in the development of character and personality and that America's future indeed lies in the hands of its children.

SUMMARY

All things considered, many sociologists have come to the conclusion that despite certain points of strain, the family in America has adapted to social and economic changes and has retained some important functions. Among

---

[16]Marlyn Coleman, Lawrence H. Ganong, and Ronald Ginrich, "Stepfamily Strength: A Review of Popular Literature," *Family Relations*, October 1985, 583–89.

[17]William J. Doherty and Hamilton I. McCubbin, eds., "The Family and Health Care," special issue, *Family Relations,* January 1985.

[18]Ann Goetting, "The Six Stations of Remarriage: Developmental Tasks of Remarriage After Divorce," in Arlene S. Skolnick and Jerome H. Skolnick, eds., *Family in Transition* (Boston: Little, Brown, 1986), 351.

Star chart for keeping track of chores. Today, there is a sincere conviction that the formative years are crucial in the development of character and personality of children. *(Weisbrot, Stock, Boston)*

these are procreation, the socialization and education of children, the economic function, the health function, recreation, and the emotional-sexual function.

Although academic study of the family is largely the province of sociologists, other groups—marriage counselors, psychologists, anthropologists, home economists, health specialists, communications specialists—have also contributed to our knowledge. Sociologists, however, are the only group who systematically study behavior and social organization from the individual and societal perspective. It is this perspective, developed within the broader framework of the family field, that is the subject of the present volume.

QUESTIONS

1. Sometimes it is said that the more things change, the more they remain the same. How might this saying apply to the American family in flux?

2. What did Ogburn mean by "changing family functions"? Would his contention apply to your own family?

3. Discuss how marriage can enhance an individual's economic status. Use figures to support your argument.

4. Most observers believe that the American family has both weaknesses and strengths. On the basis of your own observation, select what you consider to be the major weaknesses and strengths. Support your choices.

5. Do you believe that all social institutions—the state, the church, the family, the economic system—have both strengths and weaknesses, or is the duality applicable mainly to the family? Refer only to institutions within our own society.

6. It is believed that in some sections of the United States, desertions and separations exceed the number of divorces. Why should this be so? That is, what factors or combination of factors in our society might account for this phenomenon?

7. What exactly is meant by the individual-societal approach to the study of marriage
and the family? In your opinion, could this approach be used in the study of other social institutions? Defend your position.

8. How might the study of the family aid in the advancement of the individual? Of the society?

SELECTED READINGS

Baker, David P., and Doris R. Entwisle. "The Influence of Mothers on the Academic Expectations of Young Children: A Longitudinal Study of How Gender Differences Arise." *Social Forces,* March 1987, 670–695.

Bennett, William J. "The Role of the Family in the Nurture and Protection of the Young." *American Psychologist,* vol. 42, no. 3, March 1987, 246–250.

Berger, Eugenia H. *Parents as Partners in Education,* 2d ed. Columbus: Merrill Publishing Company, 1987.

Bossen, Laurel. "Toward a Theory of Marriage: The Economic Anthropology of Marriage Transactions." *Ethnology,* April 1988, 127–144.

Bradley, Robert H., Bettyle M. Caldwell, and Stephen L. Rock. "Home Environment and School Performance: A Ten-year Follow-Up and Examination of Three Models of Environmental Action." *Child Development,* vol. 59, no. 4, August 1988, 852–867.

Cheal, David. "Strategies of Resource Management in Household Economics: Moral Economy or Political Economy?" In *The Household Economy,* edited by Richard R. Wilk, 13–22. Boulder: Westview Press, 1989.

Clark, Synthia A. "Family Variables Affecting the Transmission of Religious Values from Parents to Adolescents: A Review." *Family Perspective,* vol. 21, no. 1, 1987, 1–21.

Clausen, John A. "Health and the Life Course: Some Personal Observations." *Journal of Health and Social Behavior,* December 1987, 337.

Dornbusch, Sanford M., and Philip L. Ritter. "When Effort in School Does Not Produce Better Grades: A Family Environment Affects a School Process." *Family Perspective,* 1987, 285–298.

Dutton, William H., Everett M. Rogers, and Suk-Ho Jun. "Diffusion and Social Impacts of Personal Computers." *Communication Research,* April 1987, 219–250.

Futrell, Mary Hatwood. "Public Schools and Four-Year-Olds: A Teacher's View." *American Psychologist,* March 1987, 251–253.

Glass, J., V. L. Bengtson, and C. C. Dunham. "Attitude Similarity in Three-Generation Families: Socialization, Status Inheritance, or Reciprocal Influence." *American Sociological Review,* October 1986, 685–698.

Krein, Sheila F., and Andrea H. Beller. "Educational Attainment of Children from Single-Parent Families: Difference by Exposure, Gender, and Race." *Demography,* May 1988, 221–234.

Krener, P. G., S. I. Abramowitz, and P. B. Walker. "Relation of Family Factor to Treatment Outcome for Bulimic Patients." *Psychotherapy and Psychosomatics,* 1986, 127–133.

Lee, Cameron. "Theories of Family Adaptability: Toward a Synthesis of Olson's Circumplex and the Beavers Systems Models." *Family Process,* March 1988, 73.

Maclean, Morag, P. Bryant, and L. Bradley. "Rhymes, Nursery Rhymes, and Reading in Early Childhood." *Merrill-Palmer Quarterly,* July 1987, 255–282.

Margavio, A. V., and Jerome Salomone. "Economic Advantages of Familism: The Case of the Sicilians of Louisiana." *Sociological Spectrum,* 1987, 101–121.

Nock, Steven L. "The Family and Hierarchy." *Journal of Marriage and the Family,* November 1988, 957–966.

Sprey, Jetse. "Current Theorizing on the Family: An Appraisal." *Journal of Marriage and the Family,* November 1988, 875–890.

Tavitian, Mark L., Judith Lubiner, Laura Green, Lawrence C. Grebstein, and Wayne F. Velicer. "Dimensions of Family Functioning." *Journal of Social Behavior and Personality,* May 1987, part 1, 191.

Whall, Ann L. "The Family as the Unit of Care in Nursing: A Historical Review." *Public Health Nursing,* vol. 3, no. 4, 1986, 240–249.

White, O. Z. "Some Myths Related to the American Family." In *The American Family,* edited by F. B. Burdine et al. Victoria, TX: The Victoria College Press, 1988, 75–86.

Wright, Lorranine M., and Maureen Leahey. *Families and Chronic Illness.* Springhouse, PA: Springhouse Corporation, 1987.

Chapter
2
Cross-Cultural Patterns

In every society the family fulfills certain functions necessary to sustain both the individual and society. Among these functions are reproduction, socialization of the young, transmittal of inheritance, and regulation of sexual behavior. These functions are so common throughout the world that they are called *cultural universals*.

These cultural universals vary in their application. And it is the variations that contribute to *ethnocentrism,* the feeling that one's own culture is superior to other cultures. In everyday life it seems that people tend to accentuate cultural differences more than cultural similarities, thus allowing ethnocentrism to flourish. To avoid ethnocentrism, social scientists try to evaluate each culture in terms of its own values, history, and adaptation to nature.

This concept of understanding each culture on its own terms is called *cultural relativism*. The concept is useful for observers of variations in courtship, marriage rituals, kinship structures, and orientation toward love and sex. At first, these variations may strike an outside observer as strange, unusual, or even unnecessary. Despite appearances, however, each culture maintains social order through the most universal of all regulatory institutions: marriage and the family.

THE FORMS OF MARRIAGE

Among the hundreds of different cultures in the world, none is characterized by sexual promiscuity as a dominant way of life. It can be even said that restrictions of sexual intercourse to socially acceptable partners is another cultural universal, usually practiced through marriage. Possible forms of marriage include the following:

Group marriage	Marriage of several women to several men
Polygamy	Polyandry: marriage of one woman to several men Polygyny: marriage of one man to several women
Monogamy	Serial monogamy: remarriage permitted after divorce or widowhood Strict monogamy: marriage to one spouse until that spouse's death Even stricter monogamy: no remarriage even after spouse's death

Group marriage, although it has been known to occur, is rare. Polygamy and monogamy, on the other hand, are widespread. There are specific reasons why promiscuity is not accepted as a culturally approved alternative to marriage. These reasons may offer an explanation for the universality of marriage.

Promiscuity

Although the term is often applied to casual or indiscriminate premarital sexual affairs, *promiscuity* refers to unbridled sexual interaction, or "sex without rules." In a promiscuous society, every male would be eligible to mate with every female, with blood ties no barrier. Although such a situation is found among animal species, it does not exist at the human level; all cultures have strong rules governing sexual pairings. Most of these rules are based on age and blood relationships, although some preliterate groups also have elaborate intraclan prohibitions.

Actually, promiscuity is incompatible with any known type of human social organization. If people were allowed unlimited sexual freedom, problems involving jealousy and conflict might be insurmountable. Females would be subject to sexual exploitation. Systematized promiscuity, moreover, would make it difficult to maintain an effective child-rearing program. Lacking both family life and a protective environment, children might have to fend for themselves at an early age.

Under a system of promiscuity, it is easy to visualize group bedlam; indeed, survival itself would become a problem. The human species can

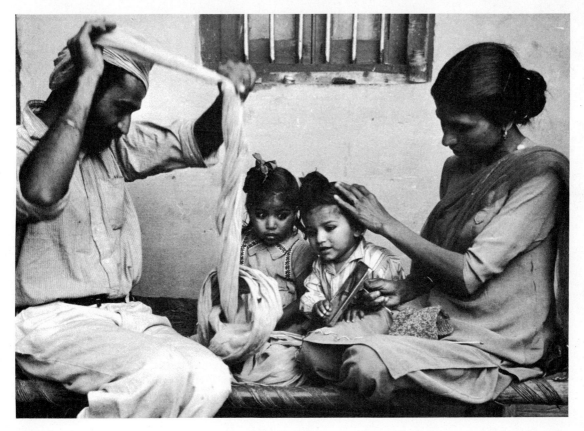

Child-rearing patterns and other elements of family life vary substantially from one culture to the next. *(Ken Heyman)*

withstand almost an infinite amount of hostility and fighting, from interfamily feuds and tribal clashes to modern warfare, but to ensure survival of the species the sexes must accommodate one another. The relationship must be enduring enough to provide protection, care, and reasonable security for the offspring. Although the forms of marriage may vary, evidence from small preliterate groups as well as from our own complex society shows that the institution of marriage and the establishment of an integrated family system are of prime importance.

Group Marriage

Earlier anthropologists such as Frazer, Morgan, Westermarck, and Briffault wrote extensively about the subject, but it seems unlikely that *group marriage* has ever existed as the dominant type of marital union. It would be more realistic to think of this form as a theoretical construct than as an institutionalized form of matrimony.

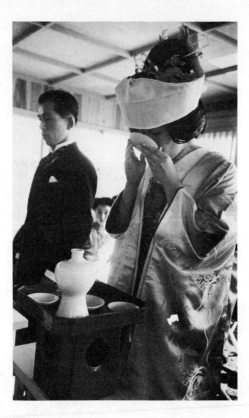

Japanese marriage ceremony. There are a number of cultural variations relating to marriage customs and wedding celebrations. The purpose of these various rituals is to impress upon young people the importance of marriage. (© *Werner Bischof, Magnum Photos*)

A moment's reflection will make it clear why group marriage is virtually nonexistent. Most important, it has no advantages over the other marital forms. Problems of jealousy on the part of both sexes would be intensified. How would the incest taboo be enforceable in group families containing dozens of children of unknown paternity? How would questions of inheritance, property rights, and lineage be handled?

Although there is a distinct difference between promiscuity and group marriage, in neither case are the advantages great enough to warrant adoption by society, especially since more practicable forms of marriage are available.

Polyandry

Polyandry, the less common form of *polygamy,* involves marriage between one woman and two or more men. Among the best-known polyandrous societies are the Todas of India, the Sherpa of Nepal, the peasants of Tibet, the Kandyan Sinhalese of Sri Lanka, and the Marquesans of Polynesia. A common characteristic of all polyandrous marriages is that the husbands usually have some prior relationship to each other. Often they are brothers or business associates.

When the prescribed pattern of marriage requires the brothers to marry the same woman, the practice is known as *fraternal polyandry*. Even when the husbands are brothers, a common problem of polyandry is the difficulty in determining *paternity*. The ethnic Tibetans in Nepal handle this difficulty in favor of the eldest brother:

> The children are linked with the eldest brother in genealogies. He is addressed by a special term for father. The eldest brother and his mother address the children in terms which translate as son and daughter. The father's younger brother, by contrast, addresses the children by the term brothers use for their sisters' children. This term is also used by the sisters for their brothers.[1]

On the surface it appears that the problem of paternity was solved in this case. According to Levine's recent field study, however, the contention over establishing rightful paternity remains a sore point among younger brothers. Tibetans do not like to discuss the problem openly, but sometimes it is so serious that it leads to court action. In general, jealousy, problems with lineage, and distribution of inheritance tend to be recurrent difficulties in polyandrous cultures.

Polygyny

Polygyny is more widespread and more acceptable than any other form of marriage. It is practiced throughout Africa, the Middle East, and South and Southeast Asia. If it were not prohibited by law, it would probably flourish in China and among some ethnic groups in the United States. Even after these legal restrictions are taken into account, polygyny is still preferred in about 70 percent of all societies.[2]

At this point, it is important to distinguish between normative forms of marriage and actual marriages. Although most societies approve and even encourage some form of polygyny, in reality it is often unattainable by most people. Individual preferences, the expenses involved in supporting more than one wife, and the limited availability of partners constrain polygyny. By definition, polygyny is legal; otherwise it's bigamy. As a result, monagamy is prevalent even in polygynous societies.

One of the most interesting exceptions to this pattern is found in the mountains of Ecuador and Peru. This region is inhabited by some 20,000 aborigines called Jivaro (Hee-varo). Jivaros are probably known best for their ability to shrink human heads to the size of an orange, and for their

---

[1]Adapted from Nancy E. Levine, "Fathers and Sons: Kinship Value and Validation in Tibetan Polyandry," *Man,* June 1987, 277.

[2]John Friedl and Michael B. Whiteford, *The Human Portrait: Introduction to Cultural Anthropology,* 2d ed. (Englewood Cliffs, NJ: Prentice-Hall, 1988), 246.

Each culture maintains social order through the most universal of all regulatory institutions: marriage and the family. (© 1987, *Joel Gordon*)

prowess in battle. Jivaros also are proud of the fact that they have never been conquered by the white man. In addition, they are known as a society where some 90 percent of the females share husbands. It has been speculated that the Jivaro males run a great risk of being killed in feuds and wars; thus polygyny is a highly adaptive form of marriage.[3]

Serial Monogamy

It is no longer realistic to speak of monogamy in American society without distinguishing *serial monogamy* from traditional or strict monogamy. Serial monagamy is a form of marriage that combines the characteristics of monogamy and polygamy. At any one time, the basic household in a serial monogamous marriage consists of the husband, wife, and children. In some ways, however, serial monogamy is like polygamy because (1) a person can have more than one spouse, although not at the same time, and (2) more than one person can be a parent with the same partner. As relationships are broken and new ones are formed legally, there is a cumulation of relationships as in polygamy.

---

[3]For an interesting study of the Jivaros' way of life see Michael J. Harner, *The Jivaro* (Berkeley, CA: University of California Press, 1984).

At least three sets of relations exist in families practicing serial monogamy that are not present in strictly monogamous families: (1) the relation between ex-spouses, legally enforceable, as in the case of child support or alimony; (2) the relation between half siblings or unrelated children; and (3) the relation between children and the spouses who are not their biological parents. These relations have been studied under various titles, including "single-parent family," "custodial family," "stepfamily," "reconstituted family," "blended family," or simply "remarriage." In any case, these studies show an emerging awareness that serial monogamy produces new family forms deserving their own classification.

Strict Monogamy

The only form of marriage accepted by all societies is *monogamy*. Even where other forms are permitted, monogamy remains the most common marital practice. Although each society thinks that its own particular form of marriage is the most desirable, it is likely that in any absolute sense, monogamy has more to recommend it than any other form. In a monogamous system the following conditions obtain: (1) those at the customary marrying age have maximal opportunity to find a mate; (2) relatively few members are "left out" of marriage, as compared with polygynous and polyandrous forms; (3) an effective method of sexual gratification is provided for both men and women; (4) intrasex jealousies and quarrels, often a problem in polygamous forms of marriage, are held to a minimum; (5) sociolegal factors involved in inheritance, property rights, and lineage are relatively easy to handle; (6) the emotional needs of the spouses—needs associated with primary-group response—are fulfilled more effectively in monogamous marriages than in any other form; and (7) child-rearing practices can be aimed effectively at establishing close emotional ties between parents and children.

Although some of these propositions can be debated, they seem to be borne out by the fact that in practice, the overwhelming majority of the earth's inhabitants follow the monogamous form of marriage.

CONSANGUINE VERSUS CONJUGAL EMPHASIS

Whatever form it takes, marriage is a way of building kinship relations between families. "Kinship" refers to relations among people who consider themselves relatives, either by birth or by marriage. The word "system" is used because each culture has its own definition of kinship roles. Individuals either are born into these roles or acquire them systematically through marriage. Kinship systems have many variations, but they all tend to emphasize either consanguine or conjugal systems of relations.

When Americans visualize marriage, often they think of a sequence that involves dating, falling in love, a fairly elaborate wedding followed by

Marriage is a way of building kinship relations between families. (© 1982, *Joel Gordon*)

a reception, a honeymoon, and a fresh start in a new home. This last item has come to signify the break with parents, for in our society, people are reluctant to marry unless they can manage on their own. Families formed in this manner, on the basis of individual mate selection and a "go-it-alone" philosophy, are known as *conjugal families*. In the strongly developed conjugal system that prevails in our society, "marriage" and the "family" tend to be functionally similar, if not synonymous.

Although the conjugal family seems natural to Americans, many non-Western societies emphasize a *consanguine family* system, in which "marriage" and the "family" are quite distinct from one another. In a consanguine family the emphasis is on blood relatives. When a couple marry, their allegiance is to their original families; in fact, they may live with or near the husband's or the wife's family, depending upon such factors as whether descent is *patrilineal* or *matrilineal*.

If we think of the two systems as extreme, or polar types, a contrasting pattern emerges. The conjugal family system emphasizes individual mate selection, romantic love, sexual attraction, independent residence, strong husband-wife ties, and bilateral descent. In the consanguine family system the emphasis is placed on mate selection by the respective families rather than by the individuals concerned, residence with the wife's or the husband's family, unilateral descent (i.e., matrilineal or patrilineal), and strong blood ties.

In a structural sense the conjugal family is fragile because divorce, desertion, or a spouse's illness or death disrupts the household, with the likelihood that the children will be affected adversely. Families based on consanguine relationships, in contrast, can withstand a variety of such stresses and strains. Death and divorce have relatively little effect on a large kinship group. The consanguine family is better equipped, economically and psychologically, to take care of aged members, a problem that has never been solved satisfactorily in our own society. In addition, it is probably true that family adjustment and cohesion are easier under a consanguine system.

On the other hand, a consanguine family tends to give relatively little heed to the sexual and romantic inclinations of its younger members, a policy that must give rise to numerous frustrations. Consanguine families also tend to grow in size. Although it cannot be demonstrated that large families satisfy the individual's emotional needs less effectively than small families, one wonders what family life is like when the numbers reach thirty, forty, fifty, or more.

PROPERTY RIGHTS AND INHERITANCE

The question of property rights and inheritance is associated with different kinship systems. Because the conjugal family is of relatively short duration, it has limited time in which to acquire property and material wealth. Moreover, whatever is acquired is normally divided among the children in every generation. The consanguine family, on the other hand, is well equipped to acquire material wealth and to "keep it in the family"; property and other holdings tend to become cumulative. In many countries consanguineal accumulation of wealth and power has been associated with privilege, titles, and social inequalities.

Despite the apparent stresses and strains involved, the conjugal family system seems to be most compatible with modern society. If the trend toward urbanism, industrialism, and mobility spreads to other parts of the world, it is possible that the consanguine type of family organization will tend to disappear along with polygamy.

THE UNIVERSAL TABOO: INCEST

Whether families are organized on a conjugal or a consanguine basis, all societies maintain strict prohibitions against sex relations and marriage between close blood relatives. This proscription, known as the *incest taboo,* is believed to be the most universal of all mores, even though sex relations between close blood relatives have been permitted or authorized in certain societies.

It has been noted, for instance, that among the Azande, a large African tribe, the highest chiefs are required to wed their own daughters. Ethnographic reports also have shown that at one time brother-sister marriages were permitted or even required in certain royal families, such as the Hawaiian nobility, the Incas of Peru, and the Ptolemies of ancient Egypt. Technically, therefore, incest would have to be defined as sex relations or marriage between persons who are *considered to be* too closely related. It should be mentioned, however, that despite the wide range of marital and sexual customs among the world's peoples, no reports of authorized mother-son marriages have ever been confirmed.

In addition to its universality, the incest taboo is one of the most rigidly enforced of all human behavioral proscriptions. Over the face of the earth, societies have used all available controls—formal and informal, sacred and secular—to ensure that sex and blood do not mix. These controls have become so effective that most people are repelled by the very thought of an incestuous relationship; indeed, it is difficult for us to visualize a functioning society in which sanctioned incest could coexist with any known type of family organization. In view of the pervasive importance of the incest taboo, it is interesting to speculate on how or why the interdiction arose.

Some of the earlier scholars, such as Hobhouse and Lowie, seemed to feel that there was an innate or instinctive aversion to sexual relations with blood relatives. There is no evidence for this belief, however. No such taboo exists among "other primates." At the human level, siblings reared apart have met as strangers, fallen in love, and married. As a matter of fact, not only does there seem to be no innate sexual aversion to blood relatives, but Freudian psychology is based on the assumption that there is an innate *sexual desire* for the parent of the opposite sex. This assumption, in turn, has been neither verified nor refuted empirically.

Another proposed explanation for the origin of the incest taboo hypothesizes that close association in the same household tends to discourage sexual attraction. This is a tempting theory, for it is known that the male animals of some species show an increase in their copulatory activity when new females are introduced into the experimental situation. At the human level it also would seem that "familiarity breeds indifference" and that adults are readily attracted to persons other than their own spouses. On the other hand, most married couples maintain a satisfactory sexual relationship over the years. Moreover, if household familiarity does foster sexual indifference or repugnance, it is difficult to explain the cases of incest that are known to occur. Incest occurs, at least sporadically, in all societies; as a matter of fact, it probably takes place more often than most people realize. In our own culture, for instance, such cases are often kept out of the newspapers.

Incidentally, in both of the foregoing attempts to account for the origin of the incest taboo—the "innate aversion" and the "close association" theories—it is hard to explain why such powerful regulations would be required for a supposedly self-enforcing restriction!

Still another proposed explanation for the existence of the incest taboo pertains to the necessity of maintaining generational roles and status within the family network. The son of a father-daughter union, for example, would be a half brother of both his mother and his uncle, the son of his own sister, and the son as well as the grandson of his father! The resultant problems involved in identity, role relationships, and lines of authority are hard to imagine.

One difficulty with this explanation is the tendency to project our own role system into the hypothetical incestuous culture. Should such a culture exist, the child of a father-daughter union would have a generational role quite different from our own. Even the "standard" kinship terms would be radically different from those we are accustomed to.

Only time will tell whether any of these theories will be refuted, modified, or substantiated. Meanwhile the research goes on, but the origin of the incest taboo remains a tantalizing mystery.[4]

COURTSHIP

Most societies consider the affectional relationship between spouses to be a desirable aspect of marriage. It is true that throughout most of the world romantic love is accorded less importance than in our own society. It is also true that in some groups it is the parents who arrange the marriage. Yet even in these societies an attempt is usually made to match partners who are believed to be mutually congenial.

The Bride Price and the Dowry

Earlier in this chapter we defined ethnocentrism, the belief that imputed negative interpretations of behavior in other cultures. To Western people the idea of *bride price,* a custom that requires the husband to pay a price to

---

[4]For current thinking on the theories of incest see Carroll McC. Pastner, "The Westermark Hypothesis and First Cousin Marriages: The Cultural Modification of Negative Sexual Imprinting," *Journal of Anthropological Research,* 42, no. 4, 1986, 573–86. See also David H. Spain, "The Westermark-Freud Incest-Theory Debate," *Current Anthropology,* December 1987, 623–45.

the bride's parents, often provokes ethnocentric interpretations, even when all parties concerned value the practice. The importance of remaining culturally unbiased under such circumstances is illustrated in the following example:

> A Colombian anthropologist was conducting field research among the Guajiro Indians in the northern part of the country and in the course of her work she learned that a particular Indian group there practiced the custom known as bride price. According to this tradition, when a man took a woman as his wife, he or his family was obliged to offer a payment (in cattle, other goods, money, or a combination of them all) to the bride's family.
>
> Although this is a fairly common practice in many non-Western societies (and elements of it can be seen in our own marriage customs, if you look closely), the anthropologist was upset by it because she felt that it challenged the dignity of a woman to be bought and sold like any other possession. It never occurred to her that while it might rob a woman of her dignity in Western society, it could have the opposite effect in the culture she was studying.
>
> Allowing her own values to come through she asked one recent bride if it didn't bother her to be purchased like a cow. The woman replied by asking the anthropologist how much her husband had paid for her when they were married. Of course, the anthropologist explained that her husband had not paid anything, that people did not do such things in her society. "Oh, what a horrible thing," replied the Indian woman. "Your husband didn't even give a single cow for you? You must not be worth anything"[5]

Next, let us consider the bride price in the Soviet Central Asian republic of Tadzhikistan. Instead of harmonious interchange among the parties concerned in marriage, recent reports from this republic tell of suicides among brides forced into marriage to men selected by parents who disregard their daughters' feelings. The guiding principle followed by these parents tends to be the size of the bride price. The man who can pay the most receives the right to marry, whether or not the bride approves. As a result, according to Soviet newspapers, 40 prospective brides in 1988 alone committed suicide by burning.[6]

The system known as the *dowry* also can have negative consequences, but usually it is benign because the parents in most cultures place their children's interests above the material value of the dowry. The dowry is a custom in which the bride's family makes payments to the groom's family as a part of the marriage contract. This custom was practiced widely in medieval Europe and still exists in India. Currently in some parts of India the dowry is suspected to be the motive behind money murders, disguised as a careless wife's "accidental" death. The practice, it seems, is for the husband to marry again and to receive another dowry. Presumably the prac-

---

[5]John Friedl and Michael B. Whiteford, *The Human Portrait: Introduction to Cultural Anthropology* (Englewood Cliffs, NJ: Prentice-Hall, 1988), 43–44.

[6]*Houston Chronicle,* Sept. 5, 1987.

tice of giving dowry is harmless if the norms of a culture support the long-term interests of the daughters as well as the sons.

Conjugal Courtship

When we turn to mate-selection practices that emphasize the role of individuals rather than that of the respective families, we are on more familiar ground. In all such practices, for example, it is rather common for young people to fall in love, even though the concept of romantic love is not so highly idealized in other cultures as in our own.

There is no need to go into the details of specific behavior during courtship. Lovemaking is much the same the world over; the male generally takes the initiative. In a few societies romantic activity is apparently less seclusive than in our own culture, and in a few groups the practice of kissing is reportedly unknown. But in general, caressing, kissing, fondling, love talk, and the desire for privacy—maneuvers that might be classified under the heading of "necking and petting" or "making out"—are more nearly the rule than the exception.

In our society a basic factor in attracting members of the opposite sex is physical appearance, and in other societies this is also true. Our standards of beauty, though, are not necessarily esteemed in other parts of the world. Anthropologists report that there are few, if any, universal standards of physical attractiveness. Some groups put a premium on thinness; others admire corpulence. Certain groups reportedly stress different traits such as eye color, skin color, or hair texture. In most societies, standards of attractiveness are more likely to be applied to the female than to the male; the latter are judged on such qualities as courage and prowess rather than on physical appearance.

PREMARITAL SEXUAL STANDARDS

Societies differ considerably in their views on premarital sex. Some groups place an extremely high premium on premarital chastity, while others take premarital intercourse for granted. Two of the most sharply contrasting societies in the world provide interesting illustrations of premarital "extremes." These are the Inis Beag, a society representing the sexual repressive extreme, and the Mangaia, a society at the opposite end of the scale.

Inis Beag, a European island community located off the coast of Ireland, is described by Hyde as follows:

> Premarital sex is essentially unknown. In marital sex, foreplay is generally limited to kissing and rough fondling of the buttocks. The husband invariably initiates the activity. The male-on-top is the only position used, and both partners keep their underwear on during the activity. The man has an orgasm

quickly and falls asleep almost immediately. Female orgasm is unknown, or at least, it is doubted to exist or is considered deviant.[7]

To illustrate the other extreme of human sexual behavior, Hyde describes the Mangaia, a South Pacific island community located 1800 miles northeast of New Zealand. In contrast to Inis Beag, sex is of paramount interest to the Mangaians. Boys begin to masturbate about the age of seven, and both boys and girls engage in sexual intercourse around the age of thirteen. Although sex is frequent and spontaneous in this society, it is not casual. The boys are trained to ensure that their partner experiences an orgasm. It would be no exaggeration to say that when males and females get together, it is for sexual purposes:

> The average "nice" girls will have three or four successive boy friends between the ages of thirteen and twenty; the average boy may have ten or more girl friends. Mangaian parents encourage their daughters to have sexual experience with several men. They want her to find a marriage partner who is congenial.[8]

Hyde further reports that around the age of eighteen, the Mangaians typically have sex every night of the week, averaging three orgasms per night. When they reach the age of forty-eight, they are reportedly having intercourse—with orgasm—two or three times a week.

Inasmuch as sexual behavior of the kind reported for the Mangaians is foreign to the views of most readers, we should ask whether such freedom is advantageous (setting ethical and religious considerations aside for the moment). From the individual viewpoint, a standard permitting premartial intercourse has much to recommend it, especially as far as young people are concerned, since they would then be permitted a legitimate sexual outlet without having to wait for the formalities of marriage. Moreover, if the stigma and social culpability attached to premarital intercourse are removed, young people are free from the guilt and remorse that might otherwise occur.

For the girl, of course, the possibility of premarital pregnancy is always present and would have to be used as an argument in the other direction—that is, toward upholding the ideal of premarital chastity. With advances in birth control techniques, however, this argument is probably diminishing in importance.

In keeping with the philosophy of this book, any absolute appraisal of premarital standards would have to meet the societal test: assuming that single people would benefit, does the sanctioning of sex before marriage actually benefit society as a whole? In one sense, this may be answered in the affirmative; that is, it can be argued that any activity that promotes the

---

[7]Janet Shibley Hyde, *Understanding Human Sexuality* (New York: McGraw-Hill, 1982), 18.

[8]Ibid., 19.

physical and emotional well-being of one segment of the population without infringing on the rights of other segments must be considered advantageous for society as a whole.

In another sense, the premarital sex question may be answered in the negative. If the only sexual activity permitted is marital coitus, a basic reason for marrying becomes that of achieving sexual gratification. When premarital relations are condoned, one of the motivating factors for marriage is removed. Since it is to the obvious advantage of society to have the bulk of its members married, premarital sexual latitude might operate against the overall societal interest. In societies where the motivation for marriage is reinforced by economic, cultural, or other considerations, premarital sexual privileges might not seriously affect the marriage rate, but in other societies the reverse might be true.

Comparative evaluations of premarital sexual patterns throughout the world are hazardous inasmuch as one can never be certain that the units of comparison are reasonably similar. In many preliterate societies, for instance, premarital sex is no great problem because, among other considerations, the age at marriage is quite low; both sexes marry shortly after puberty. Then, too, in most civilized societies the overall codes governing sexual activity are inseparable from the church and the law, both of which, as measures of social control, are often unknown among primitive peoples.

In answer to our original question, then, as to whether or not premarital sexual permissiveness benefits society as a whole, there can be no all-inclusive answer. A pattern that tends to stabilize one society might have a disruptive effect on another. Although some mores pertaining to sexual and marital behavior have near-universal value, premarital sexual regulations probably cannot be included among them.

EXTRAMARITAL SEXUAL RELATIONS

As might be expected, most societies disapprove of adultery. Where it is permitted—as will be explained below—a special situation is usually involved. This general disapproval is understandable, of course, because adultery strikes at the very heart of marriage. If marital fidelity were permitted to be taken lightly, competition over sexual partners, jealousies and clashes between spouses, neglect of children, or upsetting of homemaking routines might be expected to occur; in fact they often do occur whenever individual cases of adultery are discovered. As a result of the threat that adultery poses, most societies take measures to ensure that marital fidelity is rewarded and infractions are punished.

Some societies, nevertheless, sanction adulterous relationships during ceremonial orgies and fertility dances. These revelries are usually seasonal events, held in connection with tribal rites, such as imploring the gods to look with favor on new crop plantings. Another pertinent custom is the hymen-breaking ritual that occurs among certain primitive groups. Vividly described by earlier anthropological writers, these rituals often involve defloration and/or sexual intercourse with the bride by someone other than the husband—a tribal chieftain, for instance. Technically, this practice represents another example of sanctioned adultery.

Adultery occurs at least sporadically in all cultures for which reports are available, although how much or how often it occurs is difficult to estimate for obvious reasons. In most societies, extramarital indulgence on the part of the wife is considered more reprehensible than on the part of the husband. Because of this double standard, the incidence of adultery is higher for husbands than for wives.

Worldwide it seems likely that extramarital intercourse is increasing. This may be a reflection of a more permissive attitude toward behavior in general and toward sex in particular; "swinging" in our own society is a case in point. The social ramifications of this permissiveness, however, provide an interesting topic for debate.

Some observers believe that a tolerant, flexible attitude toward adultery is a good thing. They contend that as long as the individuals involved remain discreet in their outside affairs, as long as their own marriages are not disrupted—in short, as long as the "scandal" aspects are suppressed—the adultery, at worst, harms no one and in individual cases may actually serve to stabilize the marital relationship.

On the other hand, it can be argued that people tend to live up to and a little beyond the "rules." For example, in a twenty-five-mile-an-hour speed zone drivers tend to go thirty and thirty-five miles an hour, so that the law is only partially deterrent. But when the speed limit is raised to thirty-five miles an hour, drivers start edging up to forty- and forty-five-mile-an-hour rates. This analogy may or may not apply to sexual mores, but in the case of extramarital activities one could argue that tolerance leads to increase. It is quite possible that in most societies an overtolerance of sexual relations occurring outside marriage would have harmful effects on the institution of marriage, especially from a long-term perspective.

DIVORCE

Provisions for divorce are nearly universal and are of ancient origin, the first written regulation being incorporated into the Babylonian legal code of Hammurabi around 2000 B.C. This regulation provided that a husband could divorce his wife at will, with no stated reason required. Throughout much of Western history, divorce was considered more a prerogative for husbands than for wives, although at present most industrialized societies, including our own, accord equal rights of divorce to both spouses.

As might be expected, grounds for divorce vary from one society to the next. A review of the ethnographic literature shows that a few recurrent themes serve as the basis for divorce in most primitive groups, for example, adultery, sterility, economic incapacity, thievery, impotence or frigidity, desertion, and cruelty. These grounds also apply in most industrialized societies.

Although most groups have provisions for divorce, virtually no culture encourages it. The typical attitude seems to be that although divorce is regrettable and unfortunate, it is sometimes necessary. A number of preliterate groups have created impediments to divorce, such as imposing fines, prohibiting remarriage, levying alimony charges, or insisting that the bride price be returned. Industrialized societies, of course, apply religious, economic, and legal pressures to encourage the continuation of marriage. The one antidivorce measure used by virtually all groups is that of informal controls, including censure, gossip, disparagement, condescension, and other seemingly minor but traditionally effective social forces.

SUMMARY

As an aid to understanding our own society, this chapter describes a wide range of marital and sexual practices found in other societies. Some cultures permit sex before marriage; others impose severe restrictions. In our own society, it is illegal for a person to have more than one spouse at a time; yet in a number of cultures plural spouses are quite acceptable. Similarly, child-rearing practices, marital interaction, kinship structure, attitudes toward divorce, and other elements of family life show substantial variation from one society to the next.

Although cultural variation is important, we have also stressed underlying cultural uniformity. For instance, all societies regulate sex in some manner, and the most effective regulatory institution, in this respect, is the family.

QUESTIONS

1. What does the text mean by "cultural universals"? Give some specific examples.

2. What is the difference between polygamy and polygyny?

3. On a worldwide basis, most people practice monogamy. Why? What are the advantages of monogamy over the other forms of marriage?

4. On the scale ranging from one to ten, with one as the most permissive, where would you place contemporary premarital sexual standards in the United States?

5. A number of theories have been advanced regarding the origin of the incest taboo. Can you think of any theories or reasons other than those mentioned in the text?

6. How do sociologists and anthropologists use the terms *conjugal* and *consanguine* in regard to marriage? Do all systems of marriage belong to either the conjugal or the consanguine type?

7. In societies where a bride price is paid, how does the system actually work? Would such a practice be acceptable in our society? Why or why not?

8. Throughout the world, extramarital sex is generally regarded as more reprehensible than premarital sex. Why is this so? Is this view likely to change?

9. Do you believe that a system of premarital sex, such as that practiced by the Mangaians, would be feasible in a modern, industrialized society?

10. Provisions for divorce vary from absolute prohibition in some cultures to virtual divorce at will in others. How strict do you think divorce provisions should be in our own society? Justify your position.

SELECTED READINGS

Bernard, H. Russell, Peter D. Killworth, Michael J. Evans, Christopher McCarty, and Gene Ann Shelley. "Studying Social Relations Cross-Culturally." *Ethology,* April 1988, 155–180.

Coltrane, Scott. "Father-Child Relationships and the Status of Women: A Cross-Cultural Study." *American Journal of Sociology,* March 1988, 1060–95.

Denga, Daniel I. "Juvenile Delinquency among Polygynous Families in Nigeria." *Journal of Social Psychology,* June 1981, 3–7.

Dunfey, Julie. "Living the Principle of Plural Marriage: Modern Women, Utopia and Female Sexuality in the Nineteenth Century." *Feminist Studies,* Fall 1984, 523–36.

Engel, John W. "Marriage in the People's Republic of China." *Journal of Marriage and the Family,* November 1984, 955–61.

Haavio-Mannila, Elina, and Erkki Rannik. "Family Life in Estonia and Finland." *Acta Social,* 1987, vol. 30 (3–4), 355.

Hartung, John. "Polygyny and Inheritance of Wealth." *Current Anthropology,* February 1982, 1–8.

Hughes, Austin L. "Kin Networks and Political Leadership in a Stateless Society; The Toda of South India." *Ethology and Sociobiology,* vol. 9, no. 1, 1988, 29.

Imaizumi, Yoko. "Reasons for Consanguineous Marriages in Japan." *Journal of Biosocial Sciences,* vol. 19, 1987, 97–106.

Karki, Y. B. "Sex Preference and the Value of Sons and Daughters in Nepal." *Studies in Family Planning,* May–June 1988, 169–78.

Khatri, A. A. "Some Dimensions of the Asiatic Indian Family: A Quantitative Evaluation." *Journal of Comparative Family Studies,* Summer 1988, 261–72.

Lesthaeghe, Ron, and Dominique Meekres. "Value Changes and the Dimensions of Familism in the European Community." *European Journal of Population,* May 1986, 225–69.

Levine, Nancy E. "Fathers and Sons: Kinship Value and Validation in Tibetan Polyandry." *Man,* June 1987, 267–87.

Pastner, Carroll McC. "The Westermarck Hypothesis and First Cousin Marriage: The Cultural Modification of Negative Sexual Imprinting." *Journal of Anthropological Research,* 1986, 573–86.

Peters, John F. "Polyandry among the Yanomano Shirishona Revisited." *Journal of Comparative Family Studies,* Spring 1982, 89–96.

Poston, Dudley L., Jr., and Jing Shu. "The Demographic and Socioeconomic Composition of China's Ethnic Minorities." *Population and Development Review,* December 1987, 703.

Queen, Stuart A., Robert W. Habenstein, and Jill Sobel Quadagno. *The Family in Various Cultures.* New York: Harper & Row, 1985.

Rosenfeld, A. "Freud, Psychodynamics, and Incest." *Child Welfare,* November–December 1987, 485–96.

Spain, David H. "The Westermarck-Freud Incest-Theory Debate: An Evaluation and Reformulation with Comment." *Current Anthropology,* December 1987, 623.

Ullrich, H. E. "Marriage Patterns among Havik Brahmins: A 20-Year Study of Change." *Sex Roles,* June 1987, 615–35.

Welch, Charles E. III, and Paul C. Glick. "The Incidence of Polygamy in Contemporary Africa." *Journal of Marriage and the Family,* February 1981, 191–93.

Wilson, Barbara F., and Kathryn A. London. "Going to the Chapel." *American Demographics,* December 1987, 26–31.

Chapter
3

Historical Perspective

In the past, family texts often minimized the historical derivation of our American family system. The oversight has been remedied, fortunately, since our family system has a rich and variegated network of historical roots.

Our legal and moral codes pertaining to sex derive in large part from our Judeo-Christian heritage. Our attitudes toward women and children have been influenced by partriarchal forces starting with the early Hebrews and Greeks and continuing through the Dark Ages and the Renaissance. The concept of romantic love, once described as one of our "national problems," can be traced to the Age of Chivalry. Marital symbols, such as the engagement ring, the wedding ring, the marriage ceremony, and the honeymoon, have come to us from a variety of sources. The list of derivatives could be expanded, but—rather than deal with generalities—let us turn to some specifics.

FAMILY LIFE AMONG THE HEBREWS

The history of the Semitic peoples who roamed between Babylon and Egypt before the time of Moses is largely speculative. It was through the personality of Moses that the struggling nomadic tribes became united, and it is roughly from this point—around the thirteenth century B.C.—that Hebrew history takes on meanings that have loomed large for so many of our Western culture patterns. Basic to all Hebrew life, of course, was their rejection of idolatry in favor of the worship of one god, Jehovah.

Over the next millennium the Hebrews were first a pastoral and then an agricultural society. As was usually the case in such societies, the family was patriarchal. That is, the father was the head of the family, and women were expected to obey, show deference and respect. In these families women were first the property of their fathers and then were transferred to their husbands. Women were by no means "free" in today's sense of the word. Their roles were demanding and went far beyond motherhood and procreation. The Old Testament gives us some idea of what was expected of the "perfect" Hebrew woman:

> Who can find a virtuous woman?
> for her price is far above rubies;
> She will do him good and not evil
> all the days of her life.
> She seeketh wool, and flax,
> and worketh willingly with her hands.
> She is like the merchants' ships;
> bringeth here food from afar.
> She riseth also while it is yet night,
> and giveth meat to her household. . . .
> She considereth a field and buyeth it;
> with the fruit of her hands she planteth a vineyard. . . .
> She maketh fine linen and selleth it. . . .[1]

If she did not live up to expectations, the husband could divorce her, whereas women did not have that option. He could also take on another wife. Even though most patriarchs had only one wife, the families nevertheless tended to be large. Having twelve sons, as in the biblical account of Jacob, was not uncommon.

Similar forms of patriarchy were present in the Middle East, Europe, Africa, and Asia. As in the Hebrew culture, marriage throughout history was considered an obligation, a responsibility rather than a privilege. The idea of marrying for happiness, love, and personal fulfillment is a modern idea that will be discussed in later chapters.

Betrothal and Marriage

For a marriage to be valid, Hebraic custom required the consent of the two parties. This meant that, although the parents could *contract* for a marriage, either the boy or the girl could nullify the agreement. In view of the

---

[1]Philippe Aries, "Love in Married Life," in Philippe Aries and Andre Bejin, *Western Sexuality: Practice and Precept in Past and Present Times* (Oxford: Basil Blackwell, 1985), 131–132.

emphasis on obedience to parents, however, it seems unlikely that many sons or daughters ever vetoed parental arrangements.

In keeping with the prevailing practice, Hebrew marriages were normally consummated at an early age. According to the Talmud the legal ages were those at puberty: twelve years for the female and thirteen for the male. Marriage prior to these ages was invalid, although there was nothing in the Talmud and little in the way of public opinion to prevent the parents from *contracting* for marriage at any age.

While this contracting-for-marriage, or *betrothal,* was the source of our own *engagement,* there is a substantial difference between the two. In our society, an engagement is an informal agreement to marry. It is not a legal contract in any sense of the word, the engagement ring being purely symbolic. Among the Hebrews, the betrothal represented an actual contract and was considered to be the beginning of marriage. Faithlessness on the part of a betrothed girl was held to be just as serious as adultery, and in both cases the same harsh punishment was inflicted.

The final step was the marriage ceremony itself, which usually took place at least a year after the betrothal. The ceremony, rituals, and wedding procedures have been referred to historically as *nuptials,* although in recent years this term has fallen into disuse. At the wedding, benedictons were pronounced by the bridegroom, a rabbi, or one of the witnesses, and afterward the affair was concluded with a banquet.

Although benedictions were normally a part of both the betrothal and wedding ceremonies, neither religious pronouncements nor permission of civil authorities was required. Marriage was a private affair between the two families, a pattern which was (and is) widely followed among preliterate peoples. Religious and civil control of marriage did not become prevalent until the end of the Middle Ages.

Divorce

Although the Hebrews did not look upon marriage from the view of individual happiness or personality development, instances of marital discord did occur, as indeed they have occurred in all times and among all peoples. The Hebrew husband, in this respect, had a free hand. Legally speaking, he could divorce his wife for any reason. Moreover, this right was considered a male prerogative only, practically no provision being made for the wife. Until the advent of the Christian era, furthermore, the Hebrew husband was awarded custody of the children in all divorce suits.

In an actual case, a divorced woman would suffer no loss of community status if she were, in fact, innocent of her husband's charges. If she was adjudged guilty, however, she not only was socially disparaged but was forced to relinquish all rights to her dowry. In the event of adultery, the punishment could be much more severe; in fact, both adultery and premarital unchastity could cause her (together with her paramour) to be put to death.

In practice, Hebrew divorce procedure was not nearly so inequitable as it sounds, since group opinion in those days was much stronger than it is today, and any abuse or obvious ill-treatment of the wife would result in severe social condemnation of the husband. Also, the Hebrews did not take kindly to a husband's divorcing his wife for little or no reason, since by so doing he was reneging on his responsibility as protector and provider.

With regard to adultery, it is unlikely that the extreme penalty was often imposed. (There is no case in the Old Testament wherein an adulteress was accorded the death sentence.) In fact, so far as is known, relatively few wives actually committed adultery. Of those who did, most cases probably went undetected—even as now. And in the detected cases, there must have been many husbands who, like Joseph and Hosea, simply divorced their wives rather than become involved in a public spectacle.[2]

THE FAMILY IN ANCIENT GREECE

As was the case in other ancient cultures, marriage in Greece was largely a matter of convenience and duty. Cultural distinctions were obvious in some of the marriage customs that persist to this day. The marriage feast took place at the bride's residence and the groom would select the best man to participate in the marriage ceremony. The ceremony would take two or three days, not unlike the custom of modern Balkan families. Another ancient custom that still persists is giving of gifts to the newlyweds.[3]

The Greek marriage ceremony gives the initial impression of somewhat more equal relations between the sexes than in the Hebrew culture. In reality, however, Greek women were not educated, either formally or informally. Wives were not allowed to leave their homes without the permission of their husbands and to a surprising extent were not allowed to participate in intellectual life of the community. Historians describe husband-wife relations in ancient Greece this way:

> Indeed, her duties and achievements were hardly considered, by the husband, in a much higher light than those of a faithful slave. In prehistoric times the position of women seems to have been, upon the whole, a more dignified one.[4]

Homosexuality in Ancient Greece

The incidence of homosexuality in ancient Greece is not known; but the fact that it was accepted as a way of life can be ascertained from several

---

[2]Bernard I. Murstein, "Hebrew Marriage in the Old Testament," in *Love, Sex, and Marriage through the Ages* (New York: Springer Publishing Company, 1974), 34–46.

[3]E. Guhl and W. Koner, *Everyday Life of the Greeks and Romans* (New York: Crescent Books, 1989).

[4]Ibid., 185–186.

Greek wives were clearly subservient to their husbands and did not participate in their husbands' social activities. Here a drunken husband, returning from a night's festivities, pounds at the door while his fearful wife trembles within. *(The Metropolitan Museum of Art, Fletcher Fund, 1937)*

sources. For example, illustrations on some vases that served as utensils around the house portrayed homosexual relations. Also, the language used by Greek writers was free and open on the subject. Rather uncongenial relationships between men and women further indicate a cultural predisposition toward homosexuality. Because the Greeks subjugated their women, men often sought each other's company for intellectual and emotional support. Frequent interaction and dependence among men is believed to be responsible for much of the homosexuality in that society. Finally, the custom of older men taking under their wing young boys for years of close tutorial supervision makes it easy to see how homosexuality was far from uncommon in ancient Greece.

The Greeks, of course, had rules for acceptable sexual behavior. For example, intercourse with boys under puberty was illegal in Athens. Also, homosexuality among equal-age adult males was relatively uncommon. Presumably, homosexuality was found largely among adolescents and also between upper-class males and their adolescent pupils.

THE FAMILY IN ANCIENT ROME

By the second century B.C., the ancient customs of the patriarchal family began to weaken in Rome. The first change allowed the women to inherit property and accumulate wealth. With the gain of economic status of women the absolute power of *pater familia* (the father of the family) began to erode. Among the beneficiaries were children since the father no longer had the power of life and death over them:

> Until the beginning of the third century when abandoning a child was considered the equivalent of murder he might expose his new born child to perish of cold and hunger or be devoured by dogs on one of the public refuse dumps.[5]

Accompanying the emancipation of Roman women and children was an influx of wealth as the empire expanded. Slave labor became plentiful, and the myriad of household tasks that formerly occupied the wife came to be taken over by slaves. On the larger estates, the number of slaves would run into the hundreds. Preoccupation with food, entertainment, and gambling—by both men and women—became widespread. Even child rearing was often given over to servants and tutors.

As patriarchy faded into the past, matrimony became more and more a matter of expediency—to be entered into for political reasons, for the attainment of wealth and position, or for the improvement of one's social class. Whereas formerly marriage was considered a civic responsibility, it was now looked upon as an instrument of personal gain. And children, who were once thought of as fulfilling family traditions and sacred obligations, were now increasingly considered a burden.

Consequently, legal marriages declined and more people entered into *concubinatus,* a form of living together without legal bonds. Today we might call this "cohabitation." With the weakening of marriage, mistresses became common, prostitution flourished, and moral laxness led to adultery among all social classes. According to one writer:

> It may have been an exaggeration of Martial's to grumble that in Rome no woman ever said No, yet promiscuity was the rule, and particularly in the governing class, a colourful succession of marriages and divorces was quite usual.[6]

By the fourth century A.D., divorce and marital disruption had reached the stage of public scandal and both premarital and extramarital sex relations had become sources of official embarrassment. To state it simply, the meaning had been stripped from marriage.

---

[5]Jerome Carcopino, *Daily Life in Ancient Rome* (Harmondsworth, England: Penguin Books, 1986), 90.

[6]Karl Christ, *The Romans: An Introduction to Their History and Civilization* (Berkeley, CA: University of California Press, 1984), 101.

The disintegration of the Roman family was characterized by an influx of wealth and slave labor and a preoccupation with food and entertainment. *(Culver Pictures, Inc.)*

The birthrate fell and childlessness increased to alarming proportions. Infanticide and abortion became more and more common in spite of the enactment of many legal restrictions. Even governmental attempts to raise the birthrate through economic incentives were unsuccessful.

THE EARLY CHRISTIAN INFLUENCE

As the Roman era drew to a close, the tide of Christianity gathered momentum—and in the year 312 A.D. it was accorded legal recognition throughout the Empire. Essentially, the Christian religion was oriented toward the dignity of the individual and the brotherhood of man, with God the heavenly Father embodying infinite forgiveness and love for all His children.

Worshiping one God, whose spiritual embodiment was revealed through Christ, followers of Christianity believed that marriage was instituted for His purpose rather than for the gratification of sexual desires or the placation of ancestral spirits. And, in the eyes of God, marriage was held to be a permanent relationship between one man and one woman, indissoluble "till death us do part." Unlike the Hebrews, Christians sanctioned only monogamy; unlike the Greeks and Romans, Christians condemned all sexual activities outside of marriage; and, unlike so many other of the neighboring peoples, Christians preached against divorce.

Beneficial Effects on Family Life

Coming when it did, Christianity had many salutary effects on marriage and the family. Monogamy has already been mentioned. The followers of Christianity had originally been from among the poorer classes, and it is understandable that they would have resented the plural wives of the wealthy Hebrews and the mistresses of the Greeks and Romans. The early church preached that the Christian ideal entailed marriage between one man and one woman, with premarital chastity and postmarital fidelity. Fornication and adultery were not only severely condemned, but were considered equally culpable for *both* sexes. The church also spoke out strongly against infanticide.

Jesus taught that divorce was not permissible for any reason (Mark 10:11; Luke 16:18), although there is an inconsistency here, since in two other biblical passages he states that adultery is sufficient cause for divorce (Matthew 5:32 and 19:9). On this point church leaders have been divided for many centuries.

There were limits to the Christian influence on marriage and divorce, however, since these were still regarded as private matters rather than as affairs of state or church. Indeed, for several centuries Christianity had no patterned or formalized marriage ceremony, the role of the clergy being limited to postmarital benedictions.

Sexual Beliefs

Christian attitudes toward sex, divorce, and remarriage were more restrictive than those of the Hebrews. Some historians describe this restrictiveness as a form of rebellion against the customs of an oppressive Roman society. As the early Christians saw it, it was unchecked immorality that doomed the Roman empire.

> Christians in the early Roman Empire were subjected to a variety of humiliating experiences and not infrequently to mob violence. The emperors Decius, Valerian, and Diocletian vowed to eradicate the whole movement. Because of this hostility on the part of respected and powerful people, Church codes condemned many practices of the Christians' social "betters" and urged conduct of an opposite character. Thus there were reactions against easy divorce, "emancipation" of women, and sexual freedom.[7]

---

[7]Stuart A. Queen, Robert W. Habenstein, and Jill S. Quadagno, *The Family in Various Cultures* (New York: Harper & Row, 1985), 136.

The attitudes of the early Christians were also influenced by the Hebrews. The latter, in an effort to set themselves above their Semantic neighbors, such as the Chaldeans and the Canaanites, placed wholesale restrictions on most types of sexual activity. Among the taboos were premarital coitus, adultery, homosexuality, masturbation, and any "unnatural" carnal practices. To this list, the Christians added or emphasized such prohibitions as "contraception, abortion, the reading of lascivious books, singing wanton songs, dancing 'suggestive' dances, bathing in mixed company, and wearing improper clothing."[8] Although it was permitted, remarriage after the death of a spouse was similarly discouraged, the church preferring that both widows and widowers remain continent.

If these "supplements" seem unduly strict, it must be remembered that the early Christian leaders had been reared in a Judaic atmosphere where sex was looked upon as a procreative function. Foremost among the early leaders, of course, were Jesus and Paul, neither of whom ever married. Both were tremendous spiritual teachers, and both took a dim view of the so-called pleasures of the flesh, although Paul—distressed at the laxity he saw as he traveled the Roman road—was the most vituperative of all the apostles.

In light of the prevailing strictures of the early church, it is little wonder that the idea of virginity came to be held up as a divine state. Sex was a worldly diversion—a carnal obstruction to the attainment of higher spiritual values. Chastity came to symbolize purity of soul and dignity of person. Moreover, in the absence of strong self-control, there was the danger of internal sexual contamination. It was not necessary for one to indulge in fornication in order to sin; it was considered lecherous and sinful to have even the desire for sexual relations.

The degradation of sex and, to a lesser degree, of the marital state itself inevitably led to increases in virginity and celibacy. Persons who chose to renounce sex were increasingly considered to be select individuals. Sexual abstinence came to be one of the hallmarks of spiritual dedication, and there were continuing attempts on bishops, priests, and other ecclesiastics. In fact, centuries later, vows of celibacy on the part of the clergy were to become an integral part of the Christian dogma—a development that, in turn, played a significant role in the culmination of the Protestant Reformation.

The Controversy

It is self-evident that the teachings and writings of the early Christian leaders have had a lasting effect on our own sex codes. No one questions this fact. The controversy, from a secular view, is whether this Judeo-Christian influence has had beneficial effects, or whether it has served to foment sexual discord.

---

[8]Ibid., 146.

A number of modern writers have felt that our own moral and legal codes are still too severe and that the restrictions imposed by the early Christian leaders continue to give rise to a variety of sexual malignancies. These writers point out that under our present system, sex activity is too often accompanied by guilt feelings on the part of the person or persons involved. Masturbation, homosexuality, premarital and extramarital coitus, nudity, and verbal references to the sex act, are all—in varying degrees—looked upon as reprehensible practices.

Other writers, however, contend that the early Christian dogmatics were effective not only in reducing the more flagrant abuses of the day, but also in fostering a societally integrated sexual perspective that has lasted down to the present. They argue that while the lever of guilt has been the instrument used, pressures brought to bear in order to make people conform *always* involve the threat of either religious or secular guilt. For most people, after all, guilt is simply the realization that they have failed to follow societal convictions of right and wrong.

This is the basic position of writers who feel that our Judeo-Christian sex codes tend to promote and maintain a system of strong family values; that is, the incentive to marry is increased and the institutional aspects of the family are reinforced by permitting sex relations only between husband and wife.

The controversy over the Judeo-Christian sex codes has by no means been resolved. In recent years, however, it is true that a more tolerant attitude has been shown toward those who do not abide by the codes. Moral indignation has lessened, laws have been lightened or repealed, and sex behavior in general has come to be regarded more and more as a private matter.

THE FAMILY DURING THE MIDDLE AGES

It is difficult to characterize family life during the Middle Ages since there was no single family type as such. The Middle Ages themselves stretched for 1000 years in time, and during this period there were many changes and variations in family living. Moreover, in the centuries following the Roman collapse, the Empire was overrun by a variety of Germanic tribes—Vandals, Goths, Franks, Lombards, Saxons, and others—each of which settled in a different area; while there was much similarity in their family patterns, there were also differences among the various groups, especially as they developed into sovereign nations. And finally, the rise of feudalism resulted in differing family patterns among the various social classes: marriage and family life among the land-owning nobility was a far cry from that of the serfs. Therefore, rather than attempt to portray family life, as such, during this long medieval period, it is more feasible to describe some of the recognized forces that helped to shape marital and family values. These influences can be conveniently depicted under three headings: (1) Christianity, (2) feudalism, and (3) chivalry.

The Continuing Effects of Christianity

In the centuries immediately following the fall of the Roman Empire, the Germanic invaders held pretty much to their own marital practices and were little influenced by Christian ideals. Though most people married, marriage itself was considered a private matter between the two families, with the ceremonials being nonreligious in nature; in fact, during the Middle Ages it was not unusual for *self-marriage* to take place, in spite of much adverse public opinion. The bride and groom would simply recite the marriage ritual in the presence of one another. The actual words—analogous to "I take thee for my lawful wedded wife"—would be spoken in the present tense *with or without witnesses*. This was the origin of our present common-law marriage; in fact, as it is practiced today in the United States, common-law marriage is almost identical with the self-marriage just described.

But the church had by no means kept entirely aloof from marital affairs, and little by little, various changes could be seen in the Germanic patterns. The ascendancy of the church in this period was gradual though unmistakable, and between the fifth and eighth centuries nearly all the Teutonic groups had converted to Christianity. Concubinage was discouraged, and the church succeeded in erasing the last traces of polygyny. It is interesting that, while polygyny continued to flourish in parts of the Eastern world, the practice never again gained a permanent foothold in Western culture.

By the thirteenth century the church's control over marriage was virtually complete, the clergy having assumed the function of performing the ceremony.* The father would relinquish control of the bride so that the priest could join the couple in marriage, a procedure that now took place *inside the church*. This assumption of control by the church is reflected in the present-day religious marriage ceremony, the role of the father being implied by the question "Who giveth this woman to be wedded?" But it is the officiating clergyman who speaks for the church with the words, "I now pronounce you man and wife."

Not until the Council of Trent (1545–1563) did the church proclaim, once and for all, that marriage was a sacrament, that is, a divine creation, which only the church, as an instrument of God, could validate by bestowing its blessing. And since marriage was a creation of God, to be performed in the presence of a priest, it followed that the marital bonds could not be

---

*The use of the wedding ring also seems to have gained favor during this period, although the specific origins are somewhat hazy. It is likely that the church encouraged the custom—as part of a continuing effort to underscore the seriousness and permanence of marriage.

broken for any reason. This is the Roman Catholic position known as indissolubility.

Although the church finally succeeded in establishing the principle of the indissolubility of marriage, historical evidence indicates that the ecclesiastical courts in the Middle Ages were liberal in the granting of *annulments*—the declaration that a marriage was null and void because of some condition existing *prior* to the marriage. It is known, for example, that in some instances a distant blood relationship between spouses was sufficient cause for annulment. The church also reserved the right to grant *divortium a mensa et thoro* (divorce from bed and board), but while this action enabled the husband and wife to live apart, it did not permit either to remarry during the lifetime of the other. An annulment gave both parties the privilege of remarrying.

Feudalism: The Class System of the Middle Ages

Because local wars, plundering, and robbery were so common during the Middle Ages, some system was needed that would afford a measure of protection for the average family. Feudalism provided an answer to the problem, for under the feudal system the land was divided into estates or manors (*fiefs*), each owned by a lord, and by associating himself with one of these the common man could secure protection for his family. In return, he was obliged to perform designated services for the lord of the manor. Society thus came to be divided into a ruling class and a subject class, with a number of gradations in between.

The lowest family in the social-class hierarchy was that of the *serf*, who could not even marry without the lord's permission. Living in a one-room, smoke-filled hut, with infrequent changes of clothing and few bathing facilities, the serf had a most crude family existence. As would be expected, the infant mortality rate was high, and sickness and epidemics were widespread.

Above the serf was the *villein*, whose living conditions were somewhat better and who had certain rights with regard to personal property. Next in the social hierarchy were the middle class, or *freemen* who owned their own land. Unlike the lower classes, freemen were obligated to perform military services for the lord of the manor. At the top of the class structure were the nobility and royalty, comprising the various earls, counts, viscounts, dukes, princes, and kings.

Family life among the landed aristocracy was strikingly different from that which existed in middle- and lower-class groups. Members of the upper class saw to it that their sons and daughters were steeped in the traditions of their class, and education played an important part in the socialization process. Boys were given in-castle training as pages and squires and were taught riding and swordsmanship. They were trained in the art of warfare, and after they had demonstrated their adeptness, they could ultimately at-

During the Middle Ages, aristocratic families trained their sons in the traditions of their class. They learned the art of warfare, including riding and swordsmanship. (*Historical Pictures Service, Inc., Chicago*)

tain knighthood. Girls were taught how to spin and weave, to take care of the sick and wounded, and to become thoroughly versed in the customs and good manners of court ladies.

It was during this period that elaborate codes of etiquette were written, and fashion and decorum became the hallmarks of court society; in fact, our modern English words "courtly," "courteous," and "courtship" stem from the propriety and manners that were highly formalized in the medieval court. Women outside the circles of nobility were accorded an entirely different code of conduct, and women in the lower classes were often considered to be "fair game." Indeed, the "right of the first night," or *jus primae noctis,* gave the lord of the manor sexual privileges with the bride of a serf, although it is not known how often he availed himself of these privileges. But the lady of nobility, the upper-class lady of court and castle, was being elevated—in a very special way—to a rather exalted position.

The idealized relationship between the knight and his lady formed the basis of the concept of romantic love. *(Culver Pictures, Inc.)*

Chivalry

Certainly one of the lasting effects of the Middle Ages on family life was a glorification of the "lady" and an idealization of romantic love that crystallized within the framework of chivalry. It was in the twelfth century that the knight came to be obsessed with ideas of undying devotion, bravery, and heroic efforts—all in the service of his chosen lady. On her part, the lady of the castle was not averse to weaving ribbons and fashioning colored plumage to be worn by her knight both in tournaments and in battle. Such glorified interplay between knight and lady came to be idealized by society at large, so that, in spite of the wholesale plundering and widespread oppression characteristic of the times, there developed the concept of romantic love.

The concept captured the imagination of all classes, and, aided by the love songs of the wandering troubadours, Europe was soon engrossed with the diversionary possibilities of romantic love. The latter was not like ordinary love but was held to be an intense, subjective feeling, almost visceral in nature. Romantic love was thought of as an exalted state, *unrelated to the bonds of marriage*, but nevertheless possessing an alluring touch of inevitability. It was the destiny of every lady to meet the knight of her dreams; and for every knight there was one fair lady—somewhere. Such love was viewed as a kind of fate, over which mortal beings had little control. As thus conceived, romantic *amour* was a new concept, one which not only raised the status of women, but which, in an ideal sense, elevated the relationship between man and woman beyond the sensual level.[9]

In former periods and in other lands there had probably always been instances of strong emotional attraction between persons of the opposite sex, but not until the Age of Chivalry were such relationships institutionalized. According to our present standards, however, the romantic love of the twelfth and thirteenth centuries would have to be viewed as having a rather unique focus because, according to the tenets of chivalry, romantic love was supposed to occur *after* marriage, with a person *other than one's own spouse!*

Upper-class marriages in those days were largely prearranged, usually for purposes of solidifying social status, and it was not expected that the lord and lady of the manor would be bound by ties of love. For the lady, life in the castle was often boring, and the comings of the troubadours with songs of love were welcomed. The arrival of a battle-tested knight was even more welcome, for now the lady would have a potential opportunity to meet her romantic destiny face to face. The lord of the manor, meanwhile, was fulfilling the role of romantic knight elsewhere, his true love and devotion being shown for a lady other than his wife. Society thus held that both husband and wife had the right to love. Marriage was an obligation, but love was a privilege. And in keeping with the chivalric codes, neither lord nor lady would pry into the love affairs of the other.

Although volumes have been written about chivalry, with many questions still unanswered, one thing remains clear. As long as it was merely an extramarital diversion, romantic love could not provide the integrating values necessary for an abiding system of marriage. The romanticism of the twelfth and thirteenth centuries may have filled a class need, but this need could hardly be reconciled with the interests of society at large. With the disappearance of knighthood, therefore, it was predictable that the vine of romantic love would lose its grip and cease to flower.

On the other hand, even within a restrictive, upper-class framework, the impetus of chivalry and the glorification of romantic love were strong enough to affect both the immediate view and ultimate course of institutionalized marriage. Regarding the immediate view, chivalry implanted in the minds of men a respect for womanhood that had hitherto been lacking. Also, the possibility was raised that a gratifying emotional relationship between man and woman could be based on something other than the satisfaction of sexual needs.

From the long-range view, it should be pointed out that, while romantic

---

[9]John C. Moore, *Love in Twelfth-Century France* (Philadelphia: University of Pennsylvania Press, 1972), 87.

love ceased to flourish after the Age of Chivalry, the seed had been planted, and all that was necessary for it to take root was the proper climate and nourishment. Although these prerequisites were occasionally found in Europe, they appeared only sporadically, and it was on another continent—America—that the concept of romantic love began to thrive, not as an extra-marital adjunct, but as a *recognized basis for marriage*.

THE RENAISSANCE AND THE REFORMATION

Toward the latter part of the Middle Ages the feudal system declined. Towns and cities were beginning to emerge, and with the concentration of population in urban areas, the rigid class system gave way to a more personalized existence. There was much work to be done in urban centers, and a serf could normally secure his freedom by remaining in a city for one year. While there were still marked social distinctions among urban dwellers, people had a sense of political equality that was lacking under feudalism.

As time went on, the guild system rose in importance, and trade and commerce flourished. Because of this, there was an influx of wealth and, at least for the upper classes, sufficient leisure to indulge in educational and artistic pursuits. Thus, during the fifteenth and sixteenth centuries, interest in literature, music, architecture, drama, and painting was rekindled after an extended period of intellectual darkness. Historians have termed this scientific and artistic awakening the Renaissance, and a brief picture of marriage during this period is necessary in order to complete our historical account.

The Renaissance

During the Renaissance it was not unusual for well-to-do families to prescribe a classical education for girls as well as for boys. Also, married women in the upper classes were permitted far more latitude in their social relations than they were during the Middle Ages. These cultural amenities even filtered down, in some degree, to the middle classes. For the masses, educational achievement and cultural refinement remained at a low level, with squalor and illiteracy all too common.

Legally, the position of women remained at rock bottom, irrespective of their social class. Single or married, they had little in the way of property or inheritance rights. In England, for instance, a wife could not bequeath property except with the permission of her husband; in fact during her own lifetime even such personal effects as her clothing and jewelry belonged legally to her husband!

As in the preceding centuries, marriage during the Renaissance was divided into two parts—the betrothal and the marriage ceremony. The ceremony itself was a festive occasion, the degree of festivity and ornateness depending on the social class of the participants. It should be kept in mind that, while the *legal* class distinctions of the feudal period had largely disappeared, society during the time of the Renaissance was sharply stratified according to socioeconomic status. It was most difficult in those days for a person to improve his or her class position. After all, upper-class standing was rather carefully guarded, and, since marriages were arranged by parents, it was predictable that cross-class marriages would be rare.

Regardless of class position, once the ceremony was over, a wife found herself pretty much under the authority of her husband. And while there were undoubtedly many instances where husband and wife were faithfully devoted to each other, the familiar double standard remained in effect during the entire Renaissance period; that is, adultery on the part of the wife was severely punished, while the husband's philandering was not regarded too seriously. In the upper classes the age-old custom of keeping a mistress—sometimes referred to as a courtesan—was reportedly quite common.

The Protestant Reformation

The intellectual fervor of the Renaissance was paralleled by a growing restlessness in the spiritual realm. Both church dogma and clerical practices were being increasingly subjected to criticism, and by the sixteenth century the various dissatisfactions culminated in open revolt. Under the leadership of an Augustinian monk, Martin Luther, the Protestant Reformation had begun. Started in Germany by Luther, the reform movement spread to France, Switzerland, and Scotland, where John Calvin and John Knox led the attack against what they considered to be the abuses of the church.

Although firm in his belief that marriage was the backbone of society, Luther refused to accept the idea that marriage was sacramental in nature. On the basis of his own scriptural interpretation, he maintained that marriage was not a sacrament but a "worldly thing which does not concern the Church." It followed, logically, that marriage was a *civil* contract and that the regulation thereof should be under the auspices of the state. There is little doubt that the whole philosophy of civil marriage is largely attributable to Luther's influence.

One of the impelling reasons that led Luther to break with the church was its position with regard to marriage on the part of the clergy. For several centuries the clergy had been forbidden to marry, and Luther felt that this restriction placed an intolerable burden on the priesthood and led to violations of celibacy. He proclaimed, therefore, that the clergy had the right to marry, and he supported his contention with a scriptural interpretation.

Luther himself married a former nun, Katherine von Bora (by whom he had six children), though he was not the first reform leader to enter matrimony. A year earlier, in 1524, Ulrich Zwingli—the Swiss reformer—had publicly married one Ann Meyer, a widow. Zwingli's nuptial bond marked the first time in 500 years that a priest of the Roman church had entered into marriage.

The church bitterly opposed these marital unions, and even some of the Protestants were mildly shocked at the idea of matrimony on the part of the clergy. Eventually, however, the right of the latter to marry was accepted by all Protestant denominations, and this state of affairs has persisted down to the present.

As the Protestant movement gained headway, divorce became a growing problem. It followed logically that, if the state could regulate marriage, it could also regulate divorce. Most reformers felt that the prevailing system— whereby divorce was prohibited but annulment permitted—operated to serve the rich and penalize the poor, for the rich had the resources and the influence to establish grounds for annulment, while the poorer classes had no means of escape from an intolerable marriage. King Louis VII of France, for example, was able to have his marriage annulled on the ground that he and his wife, Queen Eleanor, were related in the seventh degree of consanguinity.

Although he disagreed with the principle of marital indissolubility, Luther himself abhorred divorce and held that the only justifications for it were desertion and the "scriptural ground" of adultery. Calvin and other reform leaders were somewhat more liberal in their views toward divorce, and in due time such grounds as cruelty and physical or mental incapacity came to be accepted.

SUMMARY

We have shown that our legal and moral codes pertaining to sex derive in large part from our Judeo-Christian heritage. Our attitudes toward women and children have been influenced by patriarchal forces starting with the early Hebrews and Greeks and continuing through the Renaissance. The concept of romantic love can be traced to the Age of Chivalry. Marital symbols, such as the engagement ring, the wedding ring, the marriage ceremony, and the honeymoon, have come to us from a variety of sources. Our religious pronouncements concerning annulment, separation, divorce, and remarriage have been molded by schools of thought that can be traced to the forerunners of the Reformation.

QUESTIONS

1. If you were asked to choose the most significant difference between family life among the ancient Hebrews and family life in modern America, what would that difference be? Explain.

2. Most historians feel that the incidence of homosexuality in ancient Greece was greater than in our society. Assuming this to be true, what was there in the social life of Greece that might have accounted for this phenomenon?

3. Some observers cite a number of parallelisms or similarities between the disinte-

gration of the later Roman family and the plight of the modern American family. How would you (a) support this position? (b) refute the whole idea?

4. What were the major effects of the early Christian influence on marriage and family life?

5. Some social historians feel that, in the sexual sphere, the influence of Christianity has been beneficial. Others believe that, overall, the influence has been harmful. Which view do you favor? Why?

6. Describe the system of chivalry, as it was practiced during the Middle Ages. Although not delineated in the text, a number of questions about chivalry remain unanswered. Can you think of some of these questions?

7. What would you say was the major difference between the class system, as it operated under feudalism, and the class system in industralized America?

8. What exactly was the Renaissance? What was the role of women during this period?

9. What were the principal effects of the Protestant Reformation on the institution of marriage? Are any of these effects still being felt? Explain.

SELECTED READINGS

Aries, P., and A. Bejin. *Western Sexuality: Practice and Precept in Past and Present Times*. Oxford: Basil Blackwell, 1985.

Atkinson, Clarissa W. "Precious Balsam in a Fragile Glass: The Ideology of Virginity in the Later Middle Ages." *Journal of Family History,* Summer 1983, 131–43.

Bell, Susan Groag, and Karen M. Offen. *Women in Family and Freedom: The Debate in the Documents*. Stanford, CA: Stanford University Press, 1983.

Bennett, Judith M. "The Tie That Binds: Peasant Marriages and Families in Late Medieval England." *Journal of Interdisciplinary History,* Summer 1984, pp. 111–29.

Burguiere, Andre. "The Formation of the Couple." *Journal of Family History,* vol. 12, nos. 1–3, 1987.

Carcopino, Jerome. *Daily Life in Ancient Rome*. Harmondsworth, England: Penguin Books, Ltd., 1986.

Dixon, Susan. "The Marriage Alliance in the Roman Elite." *Journal of Family History,* Winter 1985, 353–78.

Donahue, Charles, Jr. "The Canon Law on the Formation of Marriage and Social Practice in the Later Middle Ages." *Journal of Family History,* Summer 1983, 144–58.

Dupaquier, Jacques, E. Helin, P. Laslett, M. Livi-Bacci, and S. Songer. *Marriage and Remarriage in Populations of the Past*. Orlando, FL: Academic Press, 1981.

Ende, Aurel. "Children in History: A Personal Review of the Past Decade's Published Research." *The Journal of Psychohistory,* Summer 1983, 65–88.

Foley, Helene P. *Reflections of Women in History*. New York: Gordon & Breach, 1981.

Gautier, Leon. *Chivalry: The Everyday Life of Medieval Night*. New York: Crescent Books, 1989.

Gies, F., and J. Gies. *Marriage and the Family in the Middle Ages*. New York: Harper & Row, 1987.

Gough, Kathleen. "The Origin of the Family." In *Women,* edited by Jo Freeman, 83–99. Palo Alto, CA: Mayfield Publishing Company, 1984.

Guhl, E., and W. Koner. *Everyday Life of Greeks and Romans*. New York: Crescent Books, 1989.

Harris, Barbara. "Marriage Sixteenth-Century Style; Elizabeth Stafford and the Third Duke of Norfolk." *Journal of Social History,* Spring 1982, 371–81.

Herlihy, David. "The Making of the Medieval Family: Symmetry, Structure, and Sentiment." *Journal of Family History,* Summer 1983, 116–30.

Howard, George. *A History of Matrimonial Institutions,* 3 vols. Chicago: University of Chicago Press, 1904.

Humphreys, Sally. *The Family, Women and Death: Comparative Studies*. Boston: Routledge & Kegan Paul, 1983.

Kenkel, William F. "The Ancient Hebrew Family." In *The Family in Perspective,* 33–61. Houston: Cap and Gown Press, 1985.

Lantz, Herman R. "Romantic Love in the Pre-Modern Period: A Sociological Commentary." *Journal of Social History,* Spring 1982, 349–69.

Leits, Edmund. "The Duty of Desire: Love, Friendship, and Sexuality in Some Puritan Theories of Marriage." *Journal of Social History,* Spring 1982, 383–407.

McCarter, Kyle P., Jr. "The Patriarchal Age." In *Ancient Israel,* edited by Hershel Shanks. Englewood Cliffs, NJ: Prentice-Hall, 1988.

Veyen, Paul, ed. *A History of Private Life: From Pagan Rome to Byzantine*. Cambridge, MA: Harvard University Press, 1987.

Chapter
4

The American Family Heritage

It is probably safe to say that Americans are more interested in American history than at any time in the past. This is especially true in the area of social behavior, a topic that seems to have much more appeal for young people than does standard political history. A case in point is the American family system, including dating, courtship, and sexual conduct. Now close to 400 years old, there have been many changes in that "system." The focus of the present chapter is to describe and analyze these changes in keeping with the individual-societal perspective.

Family life in colonial America was shaped in part by the older European traditions and in part by the challenges of an unsettled and unexplored continent. On the one hand, colonists were steeped in the patriarchal tradition: it was only natural for them to look upon the husband as head of household and the wife and children as subordinates. Another carryover was the fact that the strict Judeo-Christian sex codes had been handed down almost intact, and sexual activity—except between husband and wife—was equated with sin.

On the other hand, certain circumstances in the colonies operated to bring about changes in the European family system. For one thing, conditions were severe, and the rugged day-to-day living left little time for the niceties of life, particularly in the early colonial period. For another, some of the colonies experienced a marked shortage of women. European emigration was heavily weighted in favor of males, so that colonial wives were often at a premium. In consequence, marital patterns were altered. Women began to have much more choice in the selection of a husband, and the dowry system became obsolete. Indeed, before too long, romantic love came to be a cherished part of the mate selection process.

But let us begin at the beginning. . . .

EARLY HARDSHIPS

A great deal has been written about the suffering and hardships of the English colonists in the first part of the seventeenth century. Readers are probably familiar with the fact that these early settlers—who had left England in quest of religious and personal freedom and economic opportunity—were men and women of courage. They were, however, grossly unprepared to meet the wilderness that faced them. The first settlers at Jamestown, Virginia (1607), the Pilgrims who landed at Plymouth Rock (1620), and the Puritans who settled at Massachusetts Bay (1628) were inept woodsmen and hunters. They were forced to learn by experience, and in the process these early pioneers died by the score.

The Pilgrims unwisely left England in September, and the *Mayflower* did not reach Plymouth Bay until December. By the end of that first New England winter, more than half the colony had died. In fact, during the period of their greatest distress, only a half dozen or so members were in sound health. Little wonder that later historians referred to these early Pilgrims as "babes in the wilderness."

Both the Pilgrims and the Puritans, however, had one advantage over the colonists who had settled along the James River in Virginia: they had brought their wives, whereas Jamestown was an all-male settlement. Despite the bleak New England environment, the Pilgrim and Puritan colonies grew; and despite the relatively mild Virginia climate, the Jamestown settlers became restless and discontented, and the colony was threatened with disintegration. It was not until groups of selected young women sailed from England, to become wives, that conditions in Virginia were stabilized.

And so it was throughout the colonial frontiers: family immigration and settlement made for stability, while all-male migrations carried with them the seeds of discontent.

Domestic Environment

The original colonial houses were so pitiful that they could scarcely be called "houses" at all. The settlers often dug themselves into caves, or pitched tents by using pegs and ship's canvas. On occasion, they simply used shelters that had been vacated by the Indians.

Eventually, the log cabin caught on, a development that revolutionized colonial living conditions. Nevertheless, there is abundant evidence to indicate that a typical log cabin of the 1600s was not a cheery dwelling place. The windows were small, few in number, and—until almost midcentury—made of oiled paper or cloth. The fact that the houses were dark, cramped, single-story buildings takes on added meaning when one considers the size of the average family. It was not unusual for colonial couples to have seven or eight children, and some families were much larger. (Benjamin Franklin came from a family of seventeen.) In many of the homes there was more overcrowding and congestion than there is in today's tenements. In fact, the question has been raised whether, under such conditions, the concept of privacy had any real meaning.

Like the dwelling places, household furnishings in seventeenth-century America were cruder than is generally realized. Even in the second half of the eighteenth century, housing was inadequate—at least by modern standards. As one historian puts it:

> The furniture needed for comfortable talks, the utensils necessary for true dining, the instruments and games for entertainment cannot be found. Even with the improvements, the ordinary home still looked as if the occupants expected a flash flood to sweep away their belongings at any moment.[1]

In time, the quality of the houses improved, and, eventually well-to-do colonists were erecting strongly built frame dwellings. Occasionally, a brick home could be seen, and among the wealthiest families the frame houses were two stories high. These houses were so well made that hundreds of them built in the 1600s are still standing. The number of houses remaining from the 1700s would run well into the thousands.

The Fireplace

It would be almost sacrilegious not to make special mention of the colonial fireplace. Indeed, the subject is referred to so often in American history that it almost seems as if the colonists made a career out of the fireplace—a supposition that is not wholly incorrect. For, in an almost literal sense, the fireplace was the hub around which the early American family revolved. It was not uncommon, for example, to build the fireplace *first,* and then to add one or more rooms, as needed!

Winters were long and severe, especially in New England, and, as far as houses were concerned, there was one dominant consideration: heat. And indoor heat came from one source—the open hearth. Whether the dwelling was a single-storied log cabin in the wilderness, or a double-storied frame house in Boston, there was likely to be only one chimney and one

[1]Carole Shammas, "The Domestic Environment in Early Modern England and America," *Journal of Social History*, Fall 1980, 8.

Log cabins remained a practical solution to frontier housing problems as late as the end of the nineteenth century. (*Brown Brothers*)

fireplace—which in turn meant that there was but one all-purpose room. In addition to being used for heating and cooking, therefore, the fireplace served as the center for social activity.

Early American fireplaces were perhaps the largest that have ever been built, many of them being ten feet or more in depth, and wide enough to hold the largest of logs. Keeping the fireplace lit, however, was another matter, for matches did not make their appearance until well into the 1800s. If the fire went out, it was necessary to borrow a live ember from a neighbor, or else use flint and steel in an effort to coax a spark.

On damp mornings, starting a fire was no easy task. Little wonder that, if they could help it, the early colonists never let the fire go out, most families keeping the hearthstone burning year after year!

In 1745 the Franklin stove made its appearance and threatened to supplant the open fireplace. As a matter of fact, the stove—one of Benjamin Franklin's many inventions—actually did alter American eating habits. Muffins, biscuits, flapjacks, and corn bread, for instance, all became popular when the quick-heating stove replaced the slower-heating brick of the fireplace.

But it was the fireplace that somehow captured the spirit of the colonial family, perhaps by symbolizing the hardships that were overcome; and despite the many advantages of the stove, the open hearth remained a hallmark of the American way of life. Even today, when its utilitarian value has been largely eliminated, the open fireplace can be seen in many homes—a vestigial culture trait, emblematic of the family of an earlier day.

COURTSHIP

Courtship in the early colonies was regulated according to strict, European traditions. These included legally prescribed dowries and the father's authority to control contacts with the marriageable partners. Individual initiative in mate search was even discouraged by law. New Haven colony law in 1656, for example, provided fines, imprisonment, and corporal punishment for the repeat offenders accused of "attempt or endeavor to inveigle, or draw the affection of any maide," without consent of her father or male guardian.[2]

Romantic Love

It would be wrong to generalize from the experience of a few settlements, with extreme controls over mate selection, to other areas of the colonies, Immigrants' desire to raise a family, in spite of the shortage of women, was a more powerful force than parental control or traditional European customs. Therefore, it was not long before romantic love emerged as a basis for selection and marriage.

One of the most famous romantic marriages in American history took place in 1610 between John Rolfe and an Indian princess, Pocahontas. While this has been explained in history as a "marriage of convenience" for the benefit of peaceful relations with the Indians, Rolfe's own writing reveals a man deeply in love. He did not understand his emotions toward a person "whose education has been rude, her manners barbarous, her generation accursed, and so discrepant in all nurtriture from myself."[3] However, he valued "her great appearance of love to me." Indeed, this event can be interpreted as a milestone in the American romantic courtship.

The Puritans did not exactly accept romantic courtship with open arms. They believed that love was a product of marriage and not the reason for it. Emotions, in their view, should not be permitted to interfere with such an important decision. Even the young people accepted this belief. They often

---

[2]Donald M. Scott and Bernard Wishy, *America's Families: A Documentary History* (New York: Harper & Row, 1982), 21.

[3]Ibid., 30.

The open hearth was the center and symbol of Colonial family life. (*The Bettmann Archive*)

avoided discussing their marital plans face-to-face, and wrote to each other instead.

In some settlements, letter writing was a way to get around the sharp eye and the keen ear of the chaperon. But the fact that couples wrote to each other even in settlements where face-to-face contacts were allowed indicates that the youth were serious about minimizing the influence of their emotions. Once they knew about each other's personalities, backgrounds, and plans for the future, they would then plan for marriage convinced that they were right for each other and that, sooner or later, love would emerge.

Bundling

Certainly the most famous—or infamous—courtship practice in the colonial period was that of bundling. While social historians invariably refer to the custom, very little is known about the incidence, the frequency, or the sexual overtones involved. In view of the widespread interest shown, it is surprising that there has not been more research on the subject. The major study on bundling was made in 1871 by Henry Stile who found that from 1750 through 1780 bundling "came nearest to being a universal custom."[4]

Bundling simply involved the courting couple's going to bed together

---

[4]Ellen K. Rothman, *Hands and Hearts: A History of Courtship in America* (New York: Basic Books, 1984), 46.

LIVING MADE EASY.

EASY MODE OF COURTSHIP.

In this eighteenth-century advertisement a bachelor announces his availability. (*American Antiquarian Society*)

with their clothes on. In some instances a centerboard was used to separate the parties, and there are also reported instances where the girl was required to don a "bundling bag."

The origin of bundling is somewhat obscure, although the biblical account of Ruth and Boaz may be pertinent:

> And when Boaz had eaten and drunk, and his heart was merry, he went to lie down at the end of the heap of corn; and she came softly . . . And she lay at his feet until the morning; and she rose up before one could know another. (Ruth 3:7, 14)

Since in the same passage Boaz says to Ruth, "Tarry this night," bundling is sometimes referred to as "tarrying." Whether the custom itself persisted since the biblical times is not clear. It is clear that it did not originate in America and that it was practiced in several European countries.

The custom itself was rejected by many Americans, and some went to great pains to put an end to it. One outspoken opponent blamed mothers for allowing their daughters to participate in bundling:

> Some maidens say, if through the nation,
> Bundling should quite go out of fashion,
> Courtship would lose its sweets; and they
> Could have no fun till wedding day.
> It shant be so, they rage and storm,
> And country girls in clusters swarm,

> And fly and buzz, like angry bees,
> And vow they'll bundle when they please.
> Some mothers too, will plead their cause,
> And give their daughters great applause,
> And tell them, 'tis no sin nor shame,
> For we, your mothers, did the same.[5]

It should be remembered that once parents had given their approval of the courtship, there was no suitable place for the couple to court during winter months except in bed. Any bundling that took place, furthermore, almost always involved pairs who were contemplating marriage. And finally, the parents were not only in the same house, but were in the same room with the courting couple. So the opportunity for sexual indulgence must have been limited.

MARRIAGE

In the colonial period, marriage was considered an obligation as well as a privilege. People were expected to marry, and they normally did so at a moderately young age. There was little place for the unmarried, who were generally looked upon with disfavor. For a woman, marriage was deemed to be the only honorable state. Bachelors were suspect and in most of the colonies were heavily taxed and kept under close surveillance.

Widows and widowers were expected to remarry—and they generally did, usually without much time elapsing. "The first marriage in Plymouth was that of Edward Winslow, a widower for seven weeks, and Susanna White, a widow for 12 weeks. One governor of New Hampshire married a widow of only ten days standing, and the amazing case is cited of Isaac Winslow, who proposed to Ben Davis' daughter the same day he buried his wife."[6]

Widows, incidentally, were considered to be excellent marital choices because of the property inherited from their previous marriages. They also would have had valuable experience as homemakers, a qualification that was lacking in the younger, unmarried girls. Of course, remarriages did not always work out as anticipated, a colonial epigram reading as follows:

> Colonel Williams married his first wife, Miss Miriam Tyler, for good sense, and got it: his second wife, Miss Wells, for love and beauty, and had it: and his third wife, Aunt Hannah Dickinson, for good qualities, and got horribly cheated.[7]

---

[5]Quoted in Rothman, 47.

[6]Stuart A. Queen, Robert W. Habenstein, and Jill S. Quadagno, *The Family in Various Cultures* (Philadelphia: J. B. Lippincott, 1985), 204.

[7]Anne H. Wharton, *Colonial Days and Dames* (Philadelphia: J. B. Lippincott, 1985), 105–06.

It was because the colonists held marriage in high esteem that they made certain it was bolstered by legal, as well as social, sanctions. Not only was parental consent a prerequisite, but the consent had to be given to the town clerk in writing. Throughout the colonies, provision was also made for announcing marital intentions. This was done by posting banns—public notice of intent to wed—a certain number of days prior to the marriage.In addition to the notification of consent and posting of banns, it was required that marriages be registered. The registration was done by the town clerk, who also had the duty of recording births and deaths within the township.*

Marriage Rituals

Historians report that no uniform marriage ritual existed in the early colonial period. Weddings were apparently performed at the bride's home. The wording of the ceremony—whether civil or religious—does not appear to have been standardized. It is likely that in the trying days of the seventeenth century there was neither time nor inclination to make marriage a festive occasion. At the same time, Americans have always had a proclivity for celebrations of all kinds, and before long the "quiet American wedding" had mushroomed into a panorama of relatively large dimensions. Prayers, psalm singing, music, bridal processions, and feasting became commonplace. By the eighteenth century, weddings had become recognized occasions for revelry and merrymaking. Gifts were given, drinking and dancing were on the wild side, muskets were fired, and pranks such as bride stealing were practiced. For better or worse, the American wedding had come of age.

Common-Law Marriage

Not all colonial marriages were celebrated in the foregoing fashion. Some couples dispensed with all formalities, both social *and* legal. Such marriages were referred to by a variety of terms, such as "hand-fasting," "self-gifta," "clandestine contracts," and later "common-law marriage." Historically, these unions have always been a legal and judicial headache. In the colonial period, matrimonial laws generally provided for consent, banns, officiant, and registration. But what to do with violators? What should, or could, be done when banns were not posted, or when the marriage ceremony was performed by an unauthorized person?

In general, the colonists chose to recognize such marriages as valid, even though a fine might be imposed on the violators. Common-law marriages were treated in the same manner: they were recognized as valid even

---

*Recording of divorces presented no problem because there were so few of them. In fact, the Middle and Southern colonies had no general provision for divorce. Some trace of this prohibition carried over to recent times, for South Carolina did not permit divorce for any reason until 1949.

Colonial marriage celebrations became festive occasions, with toasting, processions, dancing, and merrymaking. (*Culver Pictures, Inc.*)

though the offenders were often fined. Some colonies attempted to invalidate such unions, but the efforts proved ineffective.

It can be argued that, in view of the sanctity attributed to marriage, the colonies should have imposed heavier penalties on the violators. Actually, it was *because* matrimony was held in such high esteem that common-law marriages were accepted. After all, once a common-law wife became pregnant, what was to be gained by having the marriage invalidated? Moreover, during colonial times and throughout much of the nineteenth century the frontier was being pushed westward. Members of the clergy or authorized civil officials were frequently unavailable in sparsely settled areas, and common-law marriage was often the only recourse.

Whether or not such marriages serve a worthwhile purpose today is debatable, but in this earlier period the recognition of common-law unions was a functional necessity.

POSITION OF WOMEN

There is no doubt that colonial America was—by modern standards—a man's world. Marriage might be a purely economic arrangement or it might be a love match, but in either case the wife was destined to lead a restricted existence.

Table 4.1   OCCUPATIONAL DISTRIBUTION
FOR WHITE FEMALE HEADS OF
HOUSEHOLDS: PHILADELPHIA
1791 AND 1860

Occupational group	1791 (%)	1860 (%)
1 Hand sewers and milliners	10.3	31.8
2 Crafts, factory jobs	1.6	6.7
3 Home spinners	15.6	____
4 Retail dealers	32.5	32.8
5 Innkeepers	7.2	2.2
6 Boardinghouse keepers	18.4	6.9
7 Teachers and nurses	14.1	11.9
8 Domestic service	0.2	7.7
Number of Observations	418	494

Source: Claudia Goldin, *Journal of Interdisciplinary History,* Winter 1986: 396.

Formal education was largely a male province. In some of the colonies, girls were permitted to attend school only during the summer, when the classroom was not being used by boys. Even among the wealthier New England families, education for girls rarely went beyond "reading, writing, and the social graces." As a matter of fact, modern historical research indicates that the majority of New England women were illiterate!

Because of their illiteracy, colonial women were particularly hard pressed during widowhood; indeed, widows often had to support themselves and their dependent children. As heads of households how did they make a living in the early republic? Goldin offers some rare data on women's employment, shown in Table 4.1.

Goldin points out that in the 1790s some factory jobs occupied by women were "ironmonger, turner, tallow chandler, shoemaker, pewterer, copper, tinplate worker, glass engraver, and sieve maker." By the 1860s these had become strictly male occupations. Goldin argues that the reduced employment status for women reflects changes in the economic development of the country and not changes in ideology or in literacy levels.

While most studies are based on evidence from New England, Southern women did not seem to fare any better. Perhaps the pressure for their submission was even greater. Leslie points out that the antebellum intellectuals justified sex inequality as follows:

> Man never suffers without murmuring, and never relinquishes his rights without a struggle. It is not always so with woman: her physical weakness incapacitates her for the combat: her sexual organization, and that part which she takes in bringing forth and nurturing the rising generation, render her necessarily domestic in her habit, and timid and patient in her sufferings. If

a man chooses to exercise his power against woman, she is sure to fall an easy prey to his oppression. Hence, we may always consider her progressing elevation in society as a mark of advancing civilization, and more particularly, of the augmentation of disinterested and generous virtue. (Thomas R. Dew, 1853)[8]

How much actual difference there was in the treatment of Northern and Southern women is impossible to say. The legendary aspects of Puritan and Cavalier behavior have become almost indistinguishable from the facts. It is possible that in middle- and lower-class families regional differences were minimal. It is also likely that the differences in child socialization were minimal, and that the history of childhood in colonial America is identical in both North and South.

CHILDREN

"It is my firm conviction that if we do not reconstruct the history of childhood we will not be able to reconstruct the history at all."[9] We might add to this quotation that if we do not reconstruct the history of childhood we will not be able to understand why today's parents behave toward their children as they do.

The harsh living in colonial America was responsible for high death rates among infants and very young children. By some accounts, half of the children died before reaching maturity. One-fourth died in the first year of life. Faced with the almost inevitable death of some of their children, parents in some cases were probably reluctant to establish close emotional ties. It is easier to lose someone when emotional investment is low than when it is high.

The custom of calling parents "sir" or "ma'am," or even "esteemed parent," which today we associate with respect, might have originated as a way of keeping parents emotionally detached from their children. Also, in some families youngsters were not allowed to sit at the same table with their parents during meals, even though this was not the general rule.

Some idea of the behavioral guidelines for youngsters can be found in Christopher Dock's *One Hundred Necessary Rules of Conduct for Children*, published in 1764. Dock, a well-known colonial schoolmaster, wrote that youths should refrain "from eating in the street, urinating in public, splashing in mud puddles, throwing snowballs, and hitching rides." Children were also instructed in the subtleties of grooming, from combing their hair and

---

[8]Cited in Kent Anderson Leslie, "A Myth of a Southern Lady: Antebellum Proslavery Rhetoric and the Proper Place of Woman," *Sociological Spectrum*, Spring 1986, 36.

[9]Aurel Ende, "Children in History: A Personal Review of the Past Decade's Published Research," *The Journal of Psychohistory*, Summer 1983, 65.

brushing their teeth to the proper method of spitting and blowing the nose. They were reminded above all to show respect to their elders and to obey their parents.[10]

With regard to formal education, girls were seriously handicapped. And even for boys, schooling, in the sense that we normally use the term, was a relatively unimportant part of the overall training program. Free, coeducational public schools and land-grant colleges—both of which are instrumental in our current educational system—were virtually nonexistent in the pre-Revolutionary period.

Even when public schools did emerge, they tended to be of the fabled one-room variety. In a typical one-room country school, teenagers would be studying Latin and Greek in preparation for college; nine- and ten-year-olds would be reading history and geography; still younger children would be trying to master arithmetic and spelling; and, at the bottom rung, the beginners were being taught the alphabet! How a single teacher could keep all the students occupied and still maintain discipline remains something of a pedagogical mystery.

Actually, the most important "education" for the colonial child was to be found at home: vocational training, religious indoctrination, and "Puritan guidance" by the parents.

NONMARITAL COITUS

The early European settlers in America brought with them strict moral and legal codes governing sexual conduct. But as was the case in their homeland, there were some who "broke the rules." Sexual offenses in the colonies ran the gamut—homesexuality, bestiality, fornication, adultery, prostitution, incest—but most of them occurred infrequently. Premarital coitus and adultery, on the other hand, occurred often enough to cause the colonists some concern.

Premarital Coitus

It is clear from documentary evidence that premarital coitus, also known as fornication, was fairly common throughout New England. One historian, for example, describes it as "the most prevalent and the most popular sin in Puritan New England."[11] To ascertain the frequency of occurrence, historians have looked at long-term trends in premarital pregnancy.

The data in Table 4.2 compiled for New England reveal that during the

---

[10]Stephanie Wolf, *Urban Village: Population Community and Family Structure* (New York: Macmillan, 1927), 305–06.

[11]Morton M. Hunt, "The Puritan as Sinner and the Meaning of 'Puritanical,' " in John F. Crosby, ed., *Reply to Myth: Perspectives on Intimacy* (New York: John Wiley, 1985), 20.

Table 4.2 LONG-TERM HISTORICAL
VARIATION IN WHITE AMERICAN
PREMARITAL PREGNANCY

Period	Percentage of first births within nine months of marriage
Before 1700	11.1
1701–1760	23.3
1761–1800	33.7
1801–1840	25.1
1841–1880	15.5

Source: Daniel Scott Smith, "The Dating of the American Sexual Revolution: Evidence and Interpretation," in John F. Crosby, ed., *Reply to Myth: Perspectives on Intimacy* (New York: John Wiley, 1985), 118.

seventeenth century about 11 percent of marriages might have involved a premarital pregnancy. Of course, the actual percentage was less than that because some conceptions probably took place soon after the marriage ceremony. Also some births could have been premature. In any case, it is clear that the percentage of premarital pregnancies increased steadily throughout the eighteenth century, after which the figures declined.

It is surprising to see how many couples in colonial times engaged in premarital coitus in spite of the threat of severe punishment. One explanation is that most couples were already committed to marriage. It was probably rare for a man and a woman to become sexually involved unless they planned to marry. For one thing, if discovered, the couple could be forced to marry. In addition, men and women could be fined and lashed. There are court records of couples who after being married for many years were punished for prenuptial fornication. Such activity was usually disclosed during a public confessional.

Adultery and the Scarlet Letter

In some ways, colonial attitudes toward adultery are similar to those of the present era. The colonists considered adultery a more serious offense than premarital coitus, and this tradition has come down to us today. Premarital coitus was more prevalent among the colonists than was adultery, and this variance also persists at present. And finally, although both sexes were severely punished for adultery, women seem to have been more harshly treated than men, and—in a social sense, at least—this is probably still true.

The Puritans considered adultery a grave offense and they employed legal, as well as religious, sanctions. In almost all of the New England colonies, adultery was originally punishable by death, and court records indicate that several people (of both sexes) were actually executed for the offense.

By 1700, the death sentence seems to have been superseded by whipping, imprisonment, banishment, and branding. Branding was believed to be particularly effective as a deterrent, and the "scarlet letter"—later made infamous by Hawthorne's book of the same name—occupied a prominent place in colonial history. Under the Acts and Laws of Connecticut, to take but one example, we read that

> whosoever shall commit adultery with a Married Woman or one Betrothed to another Man, both of them shall be severely Punished, by Whipping on the naked Body, and Stigmatized or Burnt on the Forehead with the Letter A, on a hot Iron.

> And each of them shall wear a Halter about their Necks, on the outside of their Garments, during their Abode in this Colony, so as it may be Visible. And as often as either of them shall be found without their Halters, worn as aforesaid, they shall, upon Information and Proof of same . . . be Whipt, not exceeding Twenty Stripes.[12]

Unfortunately for those involved, there was no feasible way to atone for adultery once the above penalty was imposed. Branding was permanent, and when the scarlet letter was affixed to a halter or "sewed upon the upper garments," it was presumably to be worn until death. (Pennsylvania had a bizarre set of laws pertaining to adultery. The Great Law of 1682 provided that anyone who "shall defile the marriage bed" be publicly whipped and imprisoned one year for the first offense. For the second offense the punishment was imprisonment for life. But under the Pennsylvania Act of 1705, a third offender was to be marked with an "A" branded on his forehead with a hot iron. Exactly how an adulterer could become a third offender after having spent his life in jail for the second offense is something for the legal mind to ponder!)

In passing, it might be mentioned that the problem of incest gave the colonists some concern. There is no way of estimating how much incest there really was, but the laws were just as severe as for adultery. In most of the New England colonies the only difference was use of the letter "I" instead of "A." Court statistics indicate that all of the offenders were males; while the number of such cases was small, colonial records are so incomplete that figures mean little. And, of course, a variety of other sex offenders never came before the courts at all.

SUMMARY

There is little doubt that the colonists took a dim view of sexual irregularities. The Puritans believed that the only legitimate sexual outlet was in marriage—and even marital coitus was forbidden on Sunday. They felt that sexual matters should not be discussed with children; in fact, the topic was

---

[12]George Howard, *A History of Matrimonial Institutions*, vol. 2 (Chicago: University of Chicago Press, 1904), 173.

Families were important to the settlement of the United States. Children were expected to obey their parents and follow specific rules of conduct. *The Copley Family.* John Singleton Copley. (*National Gallery of Art, Washington, D.C., Andrew W. Mellon Fund*)

more or less taboo among adults. And, judging by the harsh laws of the period, sexual transgressors were looked upon as a threat to society.

If, in retrospect, the attitude of the colonists seems to have been unduly strict, it should be kept in mind that, historically speaking, our present society has become relatively tolerant. It is only recently that sex education for children has become widespread, that sex has become a respectable topic of conversation, that sexual surveys have become rather common, and that sex outside marriage—in some quarters, at least—has come to be accepted. It is interesting to find that those who attempt to support traditional moral codes are often referred to as "puritanical."

The writers know from experience that college students tend to look aghast at the severity of the colonial sex codes. But, in all likelihood, the colonists would be equally aghast at our own! For the fact of the matter is that customs and laws which "work" in one historical era may fail in another. The permissive-restrictive pendulum seems to swing back and forth. To be effective, sexual codes must meet the needs of both the individual and society, and each generation tries to decide for itself where the point of balance lies.

QUESTIONS

1. There is no doubt that the early colonists faced extreme hardships in terms of weather, Indian attacks, inadequate housing, and the like. Would these hardships tend to make for a stable or an unstable family life? Defend your viewpoint.

2. Describe the furnishings of the early (1600s) American household. If, by some mysterious process, this early colonial family were able to obtain one modern household convenience or luxury, which one do you think would be chosen? Why?

3. Can you find in the early American courtship any practices that could be advantageous for couples today? Explain your answer.

4. How did courtship in early America differ from today's practice? What were some of the factors that brought about changes in the courtship system?

5. What role, if any, do you think "bundling" played in the transition from a highly restrictive to a more permissive society?

6. In the colonies, marriage was considered an obligation and a necessity, as well as a privilege. Why was this? What measures did the colonies utilize to "boost" marriage?

7. How would you describe the position of American women in the colonies, as compared to their position today?

8. How would you characterize the treatment of children in the American colonies? Do you agree (a) with the treatment, and (b) with the philosophy behind the treatment? Defend you position.

9. Write an essay describing how the early colonists defined sexual problems, and how they sought to deal with them.

10. Hawthorne's *The Scarlet Letter* is a widely read book even today, despite the fact that our sexual codes have softened considerably. How would you account for the book's continued popularity?

SELECTED READINGS

Blumstein, Philip, and Pepper Schwartz. "The American Couple in Historical Perspective." In *Marriage and Family in a Changing Society,* edited by James M. Henslin, 34–42. New York: The Free Press, 1985.

Boles, Jacqueline, and Maxine P. Atkinson. "Ladies: South by Northwest." *Sociological Spectrum,* Spring 1986, 63–81.

Brabant, Sarah. "Socialization for Change: Cultural Heritage of the Southern Woman." *Sociological Spectrum,* Spring 1986, 51–61.

Bullough, Vern L. "Technology for the Prevention of 'Les Maladies Produites Par La Masturbation.' " *Technology and Culture,* October 1987, 828–832.

Bushman, R. L., and C. L. Bushman. "The History of Cleanliness in America." *The Journal of American History,* March 1988, 1213–1238.

Butler, Anne M. *Daughters of Joy, Sisters of Misery. Prostitution in the American West, 1865–90.* Urbana and Chicago: The University of Illinois Press, 1985.

Calhoun, Arthur. *A Social History of the American Family,* 3 vols. New York: Barnes & Noble, 1985.

Gallman, James Mathew. "Relative Ages of Colonial Marriages." *Journal of Interdisciplinary History,* Winter 1984, 609–17.

Goldin, Claudia. "The Economic Status of Women in the Early Republic: Quantitative Evidence." *Journal of Interdisciplinary History,* Winter 1986, 375–404.

Grossberg, Michael. *Governing the Hearth: Law and the Family in Nineteenth-Century America.* Chapel Hill: The University of North Carolina Press, 1985.

Hareven, Tamara K. "American Families in Transition." In *Family in Transition,* edited by Arlene S. Skolnick and Jerome H. Skolnick, 40–58. Boston: Little, Brown, 1986.

Hawthorne, Nathaniel. *The Scarlet Letter.* New York: Chatham River Press, 1984.

Howard, George. *A History of Matrimonial Institutions,* 3 vols. Chicago: University of Chicago Press, 1904.

Illick, Joseph E. "Child-Rearing in Seventeenth-Century England and America." In *History of Childhood,* edited by Lloyd de Mause. New York: Peter Bedrick Books, 1988.

Landale, Nancy S. "Agricultural Opportunity and Marriage: The United States at the Turn of the Century." *Demography,* May 1989, 203–218.

Leslie, Kent Anderson. "A Myth of a Southern Lady: Antebellum Proslavery Rhetoric and the Proper Place of Women." *Sociological Spectrum,* Spring 1986, 31–49.

Leverenz, David. *The Language of Puritan Feeling: An Exploration in Literature, Psychology and Social History.* New Brunswick, NJ: Rutgers University Press, 1980.

Lockwood, Rose. "Birth, Illness, and Death in 18th-Century New England." *Journal of Social History,* Fall 1978, 111–25.

Matthaei, Julie A. *An Economic History of Women in America: Women's Work, the Sexual Division of Labor, and the Development of Capitalism.* New York: Schocken, 1982.

May, Elaine Tyler. *Great Expectations: Marriage and Divorce in Post-Victorian America.* Chicago: University of Chicago Press, 1980.

Mintz, S., and S. Kellogg. *Domestic Revolution: A Social History of American Family Life.* New York: The Free Press, 1988.

Rothman, Ellen K. *Hands and Hearts: A History of Courtship in America,* New York: Basic Books, 1984.

Scott, Donald M., and Bernard Wishy. *America's Families: A Documentary History.* New York: Harper & Row, 1982.

Seward, Rudy Ray. *The American Family: A Demographic History.* Beverly Hills, CA: Sage Publications, 1979.

Shammas, Carole. "The Domestic Environment in Early Modern England and America." *Journal of Social History,* Fall 1980, 3–24.

Smith, Daniel, and Michael Hindus. "Premarital Pregnancy in America, 1640–1971: An Overview and Interpretation." *Journal of Interdisciplinary History,* Spring 1975, 537–70.

Wells, Robert V. "Marriage Seasonals in Early America: Comparisons and Comments." *Journal of Interdisciplinary History,* Autumn 1987, 299–307.

TWO

American Family Varieties

Chapter
5

Experimental Family Organization

Even a cursory examination will reveal that society and the individual do not necessarily agree on the most effective type of family organization. Any number of individuals, in fact, have had some rather unusual ideas regarding family structure. These individuals, furthermore, have been able to implement their experiments, often in the face of considerable outside hostility.

The number of experimental family groups in American history probably runs into the hundreds. Most of them have been short-lived, with little if any effect on the larger society. Some, however, had a genuine impact and will never be forgotten—even though they eventually failed. One such group is the Oneida Community, which achieved much "notoriety" in the nineteenth century. The Oneidians have been chosen for analysis because of their radical social and sexual parameters.[1]

By way of contrast, we have also selected Koinonia, a twentieth century commune that—after 50 years—is still prospering! Interestingly, the future

---

[1]For an interesting pictorial account, see "The Oneida Community," *Colonial Homes,* March–April 1985, 66ff.

of Kononia may depend partly on having learned from failed experiments. In any case, let us begin with lessons of history gleaned from the Oneida experiment.

THE ONEIDA COMMUNITY

The Oneida story actually begins at Putney, Vermont, in 1831, where a fierce religious revival was in progress. One of those deeply affected was John Humphrey Noyes, a twenty-year-old graduate of Dartmouth College, who was serving his apprenticeship in a local law office. Although he attended the revival meetings with great skepticism, the result was electrifying. ("Light gleamed upon my soul.")[2] Forsaking the practice of law, Noyes entered the ministry, and upon graduation from Yale Theological Seminary in 1833, he was licensed to preach.

From the very beginning, John Humphrey Noyes was an acknowledged radical. He was convinced, for example, that Christ, whose second coming was awaited by so many, *had already returned to earth,* so that redemption, or liberation from sin, was an accomplished fact. The doctrine itself—the attainability of the sinless or perfect state—Noyes called "Perfectionism." For the spreading of this alleged heresy, his license to preach was revoked.

A small group had already begun to be attracted to the Perfectionist doctrine, however, in spite of its heterodox nature. Starting as a bible class in 1839 with Noyes as the pivotal member, this small group of Perfectionists grew both in number and in scope. Their discussions centered on the idea of spiritual equality, a belief that eventually came to embrace both the economic and sexual spheres. In the Kingdom of God, all beings were to love one another equally.

Accordingly, in 1846 the Putney Community was formed. Individual members followed a share-the-wealth type of economy in which private ownership was taboo. Paralleling their collectivist economy, adult members practiced sexual communism; that is, every adult male had marital privileges with every adult female, and vice versa. As might have been predicted, however, the citizens, of Vermont were soon up in arms, and in 1847 Noyes was arrested and charged with adultery.

Released under bond, he did not wait to stand trial but fled southward. Had he chosen to fight the case in court, the outcome would probably have been of sociohistoric interest. As it turned out, neither Noyes nor any of his Perfectionist followers were ever to stand trial for their sexual practices.

Even as the Putney Community was being broken up, however, Noyes was reassembling his flock in central New York State. The new community took shape in 1848 on the old Indian lands along Oneida Creek, and hence-

---

[2]See Constance Noyes Robertson, *Oneida Community Profiles* (Syracuse, NY: Syracuse University Press, 1977), chap. 1, 1–26.

The Mansion House in Oneida, New York. (*Oneida Ltd. Silversmiths*)

forth the Perfectionists were known as the Oneida Community. It was here that the most radical of all American marriage systems took root and, for several decades, flourished.

Starting again as a small group—no more than twenty or thirty persons in all—the Oneida Colony was barely able to survive the first few winters. The original members were primarily farmers and mechanics, and while their collectivist economy had certain advantages, they found it difficult to support a growing community solely from their land yields. Fortunately, one of their members, Sewell Newhouse, invented a steel trap, which turned out to be peerless in design. Demand for the product grew, and soon the major part of the Oneida economy came to be based on the manufacture of the now-famous traps. Thereafter, the group was without financial worry.

Social Organization

What was there, in terms of social organization, that held the Oneida Community together in the face of both internal problems and external pressures? One integrating element was the fact that practically the entire membership was housed under one roof. Although, over the years, there were six different branches and hundreds of members, the Perfectionists' home base was at Oneida, New York. It was there that the original communal home was built in 1849, to be replaced in 1862 by a spacious brick building known as the Mansion House. In subsequent years, as the membership grew, wings were added as needed. The building still stands, a striking architectural form internally as well as externally.

Although each adult had a small room of his or her own, the building was designed to encourage a feeling of togetherness, hence the inclusion of a communal dining hall, recreation rooms, library, concert hall, outdoor picnic area, and so forth. It was in the Big Hall of the Mansion House that John Humphrey Noyes gave his widely quoted home talks. It was here that musical concerts, dramas, readings, dances, and other forms of socializing were held.

Occasionally, outside artists were invited, but on a day-to-day basis the community was more or less a closed group, with members seldom straying very far from home. What might be called their reference behavior related entirely to the group. The outside community was, figuratively and literally, "outside" and was always referred to as The World. It was this system of *cultural enclosure,* sustained over several decades, that served as a primary solidifying force.

It should not be thought that life in the old community was a continual round of entertainment. The Oneidans built their own home, raised their own food, made all their own clothes (including shoes!), did their own laundry, ran their own school, and performed countless other collective tasks. The following comment was made to one of the writers by a woman whose childhood had been spent in the Mansion House:

> As children, we loved to visit the various departments they used to have: the laundry, the kitchen, the fruit cellar, the bakery, the dairy, the dining room, the ice house, the tailor shop—they even had a Turkish bath in the basement. The thing is that small groups of people worked side by side in most of these places, and they were able to talk with each other as they worked.
>
> It's hard to explain, but my mother used to tell me that no matter how menial the job was, they were so busy talking to each other that the time always flew. It was this sort of thing, year after year, that gave rise to a kindred spirit.

Additionally, adults were subject to self-imposed deprivations whenever they felt the group welfare threatened, and by modern standards "group welfare" was given a most liberal interpretation. For example, although the Perfectionists ate well, meat was served sparingly, pork not at all. Alcoholic beverages were prohibited, as were tea and coffee. Smoking also came to be taboo. The reasoning behind these prohibitions is not always clear, but presumably the Oneidans were dead set against informal distractions of an "anti-family" nature. Thus, dancing was permitted, since it was a social activity, while coffee drinking and smoking were condemned on the ground that they were individualistic and appetitive in nature.

Their unique social organization was not the only thing that held the Oneida Colony together. As the membership increased, three basic principles of Noyes' teaching combined to form the very heart of Perfectionist

The Mansion House Library. *(Culver Pictures, Inc.)*

lifestyle: (1) economic communism; (2) mutual criticism; and (3) complex marriage.

Economic Communism

Members of the Oneida Community held equal ownership of all property, their avowed aim being to eliminate competition for the possession of material things. The needs of individual members were taken care of, but there was simply no concept of private ownership, even in the realm of personal belongings such as clothes, trinkets, and children's toys.

Writing of his boyhood, Pierrepont Noyes, a son of John Humphrey, states that "throughout my childhood, the private ownership of anything seemed to me a crude artificiality to which an unenlightened Outside still clung. For instance, we were keen for our favorite sleds, but it never occurred to me that I could possess a sled to the exclusion of the other boys. So it was with all Children's House property." With respect to clothing, the same author writes that "going-away clothes for grown folks, as for children, were common property. Any man or woman preparing for a trip was fitted out with one of the suits kept in stock for that purpose."[3]

---

[3]Pierrepont Noyes, *My Father's House* (New York: Farrar & Rinehart, 1937), 126–27.

In addition to the manufacture of traps, the Oneidans found a ready market for their crops, which they put up in glass jars and cans and which became known for their uniform quality. As their business know-how (and their prosperity!) increased, it became necessary to hire outside help, and eventually the Perfectionists were employing several hundred local workers.

Starting in 1877, the Oneidans embarked on the manufacture of silverware. This venture proved so successful that, when the community was disbanded, the silverware component was perpetuated as a joint-stock company (Oneida Ltd.), whose product is still widely used today.

How much of the economic success of the group was due to the communistic methods employed, and how much was due to the fortuitous invention of the trap is difficult to say. On the one hand, collectivist methods probably had certain advantages over competing private enterprise. When it became necessary to meet the deadline on a large order, for example, it was not uncommon for the entire community—including the youngsters—to turn out.

On the other hand, the fact remains that the Perfectionists were rapidly becoming bankrupt until Sewell Newhouse's trap, figuratively and literally, "caught on." By the time of the Civil War, the trap had become the standard in both the United States and Canada. The record shows that, in a good year, the community turned out close to 300,000 traps!

In order to eliminate feelings of discrimination, the various jobs within the community were rotated from year to year. Members were quick to point out that almost everyone took a turn at the necessary menial tasks. If people did their work well, they presumably had equal status whether they were farm laborers or plant superintendents. It was work, rather than a specific type of job, that was held in high regard. In fact, one of the Perfectionists' most successful innovations was their employment of the cooperative enterprise or *bee*. The latter was

> an ordinance exactly suited to Community life. A bee would be announced at dinner or perhaps on the bulletin board: "A bee in the kitchen to pare apples"; or "A bee to pick strawberries at five o'clock tomorow morning"; or "A bee in the Upper Sitting Room to sew bags."[4]

It should be mentioned that there was seldom any trouble with idlers. On the contrary, a major difficulty was to screen out most of those who made application to join the community. Relatively few new members were admitted, and those who were accepted had to undergo a long and severe probationary period.

In their efforts to promote equality, all Perfectionists were required to eat the same kind of food, wear the same type of clothing, and live in the same home. For both sexes, dress was uniformly simple, with jewelry and

---

[4]Constance Noyes Robertson, ed., *Oneida Community: An Autobiography, 1851–1876* (Syracuse, NY: Syracuse University Press, 1970), 103.

Cooperative group activity was a hallmark of the Oneida Community. Here the Community's members participate in a bag bee. (*Historical Pictures Services, Inc., Chicago*)

adornments tabooed. John Humphrey Noyes, incidentally, was responsible for a genuine innovation in the women's clothing style. Dissatisfied with ordinary female attire, he declared in the First Annual Report (1848) that "woman's dress is a standard lie. It proclaims that she is not a two-legged animal, but something like a churn, standing on castors!" Accordingly, a committee was set up to work on the problem. The costume decided upon was a short, knee-length skirt, with loose trousers (pantalettes) down to the shoes!

Mutual Criticism

The Oneida Community had neither laws nor law-enforcing officers, and there was little need for them, major infractions being all but unknown. In any organization, however, conduct problems are bound to occur, and while the Oneidans considered themselves Perfectionists, they acknowledged that individual foibles did exist. "Mutual criticism" was the method by which such problems were handled.

Whenever a member was found to be deviating from group norms, or whenever a personality or character weakness manifested itself, a committee of peers would meet with the offender to discuss the matter. The subject was required to sit quietly while each of the committee members voiced his or her criticisms. From all accounts, the system was a success—as can be seen from the following comments, which appeared during 1871–1872 in the *Oneida Circular,* the Community's weekly newspaper:

> I feel as though I had been washed; felt clean through the advice and criticism given. I would call the truth the soap; the critics the scrubbers; Christ's spirit the water.

> Criticism is administered in faithfulness and love without respect to persons. I look upon the criticisms I have received since I came here as the greatest blessings that have been conferred upon me.[5]

In the nature of human nature, it would seem that most of us resent personal criticism. How, then, can we account for the success of the Oneida venture? Levine and Bunker give the following explanation:

> Criticism, to be effective, requires that the individual being criticized respect the opinions of those who are criticizing. To respect another's opinion, one needs to believe that the criticism comes from a disinterested party, in the sense that the critic is free of personal malice or does not represent some other competing position.

> Moreover, the individual receiving criticism should feel safe enough to be receptive to the comments of others, even if hearing them is painful. To feel safe must mean that one believes the group will continue to regard him as a member and meet his needs, even if the momentary treatment feels harsh.[6]

Krinopathy The Oneidans were so convinced of the effectiveness of mutual criticism that they actually used the technique as a cure for illness! Known as "krinopathy," the criticism-cure was applied to both children and adults and was used for everything from common colds to more serious diseases. The following account appeared in the *Oneida Circular* of December 4, 1863:

> It is a common custom here for every one who may be attacked with any disorder to send for a committee of six or eight persons, in whose faith and spiritual judgement he had confidence, to come and criticize him. The result, when administered sincerely, is almost universally to throw the patient into a sweat, or to bring on a reaction of his life against disease, breaking it up and restoring him soon to usual health.

The Perfectionists not infrequently went to extremes, however, and krinopathy was a case in point. For mutual criticism sometimes continued even after a person had died! Deceased members whose personal effects—

---

[5]See Harriet Worden, *Old Mansion House Memories* (Kenwood, Oneida, NY: privately printed, 1950), 15–16.

[6]Murray Levine and Barbara Bunker, *Mutual Criticism* (Syracuse, NY: Syracuse University Press, 1975), xxi–xxii.

letters, diaries, and the like—were thought to be incriminating might find themselves (in the hereafter) being subjected to an "earthly criticism."

In spite of some excesses, nevertheless, there is no doubt that mutual criticism worked. In fact, some observers—including the present writers—feel that mutual criticism was the single most effective method of social control employed by the community.

Complex Marriage

The world does not remember the Oneidans for their economic communism or their mutual criticism, but for their system of complex marriage. Rightly or wrongly, the name "Oneida" conjures up thoughts about the unique sex practices of the community. Noyes himself coined the term "free love," although he seems to have preferred the phrase "complex marriage," or occasionally "pantogamy." Realistically, the Oneida marital system can best be described as a combination of communitarian living and group marriage.

From the Putney days, John Humphrey Noyes had no time for romantic love or monogamous marriage. Such practices were to him manifestations of selfishness and personal possession. Romantic love, or "special love" as it was called in the community, was believed to give rise to jealousy and hypocrisy and, acording to Perfectionist doctrine, made spiritual love impossible to attain.

Accordingly, Noyes promulgated the idea of complex marriage: since it was natural for all men to love all women and all women to love all men, it followed that every adult should consider himself or herself married to every other adult of the opposite sex. This collective spiritual union of men and women also included the right to sexual intercourse.

The Perfectionist leader felt strongly that "men and women find universally that their susceptibility to love is not burnt out by one honeymoon, or satisfied by one lover. On the contrary, the secret history of the human heart will bear out the assertion that it is capable of loving any number of times and any number of persons. Variety is, in the nature of things, as beautiful and useful in love as in eating and drinking. . . . We need love as much as we need food and clothing; and if we trust God for those things, why not for love?"[7]

John Humphrey Noyes was a devout person, and the Oneida Perfectionists were a deeply religious group; any assessment of their sexual practices must take these factors into consideration. Insofar as the available information indicates, the community abided by the doctrine of complex marriage not for reasons of lust, as was sometimes charged, but because of the conviction that they were following God's word.

In practice, since most of the adult men and women lived in the Man-

---

[7]Quoted in Robert Allerton Parker, *A Yankee Saint: John Humphrey Noyes and the Oneida Community* (New York: G. P. Putnam's Sons, 1935), 182–83.

sion House, sex relations were easy to arrange. There was, however, one requirement that was adhered to: a man could not have sexual intercourse with a woman unless the latter gave her consent. Procedurally, if a man desired sex relations, he would transmit the message to a central committee, who would thereupon make his request known to the woman in question. The actual go-between was usually an older female member of the committee.

The system was inaugurated, as Parker points out, so that the women members "might, without embarrassment, decline proposals that did not appeal to them. No member should be obliged to receive at any time, under any circumstances, the attention of those they had not learned to love. . . . Every woman was to be free to refuse any or every, man's attention."[8] Although the procedure varied somewhat over the years, if the central committee granted approval and the woman in question assented, then the man simply went to the woman's room at bedtime and spent an hour or so with her before retiring to his own quarters.

It should be pointed out that Oneidans were supposed to act like ladies and gentlemen at all times. Inappropriate behavior, suggestive language, overt displays of sexuality—such actions were not tolerated. As a matter of fact, sexual behavior was not openly discussed within the community, and it is doubtful whether the subject of "Who was having relations with whom?" ever became common knowledge. One male member who became too inquisitive on this score was literally thrown out of the community, an act which represented the only physical expulsion in the group's history.

Role of Women   There is no doubt that John Humphrey Noyes had a special place in his heart for the Oneida women—and in this respect he was years ahead of his time. He saw to it that they played an integral part in the day-to-day operations of the community. The following remarks, made to one of the writers, provide a good example.

> One thing that most people have overlooked is that Noyes delegated a lot more responsibility to the women here than they ever would have received on the outside. Every committee had women on it. It made a difference, too. All the old folks will tell you it made both men and women respect each other.

In the sexual sphere, also, the Perfectionist leader had advanced ideas about the role of women. Starting in the Putney period, he rejected the idea that sex was simply a "wifely duty," that is, an act tolerated by the female at the pleasure of the male. Later on, he incorporated his beliefs in the Oneida *Handbook,* as the following passage indicates:

> The liberty of monogamous marriage, as commonly understood, is the liberty of a man to sleep habitually with a woman, liberty to please himself alone in

---

[8]Ibid., 183.

his dealings with her, liberty to expose her to child-bearing without care or consultation.

The term Free Love, as understood by the Oneida Community, does *not* mean any such freedom of sexual proceediings. The theory of sexual interchange which governs all the general measures of the Community is that which in ordinary society governs the proceedings in *courtship*.

It is the theory that love *after* marriage should be what it is *before* marriage— a glowing attraction on both sides, and not the odious obligation of one party, and the sensual selfishness of the other.[9]

Although rumors aplenty were carried by the outsiders, there is unfortunately no published record of the extent to which requested sexual liaisons were vetoed by the central committee or refused by the women themselves. All the evidence is fragmentary. Some individuals, naturally, were more in demand than others. Carden, who has done research on the subject, believes that the women often had more than four different partners a month.

A physician who interviewed a number of ex-members after the break-up reported that women had intercourse every two to four days. Another report, also by a physician, quoted an obviously discontented older woman who had left the Community. She complained that young girls would "be called upon to have intercourse as often as seven times in a week and oftener."[10]

On the other hand, that there was some rejection can be inferred from Parker's finding—based on a lengthy study—that "this entire freedom of the women to accept or reject the advances of their lovers kept men as alert as during more conventional courtships. Men sought, as always, to prove themselves worthy of the favor of their sweethearts; and that made their life, they confessed, one continuous courtship."[11]

The Eugenics Program

Child rearing occupied a special place in the Perfectionist scheme of things. Having familiarized himself with the principles of Charles Darwin and Francis Galton, Noyes was convinced of the feasibility of applying scientific methods to the propagation of the race. He felt that the only people who should have children were those who possessed superior physical and mental abilities. A clear statement of his position appeared in the *Oneida Circular*.

Why should not beauty and noble grace of person and every other desirable quality of men and women, internal and external, be propagated and intensi-

---

[9]*Handbook of the Oneida Community* (Oneida, NY: Office of the Oneida Circular, 1875), 42.

[10]Maren Lockwood Carden, *Oneida: Utopian Community to Modern Corporation* (Baltimore: The Johns Hopkins University Press, 1969), 53.

[11]Parker, *Yankee Saint*, 184.

fied beyond all former precedent—by the application of the same scientific principles of breeding that produce such desirable results in the case of sheep, cattle, and horses?[12]

Although the term "eugenics" had not yet been coined, a eugenics program—in which specially chosen adults would be utilized for breeding purposes—was exactly what John Humphrey Noyes had in mind. And of course, what more logical place to put eugenic principles into actual practice than the Oneida Community? Noyes called his program "stirpiculture" (from the Latin *stirps,* meaning root or stock), and it was not long before the scientific world was discussing the implications of the unique experiment being conducted in central New York State.

For 20 years after founding their community, the Oneidans had largely refrained from bearing children. They reasoned that procreation should be delayed until such time as the group had facilities for proper child care. The first two decades, so to speak, merely served the purpose of laying the groundwork for the future growth of the colony. The birth control technique advocated by Noyes was *coitus reservatus;* that is, sexual intercourse up to, but not including, ejaculation on the part of the male. Until they had learned the necessary coital control, younger males in the community were required to limit their sex relations to women who had passed the menopause. Although the technique was claimed by many writers to be incapable of attainment, the record contradicts them.

In any case, by 1869 the group was ready to embark upon its pioneer eugenics program. Couples desirous of becoming parents (stirps) made formal application before a cabinet composed of key members of the community, Noyes apparently holding the deciding vote. The cabinet, after assessing the physical and mental qualities of the applicants, would either approve or dissaprove the requests.* The stirpiculture program was in effect for about a decade before the community disbanded, and during this ten-year period fifty-eight children were born. Noyes himself fathered upwards of a dozen children, so that evidently he was not averse to self-selection.

Children remained in their mothers' care up to the age of fifteen months, whereupon they were gradually transferred to a special section of the Mansion House. Henceforth they would spend most of their childhood in age-graded classes. Although the children were treated with kindness by their parents, sentimentalizing was frowned upon, the feeling being that under Perfectionism all adults should love all children and vice versa.

By their own reports, the children were evidently well adjusted. Recreation, schooling, medical care—all were provided in keeping with accepted child-rearing practices. As a group, the children were remarkably healthy.

---

[12]*Oneida Circular,* 27 March 1865.

*The specific criteria and methods for selecting the strips have never been revealed. It is known that a cabinet was set up to make the selection, but what system they used remains a mystery.

Mortality comparisons indicated that the products of stirpiculture had a significantly lower death rate than children born outside the community.

That most of the youngsters had a happy childhood can be seen from the following comment:

> Well, I remember one little girl wanted her mother. She'd stand outside her window and call to her, even though the mother wasn't supposed to answer. Other than that particular case, all the children seemed happy enough. Everybody was good to us. You knew you were loved because it was like a big family. Also, there were so many activities for the youngsters, so many things to do, well—believe me—we were happy children. Everybody around here will give you the same answer on that!

What was the outcome of the stirpiculture program? Were the children actually superior? Many observers thought so. A number of the young people achieved eminence in business and in the professions. And most of them, in turn, had children who were successful. There is one catch, however, in assessing the effectiveness of the program, and that is the fact that the children presumably had an advantageous environment *as well as* sound heredity.

The Breakup

As might have been predicted, outside pressures against the Oneida Community were becoming irresistible. Rumblings grew louder against such practices as "free love," "lust," and "animal breeding." Although many of the surrounding townspeople knew the Perfectionists as hard-working, devout individuals, professional crusaders such as Anthony Comstock, self-appointed watchdog of American morals, were successful in creating a storm of adverse public criticism. As a result of this ever-increasing pressure campaign, the Oneidans were forced to give up their practice of complex marriage.

Then, too, in the later years all was not well within the community itself. John Humphrey Noyes was growing old, and in 1877 he resigned as leader. One of his sons, Dr. Theodore R. Noyes, took over the leadership, but he was in no sense the leader his father was, and factionalism within the community became rife. In June of 1879—for some inexplicable reason—John Humphrey Noyes left Oneida for Canada, never to return.

In late 1879, after fearlessly defying public opinion for almost half a century, Noyes sent a message to the community (from Canada) proposing that they abolish complex marriage and revert to the accepted marital practices. Soon afterward the group disbanded, many of the members becoming formally married. Economically, a joint-stock company was organized and the stock (worth about $600,000) was then divided among the members. Last-ditch efforts to salvage some communal type of family organization failed, thus ending—in rather pathetic fashion—what was probably the most radical social experiment in America.

John Humphrey Noyes, in the early 1870s.
(*Culver Pictures, Inc.*)

The Character of John Humphrey Noyes   Any attempt to explain either
the success or failure of the Oneida Community must take into consideration the character of its leader, John Humphrey Noyes. By all accounts,
he was an original thinker with a remarkable sense of dedication, persever-
ance, and courage. He had tremendous vigor, a vigor that manifested itself
in the spiritual, the mental—and the physical. It can be no coincidence that
his utopian community included relative freedom of sex expression. At the
same time, he strove to keep the behavior of the group on a consistently
high plane. The most striking comment of John Humphrey Noyes was the
following, made to the writer by a woman whose mother had known the
Perfectionist leader quite well:

> I've often wondered about the traits that made him what he was. I just don't
> know. You might have got an answer 100 years ago. Now, maybe it's too late.
> I remember asking my mother the same question when I was a young girl.
> "Why did you live that way? What was there about him?" And I remember
> her saying: "Don't ask me to explain it. I can't. All I know is that when you

were in his presence you knew you were with someone who was not an ordinary man. . . ."

On the other side of the ledger, Noyes was often unpredictable, a trait shared by many zealots. He not only left the group for protracted periods of time, but twice—once at Putney and once at Oneida—deserted when the end appeared imminent. During his reign as leader, moreover, he apparently made no provision for the succession of authority. Had able young men been trained as potential leaders, the factionalism that developed in later years might have been avoided.

Although the Oneida Community seemed to work well enough while it was in being, the inexorable fact remains that it did not last. Noyes' personal attributes aside, the forces that held the group together and promoted group loyalty were not strong enough to make for survival. It is true that the colony lacked the usual social problems and that there was a strong measure of social cohesion; in fact, the records indicate that, on the average, only three or four persons "seceded" each year. It is clear, nevertheless, that the existing sentiments, values, and traditions were not sufficiently durable to bring about an integrated, permanent type of social organization.

Perhaps, under the circumstances, it would have been rather surprising if the Oneida Community had endured, for Noyes was attempting to create a society *without marriage and the family* as these terms are commonly understood. The human family seems to be based on sex attraction and exclusiveness, parental child rearing, and the need for primary-group association, all of which operate as powerful systematizing forces. It is quite possible, in modern society, that some other sort of familial arrangement could be worked out, but it is difficult to conceive of an Oneida-type endeavor as filling the bill. The wonder of it may well be that Noyes' experiment lasted as long as it did.

KOINONIA PARTNERS

Koinonia commune has not been studied nearly so much as Oneida, even though after forty-five years Oneida was clearly in its decline. On the other hand, after forty-five years Koinonia is still prospering. The following account is based largely on interviews with the Koinonia partners and with Mrs. Florence Jordan, cofounder of Koinonia. Another invaluable source has been Dallas Lee's *Cotton Patch Evidence*.[13]

Koinonia was incorporated as a farming commune in 1942. It began as an idea of Clarence Jordan, a white, Baptist minister from Sumpter County, Georgia. According to the recollections of Mrs. Florence Jordan, she and her husband ignored the temper of the time as they advocated fellowship

---

[13]Dallas Lee, *Cotton Patch Evidence* (New York: Harper & Row, 1971), 28.

Clarence Jordan, the founder of Koinonia Commune. *(Koinonia Partners)*

and economic sharing among people of all races. But the opposition to their views was so strong that they decided to organize a commune with others of like beliefs.

The Experiment

As the United States became absorbed in World War II, a number of Baptist ministers could not reconcile their commitment to the Sermon on the Mount with warfare and racism. They shared their concerns through a newsletter published in South Carolina. It was in this inexpensive, home-prepared newsletter, that Clarence found a letter from a missionary in Burma whose thoughts paralleled his own. According to Dallas Lee, this letter motivated Clarence to assemble several families in a close communal relationship. The gist of the letter can be viewed as an unofficial document for the beginning of Koinonia commune. Its message was clear:

> If the barriers that divide man, and cause wars, race conflict, economic competition, class struggles, labor disputes are ever to be broken down, *they must be broken down in small groups of people living side by side,* who plan consciously and deliberately to find a way wherein they can all contribute to the Kingdom according to their respective abilities.[14]

The author of the letter, the Reverend Martin England, returned with his family from Burma to the United States and met with the Jordans in

---

[14]Ibid., 28.

Mrs. Florence Jordan, co-founder of the Koinonia Partners. (*Koinonia Partners*)

1941. The two families spent a great deal of time together until they decided to find a location for their commune. They found a financial backer who made a substantial down payment on 440 acres of farm land, which they later expanded to 1100 acres. They named the commune Koinonia, pronounced Koin-oh-NEE-ah, a Greek word from the New Testament meaning "fellowship or community." They chose this name to reflect their belief in sharing.

From the beginning, the founders recognized that survival depended on profit. Without a sound economic base nothing else would be possible. Today, Koinonia derives its profit from the raising of peanuts and soybeans, and from a mail-order pecan business. However, none of the partners use any of the profit for more than simple living. They believe that acquisition of personal wealth is greed and, therefore, un-Christian. The scriptures, as used at Koinonia, emphasize this belief: "All that believe were together, and had all things in common," and "distribution was made according as he had need" (Acts 2:44 and 4:35).

For the first fifteen years of the commune, the Koinonia farm engaged local labor to work under the old share-cropping system. As Florence Jordan explained, they shared fairly with the workers:

> We paid good wages. Our rule of thumb was, if the going wage is $3.00 per day, which it very often was in 1950s, it ought to be worth at least $6.00, and we would pay $6.00. And if it was stacking peanuts and the going rate was $25.00 per stack, we'd pay $50.00. We didn't make big profits. We made enough to live and that was all we needed.

Koinonia's fair treatment of labor disturbed some local land-owners.

Equally disturbing to the surrounding community was the fact that at Koinonia there was no enforced segregation. While the partners were white they ate meals and shared other facilities with black workers. Koinonia seemed to be pointing the way toward integration at the time when that was an emotional issue in the South. Thus, anti-integration groups targeted Koinonia for more than a decade.

Struggle for the Survival

In a drive to close Koinonia, a number of local businesses organized a boycott. They would not sell to or buy from Koinonia. This boycott began around 1956 when egg production and farming were the main sources of income at Koinonia. To stay in business the commune needed chicken feed, seeds, fertilizer, tractor parts, gas, and so on. Because they could not buy these necessities it seemed that the end of the commune was inevitable.

As the Jordans and other families were getting ready to leave, a retiring couple from Albany, Georgia, offered their pecan-shelling machinery to Koinonia. Since there were a large number of pecan trees on the farm, the couple encouraged the Koinonians to shell the pecans and sell them through the U.S. mail. As it turned out, this was just the kind of help needed to get Koinonia back on its feet.

After the recovery a number of community services were started, including the opening of a summer camp for poor children. Because these camps were integrated, Koinonians were prevented from keeping them open. Health inspectors were sent over to look for possible deficiencies that could be used to close the camp. Such inspections never produced damaging evidence, but the charges of "corrupting the morals of children" were brought. Koinonians were accused of letting the children watch farm animals give birth. The grand jury summoned Clarence Jordan. Of course they dismissed the charges, but different forms of harassment continued until the camp was closed.

Closing the camp did not appease Koinonia's opponents. Eventually, the harassment turned to violence. Koinonia's roadside store was destroyed by a bomb. When they rebuilt it, it was bombed again, causing thousands of dollars in property losses in addition to lost income. Some members were shot at and one died of a heart attack during an assault. Beatings and the threat of violence lasted for several years. Pressures escalated, and the commune began to decline. Some members remained, prepared to die for their rights, but most left.

In 1968, it seemed that the end of the commune had come. Only the Jordans and one other family remained, and the boycott still continued. However, within one year Koinonia's fortune had changed: the boycott was lifted, and other families joined the commune.

With new hope for the future, Koinonians reaffirmed their original goals. They also developed a more formal organizational structure that assured democratic decision making and corporate-style leadership.

Organizational Structure and Leadership

In 1968, Koinonia incorporated under the name of Koinonia Partners Inc. Whereas before incorporation relationships and responsibilities were informal, the reorganization instituted codes of operation and created a legal status of "partners."

The Partners The "partner" is a term used to designate a member who formally belongs to the commune. Currently there are twenty-seven partners: eleven married couples, four single females, and one single male. While Koinonians have never discriminated on the basis of race, all the partners are white. The married partners have fifteen children among them, ranging in age from under one to eighteen. In addition to the partners, the commune houses fifteen to twenty volunteers. The volunteers share the goals and the ideals of Koinonia; but they do not wish to make the commitment required of partners.

Even though Koinonia has a liberal admissions policy, it is difficult for most people to make a commitment to nonmaterialistic life. Mrs Jordan explained:

> In many ways we give up a lot of the modern things people think they have to have. We don't have individual cars, we don't go and come when we want to because we don't have the means to go and come! And we don't buy a lot of luxury items. We don't go in for a lot of commercial entertainment or anything of this sort because we just don't spend our money that way.

The partners are responsible for the selection of new members. While they accept more applications than they reject, the selection of new partners is crucial. As one partner put it:

> Probably the single most important decision that we make is "Who is going to live here?" Ultimately the type of people we have here shapes all other decisions. We have set up a residence committee to decide on new resident partners. We seldom say no. That happened when the committee decided that the person was not looking realistically at what Koinonia had to offer.

The applicants are required to divest all of their assets before joining the commune. It should be emphasized that the funds from new members are not accepted for any purpose, including donations for charitable programs operated by Koinonia. Clarence Jordan established this principle to assure that money matters never come between partners. While this principle prevented hundreds from joining, one of the families joining in 1969 permanently divested three million dollars to join Koinonia!

Partners are free to leave Koinonia at will. There is neither legal nor social pressure to stay. It is understood that some may change their minds after they experience hard work, responsibility for management, and no monetary gain for oneself beyond necessities. But most partners stay two or more years. Twelve of the present partners have been there for ten years or longer.

Most who left took other challenges in service to humanity. Others left

Clarence Jordan and a local worker. From the beginning, farming has been an important source of income at Koinonia. (*Koinonia Partners*)

for various reasons. Because the partners feel that the size of membership is important for efficient operations and for maintaining close personal relations, in 1979 six partners left to start another commune based on the same organizational principles as Koinonia's. Over the last ten years two partners left because they felt that their possibilities for marriage were low at Koinonia, and two more left because they discovered that the situation at Koinonia did not suit them.

As Koinonia became more profitable and involved itself further in larger-scale community projects, money management became a complex problem. To cope with this complexity, the partners delegated the responsibility for money management to an outside board of directors. To manage day-to-day activities at Koinonia the board appoints a partner to serve as an "activity coordinator." The members of the board are volunteers who allocate funds according to community needs. The profits and any private donations are placed into The Fund for Humanity.

The Fund for Humanity   The mechanism for applying theology to economics did not fully materialize until The Fund for Humanity was established. The fund serves as a way to raise money and to channel profits toward one purpose: to build family houses for the poorest people in the area.

Over the last seventeen years Koinonia has constructed over 160 houses on their own property and elsewhere. The partners serve on the Housing

Koinonia partners and volunteers build family houses for the poorest people in the area. (*Koinonia Partners*)

Selection Committee, which chooses new homeowners based on their needs. The new owners are given a no-interest mortgage. In 1986, monthly payments were around $100 per month for a 1000-square-foot, three-bedroom, single-family house with appliances. Payments were even lower for those who could not afford $100 per month.

This service is appreciated by the local community, which no longer opposes Koinonia. But the impact has been broader. Based on the idea of The Fund for Humanity, one ex-partner in cooperation with Koionia established a similar international fund called The Habitat for Humanity, Inc. This organization has around 150 affiliates in the United States and 27 in foreign countries.[15]

Clarence Jordan lived long enough to see the first house being built. He died in 1969, but not before he was assured that the commune was to be governed by rules of the incorporation instead of the charisma of a leader. Partly as a result of this planning, the membership remained committed to the principles of incorporation even after the founder died.

[15]Mark Rockwell, "Koinonia's Housing Ministry," *Newsletter,* Spring 1986, 3.

The Extended Family

In some ways Koinonia resembles the traditional extended family. For example, three generations live in close proximity on the same farm. And, as is the case with the extended family in general, sexual relations are restricted to married couples only. The most striking aspect of the extended family is apparent in performance of family functions and in family-like relationships among the partners.

Traditional family functions—education, recreation, and the like—are largely performed within the extended Koinonian family. Even the economic function is within the realm of the family. The members raise much of their own food and make their own clothes. The money to support themselves is acquired through industries adjacent to their homes. Their many mail-order products are produced, packaged, and shipped from the farm. A package-delivery company makes daily trips to Koinonia to pick up orders for distribution from coast to coast.

On Sundays no one works. In the morning some of the members go to church services in the surrounding community. The afternoon is reserved for services at the farm. There is never a shortage of ordained people because some of the partners are ministers. Teaching religion is a family matter, much as it probably was in colonial times.

The noon meals at Koinonia are eaten together with visitors, workers, partners, and volunteers. The partners may have their evening meals in their own homes. They can have privacy whenever they choose. In practice, however, much of the time is spent with others. One of the partners explained:

> We have a lot of people with whom we share activities day after day. We are worshiping and working and playing and eating, and practically everything we do we do together. That alone gives an element of wholeness I never had before.

The partners often refer to themselves as a family. In evaluating their communal relations, one partner contrasted the life at Koinonia with an ordinary nuclear family:

> In a nuclear family when you are related to another person, you still are reserving your things for yourself and he is reserving his things for himself. When you live in this community you have said every day, day in and day out, "I trust you and you trust me."

Another partner reflected, "It's a lot like the way I grew up. The relationship between the partners is a lot like family interaction. Real close."

If there is a way to characterize relationships at Koinonia it is that of closeness. Many partners do not hesitate to use the word "love." At Koinonia the word *love* is synonymous with "concern" or "care," not with "sex." When there is a problem between spouses, siblings, or partners, the community is always ready to help. "If there is a problem," said one partner, "the whole group in love tries to work it out."

Koinonia partners have avoided leadership and sexual problems associ-

Koinonia partners and their families. In some ways Koinonia resembles the extended family. Three generations live in close proximity on the same farm. *(Koinonia Partners)*

ated with communal living. Under these conditions, it seems Koinonians have avoided major errors that brought down the Oneida and many other communes in this and in the last century.

SUMMARY

For a commune to survive, it must overcome some major causes of communal failure. These include economic fragility, weak leadership, aberrant membership, lack of commitment, inadequate social organization, failure to satisfy primary group needs, and difficulty in the socializing of children.[16] Some researchers feel that lack of privacy is also related to the failure of a commune.[17] How long Koinonia will survive in part depends on these criteria. Let us recapitulate.

First, at Koinonia economic strength has never been taken for granted. The partners studied whatever they needed to operate a profitable farming and mail-order business. Clarence Jordan, for example, was a minister and a classical Greek scholar, but he also studied agriculture at the University of Georgia.

---

[16]William M. Kephart, "Why They Fail: A Socio-Historical Analysis of Religious and Secular Communes," *Journal of Comparative Family Studies,* Autumn 1974, 139.

[17]Noreen Cornfield, "The Success of Urban Communes," *Journal of Marriage and the Family,* February 1983, 124.

The problems of membership and commitment are controlled by a stringent membership requirement. The requirement to divest possessions with no prospect of recovery is a step only a few can make. But those who do are serious about their membership.

Leadership and social organization at Koinonia go together. Equality is stressed, and leadership is seen as a role of equal value to other essential roles. Important monetary decisions are delegated to an outside board of directors. The day-to-day person in charge is called "activity coordinator." This phrase is used to avoid status distinctions which would be conveyed by such words as "director," "manager," or "executive." The rationale for equating roles is to avoid conflict between business and the equalitarian "extended family."

These concerns assure the members of Koinonia that the relationships are affectionate and caring but not suffocating. People get together because it is convenient, because they like it, or because they must solve some collective task. Privacy is respected and assured through living arrangements. Each family has its own house.

It seems that while relationships come first at Koinonia, at the same time no one is indispensable. Partners can come and go, but the roles, goals, and functions remain intact. Therefore, Koinonia is different from Oneida and, theoretically, could go on for a long time.

QUESTIONS

1. How did the lifestyle of the Oneida Community differ from that of Koinonia Community?

2. Did the two groups have anything in common in the sexual sphere? Explain why or why not.

3. Explain the differences in leadership style at Koinonia and at Oneida Community. Is this leadership a factor in longevity of each group?

4. How did Koinonia partners come to adopt the extended family as a form of social organization, and what was their rationale for this arrangement?

5. Describe the decline of Oneida community. What measures might have been taken to prevent this decline?

6. Write an essay describing the early years of John Noyes' group, that is, before they settled at Oneida, New York.

7. What role did religion play in the social organization of Koinonia community? Give some examples.

8. To what extent did economic philosophies, as practiced by each commune, contribute to their overall success? Defend your answer.

9. How did the practice of mutual criticism operate at Oneida? Would such a system be effective, say, in a modern college fraternity or sorority?

10. It might be said that the system of complex marriage at Oneida was a hundred years ahead of its time. Would you agree with this statement?

11. Why is it so difficult to assess the effectiveness of the Perfectionists' stirpiculture program?

12. Identify the factors that may contribute to continuation and others that may contribute to the possible demise of Koinonia commune. Which factors do you feel will prevail over the next ten years? Why?

SELECTED READINGS

Berger, Bennett M. *The Survival of Counterculture*. Berkeley, CA: University of California Press, 1981.

Carden, Maren Lockwood. *Oneida: Utopian Community to Modern Corporation*. Baltimore: The Johns Hopkins University Press, 1969.

Caven, Ruth Shonle. "Public and Private Areas and the Survival of Communnal Subsocieties." *Journal of Voluntary Action Research,* April–June 1984, 46–58.

Cornfield, Noreen. "The Success of Urban Communes." *Journal of Marriage and the Family,* February 1983, 115–26.

Kanter, Rosabeth Moss. *Commitment and Community: Communes and Utopias in Sociological Perspective*. Cambridge, MA: Harvard University Press, 1972.

Kephart, William M. *Extraordinary Groups: An Examination of Unconventional Lifestyles*. New York: St Martin's Press, 1987.

Koinonia Newsletter.

Lee, Dallas. *The Cotton Patch Evidence: The Story of Clarence Jordan and the Koinonia Farm Experiment*. New York: Harper & Row, 1971.

Mandelker, Ira L. "Religion, Sex, and Utopia in Nineteenth Century America." *Social Research,* Autumn 1982, 730–51.

Miller, Gale. "Work, Ritual Structures, and the Legitimation of Alternative Communities." *Work and Occupations*, February 1985, 3–22.

Minturn, Leigh. "Sex-Role Differentiation in Contemporary Communes." *Sex Roles,* January 1984, 73–85.

Muncy, Raymond Lee. *Sex and Marriage in Utopian Communities*. Bloomington, IN: Indiana University Press, 1973.

Nordhoff, Charles. *The Communistic Societies of the United States*. New York: Dover, 1966.

Noyes, Pierrepont. *My Father's House: An Oneida Boyhood*. New York: Farrar & Rinehart, 1937.

Olin, Spencer C., Jr. "The Oneida Community and the Instability of Charismatic Authority." *The Journal of American History,* September 1980, 285–300.

Robertson, Constance Noyes, ed. *Oneida Community: An Autobiography, 1851–1876*. Syracuse, NY: Syracuse University Press, 1970.

————, ed., *Oneida Community: The Breakup, 1876–1881.* Syracuse, NY: Syracuse University Press, 1972.

Scott, Donald M., and Bernard, Wishy, Eds. "Families in Utopia." In *American Families: A Documentary History,* New York: Harper & Row, 1982.

Weisner, Thomas S., Mary Bausano, and Madeleine Kornfein. "Putting Family Ideals into Practice: Pronaturalism in Conventional and Nonconventional California Families." *Ethos,* Winter 1983, 278–304.

Chapter
6

Ethnic Varieties: Religion and National Origin

THE OLD ORDER AMISH FAMILY

In contrast to radical family types such as Koinonia and Oneida, the most conservative family type is that of the Old Order Amish. The Amish are a branch of the Mennonites, an Anabaptist group that originated in Switzerland during the thirteenth century. They are named after their founder, Jacob Amman, a Mennonite preacher whose views were too conservative even for the Mennonites. Amman felt that his people had grown too lenient in their excommunication practices and too lax in their enforcement of the *Meidung,* the "shunning" of those who have been excommunicated.

It was Amman's position that the *Meidung* served as the backbone of the Mennonite religion and that without rigid enforcement there would be little deterrence for potential transgressors. Based on biblical admonition, Amman felt that the "shunning" carried with it not only religious ostracism but complete avoidance in the social, economic, and domestic (including the marital) spheres.

The *Meidung controversy,* as it has been called, was a bitter one and

An Amish family. (*Fred J. Wilson*)

led ultimately to a schism within the larger Mennonite group. The followers of Jacob Amman came to be known as the Amish, and to this day the *Meidung* remains an integral part of the religion.

Driven from Switzerland by successive waves of religious persecution, the Amish eventually became part of the ever-increasing stream of American colonists. Largely because of William Penn's promise of religious freedom, the first Amish families settled in Pennsylvania in the early 1700s. Today, Amish settlements can be found in no less than twenty states, as well as in Canada and Central and South America. Interestingly, there are no Amish in Europe, their original homeland.

Although they are often associated with Lancaster County, Pennsylvania, the Old Order Amish have large settlements in other states; in fact, approximately 75 percent of the Amish in the United States reside in three states: Ohio, Pennsylvania, and Indiana.[1] The Lancaster County group, however, is one of the oldest—and surely one of the most interesting—of all Amish groups. Much of the following account is based on personal observation and conversations with area residents.*

Life Style

Amish life, both literally and figuratively, revolves around the home. Most of the followers of Jacob Amman are born at home, work at or near home, and socialize at home. Most of their clothing is homemade, and almost all of their meals are eaten at home. The Amish also marry at home, and—as a most fitting finale—their funeral services are held at home. The term "home," however, has a special connotation, for the Old Order Amish are basically a rural people, and their dwelling might better be described as a farmstead.

Although the "land squeeze" in Lancaster County has forced an increasing number of Amish men into nonfarm occupations, most of the men are farmers—and their farms are acknowledged to be among the best in the world. In addition to dairy herds and extensive crop acreage, farmsteads include large, well-kept barns, stables, springhouses, silos, and storehouses. Also, since the followers of Jacob Amman maintain no homes for the aged, a typical farm may include two, three, or even four generations. Additions are made to the farmhouse as they are needed. The presence of oldsters on the farm serves as a kind of self-perpetuating conservative influence.

Appearance and Apparel With the possible exception of their horse and buggy, the most distinguishing feature of the Old Order Amish is their wearing apparel. Men's hats—one of their hallmarks—are of low crown and wide brim, smaller models being worn by the youngsters. Coats have no collars, lapels, or pockets, and are usually worn with a vest. Belts and sweaters, on the other hand, are taboo. Trousers are plain, without crease, and are always worn with suspenders. Shirts are also plain and are worn without neckties, the latter being considered useless adornments.

Following a biblical injunction, Amish women keep their heads covered at all times: indoors, by a small white lawn cap; outdoors, by the familiar

---

[1]*New York Times*, August 25, 1987. See also William Kuvlesky, "Some Amish Move a Lot: The Old Order Amish in Texas," paper presented at the meetings of the Southern Association of Agricultural Scientists, Nashville, TN, 1987.

*Customs of Amish groups in other parts of the country may differ somewhat from those reported here. Readers who are familiar with the Lancaster County area will recognize the picturesque names of villages in the heart of Amishland: Intercourse, Smoketown, Leola, Compass, White Horse, Bird-in-Hand, Beartown, Paradise, and others. The Lancaster County Amish are a growing group. During the 1990s, they are expected to go well over the 20,000 mark.

black bonnet. Perfume and makeup of any kind are prohibited. Dresses are of a solid color, with (variable) long skirts and aprons. In public, women also wear shawls and capes. Scott explains the latter practice as follows:

> The kerchief or cape . . . is found in many surviving folk costumes of Western Europe. Its wide appeal to pious country women is no doubt based on the modesty it provides. The extra covering is seen to conceal the neckline and the form of the bosom, and provides privacy when nursing a baby.

> A 19th-century English woman remarked on . . . the cape, "Certainly the most ingenious device ever contrived for concealing all personal advantage."[2]

Amish clothes never go out of style, although this is not the reason for their standardized mode of dress. Their attire is based on descriptive biblical passages, plus the fact that throughout Amish history their clothing "has always been so." Also, as Hostetler points out, "Amish patterns of dress form a strong basis of identity and exclusion. Like all boundary mechanisms, dress serves to keep the insider separate from the world and to identify the outsider.[3]

As might be expected, the followers of Jacob Amman do not wear jewelry of any kind. In general, whatever is worn must have utilitarian value. An ornamental exception might be the Amishman's beard, though in one sense this has recognition value; that is, prior to marriage the young men are clean-shaven, while married males are required to let their beards grow. (Mustaches are taboo at all times.)

Men and boys wear their hair long, unparted, in a Dutch bob, with an occasional trimming at home. Women and girls adhere to the age-old custom of parting their hair in the middle, combing it down flat, and knotting it at the back. They are forbidden to cut or curl their hair, shave their legs, or pluck their eyebrows.

The Ban on Autos   In their olden attire and horse and buggy, the old Order Amish appear to be driving out of yesterday. And it is true that ownership of bicycles, motorcycles, and automobiles is strictly *verboten* in the Lancaster County settlement. Any adult who bought one would be subjected to severe group pressures. The ban is unequivocal, although it is permissible to ride in someone else's car. It is also permissible to take a bus or taxicab.

A number of reasons have been suggested for the ban on automobile ownership. It has been pointed out that horses are mentioned in the bible. It is said that automobiles—and their maintenance—are expensive compared with the horse and buggy. It is also claimed that the Amish use horse-drawn vehicles because the animals can supply manure for the farm. But

---

[2]Stephen Scott, *Why Do They Dress That Way?* (Intercourse, PA: Good Books, 1986), 86.

[3]John A. Hostetler, *Amish Society* (Baltimore: The Johns Hopkins Press, 1980), 237.

while these reasons may be contributory, they are not the real reason. The real reason is that the old Order Amish feel that automobile ownership would disrupt their entire way of life.

Nonownership of autos discourages the young people from traipsing off to town, and the followers of Jacob Amman are outspoken in their criticism of the urban way of life. Attendance at sporting events, concerts, movies, and so forth, is prohibited. Travel, except for the purpose of visiting, is discouraged. And so long as the auto is banned, worldly temptations are minimized. Also, as Scott points out, "cars are often the objects of pride and ostentation, whereas humility is a central theme of Old Order doctrine."[4]

In their agrarian, conservative, slow-paced lifestyle, the followers of Jacob Amman belong at home on the farm, and unless they are visiting an Amish neighbor or a relative—in their horse buggy—the chances are that home is exactly where they will be.

Visiting, incidentally, is something very close to the Amish people's heart. As the major form of adult recreation, it not only gives them something to look forward to but serves to reinforce the web of Amish relationships. Along the same lines, the Old Order Amish are unstinting in their willingness to offer neighborly assistance. If husband or wife becomes ill, Amish neighbors will take care of the farm and housework. Even the building of new houses and barns is often a joint enterprise in which many of the district men take part.

Collective construction is also utilized in the event a fire destroys a member's building. The much-publicized barn raising, as it is called, is an amazing sight to behold. In fact, a large group of Amishmen, working as a team, can build a complete barn *in one day!* Reciprocal assistance of this type is essential, since the followers of Jacob Amman do not believe in insurance.

Amish Homes: The Old and the New

Visitors to Amishland in the 1990s are likely to notice that the houses of the younger Amish are different from those of the previous generation. The traditional Amish home was well kept and well run. It was plain, lacking in many of the modern conveniences, and solid as an oak. It had to be, for untold generations of the same family would live there. Most of these houses were, and are, fairly large. The followers of Jacob Amman have a high birth rate, and there are likely to be a number of children living at home. Also, Amish farmers tend to retire early in life, and they usually turn the house over to one of their sons while they themselves live in the adjoining *Grosdawdy house,* built for just this purpose.

In the traditional Amish house, rooms are large, particularly the

---

[4]Stephen Scott, *Plain Buggies* (Intercourse, PA: Good Books, 1981), 6.

The horse and buggy are an essential part of Amish life, helping to differentiate and perpetuate their unique culture. (*Mike Wannemacher*)

kitchen, while large quantities of food are cooked and served. (There is no dining room.) Furnishings tend to be functional, though not drab. The Amish religion does not forbid the use of color. Walls are often light blue, dishes purple. Bed coverings and towels can be almost any color. Outside the house, there is likely to be a lawn and flower garden. Fences, walls, posts, and landmarks may also be brightly colored.

Although they love colors, the old Order Amish do not believe in mixing them. Wearing apparel, fences, posts, buggies—all are of solid color only. Plaids, stripes, and prints are considered too fancy. For this reason, contrary to popular impression, the followers of Jacob Amman never put hex signs on their barns.

Special mention should be made of the fact that the Amish home is also their church. Still adhering to the original Anabaptist custom, the followers of Jacob Amman have no church buildings. All services are held in the homes of members, the meetings—which are held every other Sunday—being rotated among the district membership.

It follows, then, that the first floor of an Amish home must be large enough to seat the entire district membership (well over 100 persons) on a given Sunday. If, as sometimes happens, the house is too small, the barn may be used for church services. Each district owns a number of plain wooden benches, and these are transported form house to house in time for the forthcoming Sunday services. The Old Order Amish have no paid clergy, incidentally, the bishops, ministers, and deacons being chosen by lot, after a preliminary nomination.

Newer Amish houses differ from the traditional variety in a number of ways. They tend to be smaller, and many do not have a "farmhouse" appear-

An Amish barn raising. *(Fred J. Wilson)*

ance at all. Except for such items as electrical wiring and curtains, they may look much like non-Amish houses. In the matter of modern appliances and equipment, the differences between "old" and "new" are even more striking.

The followers of Jacob Amman have never been permitted the use of electricity furnished by public power lines. The church has been unyielding on this point, and the prohibition has served to restrict the kinds of allowable devices and appliances. Over the years, however, the Amish have come up with some rather interesting alternatives: bottled gas, batteries, small generators, air pressure, gasoline motors, hydraulic power. The net result has been a variety of modern devices that have become available to the membership, not only in their homes, but in their barns, workshops, and stores.[5]

The contemporary Amish home in Lancaster County, for example, is likely to have fashionable exterior and planned walkway. The interior would include modern plumbing and bathroom facilities, attractive flooring and cabinet work, and a moderately up-to-date kitchen. The latter would contain

[5]See the discussion in Donald Kraybill, *The Riddle of Amish Culture* (Baltimore: The Johns Hopkins Press, 1989), 150–164.

a washing machine, stove, and refrigerator, all powered by one of the non-electrical sources mentioned above.

Change: The Safety Valve

What impact have these technological changes had on Amish lifestyle? There is no denying that the Lancaster County group has experienced some significant alterations, both in their home life and in their employment. It should be pointed out, however, that many of the changes *have operated as a safety valve;* that is, they have given members some necessary leeway, denial of which might have caused internal dissension. The above-mentioned modernization, furthermore, should not distort the larger picture: resistance to change is still one of the hallmarks of Amish society. A substantial majority of all Amishmen remain in farming and farm-related occupations. Amishland is still a basically agricultural community.

Amish homes in the Lancaster area, moreover, though surprisingly modern in certain respects, are without electricity. There are no light bulbs, illumination being provided by oil lamps or gas-pressured lanterns. And the list of prohibitions remains long: dishwashers, clothes dryers, microwaves, blenders, freezers, central heating, vacuum cleaners, air conditioning, power mowers, bicycles, toasters, hair dryers, radios, television—all are taboo.[6]

There is little likelihood that change in Amishland will get out of hand. The "land squeeze," forcing more of the Amish into nonfarm occupations, will doubtless continue, but only in certain areas. Regional differences in conservatism may undergo modification. The Lancaster County settlement, for instance, was at one time among the more conservative groups, but this is no longer true. In terms of both their population growth and their distinctive quality of life, however, they continue to thrive.

Dating and Courtship

As might be expected, Amish youth are much more restricted in dating and courtship activities than are the youth of most other groups. For one thing, Amish youth work longer hours; hence they have less time for "running around." For another, Amish youngsters have a limited number of places to meet the opposite sex. They do not attend high school or college; so they are deprived of the chief rendezvous of American youth. They do not normally frequent fast food places, shopping malls, movies, bars, dances, rock concerts, summer resorts, and other recreational catchalls. Nor are their families permitted to have automobiles, which places a further limitation on their amorous activities.

In spite of all the above factors, Amish dating and courtship are at least as successful as that practiced in society at large. Since Amish youth marry about the same age as the "English" (non-Amish), both sexes have a fair

[6]Ibid.

amount of exposure to dating. In the process, most of them seem to enjoy themselves, and nearly all of them marry.

Amish courtship activities generally revolve around the "singings" held on Sunday nights. These usually take place at the same farm where the church services were held. Singings are run by the young people themselves, and often involve participants from other districts. Refreshments are served, songs are sung, and there is always a good deal of banter, joking, and light conversation. If he has a date, the boy may bring her to the singing. If he does not, he tries to get a date in the course of the evening, so that he may drive her home.

Should the girl permit the boy to drive her home, a dating situation may or may not develop, just as in the outside society. But while courting couples are assumed to have feelings of affection for one another, romantic love is not as exalted as it is in society at large. Amish youth tend, instead, to favor those traits that will make for a successful family and community life: willingness to work, reliability, fondness for children, good-naturedness, and the like. In practice, marriage is often between those who have known each other since childhood.

Girls are supposed to remain virtuous until marriage, but to what extent necking and petting would compare with such activity among the "English" cannot be ascertained. It is known that occasionally a boy will "sneak over" to his girl friend's house after the oldsters have retired. And much to the dismay of the group, premarital pregnancies sometimes occur. They are infrequent, however, especially when compared with the premarital pregnancy rate among the non-Amish.

According to custom, young people are free to select a marriage partner of their own choosing. There are two restrictions: (1) Marriage must be to someone within the Amish faith; and (2) in every case, parental approval is required. The approval is usually granted, and when all parties (including the clergy) are satisfied with the arrangements, banns are posted and the forthcoming marriage is announced at the Sunday services. There is no engagement or engagement ring; indeed, the couple themselves tend to avoid any display of affection in public.

Marriage

Amish weddings, held at the bride's home, are the most gala occasions in Amishland, and in Lancaster County alone there are more than one hundred of them every year.[7] Since the entire district membership—plus assorted friends and relatives—are invited, the celebration generally takes place in November or December, after the fall harvest.

The ceremony itself is not elaborate, though it is rather long, certain portions of the Old Testament being quoted verbatim. There are no bou-

---

[7]Stephen Scott, *The Amish Wedding* (Intercourse, PA: Good Books, 1988), 30.

quets or flowers of any kind. The bridal veil, maid of honor, best man, photographs, decorations, wedding march, instrumental music—all are missing, though there is a good deal of group singing.

The groom wears his Sunday suit, and the bride wears a white cape and white apron. (The only other time she will ever wear white is after death—when she is laid out in a casket.) At the conclusion of the ceremony, no wedding rings are exchanged, nor do the couple kiss. The bishop says simply. "Now you can go; you are married folk."

If the wedding ceremony is simple, the meal that follows is most certainly not. There are often several hundred people in attendance; in fact, some Amish persons actually attend several weddings on the same day! Like other rural people, the Amish have remarkable appetites and normally consume large quantities of food at an everyday meal. And the wedding feast is not meant to be an ordinary meal.

The writers know of an Amish bill of fare that included one dozen each of chickens, ducks, and geese; fifty loaves of bread; several bushels of potatoes; vats of assorted vegetables and sauces; sixty pies, a dozen large layer cakes; bowls of mixed fruit; and a seemingly endless supply of fresh milk.

To help in the preparation and serving of the food, women of the district volunteer their services. Kitchens are generally large enough to accommodate several cooks at a time. If not, temporary kitchens may be set up. In any case, guests are usually served in shifts.

Feast and festivities over, the couple embark on their honeymoon. But whereas most people visualize their honeymoon as a more or less luxurious trip, one aim of which is privacy, in Amishland it is simply an extended series of visits with friends and relatives. As guests on the honeymoon circuit, the couple are the recipients of many wedding presents, usually in the form of practical gifts for the home.

Following the honeymoon, the couple take their place in the community as husband and wife. In some cases they will live with the husband's parents, gradually taking over the bulk of the farming and household duties, while the parents retire to the *Grosdawdy house*. In most cases, though, the couple will live close by their parents' place in a house purchased because of the proximity.

There is an old Amish saying that the children should not live farther away "than you can see the smoke from their chimney," and the large majority of brides and grooms are born in the same county that their parents were born in. As a matter of record , about the only time an Amish family moves out of an area is (1) when no suitable land or acceptable jobs are available[8] or (2) when they have had an irreconcilable difference with the

---

[8]To repeat, while the large majority of Amishmen are still in farm or farm-related occupations, because of the "land squeeze" the number of nonfarm jobs has been increasing. However, their choice of nonfarm jobs has been highly selective. For example, while they operate a variety of craft shops, Amish men generally reject factory work as being a bad influence. For a detailed discussion of the topic, see Kraybill, *The Riddle of Amish Culture,* 188–211.

The wide-brimmed hats and beards indicate that these men are Old Order Amish. (*John Launois/Black Star*)

bishop. And even in these instances, the followers of Jacob Amman tend to move to another Amish settlement. It is because of this preference to live among "their own kind of people" that the area they inhabit tends to become rather solidly Amish.

Family and Kinship

The Amish family system is at once both simple and effective. They take great pride in their farmstead and in their work, and they have the reputation of being completely trustworthy. They are such excellent workers and so thrifty in their daily living that outsiders often believe them to be quite wealthy. In a monetary sense this is generally not so, although the Old Order Amish do possess some sizable holdings of extremely valuable land.

Since the farm is likely to be an Amish couple's daily concern, they usually have a large number of children to aid in the enterprise. Amish youngsters are generally exempt from higher education, so that compulsory school laws and child labor laws have limited meaning. Consequently, unlike other children, Amish youngsters are considered to be economic assets. Families with ten or more children are far from uncommon; in fact, the *average number* of births per couple is around seven!

To the followers of Jacob Amman, parenthood is quite in keeping with the nature of things. Birth control—of any kind—is held to be against God's will, and is prohibited. The upshot is that the Old Order Amish have one of the highest rates of increase in North America. Between 1970 and 1990 in Lancaster County alone, both the number of districts and the Amish population more than doubled.[9]

For those interested in kinship structure, the following should be noteworthy. During the colonial period the number of Amish immigrating to America was small, and since they seldom marry outsiders, most of the present membership can trace their genealogy back to the original families. Surnames today are much the same as they were in the 1700s.

Although there are now thousands of Old Order Amish in Lancaster County, a dozen or so surnames would cover most of the group. In fact, four of the names—Stoltzfus, King, Fisher, and Beiler—account for nearly 60 percent of the households. (There is an oft-told story about the one-room Amish schoolhouse in which 39 of the 48 pupils were named Stoltzfus!) Other common names include Lapp, Zook, Smucker, Glick, Riehl, Blank, and Petersheim. Oddly enough, there do not seem to be any Ammans among the Amish of Lancaster County—or elsewhere.

To add to the cognominal confusion, the Amish rely on the bible for first names. Among males, names like John, Amos, David, Jacob, Samuel, and Daniel are quite popular. For females, Mary, Annie, Katie, Sarah, Rebecca, and Lizzie predominate. Anyone who sends a letter to John Beiler or Mary Stoltzfus, with nothing more than a rural delivery address, is likely to create an interesting problem for the mailman.

Given the structure and frequency of both first and last names, how do the Amish themselves—in referring to one another—manage to communicate? The answer is that they are ingenious in their use of nicknames and employment of other identifying features.

Women and Children

Division of labor in an Amish farmstead is largely a function of age and sex. The husband arises early, completes his morning chores, and then, aided by his sons, works the fields. His wife, assisted by the daughters, cooks and takes care of the house and garden. During the planting season, however, it is not uncommon to see what appears to be an entire family in the field.

At the same time, there is little doubt that "Papa" is the boss. It is he who makes the major decisions. Amish women do not lack for affection and kindness, but theirs is a subordinate status. They cannot, for example, be considered for the clergy. And if all this seems rather strange to us today, it should not be forgotten that the followers of Jacob Amman are living in many ways like the early American colonists, who considered women to be helpmates rather than the equals of men.

---

[9]Ibid., 263. The 1990 figure was extrapolated.

Following the colonial heritage, children also have subordinate status. However, although the Old Order Amish are strict, they do not go overboard on discipline. From all indications, their youngsters have a joyous childhood. Hostetler, the foremost authority on Amish life, writes that

> early in life the child learns that the Amish are "different" from other people. Thus, he must learn not only how to play the role at home and in the Amish system, but also how to conduct himself in relation to the norms of his "English" neighbors . . . He cannot have clothes and toys just like the "English" people have. He soon learns to imitate his parents and to take pride in the difference. Amish children are raised so carefully within the Amish family and community that they never feel secure outside it.[10]

Overall, there is a good deal of evidence to suggest that the Old Order Amish maintain what is perhaps the strongest and most stable family system in America. They seldom marry outside the group. Their birth rate is usually high and is not affected by economic conditions. Illegitimacy is almost unheard of, as is adultery. Desertion is virtually unknown, and no divorces have yet been reported. In brief, practically all the Amish marry, they have large families, and they stay married until death intervenes.

So far as can be determined, the American record for the largest family is also held by an Amishman—John Eli Miller, who died at the age of ninety-five.

> He was survived by five of his seven children, 61 grandchildren, 338 great grandchildren, and six great-great grandchildren, a grand total of 410 descendants. . . . At the end of his life, the postman was bringing John Miller word of the birth of a new descendant on the average of once every ten days. What did he think about his large family? Did it worry him to see it growing so large? Indeed it did. He summarized it in one simple question: "Where will they all find good farms?"[11]

"Our Way of Life"

Are the Amish a contented people? Most of the signs would certainly indicate that they are. Economically they are well off, with little or no poverty. No Amish person has ever been on public welfare or has accepted any other type of state or federal aid, including social security. (Congress agreed to exempt the group from the social security program. Accordingly, Amish farmers neither pay social security taxes nor receive any of the benefits therefrom.)

Despite the fact that they make almost no conversions, the followers of Jacob Amman are one of the most rapidly growing groups in America: five

---

[10]Hostetler, *Amish Society,* 157.

[11]Glenn Everett, "One Man's Family," *Population Bulletin,* vol. 17, no. 8, 1961, 1ff.

thousand in 1900; thirty-three thousand in 1950; well over one hundred thousand today!

According to those who live among them, the Old Order Amish are quite content to follow their conservative, slow-paced way of life. The fact that the entire membership is following an equally severe path gives them a powerful feeling of group solidarity. It is this solidarity, plus their communality of interests and their rejection of "modernism," that leads them to a genuine enjoyment of one another's company.

Do the Amish feel threatened by the larger society? Not really. Huntington makes the following observations:

> Movies are forbidden but offer little threat to the Amish community because there is not interest in them; they are too far from the individual's experience and value system to do more than elicit passing curiosity. In many ways the Amish culture is oral rather than literary. They are not really threatened by the printed word, by radio, or even by television. Consistent with the oral tradition, the Amish stress shared knowledge and the importance of meaningful social interaction.
>
> They are so far outside the mainstream of American culture that they have little shared knowledge with the average American, and little reason to interact socially with him.[12]

On the basis of the best available evidence, then, the Old Order Amish are a well-adjusted people. They have not, obviously, created a utopia. From time to time, signs of strain appear: tourism upsets daily routine; young people—boys in particular—sometimes misbehave; farm land becomes scarce; individuals and groups secede.

Nevertheless, when the pluses and minuses are examined, the Old Order Amish come off very well indeed. They are willing to forgo personal attainment in exchange for a deeply rewarding system of family and community values. For over 250 years the followers of Jacob Amman have believed in the primacy of the group over the individual, and in the process they have achieved a lifestyle that harmonizes almost perfectly with their religious beliefs.

THE MEXICAN-AMERICAN FAMILY

A hundred years before the Pilgrims landed on Plymouth Rock, Cortez and his Spanish conquistadors conquered a thriving Aztec civilization in the central valley of Mexico. During the following decades the Jesuits established settlements throughout the southwestern part of our country. Here the Europeans lived and worked with the Indians for centuries. Out of their

---

[12]Gertrude Enders Huntington, "The Amish Family," in Charles Mindel and Robert Habenstein, eds., *Ethnic Families in America* (New York: Elsevier, 1988), 322–323.

interaction emerged a new people, a new culture, and a distinct family form.

For centuries this Mexican-American family has withstood political and economic hardships in Mexico and in the United States; it has been resilient enough to survive and to grow. For example, at the end of the war with Mexico in 1848, there were only about 74,000 Mexicans in Texas, New Mexico, Arizona, and California combined.[13] Today California alone has a population of about 5 million Mexican-Americans and Mexicans. The Mexican-origin population in this nation approached 9 million in 1980.[14] Since then, this has been the fastest-growing ethnic group in America.

This rapid growth has attracted a great deal of media coverage, most of it focusing on illegal immigrants and on the farm workers. This coverage sometimes gives the impression that the Mexican-American family is homogeneous, peasant, foreign, and illegal. Schaefer believes that even social scientists succumb to such stereotypes:

> Its characterization as the simple peasant family surviving upward mobility has not died in many accounts of the Chicano* family. Even the concept of the peasant family has received little qualification. Good and bad traits, but, usually the latter, have been assigned to Chicano families regardless of their truth.[15]

To avoid stereotypes, let us acknowledge from the beginning that the Mexican-American family is diverse. Because the generation order in the United States is an important part of that diversity, we begin with the portrayal of the first-generation Mexican-American family.

The First Generation

The family is strong in Mexico. But the economic instability in rural areas is severe enough to force people to seek opportunities elsewhere. Many come to the United States to join relatives already here. Others come legally and illegally to establish a beachhead of their own.

They also come to America for the well-being of the family left behind. They work to help and to reunite the family in their new country. They are motivated by a tradition which teaches loyalty, mutual support, unity, and respect for the elder members of the extended family. These values are often referred to as *familism*.

---

[13]Joan Moore and Harry Pachon, *Hispanics in the United States* (Englewood Cliffs, NJ: Prentice-Hall, 1985), 18.

[14]The United States Bureau of the Census, *We the Mexican Americans* (Washington, DC: Government Printing Office, 1985).

*Diversity of Mexican-Americans is reflected in the variety of terms used to refer to this ethnic group. Some authors prefer to use the term *Chicano*. Studies have shown that 50 to 75 percent of the Mexican-origin people prefer the term *Mexican-American*.

[15]Richard T. Schaefer, *Racial and Ethnic Groups* (Boston: Little, Brown, 1984), 310.

Familism   As opposed to individualism, familism places the family above individual interests. Familism includes a great many responsibilities and obligations to the immediate family and to the kin. Kutche provides some specific examples of familism among Mexican-origin families in New Mexico:

> If married children feel the need to move in with one parent or the other, the request is seldom refused. More often, unmarried wage-earning children will supplement their parents' income with occasional gifts—a stove, a refrigerator, wiring or plumbing their houses—more likely than a monthly stipend. Siblings with separate households often share garden and an orchard produce, and may work together in the *placita* if they get along particularly well.

> The migration pattern reflects such family obligations sharply; one member will get a job in an industrial city and establish a beachhead for the next whom he houses and helps to find a job (often in the shop where he works), and so on for other relatives who want to earn wages. After a few years a family, or even a village, may virtually establish a neighborhood in the city.[16]

Like any value system, familism has some positive and some negative consequences for the individual. On the positive side, sociologists have identified lower mental-illness rates, lower divorce rates, increased personal happiness, and a secure feeling about aging. The kin exchange work and skills, and they take care of each other's children. These resources, of course, are not limited to Mexican-Americans. As one group of researchers put it, "Though all of these resources are, normatively, also available within the extended kin network of most Americans, reliance on kin is carried to an extreme in the traditional Mexican-American family."[17]

If familism is carried to an extreme, the question arises whether or not its benefits outweigh its drawbacks for the individual. Some researchers reason that excessive familism may discourage individual achievement:

> To the extent that the family captures all of the significant social relations of the individual, he becomes less capable of absorbing new values and of maintaining relations with new kinds of people. Maintenance of "Mexican-ness" of both values and ethnic exclusiveness in social relations is, therefore, largely achieved through familism. . . .

> The benefits of a family's "protection" of the individual members, then, may be gained at the price of lowered individual achievement because of isolation from the larger milieu.[18]

Sacrifice of individual achievement most likely occurs among the chil-

---

[16]Paul Kutche, "Household and Family in Hispanic Northern New Mexico," *Journal of Comparative Family Studies,* Summer 1983, 158.

[17]Leo Grebler, Joan W. Moore and Ralph C. Guzman, "Chicano Culture: The Family—Variations in Time and Space," in Livie Isauro Duran, and H. Russell Bernard, eds., *Introduction to Chicano Studies* (New York: Macmillan, 1982), 409.

[18]Ibid.

dren of the itinerant farm workers. While most Mexican-Americans live in cities, some move from state to state in search of farm employment. The hardships they experience may retard upward mobility even for their American-born children. Let us discuss this possibility specifically.

Socioeconomic Hardships The first generation is more likely to experience hardships than their American-born children, because the first generation is more likely to work as itinerant laborers. Because an itinerant family does not have a permanent state of residence, their children are not covered by compulsory education laws. Consequently, some children do not receive any formal education. Nor do they receive any health care regardless of need. Bahr, Chadwick, and Strauss illustrate the plight of a Mexican-origin migrant farm family as follows:

> During the peak of the tomato harvest in Indiana, the Guerras work from dawn until dark, seven days a week. They receive no overtime pay, no health benefits, no workmen's compensation, and no unemployment insurance benefits. Their three children also work in the fields to increase the family's income. The children are not covered by the State's compulsory education law or child labor law.

> Two of the Guerras' children have abscessed teeth and are in need of dental care. They receive none. Marita Guerra suffers from influenza and is in need of health care. She receives none.[19]

Even worse, it is difficult for them to qualify for government aid when there is no work. At such times they borrow money from their employer. When the Guerras' were out of work because of drought, they could not move on to another state because of debt to the farmer who employed them. Without food or money, they applied for food stamps but were turned down "based on the estimate of income for the next month." To live until then, they borrowed again from the same farmer.

Fortunately, such dire living conditions are not common among later generations. Most are able to educate their own children and to launch them on to competition with other American ethnic groups. The immigrants who find a reasonable level of economic success, and who are able to reestablish their families in their new country, provide a better example of family organization under the Mexican-American culture.

Later Generations

Parents and Children In the Mexican-American family the children come first. During early childhood, the children are inseparable from their mother. She awakens with them in the morning, caters to their needs dur-

---

[19]Howard M. Bahr, Bruce A. Chadwick, and Joseph H. Strauss, *American Ethnicity* (Lexington, MA: D.C. Heath and Co., 1979), 65.

ing the day, and sees that they are tucked in at night. When the father comes home, he too lavishes affection and concern for the children's health and happiness. Because of the children, the mother will not work outside of the home unless forced by economic circumstances. If that happens, the children are then cared for by the relatives, usually the grandparents.

While the children are mainly their mother's responsibility, the father is also involved in decisions regarding their upbringing and their future. He may work extra hours or deny himself certain luxuries to allow the mother to be with the children without having to work. Some observers have interpreted this behavior as an expression of male dominance in a patriarchal family. The literature suggests, though, that the father and mother are in agreement on such decisions. They arrange their family life around *children* who are loved and pampered by both parents:

> The small child is regarded as an *angelito* as yet uncontaminated by human sex and error. He received adoring affection from *mother and father alike*. The father may drop his dignity to cradle a child, care for his needs or even crawl on hands and knees to play with him.[20]

This concern for the children applies not only to the larger extended family, but also to friends who are made to feel as though they are a part of the family. The phrase *como familia* (like family) is used to indicate particularly close relations with nonrelated individuals. These individuals become a part of the extended family through ritualistic roles involving important events in the life of children: baptism, first communion, confirmation, and marriage.

At baptism, the parents choose a close friend or a relative to become the child's *compadre* (godfather) or *comadre* (godmother). Additional godparents and witnesses are added for each of the remaining important events. With the children as the focus of attention, the family becomes interwoven into the network of kin and ritual kin.

When the children mature, they return their family's care and attention through a parent-child relationship known as *filial piety*. The children, now grown, maintain their respect for their parents and remain loyal to them to the extent of assuming an obligation to help them in old age. Some children feel compelled to reside close to their parents to maintain family unity and to be available to them in times of need.

From the parent's point of view, these ideals could be easily disrupted if a child marries the "wrong person." Marriage could remove a member of the family to a distant place, or it could disrupt kinship networks if the spouse belongs to a different ethnic group. In other words, from the point of view of the parents, familism can be promoted or retarded depending on

---

[20]Stuart A. Queen, Robert W. Habenstein, and Jill S. Quadagno, *The Family in Various Cultures* (New York: Harper & Row, 1985), 305.

Mexican-American children receive adoring affection from mother and father alike. (© 1980, *Janice Fullman, Picture Cube*)

who marries whom. It is not surprising, then, to find that the parents are deeply involved in their children's courtship.

Courtship and Marriage   The traditional Mexican marriage used to be arranged by parents or by go-betweens. Today, arranged marriages are rare even among the first generation. Young adults are expected to find their own mates at school, at work, in the neighborhood, at the dances, at parties organized by the Mexican-American benevolent societies, or at the church. The parents encourage their children to meet someone of the same religion, who lives in the same community. Sunday services, church socials, and church holidays provide frequent opportunities for the young people to meet under circumstances acceptable to parents.

When the children meet someone in the approved manner, both fami-

Young Mexican-Americans today are expected to find their own mates at various social activities approved by their parents. (© *1983, Menzel, Stock, Boston*)

lies may already know each other. If they do not, it is easy for them to meet at some church activity. If both families know each other, or at least if they have an easy opportunity to meet, the chances are very good that parents on both sides will approve of the match.

Traditional families forbid dating alone until the girl brings her date home to meet her parents. The first meeting at home is usually a dinner. The girl's mother and the father observe the young man, converse with him, and assess his character and his family background. If all goes well, the boy will be invited again. This also means that he is accepted by the family, and that his opportunities to meet the girl will be more frequent. But until engagement, the family participates in many dating activities such as home parties, picnics, or visits to the church or the community center. A family member may even accompany the girl to dances at night.

It would seem that in our individualistic society, the children would rebel against such parental interventions. Some point to occasional elopements as evidence of rebellion. However, while elopement does occur, it is rare. A large majority of Mexican-American couples comply with the parental rules which include (1) dating within one's own ethnic group, (2) having parental approval and some supervision of dating, and (3) complete abstinence from sexual intercourse at any time before marriage.

Table 6.1   TEENAGE MARRIAGE IN TEXAS BY ETHNIC
GROUP AND SEX, 1980

| Ethnic group | Percent ever married | | | |
| | Before age 16 | | Before age 20 | |
	Female	Male	Female	Male
Mexican-American	4.7	1.2	17.4	7.2
White	2.6	0.8	14.9	5.0
Black	2.1	1.2	8.8	3.1
Asian	1.6	0.6	12.6	2.2

Sources: Calculated from Table 205, U.S. Bureau of the Census, *Detailed Population Characteristics Texas 1980,* part 45, section 1 (Washington, DC.: U.S. Department of Commerce, 1983).

It is not clear how well the children adhere to the latter rule; but it would seem that this restriction encourages young people to marry at an earlier age than is usual for other ethnic groups. Table 6.1 shows this trend in Texas, where over 20 percent of the population is of Mexican origin.

In the state of Texas, 4.7 percent of Mexican-American girls are married before their sixteenth birthday. By their twentieth birthday 17.4 percent have been married. After age 20, marriage rates accelerate for all ethnic groups until over 90 percent of all people eventually marry.

Regardless of the age at marriage, it is an occasion for joy and celebration. The wealthier families organize elaborate balls, where hundreds of guests wear formal attire, eat catered delicacies, and listen to live music. The middle-class marriage is also an impressive affair, with a Mariachi band, ample food, and dancing long into the night. The local Mexican-American Benevolent Association Hall is a likely site for this event. In poorer families there is not less joviality, but there are fewer festivities. Families are likely to celebrate around the barbecue pit and a keg of beer in the backyard. Instead of the Mariachi, a few beers and a shot of tequila encourage some homespun musical entertainment.

The food, drinks, and music symbolize the continuation of much of the Mexican-American heritage from generation to generation. Yet, certain changes are also inevitable if an individual is to advance economically in an industrialized, individualistic society. In the next section we examine traditions that change and those that continue.

Change and Continuity

Mexicans tend to immigrate to improve the economic status of their families. Most of those who make a commitment to become U.S. citizens, and to establish a permanent family here, are ready to change their life from the day they cross the border. They know that to achieve middle-class status, at least for their children, they must compete economically with other ethnic groups in America. The question is, to what extent do they have to change to compete successfully?

Change   Changes in the Mexican-American family begin with education. Most immigrants come from Mexico with one of the lowest educational levels of any American ethnic group. But from the time they enter this country, one of their ambitions is to become better educated in English.

> One of the immigrant's principal activities in the earliest years of resettlement was the pursuit of additional formal education. As the men entered the United States *eighty-two percent* planned to seek more schooling.[21]

In spite of this high aspiration, most of these men were unable to afford the time for additional formal education. They worked long hours at low pay. Going to school requires studying in addition to attending class—a luxury which these immigrants could not afford.

What immigrants cannot attain themselves, they provide for their children. Even before the parents can speak English, they encourage their children to learn it. It is a family goal and a matter of pride to see the children advance through school. As one immigrant mother explained to an interpreter:

> He (the husband) feels very content when he hears the children speaking English. Even though they may not be saying things correctly, we want them to say them in English, because in Spanish they know more and we want them to improve in English.[22]

Higher educational attainment generally leads to higher-paid occupations and to an increased number of working wives. This alone, of course, does not guarantee sex equality any more than it does in other ethnic groups; however, the American-born families seem to be more equalitarian. For example, more than a decade ago one study found that in 83 percent of Mexican-American farm households, husbands and wives shared in the decision making.[23] The remaining households were about evenly divided between dominant husbands and dominant wives. Generally, dual-career families are changing smoothly from father-dominated to equalitarian.

As wives spend more time working away from home, the children spend more time with other relatives, usually the grandparents. With the mother and the father away from home for many hours each day, filial piety may weaken, although the data are inconclusive on this point.

---

[21]Alejandro Portes and Robert L. Bach, *Latin Journey* (Berkeley, CA: University of California Press, 1985), 173.

[22]Harriet Romo, "The Mexican Origin Population's Differing Perceptions of Their Children's Schooling," *Social Science Quarterly*, June 1984, 644.

[23]Glenn R. Hawkes and Minna Taylor, "Power Structure in Mexican and Mexican American Farm Labor Families," *Journal of Marriage and the Family*, November 1975, 807–11

Three generations of Hispanic family picnicking in a park. The familistic values seem to persist even among the third generation of Mexican-American families. (*Carey, The Image Works*)

It is also possible that with change the children will tend to move geographically in search of better occupational opportunities. If the children do move away, the familistic tradition may encourage them to bring their parents to the new location. Temporary separation, in other words, could benefit the family without sacrificing traditional values.

Continuity   The familistic values seem to persist even among the third generation. Financial assistance in time of need is still an informal family obligation. Generally, family members are available to help each other without looking for personal gain. For example, relatives consider it below their dignity to charge interest on borrowed money. Nor would they charge each other for personal services like babysitting or renovating the house. Of course, the kin do not impose on each other frivolously; but in general, the family is the first place to turn for help.

Filial piety, while modified to suit an industrialized society, also persists. Children are still brought up to be attached to their family. There is little pressure to make them "independent" or to have them go out on their own.

Today, American-born parents are less likely to follow their teenage children to dances and to accompany them on dates; but they are just as concerned about their children's marriages and family unity. Premarital sexual activity is strongly discouraged. Showing affection in public is considered in bad taste even for married couples. Observers sometimes mistak-

Mexican-American families tend to arrange their lives around children who are loved and pampered by both parents. (© *1988, Joel Gordon*)

enly interpret this behavior as aloofness or lack of feelings, when in fact it is simply an expression of a cultural norm that continues from generation to generation.

Religion also remains a dominant social force. In larger cities it is common to have a "white" Catholic church and a "Mexican" Catholic church. There is little conversion to other religions, because families still use church activities as a place for the young people to meet. In this regard, Mexican-Americans are different from other predominantly Catholic immigrant groups. Consider, for example, the findings on religious affiliation of Mexican-Americans living in San Antonio, Texas:

> In this overwhelmingly Catholic ethnic group, religious affiliation is a dominant force in the maintenance of ethnic identity. In this, Mexican-Americans are closer to Italian American Catholics than to Irish and German Catholics who have shown less continuity in religious affiliation. They are also less like the Americans from Minnesota (Protestants of Scandinavian origin) who showed markedly lower levels of continuity in religious affiliation from grandparents to grandchildren. If conversion to Protestantism is a vehicle for assimilating into the Anglo-Saxon core, there is little evidence in our data that Mexican-Americans have used this option to further their assimiliation.[24]

Mexican-Americans have proved that it is possible to succeed in America on the strengths of their own cultural heritage. American-born generations educated in English are able to participate in the economic mainstream. They see little conflict between their American nationality and the many traits of Mexican heritage that continue to characterize their family life.

SUMMARY

American population is a mosaic of ethnic groups, each with its own history and culture. Among many available groups, the Amish were discussed to show how religion can influence family life. The Amish believe in the Biblical precedent for simplicity, monogamy, frugality, filial piety, and other aspects of family life. Because the Amish have been successful in implementing these beliefs, such problems as desertion, divorce, child and spouse abuse, and elder neglect are virtually unknown in Amish land.

Cultural influences on the family are not always this easily identifiable. Nevertheless, culture goes a long way toward explaining how each of us lives and relates to family members. The Amish were easy to identify because their way of life is so much different from most other groups.

Another identifiable ethnic group are the Mexican-Americans. This

---

[24]Kyriakos S. Markides and Thomas Cole, "Change and Continuity in Mexican American Religious Behavior: A Three Generation Study," *Social Science Quarterly*, June 1984, 623.

group is characterized by their Indian and Spanish descent. Most are also immigrants or children and grandchildren of immigrants. Because immigration from Mexico has been increasing every decade this century, Mexican-Americans have become one of the largest and most written-about ethnic groups.

We showed that, when economic conditions allow, the Mexican-Americans tend to be loyal to their family, mutually supportive, and respectful of their elder family members. This is not to say that other ethnic groups do not value the same things. Most certainly do. However, Mexican-American culture provides institutionalized means for implementing these ideals. The kin, the church, and the parents interact around important family events in culturally prescribed manner. These events include baptism, first communion, confirmation, and marriage. Around each event the kin and the ritual kin reaffirm their commitments, obligations, and loyalties to the family and particularly to the children. In turn, the children are encouraged to develop respect, appreciation, and loyalty to their parents and to their kin. In this respect, traditional Mexican-American values tend to be more family oriented than individually oriented. Such value orientation in general is known as *familism* as opposed to *individualism*.

QUESTIONS

1. Homes of the younger Amish are often different from those of the previous generation. Describe the traditional Amish home.

2. Some observers feel that change in Amish land is getting out of hand. Do you agree or disagree? Defend your position.

3. How do dating and courtship in the Amish community differ from the practices of the "English"?

4. The Amish do not permit their members to own automobiles. (a) What disadvantages does this involve? (b) What are the advantages?

5. Describe—and explain—the role of women and children in the Amish community.

6. In the "social problems" area, how do the Amish compare with the larger society? Include some specific points of comparison.

7. Describe relationships between parents and children in the Mexican-American family. Give examples.

8. What are the effects of socioeconomic conditions on Mexican-American family organization?

9. What are the major differences in the life styles between the first- and second-generation Mexican-Americans?

10. How does the Amish system of courtship and marriage differ from the Mexican-American?

SELECTED READINGS

The Amish

Armstrong, Penny, and Sheryl Feldman. *A Midwife's Story*. New York: Arbor House, 1986.

Fisher, Sara, and Rachel Stahl. *The Amish School*. Intercourse, PA: Good Books, 1986.

Good, Merle. *Who Are the Amish?* Intercourse, PA: Good Books, 1985.

Hostetler, John A. *Amish Society*. Baltimore: Johns Hopkins University Press, 1980.

————, and Gertrude Enders Huntington. *Children in Amish Society*. New York: Holt, Rinehart and Winston, 1971.

Huntington, Gertrude Enders. "The Amish Family." In *Ethnic Families in America*, edited by Charles Mindel and Robert Habenstein. New York: Elsevier, 1989.

Kraybill, Donald. *The Riddle of Amish Culture*. Baltimore: Johns Hopkins University Press, 1989.

Kuvlesky, William P. "Some Amish Move a Lot: The Old Order Amish in Texas," paper presented at the 1987 meetings of the Southern Association of Agricultural Scientists, Nashville, TN.

Luthy, David. *The Amish in America: Settlements That Failed, 1840–1960*. Aylmer, Ontario: Pathway Publishers, 1986.

Scott, Stephen. *Plain Buggies: Amish, Mennonite, and Brethren Horse-Drawn Transportation*. Intercourse, PA: Good Books, 1981.

————. *Why Do They Dress That Way?* Intercourse, PA: Good Books, 1986.

————. *The Amish Wedding and Other Special Occasions of the Old Order Communities*. Intercourse, PA: Good Books, 1988.

Seitz, Ruth, and Blair Seitz. *Amish Country*. New York: Crescent, 1987.

Smucker, M. R. "How Amish Children View Themselves and Their Families: The Effectiveness of Amish Socialization." *Brethren Life and Thought*, Summer 1988, 218–36.

Mexican Americans

Alvirez, David, Frank D. Bean, and Dorie Williams. "The Mexican American Family." In *Ethnic Families in America*, edited by Charles H. Mindel and Robert W. Habenstein, 269–92. New York:Elsevier, 1983.

Cazares, Ralph B., Edward Murguia, and Parker W. Frisbie. "Mexican American Intermarriage in a Nonmetropolitan Context." *Social Science Quarterly*, June 1984, 626–34.

Duran, Livie Isauro, and H. Russell Bernard, eds. *Introduction to Chicano Studies*. New York:Macmillan, 1982.

Frazier, Donald J., and Richard R. DeBlassie. "A Comparison of Self-Concept in Mexican American and Non-Mexican American Late Adolescents." *Adolescence*, Summer 1982, 327–34.

Frisbie, Parker W. "Variation in Patterns of Marital Instability among Hispanics." *Journal of Marriage and the Family,* February 1986, 99–106.

Gann, L. H., and Peter J. Duignon. *The Hispanics in the United States: A History.* Boulder and London: Westview Press, 1986.

Gonzales, Juan L., Jr. *Mexican and Mexican-American Farm Workers.* New York: Praeger Publications, 1985.

Hawkes, Glenn R., et al. "Status Inconsistency and Job Satisfaction: General Population and Mexican-American Subpopulation Analysis." *Sociology and Social Research,* April 1984, 378–89.

Kutche, Paul. "Household and Family in Hispanic Nothern New Mexico." *Journal of Comparative Family Studies,* Summer 1983, 151–65.

Markides, Kyriakos S., and Thomas Cole. "Change and Continuity in Mexican American Religious Behavior: A Three Generation Study." *Social Science Quarterly,* June 1984, 618–25.

Markides, Kyriakos S., Harry W. Martin, and Ernesto Gomez. *Older Mexican-Americans: A Study in an Urban Barrio.* The Univesity of Texas at Austin: Center for Mexican American Studies, 1983.

Mirande, Alfredo, and Evangelina Enriquez. *La Chicana: The Mexican-American Woman.* Chicago: The University of Chicago Press, 1981.

Moore, Joan, and Harry Pachon. *Hispanics in the United States.* Englewood Cliffs, NJ: Prentice-Hall, 1985.

Murguia, Edward. *Chicano Intermarriage: A Theoretical and Empirical Study.* San Antonio, TX: Trinity University Press, 1982.

Queen, Stuart A., Robert W. Habenstein, and Jill S. Quadagno. "The Mexican-American Family." chap. 17 of *The Family in Various Cultures,* 229–331. New York: Harper & Row, 1985.

Reimers, Cordelia W. "Sources of the Family Income Differentials among Hispanics, Blacks, and White Non-Hispanics." *American Journal of Sociology,* January 1984, 889–903.

Rodriguez, Richard. "The Education of Richard Rodriguez." *Change,* October 1982, 32–35, 48–53.

Chapter
7

The Black Family

Study of the black family has loomed larger and larger in recent years. Increasingly, the question has been asked, "How did this family actually survive in spite of unparalleled difficulties and hardships?" Then, too, there are some 30 million black Americans in our society, and it is important to understand the cultural heritage of this, our largest ethnic group.

It should be mentioned also that the proportion of blacks in the population has been increasing for several decades (Table 7.1). In fact, the 1990 figure of 12.4 percent is the highest in more than 100 years. The proportion will probably continue to increase, since reproduction rates are higher for blacks than for whites. (The main reason for the relative decline in the black population before 1930 was that the tens of millions of immigrants who had entered the country were largely white.)

Actually, the 12.4 percent figure (the black proportion as of 1990) is misleading in some ways because this is a *national percentage*. Local and regional figures are vastly different. In some areas, there are few blacks whereas in certain large cities blacks make up between 25 and 75 percent of the population. It is this urban concentration that has led to the formulation of numerous research projects aimed at a better understanding of the black family in America.

Table 7.1   PERCENTAGE OF BLACKS IN THE U.S.
POPULATION, 1790–1990

Year	Percentage of blacks	Year	Percentage of blacks
1790	19.3	1930	9.7
1820	18.4	1940	9.8
1840	16.8	1950	9.9
1860	14.1	1960	10.5
1890	11.9	1970	11.3
1900	11.6	1980	11.9
1910	10.7	1989	12.2
1920	9.9	1990	12.4

Source: U.S. Bureau of the Census, *Statistical Abstract of the United States, 1989.* The 1989 and 1990 figures are the Bureau of the Census estimates reported in the same source.

For many years the chief sources of information about the black family were such works as E. Franklin Frazier's *The Black Family in the United States* (1939) and Kenneth Stampp's *The Peculiar Institution* (1956). These works depicted the black family as matriarchial, unstable, and beaten down by hundreds of years of slavery and discrimination. The authors assumed that the harsh conditions of slavery had virtually obliterated the African family heritage.

The African family heritage has been a source of strength that helped the black people to survive 400 years of slavery and discrimination. Because this heritage is an important influence on the black family, we begin our discussion with the time and place of origin: the coast of precolonial West Africa.

THE AFRICAN HERITAGE

When Europeans brought slaves out of Africa, they did not bring uncivilized savages. They brought men and women who were a part of a well-organized family and kinship system that had held together for centuries. Legitimization of marriage in Africa was no less formal, durable, or important than in Europe. The African system, however, was unknown to the Europeans, who, out of ignorance, concluded that the Africans lived in groups closer to other primates than to humans.

This attitude took a long time to change. Even those who eventually learned that there was an African civilization before European conquest assumed that African family values were too shallow to survive slavery. Only in recent years have the black pride movement and the search for roots in

Africa led to recognition of the precolonial African family. Ledner wrote about that family as follows:

> A striking feature of precolonial African society was the importance that was attached to the family unit. The extended family was highly structured, with clearly designated roles for its male and female members. Marriage was always considered a ritual that occurred not between two individuals alone, but between all the members of the two extended families. It was a highly sacred ritual that involved bride price and other exchanges of property.
>
> Often marriages were arranged by parents of the bride and groom but sometimes by the two consenting partners. The emphasis was placed upon the binding together of two individuals who represented different families, and upon the mutual duties and obligations they were to carry out for each other. The elderly were highly regarded in African society. The patriarch of the extended family, who was sometimes considered a chief, was usually an elderly man.[1]

The patriarch in this family enjoyed the right to have more than one wife, but he did not restrict a woman's economic and political power within the family. Her relationship to the children was considered important by the family, and her role was respected. Her economic role also extended beyond the family, as she was the trader in the village.[2] Whether trading and selling crafts and agricultural products for the family or for herself, she did work that could be profitable. In short, there is no evidence that precolonial African women suffered degradation or neglect as a result of polygamy.

Perhaps the greatest indication of the respect for women in Africa was the practice among many tribes whereby descent of children was traced through the mother's side, a custom known as *matrilineal descent.* (When the father is given the honor, it is called *patrilineal descent.*) This status for women may have originated as a mark of reverence for procreation. Even African legends and mythology venerate the women as important members of the family, the tribe, and the kinship network.

The woman's role in establishing kinship networks was as important as the man's. In African kinship, according to Foster, marriage did not start new families. "The couple joined a cluster of related families who resided together in a single compound."[3] The bride could join the groom's extended family, or he could join hers. These arrangements depended on the agreement and preferences of the marriageable parties and were not predetermined by gender.

The West African family was adapted to nonmigratory agricultural life,

---

[1]Joyce A. Ledner, "Racism and Tradition: Black Womanhood in Historical Perspective," in Filomina Chioma Steady, ed., *The Black Woman Cross-Culturally* (Cambridge, MA: Schenkman Publishing Company, 1981), 272.

[2]Ibid., 274.

[3]Herbert J. Foster, "African Patterns in the Afro-American Family," *Journal of Black Studies,* December 1983, 204.

with kin relationships as a center of political, economic, and religious life. Divorce was rare, even though it was not prohibited. The usual reason for divorce was the wife's infertility, but if the wife was unhappy she also could divorce (as could the husband). Even when divorce occurred, it was not a serious problem. There were dozens of kin living in the same compound who would take care of the children. The children and the aged could count on the family for whatever support they needed. In short, the African family was stable, large, and self-sufficient.

This way of family life ended for millions of Africans in the journey across the Atlantic into slavery. Today, we know that this unpleasant history did not put an end to the family itself. Instead, the family went through a traumatic phase.

MARRIAGE AND THE FAMILY AMONG AMERICAN SLAVES

Upon arrival in the new land, the kinship ties that bound and served the cultures of Africa were severed forever. This break was so complete that many social observers assume to this day that centuries of slavery and discrimination beat down the black family. Yet as early as the first years of slavery it appeared that the black family might never become established in North America. At that time conditions of bondage and the unavailability of partners seemed insurmountable.

> During the seventeenth century, slaves had few opportunities to establish a stable and independent family life. Throughout the colonies, the chances of a slave finding a spouse were quite low. In the Chesapeake colonies and the Carolinas, most slaves lived on plantations with fewer than ten slaves. These units were so small and so widely dispersed, and the sex ratio was so skewed, that it was difficult for slave men and women to find a spouse of roughly the same age. In Northern cities most slaves lived with their masters and were restricted from associating with other slaves.[4]

In addition to these problems, an extremely high death rate among the slaves meant that many would not survive long enough to marry; those who did marry had only a short time to live. Life expectancy improved only when the plantation owners realized that better treatment increased the slaves' productivity. Otherwise, general betterment in living conditions among whites did not necessarily improve the life expectancy of the slaves:

> During the first years of the eighteenth century, when improvement in agriculture, clothing, and housing brought increases in white life expectancy in South Carolina, the slave death rate actually rose and the bithrate declined—

---

[4]Steven Mintz and Suzan Kellogg, *Domestic Revolutions: A Social History of American Family Life* (New York: The Free Press, 1988), 33.

Most plantation owners encouraged the maintenance of a stable and cohesive family system among their slaves. (*Brown Brothers*)

apparently because slaveholders expanded and intensified production on rice plantations in order to purchase more slaves.[5]

Conditions of slave life improved somewhat, however, as the sex ratio in the slave population became more balanced. Sharp increases in the birth rate toward the end of the eighteenth century suggest that family life among the slaves was reemerging. By the mid-nineteenth century the family was a binding unit, even though slave marriages were not legally recognized. (Nor were they protected from their owners, who could—and on occasion, did—separate families for personal gain.)

Nevertheless, marriage was binding and the family endured because black parents resisted and rebelled against forced separations of family members. Escapes were most common when there was a possibility that one family member might be sold without the others. Parents on occasion risked lives and threatened suicide rather than enduring the breakup of their family. This threat and the possibility of escape prevented many slave owners from interfering in their slaves' family life. Margaret Garner's case illustrates this point:

---

[5]Ibid., 33.

The Strength of the Black Family. Despite the fact that slave marriages were not legally binding, slave family ties remained strong and many slave marriages lasted twenty years or more. This photograph, which was taken on a plantation near Beaufort, South Carolina, in 1862, shows five generations of a slave family. (*Courtesy of the Library of Congress.*)

Each year in the antebellum era, approximately a thousand slaves fled northward to escape bondage. Most walked on foot, traveling at night, and slept in barns and woods. Margaret Garner, a fugitive slave, killed two of her children rather than permit them to be returned to slavery. After her capture by slavecatchers, she drowned herself in the Ohio River.[6]

Although slave families in the nineteenth century became numerous, large, and cohesive, they still had to rely on the owner's goodwill. According to W. E. DeBois, the knowledge that the owner had the right to separate parents from children and lovers from each other brought uncertainty, pain, and anguish for the slave family. With time, however, owners and slaves learned to live by an unwritten code: owners would respect the slave family, and slaves would refrain from rebellion and escape.

---

[6]Ibid., caption to a picture, "Slave Mother," between pp. 92 and 93.

Most, though not all, owners lived by this code. They permitted slaves to marry and even performed the ceremony themselves. This account of a Texas slave illustrates a common marriage practice throughout the South:

> My first wife named Rachel and she lived on Double Bayou. She belong to the Mayes place. First time I see her I was riding the range seeing about cattle. I was living on Master Bob's place in Jefferson County and I have to get a pass to go to see her. I tell Master Bob I want to get married and he say, "all right." Us had a big wedding. She was dressed all in white. I had a nice hat and a nice suit of black clothes. My father was a shoemaker and he make me a good pair of shoes for me to get married in. When the time come, me and her go up and stand in front of Mr. Mayes and he read out of the Bible and marry us. There was some white folks there to see us git married. Some of them give us presents and some give us money.[7]

In a strictly legal sense, even this type of marriage was not binding. There were no marriage licenses, no marriage certificates, no rights of inheritance. The laws that regulated white sexual activity did not apply to the slaves. Therefore, there was no such thing as bigamy, adultery, illegitimacy, or fornication. Society did not care about a slave's sexual pratices or family life; it was the slaves themselves who viewed marriage and the family with esteem.

At first, marriage ceremonies appeared to be primarily a frivolous form of amusement for the masters. The master performed a simple ceremony, at the conclusion of which the slaves jumped over a broom, thereby sealing the marriage. Eventually the ceremony became more serious. A black or a white clergyman officiated, and with the passage of time the white community accepted and even participated in such marriage celebrations.

The Civil War brought an end to slavery. Blacks hoped for equal rights and freedom through Reconstruction, but instead they faced a new attack on their rights and liberties. The future seemed as dim as ever. At this time of crisis the black family helped its members to endure another phase of hardship.

POLITICAL PROCESS AND FAMILY LIFE DURING RECONSTRUCTION: 1865–1880

Although slavery is a familiar topic, our thoughts about the period following emancipation remain rather unclear. Part of the murkiness may result from films like *Birth of a Nation,* a motion picture about Reconstruction times that portrayed black people as incompetent idlers, corrupt and unable to

---

[7]Randolph B. Campbell, "The Slave Family in Antebellum Texas," in *The American Family,* Victoria College Social Sciences Symposium (Victoria, TX: The Victoria College Press, 1988), 8.

manage themselves or anybody else. These stereotypes about black people have had an enduring effect. But what actually happened to blacks during Reconstruction? Were they able to participate in the political process? What happened to their family life? These questions only recently have received scholarly attention commensurate with their importance.

Freedom

Blacks were able to achieve upward mobility for the first time immediately after the Civil War. Educated blacks became legislators and state officials. They served with distinction from Georgia to Texas, proving their ability and competence to manage and to bring about social change through the political process. During this time of confusion and corruption, black public servants earned the respect of both races. An example is Antoine Dubuclet, who was born a free man in 1880 and served as state treasurer of Louisiana.

> Antoine Dubuclet's career as State Treasurer of Louisiana was outstanding. His chief assistant and second assistant were his sons. In the "stormy days" of Reconstruction, he was untouched by scandals, and received bi-partisan praise. At his death in 1887, the conservative *Picayune* carried an extensive article, partially entitled, "Death of a Prominent Figure in the Republican Regime." . . .
>
> The political career of Louisiana's Treasurer during Reconstruction stands in sharp contrast to much of the criticism many earlier writers attributed to black officials. Perhaps Dubuclet was an exception, but the tenure of this intelligent and extremely sincere guardian of public funds for Louisiana was a challenge to the morality of the period. Along with many others of his race he contributed to the beneficial Reconstruction of Louisiana.[8]

In one sense, Dubuclet was an exception because there were only two black state treasurers at the time. In a more important sense, however, he was not an exception in terms of the competence, integrity, and eloquence exhibited by black officials throughout the South. Proceedings of legislative records after the Civil War show that many blacks were excellent administrators and eloquent speakers. Yet their ability and their hopes for improving their status through political participation were soon extinguished.

Blacks found themselves rejected on all sides. Even the abolitionists—those who had fought hardest against slavery—refused to accept the doctrine of equal opportunity. It is difficult, of course, to delineate the public opinion of the period, but for many whites, in both the North and the South, the idea of treating blacks as equals was incomprehensible. Prejudice, economic discrimination, social and political inequality—such things became hallmarks of what can be described most accurately as a split culture.

The federal government, fortunately, provided help. Military camps were

---

[8]Charles Vincent, "Aspects of the Family and Public Life of Antoine Dubuclet: Louisiana's Black State Treasurer, 1968–1878," *The Journal of Negro History,* Spring 1981, 33.

Despite severe social and economic handicaps, some blacks in the post-Reconstruction era were able to rise into the middle class. *(Frances B. Johnson, "A Hampton Graduate at Home," plate from an album of Hampton Institute, 1899–1900. Platinum print, $7\frac{1}{2}'' \times 9\frac{1}{2}''$ Collection. The Museum of Modern Art, New York, Gift of Lincoln Kirstein.)*

authorized to issue free rations to ex-slaves. The U.S. Treasury Department provided aid, as did a number of benevolent societies. In 1865, the Freedmen's Bureau was established by an act of Congress; its purpose was to encourage education, regulate labor, and provide legal assistance. Yet although the Freedmen's Bureau did help, some emancipated blacks came to believe—quite erroneously—that the government would distribute free land to them. Presumably the lands were to be expropriated from their former masters; each ex-slave was to receive "forty acres and an old gray mule."

The work of the Freedmen's Bureau was discontinued in 1869, and in 1877 the last federal troops were withdrawn from the South. Long before this time, however, it had become clear to the ex-slave that he was not going to get his forty acres. Furthermore, despite his illiteracy, he would have to compete in the open job market.

Some of the freed men were able to find employment in the semiskilled and skilled trades, but most of them turned to the occupation they knew best—agriculture. Over the years a fair number of blacks managed to buy

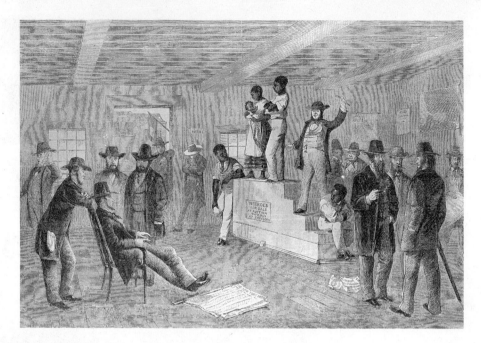

Auction sale for Negro slaves in Charleston, engraving, 1861.

and farm their own lands, but the great bulk of those who stayed in the South became general field laborers, tenant farmers, or sharecroppers.

Consequences of Reconstruction

It is difficult to generalize regarding the effects of Reconstruction on the black family. Research on this period has lagged behind that for the slave period, but it is logical to suppose that the consequences of geographical and cultural displacement were considerable. Also, as ex-slaves, blacks had no marriage certificates, and it took time for licensing procedures to become effective.

Empirical research, on the other hand, reveals a high degree of family solidarity among ex-slaves—at least, as based on official records. In her study of Walton County, Florida, Agresti reports that

> a much higher proportion of blacks in 1885 were living in family groups than had been the case in 1870, and the percentage of one-parent families was much lower in the latter year. Not only that, but many more children in 1885 were living with both parents. In many ways, the black families of 1885 were very similar to the white families of the same year.[9]

---

[9]Barbara Finlay Agresti, "The First Decades of Freedom: Black Families in a Southern County, 1870 and 1855," *Journal of Marriage and the Family,* November 1978, 697–706.

Similarly, in Gutman's study of 14 black communities covering the 1855–1880 period, the investigator found that between 70 and 90 percent of the households were classified as "husband present." Also, "most black children had two-parent families."[10]

Paradoxically, research findings have shown consistently that the freed men suffered deprivations in the *economic sphere*. Gutman reports that black representation among carpenters, painters, tailors, bankers, shoemakers, and factory workers fell drastically. Similar declines were noted in the professional and white-collar occupations.[11]

Fogel and Engerman report that in addition to their being squeezed out of various trades and crafts during Reconstruction, the life expectancy of blacks declined by 10 percent. Their diet deteriorated, and their sickness rate was 20 percent higher than under slavery:

> How could it have happened? That the proposition seems absurd is due partly, as we have tried to show, to an exaggeration of the severity of slavery. But it is also due to an exaggeration of the moral reform sought by antislavery crusaders. Few of the antislavery critics had equality of opportunity as their goal. . . .
>
> What they objected to was not the fact that slavery constrained the opportunities open to blacks, but the form which these constraints took. While physical force was not acceptable, legal restrictions were. Thus many one-time crusaders against slavery sat idly by, or even collaborated in passing various laws which served to improve the economic position of whites at the expense of blacks.[12]

URBANIZATION AND THE BLACK FAMILY

Although some ex-slaves did head northward following emancipation, the movement was slow in getting underway. As late as the turn of the century, some 90 percent of all blacks still lived in the South. Changes were afoot, however, and by World War I, blacks were streaming into nothern cities by the tens of thousands. By World War II the northward migration had reached well into the millions. And since that time, urbanization has been a major feature of the black experience in the United States. Some idea of the magnitude of the change can be seen in Table 7.2.

In nearly all cases the migrants were forced to settle in segregated

[10]Herbert Gutman, "Persistent Myths about the Afro-American Family," in Michael Gordon, ed., *The American Family in Social-Historical Perspective* (New York: St. Martin's Press, 1978), 467–89. See also Henry A. Walker, "Racial Differences in Patterns of Marriage and Family Maintenance: 1890–1980," in Sanford M. Dornbusch and Myra H. Strober, ed., *Feminism, Children and the New Families* (New York: Guilford Press, 1986).

[11]Gutman, 485.

[12]Robert Fogel and Stanley Engerman, *Time on the Cross: The Economics of American Negro Slavery* (Boston: Little, Brown, 1974), 261–63.

Table 7.2   PERCENTAGE BLACK POPULATION IN EACH
OF THE 20 LARGEST U.S. CITIES, 1940–1980

City[a]	1940	1960	1980
New York	6	14	25
Chicago	8	23	40
Philadelphia	13	26	38
Detroit	9	29	63
Los Angeles	4	14	17
Cleveland	10	29	44
Baltimore	19	35	55
St. Louis	13	29	45
Boston	3	9	22
Pittsburgh	9	17	24
Washington, DC	28	54	70
San Francisco	<1	10	13
Milwaukee	2	9	23
Buffalo	3	13	27
New Orleans	30	37	55
Minneapolis	1	2	8
Cincinnati	12	21	34
Newark	21	34	58
Kansas City	5	17	27
Indianapolis	3	21	22

[a]Cities are listed by rank in total population in 1940. *Source:* Gerald D.
Jaynes and Robin M. Williams, Jr., *A Common Destiny: Blacks and
American Society* (Washington, DC: National Academy Press, 1989),
62.

slums and ghettos, where the mainstream American standard of living has remained an unrealized dream. Drugs, crime, and poverty continue to erode the black family and the black culture.

A rural family, it seems, was better able than a ghetto family to preserve family functions, even during times of extreme hardship. Black farmers and even exploited sharecroppers toiled and supported their children, no matter how hard and how unfair the circumstances. In fact, it was the search for work that drove millions of blacks into nothern cities as the need for farm laborers declined. Instead of work, however, they found further discrimination and chronic unemployment.

Jaynes and Williams report that much of the sociological literature points to chronic unemployment as an important reason why most urban black males can no longer function as traditional fathers and husbands.[13]

---

[13]Gerald David Jaynes and Robin M. Williams, Jr., *A Common Destiny: Blacks and American Society* (Washington, DC: National Academy Press, 1989), 534.

Frustration over unemployment may lead to various forms of escape and withdrawal.

A common form of escape, which aggravates the already difficult economic situation, is the abuse of alcohol and illicit drugs. Research shows that drug abuse "increases risk of accidents, suicides, and homicides; family disruption, and poor school and job performance and may lead to acute and chronic medical conditions. Drug abuse among adolescents is highly correlated with adolescent pregnancy, poor grades, dropping out of school, and delinquency."[14]

High unemployment and rising drug abuse may be among the main reason why most black children today are raised in homes without fathers, but the immediate reason is a low marriage rate among black males. By age twenty-five, more than 27 percent of white males are married. In contrast, only about 12 percent of black males are married by the same age.[15] Edelman cites other factors that contribute to the shortage of black males of marriageable age:

1. About 5 percent of black males under 25 years of age live in prisons and mental hospitals.
2. Young black males are twice as likely as young white males to serve in the military and to live in barracks.
3. Black males are far more likely to marry white females than black females are to marry white males.
4. Young black males die at nearly twice the rate of whites. Among males in their twenties, this difference is due primarily to the excess of deaths by homicide among black males.[16]

In addition to these factors contributing to the disruption of the black family, the poorly educated, unemployed males may lack the self-confidence to become a husband. Black women, who tend to be better educated than black men and who suffer considerably less from disease, premature death, and destructive behavior, have become the bastions of the black community. They are employed at rates considerably higher than those of white women, most of whom have husbands to help them with the costs of child rearing. If a black woman is left without a job she resorts to welfare, not because she wants to do so but because she usually has limited choices.

BLACK FAMILY STRENGTHS

The foregoing account of the black experience from their African origins through recent urbanization will provide a background to the current picture. There is little doubt that in spite of certain historical forces and major

---

[14]Ibid., 413.

[15]Marian Wright Edelman, *Families in Peril* (Cambridge, MA, 1987), 10.

[16]Ibid., 10–11.

Most middle-class black families adhere to the nuclear-family model with equalitarian authority structure. (© *Greco, Stock, Boston*)

problems, the black family has served its members well. The strengths of the black family make for satisfying lives for those black men and women who have an opportunity to live as husbands and wives. A national survey conducted between 1972 and 1984 showed that married black persons, regardless of gender, tend to be happier than unmarried black persons.[17]

Most middle-class black families adhere to the nuclear-family model without abandoning their ties to the extended family. Furthermore, studies show that in most cases, husband-wife relationships tend to be egalitarian.[18] Willie also reports that "the equalitarian authority structure that has emerged in black families is a pattern that can be recommended for others. It and the participation of both parents in child-rearing and home-manage-

[17]Ann C. Zolar and J. S. William, "The Contribution of Marriage to the Life Satisfaction of Black Adults," *Journal of Marriage and the Family*, February 1987, 87–92.

[18]Charles Vert Willie, *Black and White Families: A Study in Complementarity* (Bayside, NY: General Hall, 1985), 34.

Premature deaths of young black males leave many black mothers to raise their families alone. In this photo, Gladys Thompson Anthony (seated second from left) of Dallas, Texas, though widowed at age 34, gave her seven children the encouragement and fortitude to succeed.

ment decisions could renew and reform our families."[19] These findings are supported by researchers in Georgia, who found that black husbands and fathers participate in child rearing.

> Literature particularly on black fathers of lower class tends to portray them typically as failing to project to their children the appropriate image of a father, the socially expected image. However, the data in this study support the view of husband/fathers as positive models for their children. They are their main provider, they punish them, they play with them, they are active in the decision-making process, and they set a good example for their children.[20]

A number of writers have commented on the strength of the black kinship-family network. For example, Barnes found that kinship groups are still viable institutions, kept alive by letter writing, telephoning, personal

---

[19]Ibid.

[20]Ira E. Robinson, Wilfrid C. Bailey, and John M. Smith, "Self-Perception of the Husband/Father in the Intact Lower Class Black Family," *Phylon,* June 1985, 144.

contact, mutual help, and ritual.[21] Foster notes that the proportion of such families is larger among blacks than among whites.[22] He also points out that black families are more willing than other American families to adopt children either formally or informally. Therefore, what might appear from a legalistic point of view to be family disorganization is simply another variety of American family. Its characteristics and its strengths are informality, support networks, and strong ties with the extended family.

The black family also has a strong religious orientation; the church is a part of the support system, and many researchers agree that it has been so since slavery. Today the church is especially important for the poor, who depend on "support services and spiritual sustenance."[23]

SUMMARY

The foregoing account shows the progressive decline of the Afrocentric influence on the black family. It seems that black Americans have developed norms that are closely related to the social class structure of white Americans. One significant difference is that among blacks the proportion of lower-class members is higher than among whites.

Economic weakness can be reduced in the future through vigorous social, economic, and political involvement by all concerned Americans. This chapter notes that as a part of that effort, some black scholars have proposed renewed emphasis on traditional Afrocentric values in the black community. These scholars contend that such values helped the black family to endure hardships in the past and can help to strengthen the black family in the future. At the same time, it is important to realize that the economic gap between blacks and whites remains formidable. To close the gap completely will take a concerted effort.

QUESTIONS

1. Increasing attention has been given to the black family in recent years. What are some of the social and demographic factors that account for this surge of interest?

2. Describe the African family heritage. How has it changed in the United States?

3. Slave owners have been described both as "cruel barbarians" and as "benevolent overseers." How might you, as an objective observer of the time, have characterized the typical slave owner in this respect?

---

[21]Annie S. Barnes, "The Black Kinship System," *Phylon*, December 1981, 380.

[22]Foster, "African Patterns," 231.

[23]Jaynes and Williams, 176. See also William Harrison Pipes, "Old-Time Religion: Benches Can't Say 'Amen'," in Harriette Pipes McAdoo, ed., *Black Families*, 2d ed. (Newbury Park, CA: Sage Publications, 1988), 54–76.

4. If you were asked to write an essay describing marriage and family life among plantation slaves, what would be your main points? Consider the legal status of a slave marriage.

5. Describe the major problems facing ex-slaves during the so-called Reconstruction period. What was the role of the Freedmen's Bureau?

6. How did Reconstruction affect the black family?

7. Describe the processes of urbanization and segregation that took place during the hundred years following the Civil War. Did this process continue in the 1980s?

8. Write an essay describing the strengths of the black family.

9. Looking ahead to the 1990s and beyond, what do you visualize as the major trends in black family behavior?

SELECTED READINGS

Amin, Ruhul, and A. G. Mariam. "Racial Differences in Housing: An Analysis of Trends and Differentials, 1960–1978." *Urban Affairs Quarterly,* March 1987, 363–76.

Barnes, Annie S. "The Black Kinship System." *Phylon,* December 1981, 369–80.

Beck, Rubye W., and Scott H. Beck. "The Incidence of Extended Households among Middle-Aged Black and White Women." *Journal of Family Issues,* June 1989, 147–68.

Blackburn, George, and Sherman L Richards, "The Mother-Headed Family among Free Negroes in Charleston, South Carolina, 1850–1960." *Phylon,* March 1981, 11–25.

Blackwell, James E. *The Black Community: Diversity and Unity.* New York: Harper & Row, 1985.

Blee, Kathleen M., and Ann R. Tickamyer. "Black-White Differences in Mother-to-Daughter Transmission of Sex-Role Attitudes." *Sociological Quarterly,* vol. 28, no. 2, 1986, 205–22.

Browman, Clifford L. "Race Differences in Professional Help Seeking." *American Journal of Community Psychology.* vol. 15, no. 4, 1987, 473–89.

Brown, Steven E. "Sexuality and the Slave Community." *Phylon,* March 1981, 1–10.

Campbell, Randolph B., and Donald K. Pickens. " 'My Dear Husband': A Texas Slave's Love Letter, 1862." *Journal of Negro History,* Fall 1980, 361–64.

Cazenave, Noel A. " 'A Woman's Place': The Attitudes of Middle-Class Black Men." *Phylon,* March 1983, 12–32.

Crohan, Susan E., and Joseph Veroff. "Dimensions of Marital Well Being among White and Black Newlyweds." *Journal of Marriage and the Family,* May 1989, 373–83.

Diedrich, Maria. " 'My Love Is Black as Yours Is Fair': Premarital Love and Sexuality in the Antebellum Slave Narrative." *Phylon,* Fall 1986, 238–47

Durant, Thomas J., and Joyce S. Louden. "The Black Middle Class in America: Historical and Contemporary Perspectives." *Phylon,* Winter 1986, 253–63.

Fogel, Robert, and Stanley Engerman. *Time on the Cross: The Economics of American Negro Slavery.* Boston: Little, Brown, 1974.

Foster, Herbert J. "African Patterns in the Afro-American Family." *Journal of Black Studies,* December 1983, 210–32.

Gary, Lawrence E., ed., *Black Men.* Beverly Hills, CA: Sage Publications, 1981.

Isaacs, Marla B., and George H. Leon. "Race, Marital Dissolution and Visitation: An Examination of Adaptive Family Strategies." *Journal of Divorce,* Winter 1988, 17–32.

Jaynes, David Gerald, and Robin M. Williams. *A Common Destiny: Blacks and American Society.* Washington, DC: National Academy Press, 1989.

Jones, John Paul III. "Work, Welfare, and Poverty among Black Female-Headed Families." *Economic Geography,* January 1987, 20–34.

Krech, Shepard III. "Black Family Organization in the Nineteenth Century: An Ethnological Perspective." *Journal of Interdisciplinary History,* Winter 1982, 429–52.

Lewis, Jerry M., and John G. Looney. *The Long Struggle: Well-Functioning Working-Class Black Families.* New York: Brunner/Mazel Publishers, 1983.

McAdoo, Harriette Pipes. *Black Families.* Newbury Park, CA, 1988.

Meyers, Lean Wright. *Black Women: Do They Cope Better?* Englewood Cliffs, NJ: Prentice-Hall, 1980.

Pinkney, Alphonso. *The Myth of Black Progress.* London: Cambridge University Press, 1985.

Sampson, Robert J. "Urban Black Violence: The Effect of Male Joblessness and the Family Disruption." *American Journal of Sociology,* September 1987, 348–83.

Schoen, Robert, and James R. Kluegel. "The Widening Gap in Black and White Marriage Rates: The Impact of Population Composition and Differential Marriage Propensities." *American Sociological Review,* December 1988, 895–907.

Staples, Robert. "Social Structure and Black Family Life: An Analysis of Current Trends." *Journal of Black Studies,* March 1987, 267–86.

Stewart, James B. "Perspectives on Black Families from Contemporary Soul Music: The Case of Millie Jackson." *Phylon,* March 1980, 57–71.

Taylor, Robert Joseph. "Receipt of Support from Family among Black Americans: Demographic and Familial Differences." *Journal of Marriage and the Family,* February 1986, 67–77.

Van Deburg, William L. *Slavery and Race in American Popular Culture.* Madison, WI: University of Wisconsin Press, 1984.

Vincent, Charles. "Aspects of the Family and Public Life of Antoine Dubuclet: Louisiana's Black State Treasurer, 1868–1878." *Journal of Negro History,* Spring 1981, 26–36.

Willie, Charles Vert. *Black and White Families: A Study in Complementarity.* Bayside, NY: General Hall, 1985.

Chapter
8

Social-Class Variations

Social class, it would seem, is a topic—some would say an "issue"—that nearly everyone is interested in. The popular press, surely, tends to exploit the whole idea of differential class levels, and terms like "under class," "working class," "middle class," and "ruling class" have become part of the standard reportorial vocabulary. Through the ingenious use of headlines, reader interest is both aroused and maintained, even though the real significance of the class structure is often distorted.

Sociologists are also interested in social stratification, but their approach is analytical rather than journalistic. That is, they look at social class as an *aid in understanding various facets of human behavior*. Whether the behavioral area under consideration is crime, birth and death rates, religious affiliation, sex behavior, or social and political organization, the sociologist has come to look for explanatory factors in terms of the class level. It would be expected, therefore, in the area of marriage and the family, that an investigation of social class would prove to be rewarding, and this expectation has been borne out by hundreds of studies.

THE UPPER-CLASS FAMILY

Although by far the smallest, the upper class is a tremendously powerful and influential segment of the population. Sometimes referred to as the "upper-upper," "established upper," or "elite," they show little tendency to relinquish or to share their influence. Despite criticism from the middle and lower strata, upper-class families remain substantially tied within their own cliques. Kerbo comments on this point as follows:

> After prep school, ties are formed and furthered in Ivy League colleges; in adult years the ties are strengthened through membership in exclusive social clubs. These clubs provide a social setting within which their typically upper-class members can share their ideas about common political and economic concerns and maintain social and business ties. Also important are the multiple-club memberships of upper-class people that help transform the upper-class network into national proportions. Becoming a regular member of one of these clubs in no easy task. They pride themselves on being exclusive, and to a large degree view their task as gatekeepers of the upper class.[1]

It is this relative impermeability that sets the upper class apart from other social strata. By and large, the American class structure is fairly fluid; at least, education, drive, and the accumulation of wealth usually lead to an improvement in one's class position. Failure in these spheres tends to bring about a loss of social status. This fluidity, however, does not extend to the upper class. Families neither enter nor leave this privileged group solely on the basis of economic criteria.

The Kinship System

Although it is obvious that the upper stratum is a moneyed class, pride in family name is also their hallmark. Thus, while names such as Morgan, Vanderbilt, Wanamaker, Mellon, Astor, Biddle, Harriman, Du Pont, Carnegie, Drexel, and Rockefeller are readily identified as centers of enormous financial power, the fact is that these families also reach back through generations of American history. They are historical families and place great emphasis on ancestral respect and generational accomplishments. In this sense, therefore, the upper stratum is perhaps more akin to a caste than a class.

Class or caste, the upper stratum perpetuates itself through a vast kin network. Significantly, it is difficult for an outsider to comprehend the kinship system, embodying as it does nuclear units interlocked through blood ties, marriage, and joint ownership of property. Since kinship ties extend through many generations, the upper class tends to become clanlike in struc-

---

[1]Harold R. Kerbo, *Social Stratification and Inequality* (New York: McGraw-Hill, 1983), 194–95.

ture. Cousins, uncles, aunts, siblings, in-laws, nieces and nephews, parents and grandparents—all combine to form an imposing range of familiarity.

This upper-class range is solidified not only through extensive business and personal relationships but through systematic encouragement of within-class marriage. Cousin marriages, particularly the second- and third-cousin variety, are commonplace. In a given locality, therefore, it is easy to see how a particular family can exert considerable influence. It is also easy to understand why the same names appear over and over in the Social Register.

Geographically, the upper class tends to be rather stationary, in contrast to the middle class. Whereas the middle-class family head is likely to move several times in the course of his occupational career, the upper-class male generally "stays put." The chances are that he will be born, live, and die in the same community, along with the rest of his kin. This nonmobility explains why certain upper-class names are associated with specific areas, for example, the Du Ponts in Wilmington, the Lowells in Boston, the Biddles in Philadelphia, and the Rockefellers in New York.

The concentration of specific upper-class families within a community, plus a strong affiliation with the kin network, leads to what one writer has called the "family office." According to Dunn, this family office links members of certain upper-class families together as they coordinate economic, charitable, and political activities.[2] When these family actions eventuate in major national enterprises, some writers refer to them as "dynasties."[3]

Courtship and Marriage

Predictably, courtship in the upper strata is rather circumscribed, especially for girls. Parents use both their economic and their social influence to see that their children are exposed to the "right" peers. Sociologists have found that middle-class parents also try to control whom their children will marry, but their resources are minuscule compared with those of the upper classes.

Exclusive contacts are also maintained through the practice known as the debutante ball. The debutante ball is a party for nineteen- to twenty-one-year-old upper-class girls. One purpose of this party is to present the girls to upper-class society. Another purpose is symbolic. It reaffirms class boundaries and the limits of contact for dating and marriage. This point is emphasized by the money spent for decor, food, entertainment, and the like.

For a while during the 1960s and the 1970s it seemed to some observers that the debutante custom was fading. It was felt that the solidarity of the upper class in general was weakening. And newspaper accounts did indicate that some upper-class girls were refusing to participate in the debu-

---

[2]Marvin B. Dunn, "The Family Office: Coordinating Mechanism of the Ruling Class," in G. William Domhoff, ed., *Power Structure Research* (Beverly Hills, CA: Sage Publications, 1980), 43.

[3]See Vance Packard, *The Ultra Rich* (Boston: Little, Brown, 1988), 242.

tante process. These girls thought that "the whole process was 'silly' or that the money should be given to a good cause."[4] Such girls, however, comprised a very small minority. Today, things are apparently back to "normal." The debutante balls persist—and so does the upper-class influence over the courtship process.

Nevertheless, parental control has its limits. When young people go off to college, for example, they tend to be drawn to one another through intellectual interests and emotional response rather than through parentally perceived social-class criteria. Some observers feel that this freedom to choose marriage partners is weakening the upper-class bonds. The difficulty here is that "upper-class" may be defined narrowly or broadly. But if we think of class in terms of occupation, income, and educational levels, upper-class boys and girls do not seem to be making a beeline for the class exit.

Irrespective of whether their boundaries are weakening, a relatively high proportion of upper-class youth do marry. They tend to marry at a somewhat later age than members of the other social classes. Among other things, they are expected to complete their college education before they marry. Also, finding a partner within the smallest social class in America does take time. Fortunately for those involved, these delays are not related to job considerations. Whether or not they have to work, most upper-class men do have successful careers.

Of more than passing interest is the fact that marital-prediction studies reveal a positive correlation between class position and marital adjustment. Also, divorce rates are much lower in the upper classes. Desertions, as might be expected, are virtually unknown. Marital disputes do occur, of course, and when they are serious they are likely to be reported in the press. Nevertheless, of the various social strata in the United States, the upper-class family is evidently the most stable.

The reason for upper-class stability can only be conjectured. Educational and economic advantages undoubtedly serve as influencing factors, though other considerations are probably involved. Since upper-class couples are at the apex of the social hierarchy, they need not concern themselves with the status aspirations that characterize so many middle-class families. Then, too, the upper stratum has more commitment to "family," per se, than do the other classes. That is, marriage is thought of not only as a husband-wife relationship but as an interlocking part of a broader kin network, which includes both in-laws and blood relatives.

Lifestyle

Basic to an understanding of the upper-class way of life is the fact that (1) because members are already established at the top of the social ladder,

---

[4] G. William Domhoff, *Who Rules America Now? A View for the '80s* (Englewood Cliffs, NJ: Prentice-Hall, 1983), 35.

there is no striving for status, and (2) there are generally no financial problems. Since status and wealth (preferably inherited wealth) are taken for granted, there is no need for ostentatious living. Upper-class families live comfortably—very comfortably—but they tend to shun any display of opulence. Thus they live in large houses, but not large new houses. They dress well, but probably not so well as the upper middle class. They may buy an expensive new car, or they may not, depending on their mood or fancy. They probably own precious jewelry, but wearing it is something else again. In brief, to exhibit one's wealth—or even to talk about it openly—is considered crass and ill-mannered.

Upper-class families travel a great deal both in the United States and abroad. They usually have a summer home and almost certainly have an extensive social life. It must be kept in mind that, in most communities, the upper class is a relatively small, cohesive group, whose members are well known to one another. Many of their social activities are organized and many are traditional.

It should not be thought that upper-class family life is totally without problems. Personality conflicts, disputes, arguments with in-laws—such discord occurs in all social strata. Moreover, there are certain kinds of difficulties that arise primarily at the upper-class level. Davis mentions three in particular:

1. Children of the rich may occasionally lack motivation to study, even less to work. They may spend their lives in the pursuit of pleasure. Davis refers to this segment as playboys with no interest in business or politics.[5]
2. The wealthy live in fear of kidnapping and of violence against them. As Davis puts it, "Mr. and Mrs. Smith is a lot safer than Mr. and Mrs. Rothschild." In the 1980s some wealthy families are even fortifying their homes and their automobiles. Yet they realize that even the most protected man in the world, the president of the United States, was shot by a lone villain.
3. "The late Paul Getty used to say that the loss of privacy was the biggest liability of being rich." On the one hand the rich must keep a low profile for protection and security. On the other hand, even ordinary events in their lives are popular themes for the news media.[6]

Each class has its own characteristic family-related problems. The problems of the rich are better known, because they are more publicized. However, in terms of duration of marriage and satisfaction with marriage and with life in general, the upper class has undoubted advantages. There is no

---

[5]William Davis, *The Rich: A Study of the Species* (New York: Franklin Watts, 1983), 179.
[6]Ibid., 226.

disagreement on this point among social-stratification specialists such as Tumin, who summarized the literature as follows:

> The higher the socioeconomic level the greater the chances for enjoying valued things and experiences, such as health, education, and long life. This generalization holds whether we compare people by income, educational levels or levels of occupational prestige.[7]

The Future

Will the democratization process and the changing pattern of American courtship make for modifications in the upper-class structure? Will the latter eventually lose its castelike impermeability? only time will tell. Thus far, there has been no pronounced tendency to "let down the bars." At the same time, social change takes place slowly at the upper-class level, where the stakes are very high indeed. But if there is a change—surely a big if—it may well occur through Cupid's perambulations on the college campus.

THE MIDDLE-CLASS FAMILY

Just below the upper class, described above, are those well-to-do families in which the father is usually a professional man or a business executive. This group is variously referred to as the "lower-upper" or "upper-middle" class. The next lower stratum in the social hierarchy is the middles-class proper, families of moderate means in which the husband is in the white-collar—clerical or sales—category. The line between middle and upper-middle is not always clear-cut. Men in the higher administrative or sales positions, for example, tend to merge into the upper-middle class. As a matter of fact, while the middle stratum has some identifiable characteristics, the so-called middle-class way of life—as we shall see—has been greatly oversimplified.

The Kaleidoscopic Class

For all its much-discussed uniformity, the middle class is a veritable kaleidoscope. It looks different, depending on the light and the angle, and no two people seem to see the same design. Beeghley, for example, defines the middle class primarily in terms of its white-collar occupations:

> White-collar people are those who work in nonmanual occupations, ranging from . . . social workers to office managers, insurance agents, and receptionists. As a proportion of the total work force, white-collar occupations have been steadily expanding over the past 75 years. Some middle-class occupations,

---

[7]Melvin M. Tumin, *Social Stratification* (Englewood Cliffs, NJ: Prentice-Hall, 1985), 105.

The middle class is a veritable kaleidoscope. No two people seem to see the same design. Where in the social spectrum do you think this family belongs? (*Nina Leen, Life Magazine,* © *1948 Time Inc.*)

especially among those classified as professional or managerial, are quite lucrative and involve a high amount of self-direction.[8]

Rapp finds it difficult to define the middle class strictly in terms of wages and occupations. For Rapp other factors are equally important:

---

[8]Leonard Beeghley, *Social Stratification in America: A Critical Analysis of Theory and Research* (Santa Monica, CA: Goodyear Publishing, 1978), 200

Such a category is obviously hard to define; like all class sectors, it must be historically situated, for the middle-class of early-twentieth century America differs markedly from that of our own times. To understand what middle class means for the different groups, we need to know not only their present status but also the ethnic and regional variations in class structure within which their families entered America.[9]

Levine does not see very much future for the middle-class family no matter how the class status is defined.

At present, the sociocultural and economic conditions that have done so much to improve our standard of living and enrich life by extending independence and personal fulfillment have also undercut the middle-class nuclear family's efforts to achieve stability and happiness. If such conditions persist, then the present state of marriage and family is an ill omen for the balance of this decade and, perhaps, the years beyond. Unbridled individualism will continue to trouble and disrupt marriage and family life, and children will increasingly pay the emotional and behavioral costs of negligent and inadequate parenting.[10]

What Levine points out may be summarized in a sentence: what is good for the individual is not necessarily good for the family.

Excessive individualism may be at least partially responsible for the rise in divorce among middle-class families. As spouses seek greener pastures for themselves, divorce sometimes impoverishes at least one of them, usually the mother. She is often left with the children and the responsibility to raise them on a fraction of the income they all enjoyed as a family.

While no one can deny that these problems are serious, some writers exude optimism. Eisler, for example, sees a return to more conservative work ethics in the middle-class family even when the children are not quite so successful as their more fortunate parents. She sees the decline of such things as commune membership, use of drugs, and other unconventional, rebellious lifestyles that often characterized middle-class children of the sixties. Today even a somewhat downwardly mobile middle-class person tends to work hard and exhibit self-reliance. Eisler calls these new middle-class people "savvy skidders" and describes them as follows:

Unselfconscious and guiltless, the savvy skidders carry the visible attributes of their advantages: from the perfectly straight teeth to the personable self-confidence of the well-schooled, well-nurtured upper-middle class child. Far from searching for new sexual configurations or noncapitalist forms of child rearing, many of these downwardly mobile young people are fervent believers in and builders of the most nuclear of families. The seriousness with which

---

[9]Rayna Rapp, "Family and Class in Contemporary America: Notes Toward an Understanding of Ideology," in Barrie Thorne and Marilyn Yalom, eds., *Rethinking the Family: Some Feminist Questions* (New York: Longman, 1982), 180.

[10]Edward M. Levine, "Middle-Class Family Decline," *Society*, January 1981, 78.

What middle-class characteristics are evident in this photograph?

these young men take the role of husband and father is so conservative—in the sense of preindustrial—as to be the most radical element of their philosophy. Often, their belief in the primacy of the personal explains most about their choice of work.[11]

Clearly the white-collar job, with its combination of rewards and frustrations, is central to an understanding of middle-class people. It must be remembered that these people are perched squarely in the middle of the socioeconomic ladder, and it is temptingly American to look up rather than down. This tendency to identify with the upper rather than the lower strata is probably a major reason for the white-collar workers' reluctance to unionize. Attempts to unionize white-collar employees have been made for several decades now, with a noticeable lack of success.

But if the middle-class worker does not take to the idea of unionizing, he most certainly embraces other American culture traits, such as the belief in education, a respect for hard work, and a high regard for the power of personality. In Arthur Miller's *Death of a Salesman*—one of the memorable American plays—there is a scene between Willy Loman and his son Biff. Willy, a pathetic figure as a fading salesman, tries to prime the boy for a business interview.

---

[11]Benita Eisler, *Class Act: America's Last Dirty Secret* (New York: Franklin Watts, 1983), 104.

WILLY: But don't wear a sport jacket and slacks when you see Oliver.

BIFF: No, I'll—

WILLY: A business suit, and talk as little as possible, and don't crack any jokes. . . . Remember, start big and you'll end big. Ask for fifteen. How much you gonna ask for?

BIFF: Gee, I don't know—

WILLY: And don't say "Gee." "Gee" is a boy's word. A man walking in for fifteen thousand dollars does not say "Gee!"

BIFF: Ten, I think, would be top though.

WILLY: Don't be so modest. You always started too low. Walk in with a big laugh. Don't look worried. Start off with a couple of good stories to lighten things up. It's not what you say, it's how you say it—because personality always wins the day.[12]

In the short space of a few sentences, poor Willy has completely reversed himself—and he is not even aware of it, so eager is he to move his stagnant son to right action. For Willy is convinced that the road to socioeconomic success is paved with personality. It is interesting that many middle-class workers, in real life, seem to have the same idea; for example, one of the contentions of small merchants and salespeople is that they "enjoy meeting people and learning about human nature."

One of the most poignant statements about the "personality" approach to sales is found in C. Wright Mills' classic *White Collar:*

The employer of manual services buys the workers' labor, energy, and skill; the employer of many white-collar services, especially salesmanship, also buys the employees' social personalities. . . . In a society of employees, dominated by the marketing mentality, it is inevitable that a personality market should arise. . . .

One knows the salesclerk not as a person but as a commercial mask, a stereotyped greeting and appreciation for patronage. . . . Kindness and friendliness become aspects of personalized service or of public relations of big firms, rationalized to further the sale of something. With anonymous insincerity the Successful Person thus makes an instrument of his own appearance and personality. . . .

Many salesgirls are quite aware of the difference between what they really think of the customer and how they must act toward her. The smile behind the counter is a commercialized lure. . . . In the normal course of her work, because her personality becomes the instrument of an alien purpose, the salesgirl becomes self-alienated.[13]

But are the actions and reactions of people like Willy Loman and the salesgirl really typical of middle-class behavior? We have presented several

---

[12]"Death of a Salesman," in *Arthur Miller's Collected Plays* (New York: The Viking Press, 1957), 168–69.

[13]C. Wright Mills, *White Collar* (New York: Oxford University Press), 1953, 182–84.

quotations purporting to describe middle-class life. Which one represents the true picture? The answer is that they probably all do. The middle class is larger than either the upper or lower strata and covers a much broader social spectrum. This spectrum is variegated and at times appears inconsistent. Social scientists can depict patterned behavior for the upper or the lower strata much more readily than for the diversiform middle class. It is easy to see why the latter is truly "kaleidoscopic."

Dominant Values

There are certain values that pervade the middle class, although the above caution should be kept firmly in mind. The present capsuled account will merely serve to show certain contrasts between the middle class and those at the upper and lower ends of the social hierarchy.

To begin with, "respectability" looms large in the eyes of the middle-class family. The latter may be uncomfortably close to certain elements of the lower class, and respectability sometimes represents the line of division. Middle-class parents, for example, would be heartbroken to learn that their son had been apprehended by the police, a happening that may be taken in stride by lower-class parents. It is the affirmation of respectability that makes middle-class parents fearful of permitting their children to associate with lower-class boys and girls.

There are certain outward signs of respectability that middle-class families take some pains to observe. Home ownership is important, and long-term mortgages are clearly preferred over the usual alternative—apartment living. Moreover, it is not just home ownership that is involved, but the endless trappings, such as interior and exterior improvements, alterations, attractive furniture, electrical appliances, and—of course—an automobile.

This particular style of living thus presents something of a problem. Whereas the family would dearly like to save some money for a rainy day, they are reluctant to scrimp on the middle-class status symbols. And since the necessary purchases—home, car, appliances—must frequently be made on a time basis, there is often little money left over for saving. In fact, at any given moment, the middle-class family is likely to have a fair amount of debt. It is debt that oftens prompts many of the wives to seek employment.

There is one cause for which middle-class parents try their very best to save: a college education for the children. Realistic or not, most middle-level parents sincerely want their children to improve on their (the parents') socioeconomic position, and a college degree is widely believed to be the instrument of improvement. While the upper and upper-middle classes may send a greater proportion of their children to college, it is the middle class that makes the most sacrifices.

Religion is another hallmark of middle-class persons. In fact, some sociologists feel that members of this class are the most regular churchgoers in America. And even though much literary cynicism has been directed toward "middle-class morality," it is nevertheless true that the middle-class atti-

Regular church attendance is one of the hallmarks
of middle-class families in America.

tudes are a major influence on such moral considerations as sexual behavior, divorce, obscenity and pornography, and personal ethics.

THE LOWER-CLASS FAMILY

Just below the middle class is the large working class—factory workers, electricians, bus drivers, and others in the blue-collar category. Below them, occupying the bottom rung of the socioeconomic ladder, is the lower class—unskilled workers, day laborers, the erratically employed, and the chronically unemployed. These are the poor, and in recent years they have been the focus of much sociological research.

The exact size of this class depends on how the term is defined. U.S. Census data place the figures "below the poverty line" at around 11 percent for the white population, 31 percent for the black, and 14 percent for the nation.[14] But, whatever the figure, the problems involved are immense for the family, the society, and the individual.

Members of the lower class are well aware that they are on the bottom rung of the socioeconomic ladder, and that their position is not likely to change. For many of them, welfare becomes the only way to survive. But welfare takes its toll on human dignity. Two welfare mothers in an 1988 interview with the Associated Press reporter in Albuquerque, New Mexico, made these comments:

> People think that just because you are on welfare you're stupid, you're a party animal, you don't want to work—you just want to live off the government and that you're lazy. That's not true at all. I hope to go to school one day soon. I want to finish school. I want to be in a profession of some kind, hopefully nursing.

> I can't see myself getting married and living happily ever after. It's just not in the cards for me. It's not a way out. A way out is for me to better myself.

Another mother explained her situation this way:

> It's been hard for me to be on welfare. When I first went on welfare I would go to the welfare office and I'd come home and just cry.

> How did I get here? What happened? I'm certainly not proud and I certainly don't think that the state owes me anything.

> When I was working I felt great. I don't tell anybody I'm on welfare. I'm not proud of it, not by a long shot. I don't want to be on welfare.

These women may well be speaking for those mothers who receive Aid to Families with Dependent Children as a temporary stopgap during an economic crisis in their life.[15] The crises are most frequently brought about by divorce or separation. Another frequently cited reason for crisis is having a baby out of wedlock. After two or three years on welfare, many mothers find employment or get married. In central cities, however, the lack of educational opportunity, shortage of men, and chronic unemployment for unskilled labor have created a class of families whose survival often depends on the long-term welfare dependence.

There is no denying that lower-class families are overrepresented in the "problem" area. It has become common knowledge that they account for a disproportionate share of unemployment, crime, disease, illiteracy, mental disorders, child abuse, and drug addiction. The causes for these conditions may range from unwise individual decisions to factors beyond the individual's control. As Joe and Rogers explained,

---

[14]The U.S. Bureau of the Census, *Statistical Abstract of the United States 1989*. Washington, DC, 1989, 38.

[15]William P. O'Hare, *America's Welfare Population: Who Gets What?* (Washington, DC: Population Reference Bureau, Inc., 1987), 7.

Some are poor because nature betrayed them at birth; others because a textile plant moved to Taiwan. Some are poor because they were not taught, others because they did not study. Still others . . . because men have oppressed women . . . whites have enslaved nonwhites. . . . Some are poor despite unending virtue, work and toil; a few because they revel in sloth, cunning and artifice.[16]

While the cause—or causes—may be debatable, the fact remains that poverty seems always to be with us. It is also a fact that the poor, like other social classes, desire both a decent life and a rewarding family system. Unfortunately, both the internal and the external obstacles are substantial.

Marriage and Family Living

Courtship for the middle and upper classes is a fairly elaborate sequence of events. Dating starts at an early age, dozens of persons are dated, attractions are numerous, and infatuations or love affairs are far from infrequent. This premarital screening, or trial-and-error process, is extensive enough to permit the formulation of marital criteria. The final selection of a mate, after years of experience, is anything but a hit-or-miss proposition. Lower-class youth, however, marry at a significantly younger age, and they often give the impression of just having drifted together. Instead of the extensive dating and trial-and-error procedures, there is a pattern of drift and a philosophy of "what will happen, will happen."

Roebuck and Hickson show how sexual interest develops early among lower-class children. They cite the following statement by a second grader:

I am at a football game. . . . I am watching the game but playing with my brother and his friends, since I always play with them. I can go anywhere if I do; otherwise, I have to stay at home. We are throwing rocks at some of the girls in my brother John's room at school. The girls are on the bleachers; we are underneath, looking up at their underpants. I have a crush on one of them—Rebecca, dark eyes and hair, small and full bosomed already, in the fourth grade. I like her a lot, so I am throwing rocks at her.[17]

By the time these children are in high school, they have already experienced sex, perhaps with more than one partner, and are ready to escape from home, especially if it is an unhappy home life. For the women, unfortunately, "escape" oftens proves to be illusory. Some lower-class males dominate their women and prevent them from attaining additional education.[18] Women's place, in their view, is in the kitchen.

---

[16]Tom Joe and Cheryl Rogers, *By the Few for the Few* (Lexington, MA: Lexington Books, 1985), 9.

[17]Julian B. Roebuck and Mark Hickson, *The Southern Redneck: A Phenomenological Class Study* (New York: Praeger Publishers, 1982), 154.

[18]Ibid., 152.

The wife may work if the couple cannot meet their minimum financial obligations; however, she is not supposed to advance in career or in education. The husband presumably fears that male teachers or office managers will appeal to his wife more than he does. Considering the general orientation toward one's wife, some men have legitimate fears. The following quotation from a recent study is illustrative:

> I love my wife and family and all that good (expletive deleted) but I wear the breeches. My ole lady does her thing. She cooks and keeps me and the kids happy. She works too. She's gotta work if we want to live good. I treat her good too, but she knows I'm the boss. I'm like the other boys. I got to go out and raise hell once or twice a week. You know chew the fat with the boys, drink a few beers and jes raise a little hell. I ain't looking for nothing but if a strange piece turns up I take care of it too. I ain't no chaser but. . . .
>
> And when I come home I don't want to hear no (vulgarity deleted) from the ole lady or nobody else. They don't mess around with me. I ain't no animal but they all know not to git outta line with me. I'll knock em on their ass if they need it—and they know it. I may be nobody out there but I am a big stick at home. They know I come first.[19]

On the basis of the above, it is easy to see why many working-class husbands and wives live almost in separate worlds. Ironically, in the middle class where there is less need for employment of both spouses, there is greater acceptance of educational and occupational advancement for the wives. In the lower social strata, the oppression of some women is so great that they either have to stay single or procure a divorce in order to improve their own status.

This may be one reason why some women stay single. Being on her own, a woman at the lower socioeconomic levels may have a better chance for upward mobility than a married woman. Childbearing, of course, weakens her chances for advancement, whether single or married. But if she has family help with child rearing, her chances to advance may still be better than if she is married to a husband whose fulfillment depends on keeping his wife in a subservient position.

Children

Children represent something of a special problem in lower-class families. For one thing, the birthrate is noticeably higher than in the upper classes. Birth-control measures are imperfectly understood by many lower-class couples. In brief, those who can least afford them have the largest numbers of children. The more children the family has, the less it can do for them. This generality applies to every social class, but in terms of educational attainment of children the results are often devastating for the lower class.

---

[19]Ibid., 152–53.

The large number of children in lower-class families also increases conflict among siblings, between parents, and between children and parents. The increase in family size complicates communication, requires improved management of children, and demands greater resources to provide necessities for all family members.

In part because there are more people in lower-class families, and in part because they place greater emphasis on obedience, the parents are more likely to use physical and emotional punishment to discipline their children. Frustrations and powerlessness may also find a vent in aggression toward children. In fact, there is often a narrow line between the legitimate disciplining of their children and the inflicting of bodily harm on them. If we use the latter as a measure of child abuse, then the children in poor families are sometimes in real danger.

Many social scientists go to great lengths to say that "all children, regardless of class, are at the risk of violence." They are certainly correct. No one can predict which particular child is going to be victimized; therefore, there is some risk associated with just being a child. The important question is, What are the differences in risk among children? If we accept the figures on serious physical injuries reported by hospitals and police, then lower-class children are at considerably higher risk.[20]

A recent study shows that a child born in a poor neighborhood is more than twice as likely to die before reaching age one as a child born in a high-income neighborhood.[21]

Bright Spots

In many ways the lower-class family presents a rather grim picture, but it is far from a hopeless one. As a matter of fact, in view of the many economic, educational, and social handicaps suffered, perhaps the wonder of it all is that the poor family is as stable as it is. Fundamentally, these men and women have a sincere desire to be good husbands and wives and to fulfill their family obligations, and most of them manage to succeed. Kerbo makes the following interesting observations with regard to the comparison of working-class and middle-class families:

> Findings showing different socialization patterns by class do not suggest that working-class parents have less concern for their children or are harder on their children. Also, one should not get the idea that working-class parents are less concerned about their children's future. What the studies do indicate is that middle-class parents are more concerned with higher-level occupational

[20]I. Berry Pless, et al., "Epidemiology of Road Accidents in Childhood," *American Journal of Public Health,* March 1987, 358–60.

[21]Edward G. Stockwell, David A. Swanson, and Jerry W. Wicks, "Economic Status Differences in Infant Mortality by Cause of Death," *Public Health Reports,* March–April 1988, 137.

attainment for their children, while working-class parents are concerned with their childrens' well-being without reference to occupational level per se.[22]

Another bright spot is the fact that sociologists have been devoting considerable time to the study of poverty. Formerly, research projects dealing with the poor were scarce, but this has been corrected. And while research, per se, will not solve the problems of poor families, it is hardly likely that the problems will be solved without a solid research foundation.

Furthermore, social workers who deal with lower-class children and their families are in a better position to provide help than formerly. They are better trained, and are often in a position to offer family counseling. Also, social workers have tended to renounce the moralistic approach to poverty. The trend today is toward understanding poverty in terms of the best available evidence. Only after understanding can an attempt be made to ameliorate the problem itself.

The many problems of the lower-class family will not be easy to solve. The stakes, however, are staggeringly important. From the individual's view, lower-class family members are neither partaking of cultural activities nor enjoying cultural benefits. From the societal view, the lower-class family too often represents a lost human resource. A multipronged attack by the government, by local schools and agencies, and by social scientists would seem to offer the best chance of success.

SUMMARY

Among the outside forces that influence family life, social class seems to be one of the most important. Whether measured by family income, occupation, or educational attainment, in general the higher the status the more stable the family life.

Needless to say, there are numerous exceptions to this rule. We have even discussed certain advantages that only lower-class families seem to enjoy. In fact, anomalous or not, we have shown some serious disadvantages that accompany wealth and fame. However, everything considered, adequate income and education remain as important ingredients for stable marriage and family life.

QUESTIONS

1. What is the function of the upper-class "family office?" Does such an office operate in the city or community in which you live?
2. Describe the courtship and marital system of the upper class. Are upper-class marriages more stable than those of the middle and lower classes?

---

[22]Kerbo, *Social Stratification*, 285.

3. How would you characterize the lifestyle of the upper class? What kinds of problems are characteristic only or largely of the upper class?

4. If you were to write an essay on the "future of the upper class in America," what would your prediction be?

5. Why is the middle class sometimes called the "kaleidoscopic class"?

6. Does the account of the middle class given in the text correspond to your own impressions and observations of this class? Explain.

7. What are the so-called dominant values of the middle class? In your opinion, are these values likely to change in the foreseeable future? Why or why not?

8. What are the principal features of the lower-class lifestyle? How does this mode of living differ from that of the middle class?

9. Describe how courtship operates among lower-class youth. Why does this seemingly haphazard procedure seem so foreign to the procedure employed by middle-class youth?

10. "Children represent something of a special problem in lower-class families." Why is this true? Discuss.

11. If you were asked to write an essay on the strengths of the lower-class family, what factors would you include?

SELECTED READINGS

Abbott, Pamela. "Women's Social Class Identification: Does Husband's Occupation Make a Difference?" *Sociology,* February 1987, 91–103.

Allen, Michael Patrick. *The Founding Fortunes: A New Anatomy of the Super-Rich Families in America.* New York: E. P. Dutton, 1987.

Alwin, Duane F., and Arland Thorton. "Family Origins and the Schooling Process: Early versus Late Influence of Parental Characteristics." *American Sociological Review,* December 1984, 784–802.

Auletta, Ken. *The Underclass.* New York: Vintage Books, 1983.

Beeghley, Leonard, and John Cochran. "Class Identification and Gender Role Norms among Employed Married Women." *Journal of Marriage and the Family,* August 1988, 719–729.

Bonney, Norman. "Gender, Household, and Social Class." *The British Journal of Sociology,* March 1988, 28–46.

Chevan, Albert. "The Growth of Home Ownership: 1940–1980." *Demography,* May 1989, 249–266.

Davis, Nancy J., and Robert V. Robinson. "Class Identification of Men and Women in the 1970s and 1980s." *American Sociological Review,* February 1988, 103–112.

Davis, William. *The Rich: A Study of the Species.* New York: Franklin Watts, 1983.

Demo, David H., and Rich C. Savin-Williams. "Early Adolescent Self-Esteem as a Function of Social Class." *American Journal of Sociology,* January 1983, 763–74.

Dunst, Carol J., and Hope E. Leet. "Measuring the Adequacy of Resources in Households with Young Children." *Child Care, Health and Development,* 13, 1987, 111–125.

Fussell, Paul. *Class: A Guide through the American Status System*. New York: Summit Books, 1983.

Goodwin, Leonard. *Causes and Cures of Welfare*. Lexington, MA: Lexington Books, 1983.

Haller, Max. "Marriage, Women, and Social Stratification: A Theoretical Critique." *American Journal of Sociology*, January 1981, 766–95.

Hiller, Dana V., and William W. Philliber. "Determinants of Social Class Identification for Dual-Earner Couples." *Journal of Marriage and the Family*, August 1986, 583–587.

Jackman, Mary R., and Robert W. Jackman. "Family Influences on Subjective Class." In *Class Awareness in the United States*, 139–65. Berkeley, CA: University of California Press, 1983.

Kulis, Stephen. "Socially Mobile Daughters and Sons of the Elderly: Mobility Effects within the Family Revisited." *Journal of Marriage and the Family*, May 1987, 421–433.

Lareau, Annette. "Social Class Differences in Family-School Relationships: The Importance of Cultural Capital." *Sociology of Education*, April 1987, 73–85.

Leiulfsrud, Hakon, and Allison Woodward. "Women at Class Crosswords: Repudiating Conventional Theories of Family Class." *Sociology*, August 1987, 393–412.

Levine, Steven B. "The Rise of American Boarding Schools and the Development of a National Upper Class." *Social Problems*, October 1980, 65–94.

McLanahan, Sara. "Family Structure and the Reproduction of Poverty." *American Journal of Sociology*, January 1985, 873–901.

Ostrander, Susan A. *Women of the Upper Class*. Philadelphia: Temple University Press, 1984.

Packard, Vance. *The Ultra Rich*. Boston: Little, Brown, 1989.

Payne, Joan. "Does Unemployment Run in Families? Some Findings from the General Household Survey." *Sociology*, May 1987, 199–214.

Rank, Mark R. "Fertility among Women on Welfare: Incidence and Determinants." *American Sociological Review*, April 1989, 296–304.

——— "The Formation and Dissolution of Marriages in the Welfare Population." *Journal of Marriage and the Family*, February 1987, 15.

Simpson, Ida Harper, and David Stark. "Class Identification Processes of Married, Working Men and Women." *Sociology*, April 1988, 284–293.

Smith, Dwayne M., and Lynne J. Fisher. "Sex-Role Attitudes and Social Class: A Reanalysis and Clarification." *Journal of Comparative Family Studies*, Spring 1982, 77–88.

Smith, James P. "Children among the Poor." *Demography*, May 1989, 235–248.

Suitor, Jill J. "Husbands' Educational Attainment and Support for Wives' Return to School." *Gender and Society*, December 1988, 482–495.

Tickamyer, Ann R., and Cecil H. Tickamyer. "Gender and Poverty in Central Appalachia." *Social Science Quarterly*, December 1988, 874–891.

Wright, Erik Olin, and Bill Martin. "The Transformation of the American Class Structure, 1960–1980." *American Journal of Sociology*, July 1987, 1–29.

THREE

Premarital Behavior Patterns

Chapter 9

Theories and Patterns of Mate Selection

Mate selection in middle-class America generally follows a pattern similar to that of serial monogamy. In cultures that accept serial monogamy, *the field of eligibles* for marriage is wide and includes both married and single people of both sexes. By contrast, in traditionally monogamous cultures a person enters the field of eligibles at maturity and exits at marriage. According to Farber, *permanent availability* is a rule of mate selection in serial monogamy:

> Each individual, at least theoretically, is permanently available as a potential mate to all other cross-sex individuals. An important point here is that being married does not restrict an individual with respect to his future potentiality as a mate in later marriages.[1]

In 1964, when Farber first introduced the principle of permanent availability, it applied only to a small proportion of the American people. By 1970, 31 percent of marriages involved at least one previously married part-

---

[1] Bernard Farber, *Family: Organization and Interaction* (San Francisco: Chandler Publishing Co., 1964), 109.

ner. By the mid-1980s the figure had risen to some 46 percent![2] It would seem that permanent availability is a condition of mate selection when serial monogamy becomes an accepted form of marriage.

Studying mate selection under serial monogamy requires a theoretical approach that encompasses a wide age span, both genders, and changing socioeconomic circumstances. Because one theory cannot accomplish that, we have extracted ideas from theories emphasizing socialization, exchange, and demography.

PARENTS' INFLUENCE ON MATE CHOICE: SOCIALIZATION THEORY

Parents' influence on choice of mate begins long before their children mature. Through teaching and through example, parents impart to their children values, beliefs, norms, and even mate-selection etiquette appropriate for their social class and ethnic group. At maturity this knowledge forms a part of the mental framework that directs love and attraction toward opposite-sex individuals. Through this process, parents transmit the culture and the family heritage from generation to generation.

In a heterogeneous society such as ours, parents cannot always control whom their children will marry. Usually they want their children to marry persons from the same ethnic group and with similar social standing. If the children do so, such marriages are described as *endogamous:* marriages between people of similar social backgrounds. Marriages outside one's social group are called *exogamous*. Marriages between brides and grooms who share personal traits, such as appearance and personality, constitute *homogamy*. Marriages between partners with different personal traits constitute *heterogamy*. The key question is why some persons marry homogamously while others marry heterogamously.

The answer may lie partly with the kind of feelings that the children develop toward their parents. The stronger the feeling, the greater the likelihood that parental characteristics will have an influence on marriage. Theoretically, when emotions are positive, the individual is likely to marry someone similar to the parents. On the other hand, negative emotions may lead to a departure from the family and from the culture that the parents represent. In other words, positive feelings toward parents may result in endogamy and homogamy, whereas negative feelings may result in exogamy and heterogamy. Because most people have overall positive experiences with their parents, *homogamy and endogamy tend to be the rule of mate selection.*

The socialization theory of mate selection postulates an even more specific relationship between parental influence and mate choice. It is popu-

---

[2]National Centre for Health Statistics, *Monthly Vital Statistics Reports,* vol. 38, no. 3 (July 1989), 16.

The psychoanalytic version of mate-selection theory postulates that the same-sex parent serves as the adult role model. The opposite-sex parent provides an image that guides the mate search. (*John Dominis, Life Magazine,* © *Time Inc.*)

larly believed that the image of the opposite-sex parent guides the search for a mate, and that the same-sex parent provides the adult role model. Empirical support for this idea comes from studies that found that (1) first-born sons marry at younger ages than those born later, (2) men with older fathers tend to marry at older ages, (3) people born to mixed-race marriages tend to marry into the ethnic group of the opposite-sex parent, and (4) people tend to choose mates with physical attributes of the opposite-sex parent more than with those of the same-sex parent.[3]

Parental images and emotions generated toward parents in general seem to influence mate selection, but the question of how parental influence manifests itself in a free market of mate selection remains to be answered. One possibility comes from the exchange theory.

THE EXCHANGE THEORY OF MATE SELECTION

Long before romantic interests develop, children learn to value their social status, their ethnic group, and their way of life. They learn what sociologists call *ethnocentrism:* the feeling that one's own ethnic group, family back-

---

[3]Glenn D. Wilson and Paul T. Barrett, "Parental Characteristics and Partner Choice: Some Evidence for Oedipal Imprinting," *Journal of Biosocial Sciences,* vol. 19, 1987, 157–61.

Courtship among eligibles is not likely to progress very satisfactorily unless agreement on values is reached. (© *Ian Berry, Magnum Photos*)

ground, and way of life are "better" than others. Through ethnocentrism and other patterns of socialization, children learn to attach values to personal and social characteristics as if these were commodities or *personal resources*. Accordingly, exchange theory states that enduring love and attraction are most likely to emerge when each person in a relationship perceives an advantageous exchange between contributed and received resources.

Because resources are at the crux of this theory, the following definitions of specific resources may influence the formation of romantic relationships.

1. *Person*. Even though this point is fundamental and obvious, it is not trivial to consider the person per se as a resource. All other things being equal, the value of the person from the viewpoint of others in a mate-selection network depends on the scarcity of members of the desired sex. When there are equal numbers of males and females, a person's value is greater or lesser than when there is a surplus or a shortage of one sex.

2. *Age*. Preferences of women for older men and of men for younger women are ingrained deeply in our nature. Age is associated with attractive appearance in youth and with higher socioeconomic status at the older age levels.

3. *Appearance*. Appearance includes physique, physiognomy, gestures, mannerisms, demeanor, and complexion. Of course there is

also an overall effect that defies definition, as acknowledged in the adage, "Beauty is in the eyes of the beholder." Generally, appearance is valued out of all proportion to its contribution to marital success.

4. *Status*. Status as a resource in mate selection is a combination of prestige ranking, economic well-being, education, recognition through honors, accomplishments, occupation, and family background. In mate selection a subjective evaluation of all these components is relevant to both the information and the continuation of romantic feelings.

5. *Personality*. Personality is one person's perception of another's ability to be understanding, emotional, expressive, cooperative, and so on. Many people make mistakes in this because perceptions are often tainted by expectations and because presentation of self before marriage may not convey the same personality as the unmasked exposure in everyday married life.

6. *Companionship*. More than any other resource, companionship is listed in "how to" manuals of mate selection as the characteristic to look for in a partner. This resource reflects middle-class values and is important for those who expect equality between sexes during mate selection and after marriage. Companionship means being able to share leisure, social, and intellectual activities. Good companionship involves good communication skills, ability to share, and willingness to reaffirm the other's worth as an equal partner in a relationship.

7. *Beliefs*. Religious and political beliefs are also exchange resources. People assess each other as partners on the basis of shared beliefs. Beliefs, of course, can be changed; one may relinquish beliefs in exchange for affection, commitment, status, or some other resource. People with similar beliefs have an essential resource of equal value.

Personal resources as used according to exchange theory are meaningful to the extent that they are valued by those involved in mate selection. The stimulus-value-role theory incorporates the valued resources in a three-stage process.

STIMULUS-VALUE-ROLE THEORY

One of the most interesting and most comprehensive of all mate-selection theories is the three-stage sequence proposed by Murstein.[4] Stimulus-value-role (SVR) theory holds that in a relatively free-choice situation most couples go through three stages before marriage.

---

[4]Bernard Murstein, *Who Will Marry Whom?* (New York: Springer, 1976), 107–33. Material in this section is used with the author's permission.

In the "stimulus" stage of mate selection one individual is drawn to another because of perception of each other's physical and social attributes. How would you describe physical and social attributes of people in the picture?

1. In the first or "stimulus" stage, one individual is drawn to another because of his or her perception of the other's physical and social attributes, as well as "his perception of his own qualities that might be attractive to the other person." "Although stimulus attraction is based on visual and auditory cues rather than on interaction, the first stage involves much more than simply good looks.

    Murstein points out that as a result of their previous experiences, people build up an image of their attractiveness to the opposite sex. Using social-exchange terminology, the author goes on to say:

    > A man who is physically unattractive (liability), for example, might desire a woman who has the asset of beauty. Assuming, however, that his nonphysical qualities are no more rewarding than hers, she gains less profit than he does from the relationship, and thus, his suit is likely to be rejected. Rejection is a cost to him, because it may lower his self-esteem and increase his fear of failure

in future encounters; hence, he may decide to avoid attempting to court women whom he perceives as much above him in attractiveness.

As can be seen, the first or "stimulus" stage is crucial to SVR theory. Unless there is mutual attraction, as described above, a courting relationship will normally fail to materialize.

2. If there has been a mutual "stimulus" attraction—say, at a social gathering of some kind—and the couple sits down to talk, they are now commencing the second stage, that of "value comparison." Murstein continues, as follows:

> The label "value comparison" refers to interests, attitudes, beliefs, and even needs when they are seen as emanating from beliefs. The primary focus of the value comparison stage, in short, is information gathering by verbal interaction with each other. . . . There is much public and private information that each learns about the other, such as religious orientation, political beliefs, attitudes toward people, interest in sports, the arts, dancing, and the like.

3. Whether or not a couple progresses to the "role" stage usually depends on the similarity of their values. In some cases, a couple may decide to marry on the basis of the first two stages—stimulus attraction and value congruence—but for most people it is also necessary to *function in compatible roles*.

A wife's role as defined by her husband consists of his perception of the behavior that is expected of a wife. His perception may be in part molded by his culture, but part of it may stem from his own idiosyncrasies, and this would not be found in his neighbor's definition. In like vein, the wife's definition of the wifely role would consist of her perception of what the role should embody.

Role compatibility is probably the most complex of all the stages and is probably never completely traversed, since individuals seem to be constantly adding new roles or modifying existing ones.

The above explanation of SVR theory is by no means complete and is offered here merely to acquaint the reader with some of the highlights. Murstein obviously has made a valuable contribution to mate-selection theory. Although no attempt has been made to replicate all his hypotheses, Imamura's recent study provides solid corroboration.[5] In view of the importance of the topic, it is hoped that further replication studies will be undertaken.

---

[5]Anne E. Imamura, "Ordinary Couples? Mate Selection in International Marriage in Nigeria," *Journal of Comparative Family Studies,* Spring 1986, 33–42.

COMPLEMENTARY NEEDS

Although the idea that mate selection may be a function of personality need fulfillment is fairly old, it remained for Winch to formulate a definitive theory on the subject and to put the theory to empirical test. According to Winch, an individual chooses a mate who provides him or her with maximum need gratification. Maximum gratification occurs when the specific need patterns of the man and the woman are *complementary rather than similar*. Among the specific complements that Winch poses are hostility-abasement, dominance-deference, nurturance-succulence, achievement-vicariousness.[6]

Even though Winch's own research confirmed his general theory, other research findings remain inconclusive. There is little doubt that similarity between partners is the major source of attraction, but complementarity also may be important to some people. Vinacke and his colleagues conclude, "People clearly do select and maintain relationships for reasons other than similarity."[7] So far, however, the strongest evidence for complementarity comes from clinical populations. If there are general complementary needs or personality traits, they remain to be discovered.

AVAILABILITY OF PARTNERS: THE DEMOGRAPHIC MARRIAGE SQUEEZE THEORY

Marriage squeeze is said to exist when a sizable number of individuals cannot marry because of a shortage of persons of the opposite sex. In our society, marriage squeeze is a result of combinations of monogamy, age heterogamy, and differential death rates. Under these circumstances a predictable number of people must remain single for a portion of their lives whether they want to do so or not.

Men and women from their teens to their eighties face the changing availability of opposite-sex marriage partners. At least in the United States, younger women and older men are in greater demand than younger men and older women. One reason is that marriages between younger women and considerably older men are socially acceptable.

Some young men under age twenty-five may have to wait three years or more before they can find a suitable partner. Generally, these young men are not aware that their situation is one manifestation of the marriage squeeze. As a result, they may attribute their lack of success to their own imagined inadequacies. Yet the whole process is largely out of their hands.

---

[6]Robert Winch, *Mate Selection* (New York: Harper & Brothers, 1958), 97.

[7]W. Edgar Vinacke, "Similarity and Complementarity in Intimate Couples," *Genetic, Social, and General Psychology Monographs*, February 1988, 74.

Table 9.1 NUMBER OF MALES PER 1000
FEMALES BY AGE GROUP AND
RACE, 1987

Age group	White	Black
Under 14 years	1054	1031
14–24	1029	979
25–44	1008	869
45–64	932	818
65 and over	683	671

Source: U.S. Department of Commerce, *Statistical Abstract of the United States, 1989.* Washington, DC: Bureau of the Census, 1989, 16.

A certain percentage of men simply have to wait until they become old enough for the odds to turn in their favor.

Table 9-1 shows how young women's advantage diminishes dramatically with age. Keeping in mind that a greater age difference tends to exist between an older man and his bride, one can see that most aging women remain single. Also note that a shortage of black men exists even before age 25.

AGE PATTERNS AT FIRST MARRIAGE: AN APPLICATION OF THE EXCHANGE THEORY

Age is an obvious factor in the selection of marriage partners. To begin with, women historically marry younger than men. At the turn of the century the average age of marriage was 22 years for women and 26 for men. The most recent figures indicate that the average age at first marriage is 24.3 for women and 26.2 for men.[8]

The narrowing of the age difference at marriage has been cited widely as an indication of declining gender inequality, but the averages are somewhat misleading. Table 9-2 shows that almost 20 percent of women who marry for the first time do so before age 20, whereas fewer than 8 percent of men do so by that age.

The exchange theory explains some of these differences. If we regard youth and beauty as resources for women and socioeconomic status as a resource for men, we can hypothesize as follows: the older the groom, the higher the socioeconomic status; hence he can exchange that status for his bride's youth and beauty. Conversely, the younger bride can exchange her youth and beauty for the highest socioeconomic status she can find. Al-

---

[8]National Center for Health Statistics, *Monthly Vital Statistics Reports,* 1989, 15.

Table 9.2 PERCENTAGE DISTRIBUTION
OF FIRST MARRIAGES BY AGE
OF WOMEN AND MEN, 1986

Age group	Women	Men
15–17	4.7	0.7
18–19	14.9	6.9
20–24	44.8	41.6
25–29	24.0	32.4
30–34	7.7	12.1
35–39	2.4	3.9
Over 40	1.5	2.4
Total	100	100

Source: National Center for Health Statistics, *Monthly Vital Statistics Report, Advance Report of Final Marriage Statistics,* vol. 38, no. 3, July 1989, 13.

though this hypothesis may seem out of touch with modern thinking, it has been true for many years without any appreciable change; thus it appears to be a valid empirical generalization.

RACIAL PATTERNS OF MARRIAGE

Although the rate of interracial marriages in the United States has increased somewhat, it remains low when compared with same-race marriages. Some observers contend that this is an indication of intolerance and racism, but there is another explanation. We alluded to it when we discussed the image of the opposite-sex parent as an influence on choice of mate. In part because of that image, people fall in love and marry those who resemble their parents or parent substitutes. Because children and their parents are usually of the same race, so are the people who attract them the most.

In view of the sociocultural obstacles involved, the question arises: why is it that some people marry interracially? Among many speculative answers, three seem promising. One is *negative identity:* a person who has a negative socialization experience with his or her parents may seek a mate in other ethnic groups. The rationale is that such people try to avoid disappointment by seeking a new way of life.

Another possible answer is *social mobility.* According to exchange theory, when socioeconomic status is considered to be a more important resource than race, some people take the opportunity to advance in status through intermarriage.

Another possibility is the *increasing tolerance toward intermarriage* in America. People are more likely to put love and affection ahead of racial traits. The statistics in this regard are remarkable. Gallup Poll figures show a clear

The exchange theory of mate selection postulates that youth and beauty tend to be exchanged for socio-economic status. What exchange resources are the persons in this picture attempting to portray?

trend toward "tolerance." When the question was asked, "Do you approve of marriage between blacks and whites?" the results were as follows:[9]

	Approve (%)	Disapprove (%)	No opinion (%)
1983	43	50	7
1978	36	54	10
1972	29	60	11
1968	20	72	8

---

[9]George H. Gallup, *The Gallup Poll: Public Opinion 1983* (Wilmington, DE: Scholarly Resources, 1984), 96.

People of the same religious backgrounds are more likely to marry each other than they are to marry people of different faiths. (*Eugene Richards, Magnum Photos*)

RELIGION AND INTERMARRIAGE

The extent of a religious intermarriage in the United States depends largely on the religion or denomination being considered. Among the Old Order Amish, mate selection outside the group is virtually nonexistent. On the other hand, intermarriage among the various Protestant denominations—Episcopalians, Baptists, Lutherans, Presbyterians, Methodists, and others—seems to be quite common. If husband and wife in Protestant households are usually of the same denomination, it may not be because of endogamous mate selection but because one party often "converts" after marriage.

Even when all white Protestant denominations are combined, they constitute less than 50 percent of the American population. Furthermore, the differences within that 50 percent are so great that grouping all white Protestants into one category is grossly misleading. In some areas it is often difficult to maintain strict religious edogamy without being left out of the marriage market altogether.

On the basis of recent surveys, religious endogamy is the rule of mate selection for the three major religious groups.[10] Protestants marry other Protestants in about 85 percent of marriages, Jews marry other Jews in 80 percent of marriages, and some 62 percent of Catholics marry each other. Although Protestants seem to have the highest rate of endogamy, most marry widely across the various denominations.

Again, it would be misleading to conclude that these figures indicate intolerance of religious differences, or even of intermarriage itself. Marriage is a serious decision that does not include deliberate searching for someone different. People of the same religious background are more likely to meet each other than to meet people of different faiths.

SOCIAL-CLASS PATTERNS OF MATE SELECTION

An important question in regard to mate selection and social class is whether social class is an individual or a family characteristic. Although social scientists debate the answer, we will assume that social class is a family characteristic. The reason for taking this position lies in the observation that as individuals move from family to family, their status changes accordingly. For example, if a person from a middle-class background marries into the upper class in America, that individual adopts the new status and discards the one acquired at birth. Thus an individual can move up in status through marriage.

Considering how advantageous it is for lower-class people to marry up, one would expect a great deal more cross-class dating and marriage. Such is not the case, however, because of built-in barriers to class exogamy. Eckland identified five such barriers:[11]

1. *Values.* Persons from the same class share the same values. These values may lead to mutual attraction.
2. *Propinquity.* Propinquity refers to nearness in place, or proximity. People in the same social class usually live in the same neighborhood, go to the same schools, and associate in their parents' social network. Segregation by social class decreases the possibility of cross-class contacts. Therefore, marriages tend to be more common within the same class than across social classes.
3. *Ethnic endogamy.* Eckland proposed that ethnicity and social class tend to be related. Because different ethnic groups historically

[10]Norval D. Glenn, "Interreligious Marriage in the United States: Patterns and Recent Trends," *Journal of Marriage and the Family,* August 1982, 562, and Allan L. McCutcheon, "Denominations and Religious Intermarriage: Trends among White Americans in the Twentieth Century," *Review of Religious Research,* March 1988, 213–27.

[11]Bruce K. Eckland, "Theories of Mate Selection," *Social Biology,* Spring–Summer 1982, 18–19.

have had different opportunities for self-advancement, ethnicity and class tend to go together. Therefore, class endogamy is really ethnic endogamy.

4. *Parental influence.* Students should be familiar by now with parents' ability to influence their children. Recall Chapter 8, for example, where it was shown how upper-class parents control their children's opportunities for contact.

5. *Intellect.* It seems to be a common observation that persons with similar intelligence levels tend to marry one another; this observation has been borne out by numerous studies. Because most Americans need education to advance or to maintain their social status, people of similar intellectual abilities often meet in school. College and university graduates are more likely to marry each other; similarly, high school graduates and high school dropouts tend to limit their contact opportunities to others of similar educational experience.

Whatever the reasons, social-class endogamy is another principle of mate selection. In America, however, the ascribed social class—that is, the class of family of origin—is only indirectly responsible for this form of endogamy. Eckland notes that "half of the similarity in class background of mates is due to assortative mating by education."[12] It would seem that American young people get more than education at colleges; they also tend to get their spouses.

SUMMARY

Mate selection in all societies operates within formal or informal boundaries; American society is no exception. Most Americans, for example, marry within the same race, and to a lesser extent within the same religion and social class. Also, the marriage of older-male, younger-female persists in spite of efforts to increase equality between the sexes.

Although surveys taken over the last two decades show an increasing "tolerance" toward exogamy, endogamy continues to prevail. Among other reasons, young people tend to marry those whom they are most likely to meet in everyday life. As long as this is the case, most Americans will continue to marry within their race, religion, and social class.

QUESTIONS

1. How have the boundaries of the field of eligibles changed? Has this change affected family life in America?

2. Parents can influence their children's mate choice directly and indirectly. What

---

[12]Ibid., 19.

are these influences, and which do you think may have the greatest effect on children?

3. In your experience, what are the resources in mate selection? Are they valued equally by each sex? Explain.

4. Explain how marriage squeeze may influence a person's self-perception. If you encountered such a case, what advice would you give?

5. Relying on the exchange theory of mate selection, explain the fluctuation in age differences at marriage for men and for women. Do you agree with this theoretical explanation? Why or why not?

6. Do your own experience and observations support or refute Murstein's stimulus-value-role theory?

7. It has been said that low rates of interracial marriage indicate racial intolerance in America. Critique this statement.

8. How can you reconcile low rates of interreligious marriage with the fact that the overwhelming majority of Americans approve of interfaith marriages?

9. Explain theoretically why interreligious marriage is more likely to occur than interracial marriage. (Hint: Think of indirect parental influence.)

10. Empirical studies have shown clearly that Americans marry within their own social class. Why is this so? Discuss in detail.

11. What is the indirect role of colleges and universities with respect to social-class endogamy?

SELECTED READINGS

Atkinson, Maxine P., and Becky L. Glass. "Marriage Age Heterogamy and Homogamy, 1900 to 1980." *Journal of Marriage and the Family,* August 1985, 685–700.

Basavarajappa, K. G., M. J. Norris, and S. S. Halli, "Spouse Selection in Canada, 1921–78: An Examination by Age, Sex and Religion." *Journal of Biosocial Sciences,* 1988, 211–23.

Buss, D. M., and M. Barnes. "Preferences in Human Mate Selection." *Journal of Personality and Social Psychology,* March 1986, 559–70.

Cate, Rodney M., Sally A. Lloyd, and Edgar Long. "The Role of Rewards and Fairness in Developing Premarital Relationships." *Journal of Marriage and the Family,* May 1988, 433–52.

Davis-Brown, Karen, Sonya Salamon, and Catherine A. Surra. "Economic and Social Factors in Mate Selection: An Ethnographic Analysis of an Agricultural Community." *Journal of Marriage and the Family,* February 1987, 41–55.

Dimaggio, Paul, and John Mohr. "Cultural, Capital, Educational Attainment and Marital Selection." *American Journal of Sociology,* May 1985, 1231–61.

Gray, Alan. "Intermarriage: Opportunity and Preference." *Population Studies.* 1987, 365–79.

Gudelunas, William, and Patrick D. Nolan. "Marriage to Non-Catholics: German, Italian, Lithuanian, Slovak, Polish, and English-Speaking Catholics, Schuylkill County, Pennsylvania, 1964–1979." *Social Science Research,* January 1987, 95–98.

Guttman, Ruth, and A. Sohar. "Spouse Similarities in Personality Items: Changes over Years of Marriage and Implications for Mate Selection." *Journal of Behavior Genetics.* 1987, 179–89.

Heaton, Tim B., and Kristen L. Goodman. "Religion and Family Formation." *Review of Religious Research,* June 1985, 343–59.

Jedlicka, Davor. "Indirect Parental Influence on Mate Choice: A Test of the Psychoanalytic Theory." *Journal of Marriage and the Family,* February 1984, 65–71.

Labov, Teresa, and Jerry A. Jacobs. "Intermarriage in Hawaii, 1950–1982." *Journal of Marriage and the Family,* February 1986, 79–88.

Leigh, G. K. "An Empirical Test of Sequence in Murstein's SVR Theory of Mate Selection." *Family Relations,* 1984, 225–31.

Murstein, Bernard I. *Paths to Marriage.* Family Studies Text Series, no. 5. Beverly Hills, CA: Sage Publications, 1986.

Petersen, Larry R. "Interfaith Marriage and Religious Commitment among Catholics." *Journal of Marriage and the Family,* November 1986, 725–35.

Schoen, Robert, and John Wooldredge. "Marriage Choices in North Carolina and Virginia, 1969–71 and 1979–81." *Journal of Marriage and the Family,* May 1989, 465–81.

Siddiqi, Musab U., and Earl Y. Reeves. "A Comparative Study of Mate Selection Criteria among Indians in India and the United States." *International Journal of Comparative Sociology,* 1986, 226–33.

South, Scott J. "Sex Ratios, Economic Power, and Women's Roles: A Theoretical Extension and Empirical Test." *Journal of Marriage and the Family,* February 1988, 19–31.

Stephen, Walter G., and White Cookie Stephen. "After Intermarriage: Ethnic Identity among Mixed-Heritage Japanese-Americans and Hispanics." *Journal of Marriage and the Family,* May 1989, 507–19.

Straus, A. L. "The Influence of Parent-Images on Mate Choice." *American Sociological Review,* October 1946, 554–59.

Wheeler, Raymond H., and B. G. Gunter. "Change in Spouse Age Difference at Marriage: A Challenge to Traditional Family and Sex Roles?" *Sociological Quarterly,* 1987, 411–21.

Chapter
10

Modes of Mate Selection

S ometimes overlooked by students of the family is the following truism: To a considerable degree, who marries whom depends on the *mode of mate selection*. A decade or two ago, for example, chance encounter followed by dating was the only mode of mate selection that young people really considered. Today, however, the picture may be changing.

In the 1990s, hundreds of thousands of Americans are trying innovative modes of mate selection. These include the use of modern technology, personal advertisements, agents, singles' groups, and social networks. Those eligible for marriage have thus expanded the field of eligibles far beyond schools, neighborhoods, and the usual chance encounters. In effect, they have overcome distance and culture as barriers to love and marriage. Dating, of course—however initiated—remains the most popular form of mate selection, especially on college campuses.

TRADITIONAL DATING

Although there is some disagreement about when dating in America started, it was in full bloom by the period between World War I and World War II. By the 1950s and 1960s, certain recognizable patterns could be

In the stimulus stage of mate selection, one individual is drawn to another by physical and social attributes. What attributes can you observe in this picture? (*Gatewood, The Image Works*)

discerned. For one thing, young people seemed to start dating at an earlier and earlier age. (At the present time it is quite common for young people of both sexes to have their first date before they are fourteen.)

Another pattern that emerged was the tendency for dating to assume a competitive quality. Boys could achieve status by dating the prettiest girls, while girls set their sights on the most popular or best-looking boys. Because good looks are always in short supply, some young people felt left out.

Still another development in the dating game was the parrying involved in the dating situation itself. There were all kinds of dating arrangements, but in one common game plan the boy would call for the girl (preferably in a car) and take her out for an evening's entertainment. Depending on the boy's economic resources, the "entertainment" might range from a local movie to a full-course dinner and show. Throughout the evening the boy would use his "line," while the girl—with equal skill—would employ various counterplays. For the boy, of course, the whole idea was to obtain demonstrable favors from the girl. For the girl, the idea was to remain in control of the situation without appearing to be too standoffish.

Admittedly the foregoing account is greatly oversimplified, but it is true that the dating game—as it came to evolve—embodied certain adversarial features.

The point is that although young Americans seemed to adapt quite readily to the dating game—indeed, many seemed to enjoy it—a number of criticisms were voiced, both by the participants and by the adult members of society.

The young complained about the competitive and adversarial aspects of dating, mentioned above. They also questioned the sexual rules—or the lack of them. On the one hand, sex during dating was held to be taboo. On the other hand—from all reports—"everybody seemed to be doing it." Furthermore, the system appeared to be contradictory. Boys were supposed to pursue, girls to resist—a prime example of the double standard.

Young people also complained about what they felt was undue parental interference in dating. Conflict between parents and offspring over the lat-

Traditional dating scene from the 1950s.
(*Sybil Shelton/Peter Arnold, Inc.*)

ter's choice of dates came to be a standard symptom of intergenerational conflict.

On their part, parents complained that they were losing control over the children. As the parents saw it, young people too often made unwise choices in their dating partners. Religious and social class lines were crossed increasingly. There was too much carousing, too much sex. In brief, the older generation felt that the dating game was a rather poor preparation for marriage.

MODERN DATING

Some of the negative aspects of dating still remain. Rose and Frieze, for example, found that in the late 1980s women were still significantly more likely than men to wait to be asked for a date and to worry about their appearance.[1] In addition, as Table 10-1 shows, dating scripts for men include

[1]Suzana Rose and Irene Hanson Frieze, "Young Singles' Scripts for a First Date," *Gender and Society,* June 1989, 258–268.

Table 10.1 FIRST-DATE SCRIPTS

A woman's first date	A man's first date
Tell friends and family.	Ask for a date.
Groom and dress.	Decide what to do.
Be nervous.	Groom and dress.
Worry about or change appearance.	Be nervous.
Check appearance.	Worry about or change appearance.
Wait for date.	Prepare car, apartment.
Welcome date to home.	Check money.
Introduce parents or roommates.	Go to date's house.
Leave.	Meet parents or roommates.
Confirm plans.	Leave.
Get to know date.	Open car door.
Compliment date.	Confirm plans.
Joke, laugh, and talk.	Get to know date.
Try to impress date.	Compliment date.
Go to movies, show, or party.	Joke, laugh, and talk.
Eat.	Try to impress date.
Go home.	Go to movies, show, or party.
Tell date she had a good time.	Eat.
Kiss goodnight.	Pay.
	Be polite.
	Initiate physical contact.
	Take date home.
	Tell date will be in touch.
	Kiss goodnight.
	Go home.

Source: Suzana Rose and Irene Hanson Frieze, "Young Singles' Scripts for a First Date," *Gender and Society,* June 1989, 258.

more action, more leadership, and more initiative. Today's dating script seems to have much in common with that of yesteryear.

The main difference between modern and traditional dating is that not all young people adhere to the same scripts. Many find dating much less formal than in the past. Dress is more casual; so are the occasions. Instead of being planned a week or more in advance, with the evening's entertainment carefully mapped out, today's dates are much more likely to be spontaneous, spur-of-the-moment affairs. The man is still more likely to pay for the entertainment and food, though this practice is no longer invariable.

Perhaps the most important change in the dating system is that young men and young women can talk to one another as equals. Traditionally, women on dates often "played dumb" to make the man appear more important and more intelligent. This demeaning experience is less likely to occur now because of the equalization of gender roles.

Sex, we should add quickly, is frequently a part of modern dating. In

Table 10.2   NUMBER AND PERCENTAGE OF IMMIGRANTS
ADMITTED INTO THE UNITED STATES THROUGH
MARRIAGE TO U.S. CITIZENS, 1982–1987

Year	Number of immigrant spouses[a]	Percentage of all marriages[b]
1982	104,218	4.1
1983	112,666	4.4
1984	116,596	4.5
1985	129,790	5.1
1986	137,597	5.2
1987	132,452	—

[a]U.S. Bureau of the Census, *Statistical Abstract of the United States, 1989.* Washington, DC, 1989, 11.

[b]Calculated on the basis of recorded marriages in the United States. See U.S. Department of Health and Human Services, "Advance Report of Final Marriage Statistics, 1986." *Monthly Vital Statistics Reports,* National Center for Health Statistics, July 1989, 9.

fact, the scenario shown in Table 10-1 includes initiation of physical contact by the male even on the first date. Sex is so much a part of dating that the next chapter will be devoted to that subject.

ASSESSMENT OF THE DATING SYSTEM

For many individuals the benifits of the American dating system are numerous: dating serves as an aid in socialization and personality development at a most important time in life; it provides young people with opportunities for learning to get along with the opposite sex; and, of course, although dating is enjoyable for its own sake, it also establishes a measure by which a marriage partner is ultimately chosen.

Despite all its advantages, however, there may be good reasons for some people to reject the dating system. As tolerance toward different lifestyles and cultures increases in America, so does the demand for varied premarital experiences. This demand is met by innovative modes of mate selection that can bring people together not only from across cities but from across countries.

INTERNATIONAL MATE SELECTION

Table 10-2 shows that well over 100,000 Americans are finding their spouses in other countries *every year*. This figure is by no means negligible: in fact, it is higher than the number of marriages in all but a handful of

Any person can find a mate almost anywhere in the world through the assistance of international correspondence agencies. (*John A. Broussard*)

states. And while there is some fluctuation from year to year, it is safe to say that international mate selection has become a major component of marriage in the United States.

Most American-international marriages take place between persons of the same race and ethnicity, although in recent years tens of thousands have involved Caucasian men and Asian women. For some reason, these marriages have attracted an inordinate amount of media coverage. Americans seem to be curious about the men and women who cross oceans and ignore boundaries in pursuit of marriage and happiness.

Who are these individuals? What is their background, and what is their motivation? In our ongoing study, we tried to answer these and other questions by applying Murstein's stimulus-value-role theory, discussed in the previous chapter. Interestingly, we found that the theory applies even when the initial contacts are not face-to-face!

Stimulus-Value-Role

In our survey we conducted personal interviews and examined the advertisements of many foreign participants. Findings indicate that physical appearance is valued highly in these relationships. Participants decide whom to contact by viewing photographs. In this respect the stimulus stage depends as heavily on appearance in international mate-selection networks as in ordinary dating. An exchange of comments in a newsletter published for clients of one agency illustrates this point:

CLIENT'S COMMENT: I have made the mistake of writing to the prettiest girls. . . . You write them one or two letters, they write back and ask for your photo. You send it, and that's the last you hear of them. . . . I guess the only disillusionment I have is the sad discovery that the majority of attractive women in the world are stuck up (not just the U.S.).

AGENT'S RESPONSE: I don't think the man ever did catch on to the fact that he was getting some of his own medicine. If the ladies are only willing to correspond with the most attractive men, he labels them "stuck up" . . . yet he was only willing to write to the prettiest ladies.[2]

We found that the exchange of photographs was an important part of the stimulus stage. Participants began serious correspondence only after they found each other's appearance acceptable. We never read their letters, but we were told that the letters tend to be long and frequent. Correspondents discuss mutual idiosyncrasies, attitudes, values, hobbies, likes, dislikes, and plans for the future. They thoroughly explore their values and, in more serious cases, their role expectations in marriage.

The role stage of the relationship, of course, is the most serious. At that point a pair decides whether or not to marry. This decision gains significance when long distances, travel, and money are involved. Before this commitment is made, according to an agent in California, most Americans go abroad to continue their courtship face-to-face. For some, the courtship abroad may take weeks or months. If young people are involved, the courtship rules are followed to the parents' satisfaction. If everything goes well, the couple marries before coming to the United States.

Until January 1987, it was also possible for thousands of individuals to come to the United States and marry a person whom they had never met. The marriage-fraud provision of the 1986 Immigration Act, however, now prohibits this practice.

Another scenario involves marriages after prolonged, intimate correspondence with multiple partners. It is neither uncommon nor considered unethical in international mate-selection networks to correspond with several people at the same time. At first, both men and women may initiate contacts with a hundred or more people, and then may reduce that number to only one partner. In some cases, however, similarities among participants are so great that multiple correspondence may go on for a year or longer.

---

[2]Kelly Broussard, *Hotline* (Honokaa, HI: May–June 1982), 1.

Participants' Profiles

To discern the profile of American participants we mailed a questionnaire to 607 clients of one international agency operating out of Hawaii. Two hundred and sixty-five, or 44 percent, returned usable questionnaires. Their profile is based on these results.

The overwhelming majority of American participants are men—half of them age thirty-seven or older. They are predominantly urban; 84 percent live in major metropolitan areas across the country. Their occupational attainment is considerably above average; 42 percent are professionals, executives, and managers. Their individual income was also above average; more than 63 percent earned more than $20,000 a year. Their income levels are commensurate with their above-average educational attainment. Only five did not complete high school, more than half had two or more years of college, and 6 percent had a Ph.D. or M.D.

Their religious affiliations were commensurate with that of the country at large: 48 percent Protestant, 23 percent Catholic, 15 percent all other religions, and 14 percent no religious affiliation. Politically, most viewed themselves as conservative. They were also conservative about sex and marriage; about 90 percent believed that sex should be restricted to marriage or to live-in partners. However, 91 percent felt that marriage is the ideal living arrangement.

The data on our foreign participants are limited to personal advertisements in matrimonial publications directed at American clients. We selected publications specializing in Asia because half of the foreign clients of matrimonial agencies live in Asiatic countries. The following findings are based on an analysis of 665 personal advertisements appearing in American matrimonial publications.

All the Asian advertisers were women. Their ages varied from fifteen to fifty, but more than half were age twenty-five or less. Most were well-educated and fluent in English. Some may have used another person's services to write their letters, but that kind of deceit would be discovered easily and certainly would lead to rejection. Most of those who lacked proficiency in English were candid about it and were willing to learn. In fact, most of the foreign participants were college students. Another 30 percent were managers, professionals, and clerical workers. Fewer than 10 percent came from rural areas or had held menial jobs. In general, the profile of the Asian clients seems to correspond to that of their American suitors: well-educated, urban, and in middle- and higher-status professions.

Motives for Seeking Spouses Abroad

The best clue to why Americans seek spouses abroad comes from the data on marital histories. More than 57 percent of the American participants were divorced. Most of the others had had unpleasant experiences during courtship and engagement. Frequently they revealed that they had been victims of deceit, unfaithfulness, loss of wealth due to divorce, and even fraud. A full 75 percent of the American participants had experienced some kind of trauma. As a result, many were trying to avoid repeating the experience by finding someone geographically removed and culturally different.

Twenty-five percent, however, were simply interested in expanding their cross-cultural experiences. They used this mode of selection in addition to ordinary dating at home. Actually, more than 90 percent of the American participants feel comfortable with any mode of mate selection, including face-to-face chance encounters. Only 10 percent use agencies and correspondence because they feel that their temperament, personality, or lifestyle is better suited for this mode of mate selection.

One can only guess about the motives of foreign participants. Yet in view of the fact that in many Third World countries women are more likely than men to graduate from college, we believe that the educational imbalance is a major reason. This imbalance would explain why so many foreign participants are college students or college graduates.

One benefit for all participants is the expansion of their field of eligibles. Whether abroad or at home, innovative modes of mate selection can bring into contact people who otherwise would never have a chance to meet.

COMPUTER DATING

In 1977, the National Science Foundation sponsored a study on computer applications in information exchange. About 500 scientists in various disciplines throughout the United States and Canada participated. Using their computer terminals, these scientists dispatched messages, research findings, and answers to inquiries. As the experiment progressed, those with common interests formed alliances and strengthened their professional ties. For the sociologists among them this experience led to the next logical question: could similar procedures be applied to people interested in the search for love and marriage?

This question led to a study titled "Automated Go-Betweens: Mate Selection of Tomorrow?"[3] A few years later that "tomorrow" had arrived. Computers are now matching hundreds of people every day. Regardless of place of residence or availability of partners in one's locality, anyone with access to a personal computer can get in touch with others through computer-dating networks called "dial-your-mate."

"Dial-your-mate" refers to mate selection with the aid of personal computers. Unlike other innovative modes of mate selection, dial-your-mate is gaining acceptance rapidly. Because tens of thousands of people are experimenting with it, let us examine how it works.

---

[3]Davor Jedlicka, "Automated Go-Betweens: Mate Selection of Tomorrow?" *Family Relations,* July 1981, 373–76.

To participate, one must have a telephone, a personal computer, and a *modem*—a unit that connects the computer to the telephone. The cost of this equipment can vary from around $300 to more than $3000. (If there is no dial-your-mate service available locally, long-distance telephone charges could be a substantial part of the searching cost.) There are no membership fees, because the system is operated by hobbyists and computer clubs throughout the country.

To use this service the participant must have a telephone number to reach one of the computers in the dial-your-mate network. These numbers are available from local computer clubs anywhere in the United States. Because the demand for these services is so high, it may take several hours to reach a number, but sooner or later everyone gets through.

Once the participant is on the line, there is no need for any knowledge of computer programming. Each caller is prompted step by step to provide the information necessary for mate searching. The questions appear on the screen with instructions for answering. Although the questions vary from network to network, our perusal of various services indicated that they are based on popular notions of what is important to people looking for dates.

The most frequently asked questions assess one's appearance, as follows:

> What is the color of your hair?
> What is your height?
> How would others rate your appearance? A. Very attractive B. Good looking C. Average D. Nothing special.

There are also questions about personal characteristics such as age, race, educational level, marital status, occupation, religious preference, and political affiliation.

Other questions probe personal hobbies, racial preferences, level of commitment sought, musical preferences, and so on. Once all the questions are answered, the computer compares the answers with those of all opposite-sex participants and ranks them on percentage of agreement. If two people gave similar answers to every question, they would agree 100 percent. On the opposite end of the scale, 0 percent would show that they have no answers in common. As soon as these comparisons are completed, the participant is provided with the code numbers of those with the highest percentages of agreement.

The recipients' responses have not been studied. Those involved can ignore the messages, exchange more messages, or terminate interactions for any reason. Both senders and recipients are spared the unpleasantness of face-to-face rejections because communications remain anonymous until the individual decides otherwise.

Anonymity in the absence of visual stimuli means that the value stage of a relationship precedes the stimulus stage. Even appearance becomes another value that people use to evaluate each other before making arrangements for face-to-face dates. For example, attractive individuals may resent those who consider appearance as the primary criterion for initiating relationships. They may consider other aspects of self more important. Through the computer, they may reveal their important values without interference from visual stimuli. Thus the stimulus-value-role sequence of ordinary courtship becomes value-stimulus-role in the computer-dating sequence. Whether this mode of mate selection enhances the search for love, sex, and affection remains to be studied.

CLASSIFIED ADVERTISEMENTS

Any person, whether single or married, can find a mate through personal advertisements. Bookstores, grocery stores, and newsstands across America sell newspapers that carry personal advertisements for mate selection. Although it may seem strange or unusual for people to advertise themselves, this mode of mate selection dates back to the frontier days. As the men in the nineteenth century moved west, they advertised in newspapers for brides. In his 1867 book on marriage in America, Carlier was among the first to note this frontier American innovation:

> Circumstances sometimes prevent the immigration of women and the gloom and languor which pervade these sections can scarcely be imagined. Thus, in some of the rapidly formed territories, we may perhaps find only men—it having chanced that women had not thought to go in this direction. We soon find appearing in the papers positive supplications from those unfortunate men to the young women of the other states, entreating them their choice, and promising dowries quite comfortable and well assured.[4]

There is evidence that personal advertisements in newspapers appeared even in colonial times. On the frontier, however, this became a common mode of mate selection. Ever since that time, specialized magazines and newspapers have carried matrimonial advertisements. Until the mid-1970s such publications were sold nationally. Today they are increasingly local or regional.

VIDEO DATING

Video dating, a relatively recent innovation, is restricted to walk-in clients who seek assistance from an agent. Part of the agent's responsibility is to prepare an audio and a video presentation for the clients. This service usually costs $600 or more. Some agencies minimize the cost of taped videos by charging viewing fees and by selling addresses on request. This procedure

---

[4]Auguste Carlier, *Marriage in the United States* (New York: Arno Press, 1972), 44–45.

minimizes third-person involvement and lowers the cost for participants, but it appeals only to those for whom identity protection is not important.

Most agencies, though, guard their clients' identities by restricting participation to paid-up members. To be a member, one must have prepared a videotaped presentation, which then is viewed by other members in consultation with the agent. In this capacity the agents act as counselors. They give advice, answer questions, and suggest good matches.

If we may judge by the number of agencies emerging throughout the country, it seems that the clientele for video dating is increasing despite the high cost of membership. Some agencies have grown so fast that they need computers to keep track of their clients and to help them with the matching process. They administer computerized questionnaires similar to those found in dial-your-mate networks. This information is used together with the video as an aid in choosing a mate

Lest the reader forget during this discussion of technology, romantic love is not abandoned regardless of the mate-selection method. Whether chance, a third person, or a technological device is used, mate selection remains generally a quest for romantic love.

ROMANTIC LOVE

No matter how one finds romantic love, it is difficult to define. Those who have been in love seem to think that they know what it is, but researchers have found at least *six styles of love*. They have given each style a Greek or Roman name and the following definitions:[5]

    Eros: A strong and immediate physical attraction to a particular physical ideal.
  Ludus: A light-hearted, casual relationship.
 Storge: Friendship.
 Mania: Anxious, obsessive love.
Pragma: A pragmatic relationship.
 Agape: Unconditional, altruistic love.

Researchers generally agree that love cannot be defined by any single style. Different styles may be present in various combinations, and an individual may change the style over time. Yet, however one classifies the style of love, the essence of romance remains physical attraction, emotional involvement, and idealization.

According to popular opinion girls are more "romantic" than boys, but this belief may be oversimplification in terms of love styles defined above. For example, Hendrick and Hendrick found no significant differences between currently-in-love males and females regarding physical ideals (eros),

---

[5]Duncan Cramer, "Lovestyles Revisited," *Social Behavior and Personality,* 15(2), 1987, 215.

obsessive behavior (mania), or altruism (agape).[6] They found, however, that men were more ludic (casual) and women more storgic (friendship-oriented) and pragmatic (practical).

These differences are not entirely unexpected. Men and women follow different time schedules with regard to romance and marriage. Women start dating earlier and marry earlier. Even when they delay marriage, they are not likely to choose younger men. All in all, the romantic process seems to favor younger women more than younger men. As long as this dichotomy persists, it is reasonable to expect some differences between men and women in their romantic orientations.

SUMMARY

Mate selection is one of the most important factors in the development of family relationships. Dating initiated by chance encounter is the most prevalent mode used by young Americans, but other modes are increasing in popularity. For reasons ranging from lack of time to geographic isolation, significant numbers of Americans rely on innovative methods of mate selection, including participation in international networks, computer dating, video dating, and personal advertisements. Not all of these methods work for everyone, but for many people the innovative methods lead to love, romance, and marriage.

Romantic love is the basis of mate selection whether conventional or less conventional methods are used. Romantic love, although difficult to define, has been classified into *six styles:* eros, ludus, storge, mania, pragma, and agape. These styles may be present in various degrees in each individual, and they may also vary with each individual over time. Some differences in love styles between the sexes also have been discovered.

QUESTIONS

1. What is meant by the "adversarial aspects" of the American dating system? Are some of these aspects still with us, or are they a thing of the past? Discuss on the basis of your own observations and experiences.
2. What are some of the differences between modern dating and traditional dating? What would you say is the most important difference?
3. Is the usual search for dating partners suited for everyone? Explain.
4. Discuss the differences between the stimulus-value-role sequence and the value-stimulus-role sequence in mate selection. What are the advantages or disadvantages of each mode?

---

[6]Clyde Hendrick and Susan S. Hendrick, "Lovers Wear Rose Colored Glasses," *Journal of Social and Personal Relationships,* 5, 1988, 161–182.

5. What are some theoretical reasons for international mate selection? Are the reasons the same for American participants as for their foreign partners?

6. Some people fear computers as a dehumanizing influence on society. Do you share that sentiment with respect to computer applications in mate selection? Explain in detail.

7. Consider a person's age, marital history, social status, and geographic location; which mode of mate selection do you think may be best suited for various categories of eligibles?

8. Classified personal advertisements have a long history in the United States. Explain how this mode of mate selection originated, why it exists today, and whether you think it will be useful in the future.

9. What is romantic love? Why is it so difficult to make generalizations about the subject?

SELECTED READINGS

Boling, Rosemary, Peter J. Stein, and Patrick C. McKenry. "The Self-advertisement Approach of Dating: Male-Female Differences." *Family Relations,* October 1984, 587–92.

Cramer, Duncan. "Lovestyles Revisited." *Social Behavior and Personality,* 15(2), 1987, 215–219.

Danziger, James N. "Social Science and the Social Impact of Computer Technology." *Social Science Quarterly,* March 1985, 3–21.

Dissanayake, Wimal. "Newspapers as Matchmakers: A Sri Lankan Illustration." *Journal of Comparative Family Studies,* Spring 1982, 97–108.

Gordon, Michael. "Was Waller Ever Wright? The Rating and Dating Complex Reconsidered." *Journal of Marriage and the Family,* February 1981, 67–76.

Hansen, Sally L., and Mary W. Hicks. "Sex Role Attitudes and Perceived Dating-Mating Choices of Youth." *Adolescence,* Spring 1980, 83–90.

Hendrick, Susan S., and Clyde Hendrick. "Research on Love: Does It Measure Up?" *Journal of Personality and Social Psychology,* 56(5), 1989, 784–794.

Imamura, Anne E. "Ordinary Couples? Mate Selection in International Marriages in Nigeria." *Journal of Comparative Family Studies,* Spring 1986, 33–42.

Jedlicka, Davor. "Automated Go-Betweens: Mate Selection of Tomorrow?" *Family Relations,* July 1981, 373–76.

———. "Formal Mate Selection Networks in the United States." In *Marriage and Family,* edited by Leonard Cargan, 102–7. Belmont, CA: Wadsworth, 1985.

Jeffries, Vincent. "Love as Virtue, Love as Attraction, and Relationship Quality." *Family Perspective,* 22(2), 1988, 107–128.

King, Charles E., and Andrew Christensen. "The Relationship Events Scale: A Guttman Scaling of Progress in Courtship." *Journal of Marriage and the Family,* August 1983, 671–78.

Laner, Mary Riege. "Competition in Courtship." *Family Relations,* April 1986, 275–79.

McCabe, Marita P. "Toward a Theory of Adolescent Dating." *Adolescence,* Spring 1984, 159–70.

Parks, Malcolm R., Charlotte M. Stan, and Leona L. Eggert. "Romantic Involvement and Social Network Involvement." *Social Psychology Quarterly,* June 1983, 116–31.

Peres, Yochanan, and Hanna Meivear. "Self-Presentation during Courtship: A Content Analysis of Classified Advertisements in Israel." *Journal of Comparative Family Studies,* Spring 1986, 19–32.

Philbrick, J. L. "Sex Differences in Romantic Attitudes toward Love among Engineering Students." *Psychological Reports,* 61, 1987, 482.

Rubin, Zick, Letitia Anne Peplau, and Charles T. Hill. "Loving and Leaving: Sex Differences in Romantic Attachments." *Sex Roles,* August 1981, 821–35.

Tingle, Vonell C. "Immigration Marriage Fraud Amendments of 1986: Looking in by Looking Out?" *Journal of Family Law* 27(3), 1988–1989, 733–752.

Woll, Stanley B., and Peter Young. "Looking for Mr. or Ms. Right: Self-Presentation in Videodating." *Journal of Marriage and the Family,* May 1989, 483–488.

Chapter
11

Premarital Sexual Attitudes and Behavior

*F*rom a sociological viewpoint, the topic of premarital sex is fascinating. On the one side are the young people, who in the fullness of youth have a natural tendency to explore the complexities of sex. On the other side are the ever-present forces of social control: the law, the church, public opinion, parents, and the like. This is an oversimplification, of course. Not all young people are on the same side of the issue, though most seem to be. In fact, not all the forces of social control are on the same side! To make matters more complicated, today's young people are tomorrow's parents—a role that frequently calls for switching sides.

In any case, it may come as a surprise to learn that earlier texts dealing with the family did not even include the topic of premarital sex. Not only was the incidence of sex before marriage much lower than it is today, but the subject itself was unacceptable as a topic for either conversation or publication.

Rates of premarital sex in the United States increased only gradually over most of the decades following colonial times. By the 1930s, some 15 percent of American women had experienced premarital coitus at least once.[1] Over the next 30 years that percentage more than doubled. In the 1960s the acceptance and practice of premarital sex became so common that the term "sexual revolution" came into use.

Throughout the 1970s, rates of premarital coitus continued to increase; young people's attitudes reflected their belief that premarital sex was a personal matter and not something to be regulated by outside agencies. Movies and popular music encouraged these attitudes and even championed them, in the view of many people.

Today, as we head into the 1990s, the trend seems to have stabilized. The sexual revolution has apparently run its course. Yet its influences remain controversial not only for religious and moral reasons, but also because of problems regarding the health and welfare of the participants.

Obviously these are difficult problems. We hope that this and the following chapter will bring the problems into sharper focus.

TRENDS IN PREMARITAL SEXUAL ACTIVITY: THE OLD DOUBLE STANDARD

Only twenty years ago premarital sexual behavior was characterized by a double standard. At that time it was considered acceptable for single men to have intercourse, but not for single women. The sexual revolution, which began in the 1960s, advanced the notion that if men were involved, women should be also. Only a minority argued for the opposite solution: if women were abstaining, let men do the same. Needless to say, that argument was among the first casualties of the sexual revolution.

During the era of the double standard, the question was often asked: "If so few women are sexually active, whom do the men have as partners?" It seemed illogical that the sexes would participate unequally in an event that involves one member of each sex. Some people have argued that this apparent discrepancy may reflect females' reluctance to divulge sexual experience and males' tendency to exaggerate it.

In retrospect, however, lack of candor seems to be an unlikely explanation. For one thing, questionnaire data are not the only source of information used by sociologists. They also use rates of venereal disease and rates of premarital pregnancy, both of which corroborate student questionnaire data over the last two decades. Whatever errors were present from surveys were small enough to permit a realistic assessment of trends. Therefore, it would seem that the answer to the above question lies elsewhere.

The number of possible answers is limited. An obvious one is that college men consort with noncollege women. Another possibility is that men

---

[1]Edward Shorter, "The Two Sexual Revolutions," in John F. Crosby, ed. *Reply to Myth: Perspectives on Intimacy* (New York: John Wiley, 1985),147.

solicit prostitutes. A third possibility is that a small number of women engage in recreational sex with numerous partners. Actually, a combination of all three possibilities accounted for men's and women's differential sexual experience.

In any case, the sexual double standard was a reality, and in the mid-1960s the drive toward "sexual equality" was based on eliminating it. By 1975, premarital intercourse reportedly had become a norm for the majority of single college students of both sexes.[2] This trend, as shown in Table 11.1, continued through about 1980. At that time many people assumed that males' and females' rates would continue to converge toward a common level. According to the 1985 observations, however, that prediction was not realized. Instead the rates seem to be stabilizing at different levels for each sex.

Petting refers to physical contact that does not involve sexual intercourse but may involve orgasm. Petting levels as noted in Table 11.1 represent the following forms of behavior:

Light petting—tongue and lip kissing

Moderate petting—oral or manual breast manipulation

Heavy petting—oral or manual manipulation of genitals

Petting rates, like intercourse rates, are stabilizing at somewhat higher levels for males than for females. Are these differences large enough to confirm that the old double standard still persists? Even though this is a subjective matter, it seems safe to say that the old double standard is not as strong as it used to be.

RESPONSIBILITY FOR CONTRACEPTION: THE NEW DOUBLE STANDARD

In general, a double standard is said to exist when the meaning of some behavior depends on the characteristics of persons rather than on the nature of the behavior. For example, expectations of virginity before marriage for women only represent a double standard. A single standard—whether condemnation or condonation—would apply equally to males and to females.

The double standard applies to the differential expectations of men and of women in their responsibility for contraception during premarital intercourse. Biology is partially a factor here because only a few contraceptive methods are available to men: the condom, withdrawal, and vasectomy. Women, on the other hand, can use the pill, intrauterine devices, diaphragms, spermicides, and sterilization.

---

[2]Ira E. Robinson and Davor Jedlicka, "Change in Sexual Attitudes and Behavior of College Students from 1965 to 1980: A Research Note," *Journal of Marriage and the Family,* February 1982, 238.

Table 11.1   SEXUAL BEHAVIOR AMONG COLLEGE STUDENTS, 1965–85

Year and behavior	Males		Females	
	Percent	Number	Percent	Number
None				
1965	1.6	3	8.7	10
1970	2.2	3	1.3	2
1975	2.6	3	3.4	9
1980	3.0	5	1.8	4
1985	3.8	8	2.0	5
Light Petting				
1965	11.6	15	32.3	37
1970	8.9	12	19.5	30
1975	6.9	8	12.7	34
1980	6.6	11	12.9	29
1985	4.3	9	8.6	22
Medium Petting				
1965	14.7	19	24.3	28
1970	9.6	3	19.5	30
1975	10.3	12	16.6	31
1980	5.4	9	12.4	28
1985	8.7	18	12.2	31
Heavy Petting				
1965	71.3	92	34.3	40
1970	79.3	107	59.7	92
1975	80.2	93	72.7	195
1980	84.9	141	72.9	164
1985	81.2	169	74.1	189
Intercourse				
1965	65.1	129	28.7	115
1970	65.0	136	37.3	158
1975	73.9	115	57.1	275
1980	77.4	168	63.5	230
1985	79.3	208	63.0	257

Source: Courtesy of Dr. Ira E. Robinson, Department of Sociology, the University of Georgia.

As a result, the tendency to think of contraception primarily as women's responsibility is evident throughout society. For example, family planning agencies systematically tend to exclude men. Family researchers rarely study males' contraceptive behavior or fathers' responsibility for children born out of wedlock. Some social scientists recognize this bias, but the overall focus remains on the sex that can use the pill.

Researchers agree that sexual intercourse is not always planned by either party. It may be planned by one person—usually the male—or by neither. Without planning, and with the expectation that contraception is the woman's problem, it should not be surprising that well into the 1980s, 53 percent of couples used no contraception during their first sexual intercourse.[3] Most women have used the pill at some point before marriage, but not in preparation for their first intercourse. The use of the condom during first intercourse has actually declined since the introduction of the pill, from about 22 percent in the 1960s to 17 percent in more recent years.[4]

INDUCEMENTS TO PREMARITAL INTERCOURSE

Most public attention today is focused on the morality of premarital intercourse rather than on responsibility. Some people argue that the only correct behavior is complete abstinence; others encourage sexual freedom. Young people are sometimes caught between the two arguments, and are bewildered by conflicting messages. Because of this lack of agreement, they adopt one of several possible codes of premarital sexual standards. At one extreme is strict abstinence; at the other is promiscuous sexuality. The majority, who do not adapt these extremes, eventually become sexually active under the influence of situational or societal inducements.

Sex and Drugs

Various substances have a reputation for their ability to reduce sexual inhibitions. Although many drugs belong to this category, marijuana and alcohol are used most frequently. A study of marijuana users confirmed what many people already suspect or know through experience: "One-half felt that drug use made them more willing to have intercourse the first time."[5]

Drug use is not always a self-induced "nudge" to reduce inhibition. On the contrary, while using drugs "one-half of both men and women had had unwanted intercourse (intercourse they did not seek and later regretted)."[6] Another study using a broad spectrum of college students showed that drugs were "important circumstantial factors influencing the decision to have intercourse."[7] The same study, however, showed that drugs were not

---

[3]William D. Mosher and Christine A. Bachrach, "First Premarital Contraceptive Use: United States, 1960–1982," *Studies in Family Planning,* April 1987, 85.

[4]Ibid, 85.

[5]Ronald A. Weller and James A. Halikas, "Marijuana Use and Sexual Behavior," *The Journal of Sex Research,* May 1984, 190.

[6]Ibid.

[7]F. Scott Christopher and Rodney M. Cate, "Factors Involved in Premarital Sexual Decision-Making," *The Journal of Sex Research,* November 1984, 369. See also Frank L. Mott and R. Jean Haurin, "Linkages between Sexual Activity and Alcohol and Drug Use among American Adolescents," *Family Planning Perspectives,* May/June 1988, 128–136.

A girl in a "punk" hairstyle draws a predictable response from her peers at a Huntington Beach, California, junior high school. Peers are generally a strong force in encouraging permissiveness.

so important in ongoing relationships, in which love for the partner, commitment to the relationship, and the number of dates with the same partner were the important considerations.

The research on drugs and sex is clear on one point: drugs and initial sexual encounters tend to go together. Under this influence, even without prior intent, men and women are more likely to indulge. After the drug effects wear off, the participants often feel indignant about the affair.

The use of drugs before sex is sometimes seen as part of peer-group influence. Drinking alcoholic beverages, smoking marijuana, and using other drugs are often commonplace within certain groups. Peers—people of similar age and social status—are generally a strong force in encouraging permissiveness. Their influence deserves consideration in its own right.

Sex and Peers

Wherever parents draw the line of acceptable premarital behavior, the children's peer group is often on the other side. This disagreement between parents and children is sometimes called the generation gap. From colonial times through the present day, each generation of parents has complained about young people's sexual morals. It seems likely that the biology of puberty and the youthful sex drive contribute to the generation gap. In this respect, youth of the past had much in common with today's youth. The difference is that parental control over children's sexual activity was stronger then than it is today.

In the past, schools, churches, the media, and public opinion were unified on the parents' side. It was not until the beginning of this century that the long-standing alliance started to crumble. The press was the first to lose its enthusiasm for "the old morality." Alarmed at this wavering by the press, one observer wrote as follows in 1922:

> Sensational criticism of our young people has been reaching us from time to time from the churches, the colleges, and numerous scandalized members of the younger generation itself. If the newspapers are less outspoken than a year ago, when THE DIGEST investigated these matters by questionnaire, the change appears to be not so much a result of improvement in our young people as of indifference toward conditions that have lost their "news punch." To many an observer this indifference is alarming, as it seems to indicate that we are acquiescing in what such observers call a moral and spiritual revolution whose consequences can hardly be other than subversive.[8]

These developments seemed to mark the start of the erosion of parental influence. Families were stronger at that time, however, and were better able to teach their children to be restrained. Then, around the mid-1960s, the tide seemed to shift in favor of the younger generation. The large cohort of young people born after World War II—the baby-boom generation—gained political and economic power unprecedented for that age group. They used their power to launch a change in standards of education, consumer taste, entertainment, and sexual behavior. Simultaneously, parents seem less able, if not less willing, to influence their children. The peer group replaced them as the paramount influence on sexual life.

Peer influence now operates through persuasion, example, and the providing of situations conducive to intercourse. Parties, drinking, smoking marijuana, and various singles activities are obvious means by which peers influence sexual behavior. In addition, young persons' attitudes establish normative standards for sexual morality; and the peer group under weaker parental control has become the beacon of premarital sexual norms by default.

Some people argue that society, through its various institutions, not only is neutral toward permissive behavior, but—through music, movies, and fashions—actually may be reinforcing pubescent standards of sexual behavior. As we will see, these arguments are based on evidence.

Popular-Culture Focus on Sex

Adolescents and preadolescents buy more records and tapes than any other age group. They also listen to the radio, watch television, and follow fash-

---

[8]"The Case against the Younger Generation," *Liberty Digest,* 17 June 1922. Cited in Donald M. Scott and Bernard Wishy, eds., *America's Families: A Documentary History* (New York: Harper & Row, 1982), 540.

Two teenagers hug tight in a parking lot. Some people argue that society, through its various institutions, may be reinforcing pubescent standards of sexual behavior.

ions. Consequently the popular culture caters to their tastes and appeals to their concerns. Some observers have gone so far as to say that sexually oriented advertisements and entertainments have led the sexual revolution. What does the evidence suggest in this regard?

Most observers place the beginning of the upswing in permissive premarital sex around the mid-1960s. Yet at that time the media and the entertainment industry were still conservative by today's standards. By the early 1970s the term "sexual revolution" had become a household word, but little change was reflected in the popular culture. One study reports that as late as 1973 "only a tiny number" of songs were sexually explicit.[9]

---

[9]Samuel S. Janus and Cynthia L. Janus, "Children, Sex, Peers, Culture: 1973–1983," *The Journal of Psychohistory*, Winter 1985, 369.

According to the same study, sexually explicit entertainment for youth increased steadily after that point until it reached new highs in the 1980s. By 1983, 62 percent of the weekly top ten songs were sexually explicit or suggestive. Parents and church groups are concerned about the influence of such entertainment on young people, but they have been largely unsuccessful in reducing the appeal of such material.

There is no doubt that some elements of popular culture appeal to the prurient interests of youth, and that concerned groups have a right to oppose offensive cultural elements. The research, however, is silent about whether the media raise sexual expectations on dates. Although the commonsense answer is that they may do so, empirical proof is not available.

It is well known that in addition to sexual explicitness, the media portray a great deal of violence, sometimes in conjunction with sex. Because most sexual violence in the media is directed toward women, the question arises again: "Do the media reflect reality or do they influence it?" Although casual connections, if any, are not clear, forced sex occurs with surprising frequency in everyday life. This finding is particularly puzzling when we recall that only a few years ago experts predicted that increased sexual freedom would lower the rates of rape and other forms of sexual violence. Today enough research is available to evaluate that prediction.

SEXUAL COERCION AND RAPE

Looking back over the decades before the sexual revolution, one finds among some academic disciplines a theoretical view that attributes sexual victimization of women to an absence of sexual outlets for men. Sometimes referred to as the *frustration theory,* this view held that strict moral standards and abstinence frustrate men and therefore increase women's vulnerability. This school of thought predicted that the sexual revolution would solve the problem.

Sociologists, however, were also making predictions. They applied the relative frustration theory, which postulates that "it is sexually less frustrating to be rejected by a woman in a sexually restrictive society than in a sexually permissive setting."[10] According to this theory, the rates of rape go up, not down, as the society becomes more permissive.

While researchers continue to study the validity of various theories, rates of rape have increased—with some exceptions—year after year. Consider, for example, the data presented in Table 11.2. It is debatable whether the relative deprivation theory can account for these increases, but it is crystal clear that the increase in sexual freedom *has not* reduced sexual violence against women. In fact, the number and the rate of rapes have nearly quadrupled since the beginning of the sexual revolution in the 1960s.

---

[10]Eugene J. Kanin, "Date Rapists: Differential Sexual Socialization and Relative Deprivation," *Archives of Sexual Behavior,* June 1985, 220.

Table 11.2 FORCIBLE RAPE
CASES IN THE
UNITED STATES

Year	Number	Rate
1963	17,650	9.4
1967	27,620	14.0
1971	42,260	20.5
1975	56,090	26.3
1980	82,088	36.4
1985	87,671	36.7
1986	91,459	37.9
1987	91,111	37.4
1988	92,486	37.6

Source: U.S. Department of Justice, *Uniform Crime Reports,* Washington, DC, issued yearly. The rate is per 100,000 inhabitants.

Relative frustration theory gained additional support in a recent study by Jaffee and Straus, who found that "the more sexually liberal and permissive the attitude in a state, the higher the reported rape rate."[11]

This finding can be interpreted two ways. One is that women are more likely to be raped in states with liberal sexual attitudes. If that is the case, such a finding is consistent with the relative frustration theory. Critics of that theory point to a different interpretation, which concludes that in states where sexual attitudes are open and permissive the women are more likely to report rape. Although it is not certain which interpretation is correct, we cannot ignore "a strong relationship between rape and the aspect of sexuality measured by readership of sexually explicit magazines."[12]

Other studies also have shown increases in risk of sexual assault. A survey of 516 adult women in New Mexico revealed that 60 percent had experienced at least one episode of sexually stressful events; many had experienced more than one. These events ranged from obscene phone calls, exposure, harassment, and peeping to uninvited fondling, attempted rape, and rape.[13] This study also suggests strongly that the number of rapes reported to the police is less than the number of rapes committed.

---

[11]David Jaffee and Murray A. Straus, "Sexual Climate and Reported Rape: A State-Level Analysis," *Archives of Sexual Behavior,* 16 (2), 1987, 116.

[12]Ibid., 116.

[13]Peter V. DiVasto et al., "The Prevalence of Sexually Stressful Events among Females in the General Population," *Archives of Sexual Behavior,* February 1984, 64.

The threat of sexual violence against women does not seem to be abating:

> A finding of primary importance is that many college students have deleterious attitudes concerning sex, dating, and date rape. These attitudes are strongly related to gender with males far more likely than females to hold attitudes that condone aggressive sexual behavior. . . .
> The data also indicate that males are as likely to agree as disagree with the statements "Females who ask males out on dates are probably looking for sex" and "In the dating game, males are the predator and female the prey." American society is indeed not a safe place for the woman who dates.[14]

In view of these developments it is no wonder that college students across the country express concern with the direction that the sexual revolution has taken. In the race toward sexual intercourse there seem to be few constraints and many inducements for immediate sexual gratification.

The constraints obviously are less effective than the inducements, but they are also an important part of the circumstances surrounding sexual activity.

CONSTRAINTS ON PREMARITAL INTERCOURSE

"Sexually transmitted diseases threaten to undo the sexual revolution" has been heard often in recent years. It would seem that enough fear has been generated to reverse the trends in premarital intercourse rates, but moral convictions still seem to be more effective than the fear of disease.

Sexually Transmitted Disease

Among the many forms of sexually transmitted diseases monitored by the Public Health Service, gonorrhea is reported most frequently. Because men are more likely to have higher premarital intercourse rates than women and generally have more partners, they also have higher rates of gonorrhea and other sexually transmitted diseases. As shown in Table 11.3, 381 males were infected with gonorrhea in 1987 for every 100,000 persons, in contrast with about 269 females.

This table also reveals a predictable fact: younger women are at a higher risk of contracting gonorrhea than are men of the same age. This is precisely what one would expect on the basis of our knowledge about mate selection in general. We know that the male partner is more likely to be older and to remain single longer. The longer period of singlehood brings a greater degree of sexual experience and a greater risk of contracting a sexually transmitted disease.

---

[14]R. Thomas Dull and David J. Giacopassi, "Demographic Correlates of Sexual and Dating Attitudes: A Study of Date Rape," *Criminal Justice and Behavior,* June 1987, 188.

Table 11.3 GONORRHEA RATES FOR 100,000
POPULATION BY AGE GROUP
AND SEX, UNITED STATES, 1987

Age group	Male	Female	Total
10–14	21.0	65.6	42.7
15–19	793.2	1269.2	1028.1
20–14	1758.5	1306.3	1527.2
25–29	996.8	488.0	738.2
30–34	509.3	181.5	344.0
35–39	247.6	73.0	158.6
40–44	151.6	40.1	94.5
45+	35.4	6.7	19.6
All ages	381.3	268.6	323.1

Source: U.S. Department of Health and Human Services, *Sexually Transmitted Disease Statistics,* Atlanta: Centers for Disease Control, 1988, erratum to Table 3, p. 5.

Table 11.4 PERCENTAGE OF AIDS CASES BY EXPOSURE
CATEGORY, REPORTED THROUGH MAY 1989

Exposure category	Percentage	Number of cases
Male homosexual/bisexual contact	61	58,389
Intravenous (IV) drug use	20	19,497
Male homosexual contact and IV use	7	6,824
Heterosexual contact	5	4,305
Undetermined exposure	3	3,273
Receipt of blood transfusion	2	2,361
Hemophilia	1	912
Total adult cases	100	95,561

Source: U.S. Department of Health and Human Services, Centers for Disease Control, *HIV/AIDS Surveillance,* June 1989, Table 3, 8.

AIDS and Sexual Behavior

AIDS—acquired immune deficiency syndrome—is transmitted sexually in most cases. (See Table 11.4 for a more complete listing of exposure categories.) AIDS is generally fatal and is still incurable. Thus it is reasonable to expect that the fear of this disease will have at least some effect on sexual behavior.

That effect has not yet been reflected, however, in any reduction in the number of sexually active unmarried people. Premarital sexual coitus, especially among college students, seems to have stabilized at about three-quarters of the population. It is likely, though, that this sexually active segment is less casual about sex, more cautious about sex with strangers, and more likely to have fewer partners. The evidence of this change is the overall reduction in sexually transmitted disease rates since 1980. It is hypothesized that at least a part of this reduction may be due to fear of AIDS.

We should keep in mind that most heterosexual college students are unlikely to perceive themselves or their partners as being at risk for any sexually transmitted diseases. Assessing risk in sexual behavior may be compared with smoking or with not wearing seat belts. Each activitiy has been shown to be potentially deadly, yet some people continue to rationalize that such things only happen to others.

Although the effect of AIDS on sexual behavior is still a matter of opinion, research suggests that moral convictions tend to be more important determinants of sexual behavior than the fear of deadly diseases.

Moral Conviction

Sex before marriage seems to be less of a moral matter today than at any other time in American history. Yet when asked to rank constraints by importance, 54 percent of the women and 26 percent of the men ranked moral considerations as the most important influence in the decision to have or not to have intercourse.[15] At the same time, the percentage of students who responded affirmatively to "I feel that premarital sexual intercourse is immoral" has declined since 1965, as shown here:[16]

Year	Men	Women
1965	33.0	70.0
1970	14.0	34.0
1975	19.5	20.7
1980	17.4	25.3
1985	15.9	17.1

Why do so few students think premarital intercourse is immoral, while a larger number consider morality as the most important influence in the

---

[15]Davor Jedlicka and Ira E. Robinson, "Fear of Venereal Disease and Other Constraints on Occurrence of Premarital Coitus," *The Journal of Sex Research*, August 1987, 393.

[16]Ira E. Robinson, work in progress.

The moral concern around singles today is more likely to be when and with whom to engage in intercourse than whether or not to do it at all.

decision to have or not to have sex? This contradiction is resolved easily when we consider that virginity before marriage is not a moral issue for the large majority of students. Nevertheless, moral convictions do enter into the decision to have—or not to have—intercourse. The moral concern today is more likely to be *when and with whom* to engage in intercourse than whether to do it at all. For example, sex without love and sex with many partners may be considered immoral, but sex with love for one partner may be regarded as permissible.[17]

Overall, the influence of constraints seems to be outweighed by the influence of inducements to premarital intercourse. This situation is particularly noticeable in the high rates of pregnancy among unmarried teenage mothers. As we show in the next chapter, teenage pregnancy has become a major social and health problem in the United States.

SUMMARY

Sexual attitudes seem to be more conservative today than in recent years, but the proportion of sexually active single people has not been reduced. Among male college students, more than three-fourths have experienced

---

[17]Albert D. Kossen, Colin J. Williams, and Eugene E. Levitt, *Sex and Morality in the United States* (Middletown, CT: Wesleyan University Press, 1989), 27–28.

coitus at least once; more than sixty percent of women have had the same experience. The old double standard of sexual behavior is less prevalent today, but a new double standard has emerged. This new standard places greater responsibility for contraception and pregnancy on women than on men. The sexual revolution has freed most women from the inequities of participating in sexual activity, but it has not freed them from the unequal sharing of responsibility that accompanies that freedom.

Inducements to sexual intercourse are found among peers in the drug environment, and in popular culture. Constraints arising from the fear of venereal disease seem to have less effect on behavior than is generally believed. Moral constraints, on the other hand, are far more important in the decision to become or not to become sexually active.

QUESTIONS

1. Some observers feel that sex is a private matter, and therefore should not be regulated. Others feel that if sex is not regulated, there will be adverse societal effects. Which of these two views do you support? Why?

2. Forcible-rape cases in the United States seem to increase year after year. In your opinion, why is this?

3. Explain the influence that the peer group may have on the occurrence of premarital intercourse.

4. Moral convictions are a major constraint on the occurrence of premarital intercourse; yet, only a few students feel that premarital intercourse is immoral. Resolve this apparent contradiction.

5. The fear of venereal disease has not had the influence on the occurrence of premarital intercourse that people think it has. Why is this a weak constraint?

6. Why do females under twenty have higher venereal disease rates than men of the same age? Explain male-female differences in rates of venereal disease in general.

7. Why do some teenagers desire to become pregnant without getting married?

8. What is meant by "the new double standard?" How is it different from the old double standard?

9. How would you characterize the influence of mass media on premarital sex? Why have the media taken this position?

SELECTED READINGS

Amick, Angelynne E., and Karen S. Calhoun. "Resistance to Sexual Aggression: Personality, Attitudinal, and Situational Factors." *Archives of Sexual Behavior,* 16(2), 1987, 153–63.

Byers, Sandra E., and Kim Lewis. "Dating Couples' Disagreements over the Desired Level of Sexual Intimacy." *Journal of Sex Research,* 24, 1988, 15–29.

Carlson, Bonnie E. "Dating Violence: A Research Review and Comparison with Spouse Abuse." *Social Casework,* January 1987, 16–23.

Darling, Carol A., and Kenneth Davidson, Sr. "The Relationship of Sexual Satisfaction to Coital Involvement: The Concept of Technical Virginity Revisited." *Deviant Behavior,* 8, 1987, 27–46.

Forste, Benata T., and Tim B. Heaton. "Initiation of Sexual Activity among Female Adolescents." *Youth and Adolescence,* March 1988, 250–68.

Furstenberg, Frank F., S. Philip Morgan, Kristin A. Moore, and James I. Peterson. "Race Differences in the Timing of Adolescent Intercourse." *American Sociological Review,* August 1987, 511–18.

Howard, Judith A. "A Structural Approach to Sexual Attitudes: Interracial Patterns in Adolescents' Judgements about Sexual Intimacy." *Sociological Perspectives,* January 1988, 88–121.

Jedlicka, Davor, and Ira E. Robinson. "Fear of Venereal Disease and Other Perceived Restraints on the Occurrence of Premarital Coitus." *Journal of Sex Research,* August 1987, 391–96.

Klassen, Albert D., Colin J. Williams, and Eugene E. Levitt. *Sex and Morality in the U.S.* Middletown, CT: Wesleyan University, 1989.

McDonald, James R. "Censuring Rock Lyrics: A Historical Analysis of the Debate." *Youth and Society,* March 1988, 294–313.

Miller, Brent C., and Raymond Bingham. "Family Confirguration in Relation to the Sexual Behavior of Female Adolescents." *Journal of Marriage and the Family,* May 1989, 499–506.

Mills, Randy K., "Traditional Morality, Moral Reasoning and the Moral Education of Adolescents." *Adolescence,* Summer 1987, 371–75.

Moore, Kristin A., James L. Peterson, and Frank F. Furstenberg. "Parental Attitudes and the Occurrence of Early Sexual Activity." *Journal of Marriage and the Family,* November 1986, 777–82.

Remafedi, Gary J. "Preventing the Sexual Transmission of AIDS During Adolescence." *Journal of Adolescent Health Care,* 9, 1988, 139–43.

Roscoe, Bruce, Donna Kennedy, and Tony Pope. "Adolescents' Views of Intimacy: Distinguishing Intimate from Nonintimate Relationships." *Adolescence,* Fall 1987, 511–16.

Shotland, Lance R., and Jane M. Craig. "Can Men and Women Differentiate between Friendly and Sexually Interested Behavior?" *Social Psychology Quarterly,* 51(1), 1988, 66–73.

Smith, M. Diwayne, and Carl Hand. "The Pornography/Aggression Linkage: Results from a Field Study." *Deviant Behavior,* 8, 1987, 389–99.

Sprecher, Susan, Kathleen McKinney, Robert Walsh, and Carrie Anderson. "A Revision of the Reiss Premarital Sexual Permissiveness Scale." *Journal of Marriage and the Family,* August 1988, 821–28.

Stets, Jan E., and Maureen A. Pirog-Good. "Violence in Dating Relationships." *Social Psychology Quarterly,* 50(3), 1987, 237–46.

Studer, Marlena, and Arland Thornton. "Adolescent Religiosity and Contraceptive Usage." *Journal of Marriage and the Family,* February 1987, 117–28.

Thornton, Arland, and Donald Camburn. "The Influence of the Family on Premarital Sexual Attitudes and Behavior." *Demography,* August 1987, 323–40.

Udry, Richard J. "Biological Predisposition and Social Control in Adolescent Sexual Behavior." *American Sociological Review,* October 1988, 709–22.

———, and John O. G. Billy. "Initiation of Coitus in Early Adolescence." *American Sociological Review,* December 1987, 841–855.

U.S. Department of Health and Human Services. *AIDS Recommendations and Guidelines.* Atlanta: Centers for Disease Control, 1988.

Williams, John D., and Arthur P. Jacoby. "The Effects of the Premarital Heterosexual and Homosexual Experience on Dating and Marriage Desirability." *Journal of Marriage and the Family,* May 1989, 489–97.

Chapter 12

Pregnancy and Parenthood without Marriage

*P*regnant, unwed young women in our society have a mixed image. On the one hand are popular entertainers who have glamorized unwed motherhood by joining the trend toward nonmarital pregnancy. On the other are the downtrodden, forlorn young women apparently doomed to a lifetime of poverty. The reality lies somewhere between these extremes. Pregnancy with or without marriage is not automatically a road to failure. At the same time, however, it is easier for families to improve their standard of living when women delay childbearing and when both parents are raising the children. Yet despite these advantages, nonmarital childbearing, including that among teenagers, has increased to unprecedented levels.

CHILDBEARING TRENDS AMONG NEVER-MARRIED TEENAGE WOMEN

Teenage fertility rates have declined over the last two decades, but conception rates have not declined. When the number of abortions is added to the number of live births, the pregnancy rates for teenage population remain at high levels.[1]

---

[1]U.S. Department of Health and Human Services, *Teenage Pregnancy in the United States* (Atlanta: Centers for Disease Control, 1987),

Table 12.1 LIVE BIRTHS PER 1000 UNMARRIED
WOMEN UNDER 18 YEARS OF AGE,
BY RACE OF CHILD: UNITED
STATES, 1970–1986

Year	White	All others	All races
1970	7.5	73.3	17.1
1975	9.6	70.7	19.3
1980	11.8	63.1	20.6
1985	14.2	59.1	22.5
1986	14.6	59.1	22.9

Source: National Center for Health Statistics, *Advance Report of Final Natality Statistics,* 1986. Monthly Vital Statistics Report, vol. 37, no. 3, Public Health Service, Hyattsville, MD, 1988.

Despite abortions and the resulting decline in the teenage fertility rate, Table 12-1 shows that fertility among unwed teenage mothers continues to increase. The table also reveals that the increase is due to the changes in white teenagers' sexual behavior. Historically, white teenagers had low rates of unwed fertility. In 1970, after the beginning of the sexual revolution, the rate climbed to approximately 7 births per 1000 girls below 18 years of age. In that year, girls of other races were ten times more likely than white girls to give birth outside marriage. Over the next twenty years, however, the trends reversed: the birth rates for nonwhite girls declined to 59 births per 1000 girls under 18, while the rate for white girls of the same age nearly doubled to 14.6.

These rates are a convenient way to compare births over time and across different populations, but they do not portray the magnitude of the accompanying health problems and social problems. For example, they do not reveal the numbers of mothers and children involved. Because the white population in the United States is much larger than the nonwhite population, the magnitude of problems associated with youthful pregnancies is far greater than the rates imply.[2]

ABORTION

In an interview with a reporter, an eighteen-year-old explained her decision to have a baby in this way: "I was going to have an abortion, but I spent the money on clothes." It is difficult to tell how many of the 300,000-plus abor-

---

[2]Ibid., 34.

In recent years the birth rate increased substantially among women under 20. (*O'Brien, Archive Pictures*)

tions per year among American teenagers are decided so frivolously.[3] It is certain that most teenage pregnancies, whether aborted or not, were not intended. Poor planning, high rates of premarital intercourse, and a raging political debate over abortion seem to have produced confusion and fatalism among large numbers of young people.

Abortion is a relatively recent political issue in the United States. English common law accepted abortion before quickening—the point at which fetal movement first could be felt.[4] This practice, according to a study by Vern and Bonnie Bullough, was carried over to the American colonies and was "well established in the canon law of the Roman Catholic Church."

The first challenge to this practice came from American physicians in

---

[3]Ibid., 34.

[4]Vern and Bonnie Bullough, "Abortion in Historical Perspective," *Free Inquiry,* Spring 1989, 5–6.

the first half of the nineteenth century. They argued that abortion, which at that time was in the hands of the midwives, was an unsafe procedure and should be performed only by physicians for therapeutic reasons. Soon this view prevailed; states enacted legislation to prohibit midwives from performing abortions under any circumstances and to limit the physicians to therapeutic abortions. In 1869, the opposition to abortion stiffened when Pope Pius IX eliminated the use of quickening as a demarcation point for legal abortions.

The Pope's proclamation and the continued conflict between physicians and midwives set the stage for the eventual prohibition of all nontherapeutic abortions in every state. The last two states to outlaw abortion for any nontherapeutic reason were Arkansas in 1947 and Mississippi in 1956.

As each state outlawed legal abortions, illegal abortion rates increased. Physicians were not willing to risk going to jail or losing their practices by performing nontherapeutic abortions. Consequently, illegal practitioners, usually poorly trained and operating in unsanitary conditions, offered their services to the poorer women. Women with money had their abortions performed legally by specialists in Europe or Japan.

Deaths due to complications from abortions became a major concern of the public health agencies, and political groups organized to change the laws. A key legal challenge was presented to the Supreme Court by Jane Roe of Dallas County, Texas. She charged that the denial of abortion violated women's constitutional rights. In 1973, in a decision known as *Roe v. Wade,* the Supreme Court ruled that "a woman's right to choose abortion was part of her fundamental right to privacy."

Since that time abortion rates have increased steadily, especially among unmarried women.[5] The number of abortions, which has been greater than a million per year for a number of years, shows that many single women become pregnant accidentally or that many couples regard abortion as a method of birth control.

In either case, the new abortion pill, RU 486, developed and tested in France in 1987, can theoretically reduce the number of surgically induced abortions to a fraction of the current number. The pill is not likely to eliminate the moral and political controversy over termination of pregnancy, but the debate in the 1990s is likely to take some new directions.

ADOPTION

One possible resolution of the debate over unwanted pregnancy is adoption. As the number of women delaying marriage and childbearing increases, so will the number of couples who wish to have children but cannot because *fecundity* (the ability to conceive) decreases with age.

---

[5]Centers for Disease Control, *CDC Surveillance Summaries,* MMWR 38(SS-2), September 1989, 43.

We mentioned in Chapter 1 that certain European countries are on the verge of population decline. Some demographers believe that the middle class in America is facing the same predicament. Should that happen, adoption could maintain the numbers of a group that otherwise would decline.

In view of the increase in demand for adoption, it may be surprising that as abortion rates increased dramatically, adoptions decreased rather than increased. According to one social scientist, the reasons for declining use of adoption include the following:[6]

- Increased availability of abortion
- Fewer social sanctions against unmarried mothers
- Hesitation on the part of adoption agencies to embrace adoption practices in keeping with changing attitudes about parenting arrangements

Hundreds of thousands of infants born to unmarried teenage mothers could actually be placed for adoption if the mothers knew the procedure for doing so. Most mothers think of adoption as "closed"—an arrangement whereby the birth mother relinquishes her child and her right to know its fate. Modern adoption procedure, however, called "open adoption," permits the birth mother to participate in the selection of potential adopters. She may inspect biographies of applicants and may interview them, along with the social worker in charge of her case.

The way in which an unwed mother resolves her pregnancy often depends on how much responsibility the father takes for his child. Unfortunately, the father often disappears after the pregnancy, and the authorities are often reluctant to apprehend him. Yet the father's role and responsibility may be crucial for both the mother and the child.

THE ROLE OF THE UNMARRIED FATHER

Fathers of children born outside marriage are sometimes portrayed as lacking a sense of responsibility for their actions. At other times they are depicted as individuals who would like to be responsible for their children if circumstances permitted them to do so. Both of these images are apparently true. Some fathers take responsibility for their children; others would do so if they could; still others fit the worst stereotypes.

Attitudes of Teenage Fathers

In a recent survey, high school male students in a large metropolitan area were presented with the following hypothetical situation:

---

[6]Richard P. Barth, "Adolescent Mothers' Beliefs about Open Adoption," *Social Casework,* June 1987, 323.

You have been dating the same girl who is about your age for the past year and she told you last week that she was 2 months pregnant with your child. For the purposes of this survey assume that your girlfriend wants you to live with her and your child.[7]

Pregnancy after one year of dating indicates a high degree of commitment. Yet even in these highly favorable circumstances the men showed a great deal of reluctance to assume responsibility for their actions. These were their responses:[8]

Group	Extremely or quite unlikely	Slightly unlikely	Neither	Slightly likely	Extremely or quite likely
Total	16.4	7.8	7.1	20.8	47.8
Black	16.2	9.5	6.7	23.8	43.8
White	16.4	6.8	6.3	20.0	50.5

Public policy toward reluctant fathers has been rather lenient. There seems to be a lingering feeling that the mother must be penalized for allowing herself to become pregnant. Historically, punishment in the United States extended to the child, who was labeled "illegitimate" and was denied the legal protection granted to children who were born to married parents. Not until 1968 did the U.S. Supreme Court rule that all children are entitled to equal legal status.

> The status of illegitimacy has expressed through the ages society's condemnation of irresponsible liaisons beyond the bonds of marriage. But visiting this condemnation of the head of an infant is illogical and unjust. . . . Obviously, no child is responsible for his birth and penalizing the illegitimate child is an ineffectual—as well as an unjust—way of deterring the parent.[9]

Theoretically, having both parents could be viewed as a fundamental right of children. In reality, however, the responsibility for the child falls primarily on the mother. In an earlier chapter we used the term "the new double standard" to describe gender inequality in responsibility for contraception, resolution of pregnancy, and parenthood. The roots of this double

---

[7]William Marsiglio, "Commitment to Social Fatherhood: Predicting Adolescent Males' Intentions to Live with Their Child and Partner," *Journal of Marriage and the Family,* May 1988, 431.

[8]Ibid., 429.

[9]Ann Nichols-Casebolt, "Paternity Adjudication: In the Best Interests of the Out-of-Wedlock Child," *Child Welfare,* June 1988, 247.

standard go deep into history, but its impact on women is still great. Consider the following evidence.

Before the 1960s, pregnancy outside of marriage was almost always followed by marriage. In 1960, there were only 21,000 families with children headed by never-married women between fifteen and forty-four years old.[10] In a country the size of the United States, that number was hardly noticeable; on the average, it was equivalent to approximately six such families per county. By 1981, the number had increased to 343,000. Since that time, it has continued to grow, even without including households of divorced and widowed women.

Of course, not all households headed by women are in the "problem" category; some women choose and can afford a single lifestyle. It is misleading, however, to think that most unmarried mothers lead comfortable lives. Far too many are poor, struggling to raise their children, and in need of help from the children's fathers.

Getting the Fathers Involved

Whether the unmarried father supports his child depends in part on his age and financial status. Many young fathers would like to contribute to their children's social and financial well-being if they had the means to do so, but they themselves tend to live in poverty, to be unemployed, and to lack education.[11] Furthermore, social agencies try to help the mother and her child but tend to exclude the father, whether or not he wants to be excluded. One study found that when unwed fathers were offered an opportunity to work or to improve their skills, the majority accepted it.[12]

Vocational training was the most popular program for these teenage fathers. Soon after they gained some competence as breadwinners, they showed interest in becoming dependable fathers. The counselors taught parenting skills to both parents; their joint responsibilities included limiting their family size. The counselors found that many of the young men had never had a loving home or a caring father. These men often remarked, "I want to be a better father than my father was to me. I want something different for my child than what I have."

It seems that the more we know about teenage fathers, the more we can help them learn how to be responsible parents. The surprising fact is that behind the "macho," "cool," "superstud" image which many sexually

---

[10]Phillips Cutright, "Child Support and Responsible Male Procreative Behavior," *Sociological Focus,* January 1986, 28.

[11]Joelle Hevesi Sander and Jacqueline L. Rosen, "Teenage Fathers: Working with the Neglected Partner in Adolescent Childbearing," *Family Planning Perspectives,* June 1987, 108.

[12]Ibid., 108.

active men project, there is often a person with low self-esteem, longing to be the father he never had.

CORRELATES OF ADOLESCENT PARENTING

Are the young women who become mothers different somehow from those who do not? The differences are not always clear, but when they can be identified, the most striking contrast lies in socioeconomic status.

Single parents, both black and white, are found most often among the inadequately educated and the poor.[13] Consequently, many young single parents are on welfare. Yet contrary to popular belief, single mothers, black or white, are more likely to work than married mothers; most of their income comes from work, not from welfare.[14] They are likely to need welfare because the money they earn is not enough to support a child.

One study found no appreciable differences between married and unmarried mothers regarding major psychiatric problems, learning of social skills, or prevalence of alcohol or other drugs.[15] Instead it was concluded that "the problems faced by single parent women may be a reflection of poverty and stress in families and not of psychiatric disorders or poor social relations in mothers."

This conclusion leads to the next important question: What causes social class to be associated with the high risk of teenage pregnancy? The answer is not certain, nor is it likely that there is only one correct answer. Nevertheless, there is a growing consensus among researchers that teenage motherhood may be motivated by what sociologists call *status deprivation.*

Status deprivation usually is found in the lower socioeconomic strata; it may exist when the usual avenues for advancement are not open. Poverty deprives many people of employment opportunities, a good education, and sometimes even of love and affection at home. According to Shtarkshall,[16] deprivation may motivate childbearing for several reasons:

---

[13]Myrna M. Weisman, Philip J. Leaf, and Martha Livingston Bruce, "Single Parent Women," *Social Psychiatry* 22, 1987, 35. See also Mark R. Rank, "Fertility among Women on Welfare: Incidence and Determinants," *American Sociological Review,* April 1989, 296–304; Lynda Henley Walters, James Walters, and Patrick C. McKenry, "Differentiation of Girls at Risk of Early Pregnancy from the General Population of Adolescents," *Journal of Genetic Psychology,* March 1987, 19–30.

[14]Ann M. Nichols-Casebolt, "Black Families Headed by Single Mothers: Growing Numbers and Increasing Poverty," *Social Work,* August 1988, 310.

[15]Weisman et al., "Single Parent Women," 29.

[16]Ronny A. Shtarkshall, "Motherhood as a Dominant Feature in the Self-Image of Female Adolescents of Low Socioeconomic Status," *Adolescence,* Fall 1987, 568.

- A child may be perceived not only as an object of love but also as a source of love, strength, and support to its mother. In a way, a young woman's self-esteem may be enhanced by giving birth.
- From a sociological point of view, especially among feminists, this phenomenon might be the result of the fact that the only status roles permitted to women in this subculture are those of daughter and mother.
- Another possible explanation is that socially and educationally deprived young women perceive themselves in other roles but are unable to deal cognitively or emotionally with multiple roles.

Each of these explanations assumes that parenthood enhances status and brings fulfillment to men and women alike. Probably it does so for many people, but the risks of youthful parenthood seem to overshadow whatever benefits may exist.

CONSEQUENCES FOR THE MOTHER

Childbearing without marriage can be a chosen lifestyle. Some professional women, for example, may choose to have children but not a husband. These women usually have completed school and are established in a profession before they decide to become mothers. Their children are wanted, usually they are well cared for, and they are unlikely to become a financial burden to their mothers or to society.

Obviously, most teenaged unwed mothers do not fall into this category. A typical teenage mother is poorly prepared to raise children alone. Her education is likely to be inadequate, and her emotional maturity may not be well developed. If she is particularly young, her health and that of her child also may be endangered. Because of these problems, teenage pregnancy continues to be an issue of great concern in the United States.

Many difficulties are associated with adolescent childbearing. They include health problems, rapid subsequent fertility, large families, low educational attainment, low earnings, welfare dependency, low perceived personal efficacy, and high rate of marital disruption.[17]

Marital disruption seems more likely to occur if the birth occurs before marriage.[18] It seems hardly to matter whether the mother *conceived* before or after the marriage; marital instability appears to increase only if the marriage occurs *after the birth*.

Most of the disadvantages to adolescent mothers are well known and

---

[17]John O. G. Billy, Nancy S. Landale, and Steven D. McLaughlin, "The Effect of Marital Status at First Birth on Marital Dissolution among Adolescent Mothers," *Demography*, August 1986, 329. See also Eugene B. Gallager and Michael G. Farrall, "Adolescent Vicissitudes and Medical Judgment: A Case Study," *Adolescence*, Fall 1987, 671–80.

[18]Ibid., 344.

widely discussed. In view of the number of pregnant teenagers, this topic can hardly be overemphasized. Nevertheless, according to one study of 300 urban black women who gave birth as adolescents, "the majority completed high school, found regular employment and, if they had been on welfare at some point, they eventually managed to escape dependence on public assistance."[19] Adolescent mothers as a group, though, do not fare as well in the long run as mothers who postpone childbearing. Unfortunately, neither do their children.

CONSEQUENCES FOR CHILDREN

The problems for children of adolescent mothers begin at birth. Premature births and low birth weights are associated closely with the mother's age.[20] This risk also is higher than average for mothers over age forty, but older women are much less likely to become pregnant than teenagers. The most favorable childbearing age in terms of the infant's weight is between twenty-five and thirty-four. For the sake of the infant's health, most women would do best to plan their first child after age twenty-five. In fact, that is the case for women who marry before they have children; about two-thirds of all births to married women take place after age twenty-five.[21] In contrast, about 70 percent of unmarried women have their children before that age.

Infants in the care of young mothers are at greater risk of other misfortunes as well. In general, "adolescent mothers provide parenting of lower quality than adult mothers."[22] The reasons are speculative, but they point to a lack of preparedness for parenting.

Lack of parenting skills may result in curtailed school achievement not only for the adolescent parents but also for their children. The lower the mother's educational attainment, the lower her child's educational attainment, regardless of her age.[23] Having a child outside marriage at an early age impedes a young woman's ability to go to school and earn good grades. In turn, the children of mothers with poor education tend to be poor students themselves.

---

[19]Frank F. Furstenberg, Jr., J. Brooks-Gunn, and S. Philip Morgan, "Adolescent Mothers and Their Children in Later Life," *Family Planning Perspectives,* August 1987, 142.

[20]National Center for Health Statistics, "Advance Report of Final Natality Statistics, 1986." *Monthly Vital Statistics Report,* 37(3), Public Health Service, Hyattsville, MD, 1988, 6.

[21]Proportions of births by age and marital status were calculated by the authors.

[22]Michael E. Lamb, D. Hopps, and A. B. Elster, "Strange Situation Behavior of Infants with Adolescent Mothers," *Infant Behavior and Development,* March 1987, 39.

[23]E. Milling Kinard and Helen Reinherz, "School Aptitude and Achievement in Children of Adolescent Mothers," *Journal of Youth and Adolescence* 16(1), 1987, 69.

SOCIAL COSTS

The budget of the United States faces almost unlimited demands for a variety of worthy causes. Money is needed to reduce infant mortality rates, improve the quality of education, provide day care for children, and wage war on drugs. Whether or not the amount spent is enough is a political question beyond the scope of this book. Whatever the size of that amount, however, a substantial portion is spent on the support of teenage mothers and their children.

The Center for Population Options estimated these costs for the mid-1980s as follows:[24]

- In 1985 the United States spent $16.6 billion on families that were begun when the mother was a teenager. This amount includes AFDC (Aid for Families with Dependent Children), Medicaid, and food stamps. (It does not include other social services such as housing, special education, child protective services, foster care, and day care).
- If all teenage births were delayed to age twenty, the United States would save about $2.1 billion per year.
- Two out of three teenage mothers do not receive public assistance. The estimated public cost per teenage parent who did receive public assistance was $36,508.

Concerned citizens often ask, "Are these payments encouraging women to have children?" Although the total amounts expended are large, the amount received directly by the women seems to be too small to serve as an inducement. Most of the money is spent to operate the programs and to protect the child's health rather than for the mother's benefit. Nevertheless, these costs could probably be reduced through preventive programs.

SOCIAL POLICIES REGARDING TEENAGE PREGANCY

Few issues in America today are more controversial than public policy regarding teenage pregnancy. Religious beliefs, moral convictions, and even disagreement among social scientists contribute to confusion and inaction. Meanwhile, pregnancy among unwed teenagers continues to increase.

Ideally, to reduce the problem, adolescents need to stay in school, find employment, and marry compatible partners. To bring about that improvement, effective programs could teach values (including the importance of

---

[24]Debra W. Hafner, "Coping with the Costs of Teenage Pregnancy," *New England Journal of Social Services* 7(1), 1987, 5–6.

individual responsibility), and in general help parents to control their children's sexual behavior. There is no single way to accomplish this goal, nor are all proposals equally realistic.

Abstinence

One idea that carries wide popular support is that of greater abstinence from coitus. The age for socially approved intercourse varies from one society to the next. Probably because we are a multicultural nation, different groups in the United States have different notions about what that age should be. Some groups, on the basis of their religious convictions, believe that sex should take place only within marriage, regardless of how long a person delays marriage. If we judge by the onset of premarital coitus discussed in the previous chapter, however, such beliefs have had little influence on overall behavior. Among certain groups, of course, restrictive teachings have been quite effective.

Abstinence certainly is the most effective method for preventing unwanted pregnancies and the many problems that follow. It is not surprising that churches, schools, and parents advocate this method strongly, but they seem to lack definite programs that could assist young people to abstain.

It would be helpful if young people had more opportunities to be in adult company. Volunteers might use public facilities for supervised recreation, such as visual arts, music, and sports. These activities would reduce the amount of unsupervised time that young people spend together, and the opportunities for coitus could thus be reduced. More important, alternative forms of status advancement could reduce a major motivation for teenage parenthood.

In practice, however, except for halfhearted rhetoric, communities have been unwilling or unable to promote abstinence. Instead, public policy is focused on birth-prevention programs, which—ironically—are even more controversial.

Contraception

In the absence of successful programs to help young people abstain from sexual activity, many health professionals advocate educational programs to encourage the use of contraceptive devices. Such programs, however, either are not implemented widely enough or are simply ineffective. As a result, many young people remain uninformed even about their own anatomy and physiology. (For any readers who may lack some of this information we have included an Appendix, "The Physiological Basis of Marriage.")

Given the number of abortions and unwanted births in this country, it may be that an environment that is unconducive to abstinence is also unconducive to sex education. In any case, from the young people's viewpoint, the situation must be rather bewildering. Most sexually active teenagers, for example, had their first intercourse without contraception, even though about 80 percent favored the use of effective birth-control methods.[25] Their contraceptive inefficiency was due in part to a lack of knowledge about basic reproductive biology.

- More than one-third did not know that the effectiveness of the rhythm method depends on abstaining from coitus at midcycle.
- About one-third did not know the point during the menstrual cycle when pregnancy is most likely to occur.
- The length of the period during which fertilization can occur was underestimated by 27 percent.
- More than half of the respondents did not know how long sperm remains viable.

The paucity of knowledge shown in this study was particularly remarkable when we consider that the subjects were college students over 18 years old. Younger students who are not college-bound probably would fare considerably worse. Because ignorance is not conducive to abstinence, many educators promote sex education and the teaching of contraceptive methods in public schools.

SUMMARY

Teenage fertility rates in the United States continue to decline. Although from a public health point of view, this is a positive trend, teenage pregnancies *among the unmarried* remain high. In fact, among whites the rates have actually increased. In the eyes of many authorities, the overall problem is grim indeed.

It is clear that teenage fertility has declined primarily because hundreds of thousands of abortions are performed every year. It would seem that, from the broad picture, both the family and society have failed to provide an environment conducive to abstinence. At the same time, sex education programs, and the use of contraceptive measures by the young people themselves, continue to be the focus of continued community debates and heated public discussion.

QUESTIONS

1. What have been the trends in teenage conception and childbearing in the 1980s?
2. What has been the history of abortion in America? Why is "quickening" no longer accepted as the demarcation point for legal abortion?

---

[25]Candace S. Lowe and Susan M. Radius, "Young Adults' Contraceptive Practices: An Investigation of Influences," *Adolescence*, Summer 1987, 295.

3. What are some of the major considerations determining whether a mother will have an abortion, place a child for adoption, or raise the child herself?

4. Why are unwed mothers becoming less likely to place their children for adoptions? Do you think this trend may continue through the year 2000? Explain your answer.

5. What are some reasons for an unmarried father's failure to support the mother and his child? How have some programs tried to involve fathers? What were the results?

6. In general, how are young women who become parents different from those who do not? How are they similar?

7. Explain how status deprivation may lead to wanted pregnancy among young people.

8. What are some problems of early childbirth to (a) the mother, (b) the child, and (c) the society?

9. Propose a program that would promote abstinence from coitus among teenagers under age eighteen in some specific community. Be specific and realistic.

10. Explain why a low level of abstinence from coitus seems to coincide with inefficient contraceptive practices.

SELECTED READINGS

Barth, Richard P. "Adolescent Mothers' Beliefs about Open Adoption." *Social Casework,* June 1987, 323–31.

Brazzell, Jan F., and Alan C. Acock. "Influence of Attitudes, Significant Others, and Aspirations on How Adolescents Intend to Resolve a Premarital Pregnancy." *Journal of Marriage and the Family,* May 1988, 413–25.

Bumpass, Larry, and Sara McLanahan. "Unmarried Motherhood: Recent Trends, Composition, and Black-White Differences." *Demography,* May 1989, 279–86.

Cahill, Lisa Sowle. " 'Abortion Pill' RU 486: Ethics, Rhetoric, and Social Practice." *Hastings Center Report,* November 1987, 5–8.

Cutright, Phillips. "Child Support and Responsible Male Procreative Behavior." *Sociological Focus,* January 1986, 27–45.

Darling, Carol A., and Kenneth Davidson, Sr. "Coitally Active University Students: Sexual Behaviors, Concerns, and Challenges." *Adolescence,* Summer 1986, 403–19.

Furstenberg, Frank, Jr., J. Brooks-Gunn, and S. Philip Morgan. "Adolescent Mothers and Their Children in Later Life." *Family Planning Perspectives,* August 1987, 142–51.

———. "Bringing Back the Shotgun Wedding." *The Public Interest,* Winter 1988, 121–132.

Gruber, Enid, and Christopher V. Chambers. "Cognitive Development and Adolescent Contraception: Integrating Theory and Practice." *Adolescence,* Fall 1987, 661–70.

Kelley, Kathryn, George Smeaton, Donn Byrne, D.P.J. Przybyla, and William A.

Fisher. "Sexual Attitudes and Contraception among Females across Five College Samples." *Human Relations,* 40(4), 1987, 237–54.

Kinard, E. Milling, and Helen Reinherz. "School Aptitude and Achievement in Children of Adolescent Mothers." *Journal of Youth and Adolescence,* 16(1) 1987, 69–87.

Kochanek, Kenneth D. "Induced Terminations of Pregnancy: Reporting States, 1985 and 1986." *Monthly Vital Statistics Reports,* April 28, 1989, 1–32.

Krein, Sheila Fitzgerald, and Andrea H. Beller. "Educational Attainment of Children from Single-Parent Families: Differences by Exposure, Gender and Race." *Demography,* May 1988, 221–34.

Lowe, Candace S., and Susan M. Radius. "Young Adults' Contraceptive Practices: An Investigation of Influences." *Adolescence,* Summer 1987, 291–304.

McLanahan, Sara S. "Family Structure and Dependency: Early Transitions to Female Household Headship." *Demography,* February 1988, 1–16.

Miller, Brent C., and Stephen R. Jorgensen. "Adolescent Fertility-Related Behavior and Its Family Linkages." In *Social Stress and Family Development,* edited by David M. Klein and Joan Aldous, 210–33. New York: The Guilford Press, 1988.

Mitchell, Faith, and Claire Brindis. "Adolescent Pregnancy: The Responsibilities of Policymakers." *Health Services Research,* 22(3), 1987, 399–438.

Nichols-Casebolt, Ann. "Paternity Adjudication: In the Best Interests of the Out-of-Wedlock Child." *Child Welfare,* May–June 1988, 245–54.

Rank, Mark R. "Fertility among Women on Welfare: Incidence and Determinants." *American Sociological Review,* April 1989, 296–304.

Reis, Janet S., and Elicia J. Herz. "Correlates of Adolescent Parenting." *Adolescence,* Fall 1987, 599–609.

Streetman, Lee G. "Contrasts in the Self-Esteem of Unwed Teenage Mothers." *Adolescence,* Summer 1987, 459–64.

Unger, Donald G., and Lois Pall Wandersman. "The Relation of Family and Partner Support to the Adjustment of Adolescent Mothers." *Child Development,* 59, 1988, 1056–60.

Walters, Lynda Henley, James Walters, and Patrick C. McKenry. "Differentiation of Girls at Risk of Early Pregnancy from the General Population of Adolescents." *Journal of Genetic Psychology,* March 1987, 19–30.

Yamaguchi, Kazuo, and Denise Kandel. "Drug Use and Other Determinants of Premarital Pregnancy and Its Outcome: A Dynamic Analysis of Competing Life Events." *Journal of Marriage and the Family,* May 1987, 257–70.

FOUR

Marital Interaction and the Family Life Course

Chapter
13

Marital Adjustment

*I*f mate selection were a more efficient process, there would be much less need for a chapter on marital adjustment. Brides and grooms would know before marriage how to fulfill each other's expectations and how to attain lasting happiness, love, and affection. Unfortunately, however, some of the most desirable dating partners may be incompatible as spouses. Personalities, role expectations, and involvements outside the family often do not mesh after marriage as well as anticipated before marriage. Spouses may require a great deal of negotiation, clear communication, and flexibility to adjust to each other and to the world around them. If they fail to adjust, then strife, prolonged unhappiness, divorce, or even abuse and violence may occur.

Although these difficulties are well publicized, more than 90 percent of Americans continue to marry—and continue to hope for fulfillment and happiness. The fact that one-half of the marriages may not succeed is a further indication that young people need to know as much as possible about the various dimensions of marital adjustment. The present chapter discusses some of these dimensions, especially as they relate to long-term marital satisfaction.

DETERMINANTS OF MARITAL POWER

About a decade ago, researchers found that "in modern urban settings, exclusive male dominance in conjugal decision making is on the decline."[1] The reason is that in such settings an increasing number of women are employed. It is theorized that income from their employment increases their bargaining power in family decision making. If the wife has no income, she is more likely to be totally dependent on her husband.[2] Some women even feel helpless and trapped in intolerable marriages.

Obviously, increases in educational attainment, better jobs, and higher income can minimize the husband's domination. Men, however, are more likely than women to obtain marital power from many different sources, including "control of resources, physical force, influence, manipulation of interests, strategic scheming, intimidation, and knowledge,"[3] Consequently, the decision-making process in the family is still dominated by men.

In what has come to be regarded as the original study, Blood and Wolfe interviewed several hundred wives in the Detroit area. They selected a number of decision situations (what kind of car to buy, where to go on vacation, whether the wife should work, whether to buy life insurance, and so forth) and then asked who would make the decision: husband, wife, or both.

Findings revealed that white-collar husbands had more power over their wives than did blue-collar husbands. It was also found that husbands' power increased with their income. Conversely, the husbands' power decreased in instances where the wife was gainfully employed.

On the basis of such findings, the authors formulated the well-known *resource theory* of marital power: the spouse with greater resources, such as education, occupation, or social status, wields the greater decision-making authority.[4]

In the years since the Blood and Wolfe findings first appeared, women's status has improved. Today more women work in white-collar occupations, earn higher incomes, and attain more education. Therefore, most couples expect equality in marriage, especially if the wife is employed. In reality, however, the wife's employment does not seem to influence bargaining

---

[1]Ruth Katz, "Conjugal Power: A Comparative Analysis," *International Journal of Sociology of the Family,* Spring 1983, 98.

[2]Francis Klagsburn, *Married People: Staying Together in the Age of Divorce* (Toronto: Bantam Books, 1985), 49.

[3]Richard F. Curtis, "Household and Family in Theory on Inequality," *American Sociological Review,* April 1986, 171.

[4]Robert Blood and Donald Wolfe, *Husbands and Wives: The Dynamics of Married Living* (Glencoe, IL: Free Press, 1960). For a critique of this theory see Aafke Komter, "Hidden Power in Marriage," *Gender and Society,* June 1989, 187–216.

While much progress has been made toward sex equality, the decision-making process is still dominated by men. What do the facial expressions tell you about this couple? (*Catherine Ursillo*)

power and the sharing of labor as strongly as the theory predicted. Instead, the male's dominant role remains evident.[5] For example, it is still customary to refer to the male as "head of the household."

Judging from these studies, it would appear that impediments to equality in marriage loom large in our society. This fact is generally known, but it is not well understood. Some people blame the economic system and invoke political reform; others want to bring about educational changes. There is no doubt that some blame may fall in each of these areas, but is it also possible that there is an overlooked impediment to equality in marriage?

Such an impediment might be found in the way men and women select each other for marriage. Particularly with respect to age differences, most couples enter marriage as *unequal partners*. The older spouse is more likely to have attained higher educational status and to have greater opportunity for employment or promotion. The younger spouse, regardless of sex, starts the relationship in a position of less power.

---

[5]Dana V. Hiller and William W. Philliber, "The Division of Labor in Contemporary Marriage: Expectations, Perceptions, and Performance," *Social Problem* 1986, 199.

This inequality is likely to lead to domination of family decision making by the older spouse. Age tends to give a person experiential advantage and a savoir faire respected by the younger spouse. These differences, although subtle, can influence dominance within marriage.

Only one early decision in favor of the career of one spouse is needed to influence a lifelong series of decisions in favor of the same spouse. For example, the couple may decide to move the household so that the older spouse can accept a 'better job in a distant community, or the younger spouse may decide to stay home with a child while the older one works. Decisions like these routinely favor the professional development of the older spouse at the expense of the younger. It seems reasonable to expect that as long as wives continue to be younger than their husbands, their marital power disadvantage is likely to continue.

MARITAL-ROLE ARRANGEMENTS

Modern marriage differs in many respects from the marriage of fifty or even thirty years ago. One of the chief differences relates to marital roles. Today's young wife is better educated than in the past, and the chances are that she will be employed outside the home. Certainly within the home she will expect to share in the decision-making process with her husband. And her husband will be expected to do his share of the household tasks.

The difficulty is that some people see the traditional division of labor by sex as the correct marital role arrangement, and others see role sharing as correct.

Traditional Role Arrangements

According to family historians, male-female division of labor in the family predates the Roman, Greek, and Hebrew cultures. Ever since the hunting and gathering period of history, succeeding civilizations have passed along the principles of gender division of labor. The most persistent of these rules involved nurturant and submissive roles for women and provider and dominant roles for men. Today we call these expectations traditional marriage roles.

Theoretically, division of labor by gender might have helped ancient families to survive. Males' physical strength was required for hard agricultural labor, hunting, and protecting the family. Women were likely to be pregnant throughout their fecund period, so that they were even more dependent on the males. Some scholars argue that centuries of such dependence created a cultural expectation of submissive females, restricted to taking care of home, husband, and children.

Although confinement of women to the home was understandable in ancient times, today many people perceive it to be an anachronism. Clearly,

Increasing numbers of couples today expect to share the responsibility for raising children. (© *Scherr, Jeroboam*)

the husband's domination of the wife and her confinement to home are losing much support throughout the developed world. Educated people understand that one's qualifications for working outside the home now depend on education, intellect, and ability, not on gender. Although there are still jobs that require more brawn than brains, these jobs are fewer and usually less well paid than skilled or professional occupations.

In spite of these changes, some couples deliberately choose traditional role arrangements because of religious or personal convictions. Other couples experiment with various role-sharing arrangements.

Role Sharing in Marriage

Increasing numbers of couples today expect to share the responsibility for performing various household tasks: providing family income, doing household chores, raising children, maintaining contacts with relatives, and in general participating equally in decision making. Some couples even put these expectations in writing before marriage. In one way or another, most try to avoid division of labor based on gender.

In practice, that ideal has not been easy to implement. For one thing, demands outside the home may be different for each spouse, thereby under-mining the couple's intentions to share tasks equally. Consider, for exam-ple, some events that can disrupt role-sharing plans: job promotions requir-ing migration, irregular work hours, loss of job or reduction in income, having a child, ill health, or need for additional education. Surely the reader can think of many other considerations. It is understandable that in the face of such contingencies, many couples become frustrated. Some give up and divorce; others try to be innovative.

Whichever method of sharing couples try, the fact is that in spite of their best intentions, most couples either divorce or the wife assumes major responsibility for the home even when she is employed. Sociologists call this inequality the *double burden*.[6]

The sociological forecast for the 1990s is that division of labor will be-come more egalitarian. Future research, as Blumberg and Coleman sug-gest, will focus on the "niceness versus nastiness" of household tasks. These researchers point out that "even if a couple divides the work load more or less evenly, there is still some untapped power if he gets to mow the lawn, grocery shop, cook gourmet meals, and take the kids to the zoo while she scrubs the toilets, scours the pots and pans, and washes the dia-pers."

Role sharing is a noble, timely idea, but often it does not seem to work well. Certainly many couples find happiness in their marriage and satisfac-tion with their marriage-role arrangements, but unfortunately, failure is fre-quent enough to justify asking whether another marriage-role arrangement would work better for more people. At least theoretically, some sociologists say yes. They offer random role assignment as a possible solution in the future.

Random Role Assignment

Although more progress has been made toward gender equality, most family sociologists admit readily that disadvantages for married working women persist. At the same time, most believe that strides toward equality will con-tinue. A few even think that at some time in the future, men will be as likely as women to take care of children, cook, and do other household chores that traditionally have been labeled as "women's work." In short, role assign-ments will depend on ability, merit, and interest. With respect to gender, roles will be assigned randomly.

The reader should not confuse the idea of random role assignment with the practice of role reversal. The term "role reversal" is used in reference to traditional sex-role arrangements and means that each sex takes on the responsibilities of the other. The idea of role reversal retains a division of

---

[6]Rae Lesser Blumberg and Marion Tolbert Coleman, "A Theoretical Look at the Gender Bal-ance of Power in the American Couple," *Journal of Family Issues*, June 1989, 242–43.

labor by gender. In contrast, random role assignment implies no distinction between men's work and women's work.

Random role assignment may be the answer for couples who find that role sharing is too much of a burden for both husbands and wives. Some people find it difficult to care for the family and pursue a career. At the same time, they might reject the idea of arbitrarily assigning sex roles according to the dictates of the traditional role arrangements. They may decide, without regard to gender, that one partner will take on the major responsibility for home and children while the other pursues income with minimum interference from obligations at home.

No solution, including random role assignments, may work for everyone, but a society that is receptive to random role assignments also could remain receptive to those who prefer the challenge of role sharing. For that matter, there could also be a place for those who prefer traditional role arrangements. Perhaps the solution to sexual inequality lies not in any one marriage role but in a choice among options that can fulfill varied abilities, interests, and personalities.

NIGHT PEOPLE AND MORNING PEOPLE

Some research suggests that marital adjustment may depend more on a *fitting* of the two personalities than on the personalities themselves. One example of personality fit is that of "night people" and "morning people." The terms are virtually self-explanatory; most of us know individuals who fall into one category or the other. A night person is one who hates to get up in the morning, whose energy seems to build up during the day, and who by nighttime (especially late at night!) is "raring to go." Conversely, a morning person likes to get up with the sun and enjoys the daylight hours, but by nightfall tends to lose energy and to yearn for bed.

The above description simply bears out common observation and experience but it remained for two family specialists, Bert Adams and Ronald Cromwell, to put the matter to empirical test. Working with a small group of married persons, the investigators attempted to find out whether nightness-morningness was a researchable topic and whether married persons saw the distinction as an important aspect of their lives. The answer to both questions was a definite yes.[7]

In a book on this topic, Murray Melbin noted that every home routine is affected when husbands and wives have different working schedules.[8] According to the couples whose nightness and morningness are

---

[7]Bert Adams and Ronald Cromwell, "Morning and Night People in the Family: A Preliminary Statement," *The Family Coordinator,* January 1978, 5–13.

[8]Murray Melbin, *Night as Frontier: Colonizing the World After Dark* (New York:Free Press, 1987), 111–14.

Being on different schedules of nightness or morningness can sometimes affect a relationship and give a feeling of being out of phase with one another. (*Suzanne Szaz/Photo Researchers, Inc.*)

mismatched because of work requirements, their sex lives are affected particularly. Some make love only on the weekends. Others make careful plans in advance and find that the only time for intimacy is during the day.

Melbin also found that some couples are "averse to making love in the daytime." Not only are they apprehensive about possible interruptions, but night people seem to be averse to daytime romance under any circumstances. When work schedules force them to behave against their inclinations, the strain on marriage may become intolerable.

Why are some of us night people and others morning people? It is possible that some internal biorhythm is operating. It is also possible that nightness and morningness are learned or are adaptive responses to social situations. It may be, as Adams and Cromwell theorized originally, that nightness and morningness are points on a continuum rather than a simple dichotomy.

When family routines are disrupted by differences in time orientation or by work at night, the child-parent relationship may also create problems.

Little is known about this complication, but it is reasonable to assume that the presence of children would make marital adjustment even more difficult.

THE EFFECT OF CHILDREN ON MARITAL HAPPINESS

Our attitudes toward children—in some respects, at least—may be changing. Perhaps it is no accident that the long-term trend of the birth rate has been downward, and that families with three, four, and five children are becoming scarce. One reason, of course, is that children cost money—a great deal of money. In an economic sense the cost must be figured in two ways: (1) the direct maintenance costs (the actual expenses involved in child care, such as food, clothing, and education), and (2) the opportunity costs (the income that parents forgo by staying at home or by leaving school to support the family).

In addition, there are nonmonetary costs—the worries, the day-to-day problems, and the sense of being tied down. Are these costs outweighed by the rewards—in the form of emotional satisfaction—that so many parents seem to gain from their youngsters?

The answer is no for couples who were poorly adjusted before they had a child.[9] It seems that adding a child when there are unresolved differences between spouses only increases stress and exacerbates existing problems. Readers may be surprised to learn that in general, children detract from marital happiness rather than contribute to it.

Glenn and McLanahan explored the possibility that older couples would be happier if they had grown-up children. As the old saying goes, "Children are a comfort in old age." Yet even this seemingly commonsense belief was not supported by the data. These researchers found that "having had a child or children has had no important effects on the psychological well-being of older Americans."[10]

SEXUAL ADJUSTMENT

Couples would be well advised to consider their sexual compatibility before having children. If a sexual problem exists, it will be more difficult to solve after the children are born than before. Infants require care and affection, thus reducing the time and energy the parents have for each other. Infants also are notorious for having a schedule of their own, which often interrupts

---

[9]Lynda Cooper Harriman, "Marital Adjustment as Related to Personal and Marital Changes Accompanying Parenthood," *Family Relations,* April 1986, 238.

[10]Karen Secombe, "Children: Their Impact on the Elderly in Declining Health," *Research on Aging,* June 1987, 312–26.

parents' sleep. It takes a well-adjusted couple to assume responsibilities for children and still remain sexually satisfied with each other.

Although this might not always have been the case, sexual intercourse today is regarded by both husbands and wives as an integral part of marriage. For most young people, certainly, the prospect of marriage without sex would be grim indeed. Under such conditions it is problematical to imagine what proportion of single males and females would ever marry.

A generation or two ago, sex was likely to be considered an obligation or a duty as far as the wife was concerned. Sexual gratification was felt to be a prerogative of the husband rather than a joint venture of husband and wife. The latter was presumed to "submit" to her mate's desires; if in the process she received any gratification herself the fact was likely to be kept secret, because sex was neither written about nor discussed as it is today. And if the wife was left sexually unsatisfied in the process of satisfying her husband's needs, it was unlikely that she would voice her complaints, because any manifestation of her own sexual needs or desires was considered "unladylike."

Today conditions have changed; now it is recognized that women as well as men have sexual needs. Indeed, unless this fact is recognized by the couple, the chances of a happy marriage may be reduced substantially. Therefore, as a working definition, we consider a married couple to be sexually adjusted when the frequency of coitus and the physical and psychoemotional responses involved are mutually satisfactory. It is recognized that this definition depicts an ideal type, and that in reality sexual adjustment is more likely to be a matter of degree.

SEXUAL MALADJUSTMENT

From all accounts, sexual discord is fairly widespread in the United States. Research findings from a variety of sources—divorce courts, clinics, marriage counselors, questionnaire and interview surveys—have shown sexual difficulties to be among the marital complaints that are mentioned most often. Masters and Johnson, two of the best-known practitioners in the field of sex therapy, went so far as to state that "half of all American marriages are troubled by some form of sexual distress ranging from disinterest and boredom to outright sexual dysfunction."[11]

It is ironic that sexual maladjustment is so prevalent today even though sexual matters are discussed more openly, premarital sexual experience has increased, sexual clinics have sprung up, and a staggering number of books

---

[11]William H. Masters, Virginia E. Johnson, and Robert C. Kolodny, *Masters and Johnson on Sex and Human Loving* (Boston: Little, Brown, 1986), 440.

and articles on the subject have appeared. Sexual discord remains an important problem in the lives of many couples.

The exact source of the problem is difficult to determine. For instance, if husband and wife cannot agree on how often to have intercourse, it is likely that this disagreement will adversely affect their day-to-day congeniality. Conversely, if congeniality is low, it seems likely that sexual adjustment would be affected adversely, even if the partners have an otherwise equal interest in sexual relations.

Lawyers who handle divorce cases often believe that sexual discord is the most important cause of marital unhappiness. This belief is shared by many doctors. Most family researchers, however, although conceding the importance of the sexual factor, would hesitate to label it the leading culprit. On the basis of our own research and general familiarity with the sociological literature, we would judge that sex is about as important a part of marriage as any other single factor.

There is no need to go into detail regarding the specific sexual complaints that are heard—premature ejaculation, failure of wife to reach orgasm, disagreement about coital techniques, lack of affection on the part of one spouse—because they have been well publicized in both clinical and popular literature. There is a real need, though, to look carefully at a more tragic problem—the occurrence of marital violence.

SPOUSE ABUSE

After years of increases in wife abuse, the efforts to curb it seem finally to be paying off. "Shelters and treatment programs have decreased the incidence of spouse abuse over the last decade," writes Murray Straus, co-director of the Family Research Laboratory at the University of New Hampshire.[12] According to this report, later age at marriage and an increase of women in the paid labor force also are responsible for favorable changes.

Although such a reversal of trends is welcome, family violence remains a major problem. Straus reports that even after reductions in rates, more than three million spouses are assaulted seriously each year; two husbands and three wives die of their wounds each day. These statistics are a reminder that a family, on the one hand, is a source of love and affection; on the other, it is the most violent institution in our society.

There is little doubt that the persistence of male dominance and chal-

---

[12]Murray A. Straus, "Family Violence," in David H. Olson and Meredith Kilmer Hanson, eds., *2001: Preparing Families for the Future* (Minneapolis: National Council on Family Relations, 1990), 26.

lenges to this dominance are fundamental causes of wife abuse.[13] Generally, the more power a husband has in relation to his wife, the greater the likelihood that the wife will be abused physically. It may be that greater power encourages some husbands to lash out emotionally at their helpless wives. Another possibility is that wives with few marital resources act out their frustrations in violent outbursts against their husbands, who in turn escalate the level of violence. In this cycle of violence the wives are more likely to receive serious injuries.[14]

Perhaps the strangest reason why husbands use violence against their wives is the belief held by some couples that verbal provocation gives a husband the right to hit his wife. "I kept at him and at him. He finally turned around and belted me. It was my fault, I asked for it," said one wife to an interviewer.[15] Offending husbands sometimes justify their actions as necessary to "knock her to her senses."[16] For these couples violence is a normal form of marital interaction; it would not be reported to the authorities unless death or a serious injury occurred.

The problems of marital violence and the reasons for the problems are known somewhat better today than in the past, but the solutions are not easy. The degree of marital maladjustment, ranging from simple discontent to genuine violence, requires us to look carefully at some of the proposed solutions.

Different problems in marriage require different approaches. Marital violence may require societal solutions ranging from legal intervention to improvement of women's status through education and employment. Local communities also could contribute by making shelters for battered women available. On the other hand, problems such as sexual maladjustment are handled most effectively through family counseling and sex therapy. The following discussion should be regarded simply as examples of the approaches that might be taken.

LEGAL SOLUTIONS FOR DOMESTIC VIOLENCE

Legal reformers believe that as it operates presently, our criminal justice system is inadequate to reduce the incidence and severity of domestic violence. One writer describes this inadequacy as follows:

---

[13]Avonne Mason and Virginia Blakenship, "Power and Affiliation Motivation, Stress, and Abuse in Intimate Relationships," *Journal of Personality and Social Psychology* 52 (1), 1987, 203.

[14]R. L. McNeely and Gloria Robinson Simpson, "The Truth about Domestic Violence: A Falsely Framed Issue," *Social Work,* December 1987, 486.

[15]Richard J. Gelles, *The Violent Home* (Newbury Park, CA: Sage Publications, 1987), 59–60.

[16]Ibid., 61.

Criminal assault and battery statutes offer little protection for a battered wife since few states define wife-beating as a felony. The misdemeanor status of wife-beating often serves to compound the problem by extracting fines and jail sentences small enough to be only minor deterrents but large enough to incite anger and greater violence.[17]

As a step in the prevention of domestic violence, reformers argue for removal of statutes that treat domestic violence differently from other forms of violence. New statutes have been proposed in various states that would treat each violent act in the same way, whether it occurred at home between spouses or on the street between strangers. The rationale for this change is deterrence; that is, a husband might be less likely to batter his wife if he knows that he could be punished for doing so.

Also on the reformers' agenda are laws that would make it illegal for a husband to rape his wife. Marital rape is defined as a form of violence in which the husband physically restrains, forces, or threatens the wife with bodily harm to have sexual relations with him against her will.

Legal reforms of this nature have been introduced in a number of countries. One of the first countries to abolish marital rape exemption was Poland in 1932. After World War II, Czechoslovakia, the USSR, Sweden, Denmark, and Norway followed with similar legislation.[18] In these countries, at least in theory, sex is a consensual act. The husband does not have a right to force his wife to have sexual intercourse.

Some reforms include mandatory arrest laws. Research shows that when family violence is treated as a crime and when perpetrators are arrested and persecuted, abuse declines.[19] The punishment fitting the crime seems to serve as a deterrent in the case of family abuse. So far, however, only a few states have mandatory arrest laws. Among these is Oregon, where "an officer at the scene of domestic disturbance may arrest and take into custody an alleged assailant or potential assailant if in the Officer's judgement 'one person has placed the other in fear of imminent serious physical injury.' "[20]

Other states are moving very slowly in this direction because legislators seem to believe that marital problems call for sociopsychological rather than legal solutions. As a result, individually oriented programs for the solution

---

[17]Michael A. Buda and Teresa L. Butler, "The Battered Wife Syndrome: A Background Assault on Domestic Violence," *Journal of Family Law,* April 1984–85, 365.

[18]Michael D. A. Freeman, "But If You Can't Rape Your Wife, Who(m) Can You Rape?: The Marital Rape Exemption Re-examined," *Family Law Quarterly,* Spring 1981, 26.

[19]Nanet J. Davis and Sarah Randles Hardin, "The Mandatory Arrest Law in Domestic Violence Cases: The Limits of Criminal Justice Intervention," in Zvonimir Paul Sheparovich and Wanda Jameson, eds., *Domestic Violence,* selected papers given at the International Workshop on Domestic Violence, World Society of Victimology, Dubrovnik, Yugoslavia, 1988, 63.

[20]Ibid., 19.

of marital problems abound in the United States. Perhaps the most publicized are those based on sex therapy.

MARITAL THERAPY AND SEX THERAPY PROGRAMS

Family violence is one of many possible problems that can beset a family. Other problems include personality mismatches, addiction, failure to communicate, failure to perform family roles, and so-called sexual dysfunctions. In recent years couples with serious sexual problems frequently have been advised to seek sex therapy in specialized centers or clinics. Sex therapy programs have become so popular that they number in the thousands.

Serious scientific concern with human sexuality began about one hundred years ago. Scientists of the Victorian era viewed sex as a dangerous activity. Masturbation, for example, was viewed as a cause of "epilepsy, eye disease, acne, asthma, headaches, mammary hypertrophy, warts on the hands, deafness, cardiac murmur, painful menstruation, feeble mindedness, insanity, and criminality."[21] Because of such misconceptions it is not difficult to see that orgasm, especially for women, was considered a health hazard, something to fear and to engage in only sparingly.

Much as the field of chemistry emerged from the age of alchemy, sex therapy emerged from the misconceptions of the Victorian era. Sex research conducted over the decades discounted medical dangers and disclosed that sex in marriage was an important bond.

Failure to develop such a bond may result in difficulties in matters unrelated to sex. Personality conflicts, role disagreements, and many of the faults that couples find with each other may be easier to overlook when the partners have a satisfying sex life than when they have a problem in that area. Because of this close interrelationship between sex and other marital functions, there is an increasing tendency to integrate marital therapy and sex therapy into one profession. The rationale is that a counselor trained to deal with the total family has the flexibility to understand multidimensional problems. For some couples, the major dimension may be sex per se; for others, role expectations or personality mismatch may be more important, and in turn could interfere with sexual performance.

A drawback to the most practical therapeutic approaches, however, is the fact that they are designed to cure existing problems rather than to prevent them. Even if a sufficient number of reputable practitioners could be trained, the percentage of couples with various sexual and marital adjustment problems would remain high. Therefore, to be of maximal individ-

---

[21]Joseph LoPiccolo, "The Reunification of Sexual and Marital Therapy." Plenary session presentation, National Council of Family Relations, New Orleans, November 1989.

ual and societal value, programs aimed at reducing sexual discord must embody a preventive philosophy.

THE MARRIAGE-MANUAL APPROACH

Marriage manuals are generally small, inexpensive books or booklets that advise married couples on the fine points of sexual adjustment. Dozens of such books are for sale in stores and on newsstands, and although they vary widely in content, these books generally view the "past" as the scapegoat for current sexual problems. Because the past is regarded as "producing a very inhibited, nonliberated view of sexuality," it is up to the couple to throw off the shackles and to participate as fully (and as often) as possible in a wide variety of sexual activities. In short, as Brissett and Lewis explain, the message is one of liberation. "Permissive sex is in."[22]

As a means to achieve liberation, an ingenious variety of orgasm-attaining techniques, positions, and sexual "skills" are advocated and described—often in amazing detail. In fact, after an extensive investigation of the major marriage manuals, Brissett and Lewis entitled their article "The Big Toe, Armpits and Natural Perfume: Notes on the Production of Sexual Ecstasy."[23]

Moreover, if the recommended techniques are followed, the rewards are great—or at least so the manuals contend: "Sex keeps your weight down. It's good for your complexion. It keeps you young." "The sexually happy man gets a better job, more money, and a better house." "A sexually satisfied woman is a healthier, livelier person. . . . The eyes are clearer. Many of the psychosomatic ailments disappear. . . ."[24]

In recent years—as might have been predicted—marriage manuals have been criticized heavily. Even though sales of these manuals have run well into the millions, the truth is that sexual adjustment is much more than a simple game of genital skills. For example, the manuals do not take into consideration the great range of individual differences in human sex drive. Some individuals are highly sexed; others experience sexual desire infrequently. For the latter group, it is unlikely that recourse to erotic techniques would alter the basic sexual pattern.

Nor are the "rewards" as great as the marriage manuals would have us believe. Indeed, both husbands and wives bring a lifetime of experiential

---

[22]Dennis Brissett and Lionel Lewis, "The Big Toe, Armpits, and Natural Perfume: Notes on the Production of Sexual Ecstasy," in Leonard Cargan, ed., *Marriage and Family: Coping with Change* (Belmont, CA, Wadsworth Publishing Co., 1985), 76–88.

[23]Ibid.

[24]Ibid.

values to the marriage bed, and if these attitudes and beliefs are not in keeping with the techniques advocated in the manuals, it is possible that an attempt to apply new "skills" will do more harm than good.

In addition, many couples enjoy sexual intercourse even though the wife does not regularly experience orgasm. In this instance, the advice given in the marriage manuals—stressing a wide range of amatory techniques for attaining orgasm—may (1) cause the wife to feel that something is wrong with her sexuality and (2) engender feelings of inadequacy on the part of the husband.

A SOCIOLOGICAL APPROACH

Basic to any sociological approach is the premise that sexual adjustment, like so many other aspects of marriage, is a fairly complex phenomenon that cannot be solved by recourse to a few simple maxims. To begin with, the sociologist is highly aware of the existence of individual differences. Virtually all research surveys have revealed wide differences in sex drive, and a couple's understanding of such differences would seem to be prerequisite to their sexual compatibility.

Over and above the matter of individual differences, the sociologist also would consider sexual adjustment as linked inextricably with the total personal interaction of the two spouses. Sexual discord often is held up as the cause of marital unhappiness; all too seldom is it realized that marital difficulties may precede sexual maladjustment. If a husband drinks incessantly and is otherwise rude and inconsiderate, it is unlikely that his wife would show much sexual enthusiasm. The futility of the marriage-manual approach in such a case becomes obvious. It seems likely that the better a couple's all-around adjustment, the easier it will be to achieve sexual harmony. In any case, however, before attributing sexual incompatibility to strictly sexual factors, the sociologist would want to know more about the overall level of marital adjustment.

As mentioned above, women's orgasmic response is a controversial phenomenon. On the one hand, it is well established that some wives attain multiple orgasms during intercourse, a capability beyond that of their husbands. On the other, only about 63 percent of women achieve orgasm in more than half of their coital experiences.[25]

Darling and Davidson acknowledge that it is perfectly acceptable not to achieve orgasm consistently. Yet they found a large number of women who pretend to have an orgasm. These women, it seems, may be reacting to social expectations even in the privacy of their own bedrooms. Ironically,

---

[25]Carol A. Darling and J. Kenneth Davidson, "Enhancing Relationships: Understanding the Feminine Mystique of Pretending Orgasm," *Journal of Sex and Marital Therapy,* Fall 1986, 183.

not too long ago women were under pressure to pretend *not* to have reached an orgasm; the husband might worry that he was harming her health. Today he might worry that his performance is not meeting expected standards. Throughout both periods of history it seems that women have continued to adjust by feigning.

While there are a number of approaches to the problem of marital sex adjustment, most sociologists would be inclined to stress the advisability of research. Sex is no longer the hush-hush topic it used to be, and there is every reason to believe that, as time goes on, more and more worthwhile surveys will be undertaken. In turn, findings from these surveys should be of help to couples who have sexual problems. In the past, unfortunately, advice to couples has sometimes outstripped the factual information available at the time.

SUMMARY

The final word on marital adjustment has not yet been written. It is hoped that further research will clarify some of the developmental aspects of the subject. Meanwhile, couples should realize that marriage is a dynamic rather than a static relationship. It is not to be taken for granted. Yet we have observed that college students often work harder at making their courtship happy than at making their marriages a success.

The fact seems to be that spouses change, and their roles and outlook change. Unless both husband and wife make a conscious effort, they are likely to find that change has sent them in different directions. If they expect change and anticipate certain problems in role arrangements, most couples should be better prepared to live "happily ever after."

QUESTIONS

1. In your estimation, would our forebears have found it difficult to envision a chapter on husband-wife relationships? Explain your answer.

2. What is the resource theory of marital power? Has the theory been substantiated by research? Explain.

3. Role compatibility as a factor in marital adjustment is probably more important today than a generation ago. Why? Explain.

4. What is the significance of "night people" and "morning people" regarding marital adjustment? Explain, using real or hypothetical examples.

5. True equality has been difficult to attain in marriage. Why? What solutions would you propose?

6. If you were given the task of consulting with your state legislature on how to reduce spouse abuse, what would you propose? Be specific. Justify your proposal.

7. Research surveys over the past twenty years seem to show rather clearly that children tend to detract from, rather than contribute to, marital happiness. Why should this be so? After all, haven't Americans always cherished their children?

8. What is meant by the "marriage-manual approach" to sexual adjustment? Has this approach been successful?

9. What does the text mean by a "sociological approach" to sexual adjustment? What are some of the factors that a sociologist would consider?

10. How does paid work influence family functions in general? Consider the roles of husbands and of wives as participants in the paid labor force.

SELECTED READINGS

Atkinson, Jean, ed. *Journal of Family Issues*. Special issue on gender roles in the family, March 1987.

Daniels, Arlene Daplan. "Invisible Work." *Social Problems*, December 1987, 403–15.

Darling, Carol A., and J. Kenneth Davidson. "Enhancing Relationships: Understanding the Feminine Mystique of Pretending Orgasm." *Journal of Sex and Marital Therapy*, Fall 1986, 182–96.

deTurck, Mark A., and Gerald R. Miller. "The Effects of Husbands' and Wives' Social Cognition on Their Marital Adjustment, Conjugal Power, and Self-Esteem." *Journal of Marriage and the Family*, November 1986, 715–24.

Hansen, Gary L. "Reward Level and Marital Adjustment: The Effect of Weighing Rewards." *Journal of Social Psychology*, May 1987, 549–51.

Madden, Margaret E. "Perceived Control and Power in Marriage: A Study of Marital Decision Making and Task Performance." *Personality and Social Psychology Bulletin*, March 1987, 73–82.

Mirowsky, John, and Catherine E. Ross. "Belief in Innate Sex Roles: Sex Stratification versus Interpersonal Influence in Marriage." *Journal of Marriage and the Family*, August 1987, 527–40.

Ramu, G. N. "Marital Roles and Power: Perceptions and Reality in the Urban Setting." *Journal of Comparative Family Studies*, Summer 1988, 207–27.

Sorensen, Annette, and Sara McLanahan. "Married Women's Economic Dependency, 1940–1980." *American Journal of Sociology*, November 1987, 659–87.

South, Scott J. "Sex Ratios, Economic Power, and Women's Roles: A Theoretical Extension and Empirical Test. *Journal of Marriage and the Family*, February 1988, 19–31.

Trent, Katherine. "Sex Ratios, and Women's Roles: A Cross-National Analysis." *American Journal of Sociology*, March 1988, 1096–1115.

Zimmer, Dirk. "Does Marital Therapy Enhance the Effectiveness of Treatment for Sexual Dysfunction?" *Journal of Sex and Marital Therapy*, Fall 1987, 193–208.

Spouse Abuse

Anderson, C., and L. P. Rouse. "Intervention in Cases of Women Battering: An Application of Symbolic Interactionism and Critical Theory." *Clinical Sociology Review* 6, 1988. 209–23.

Campbell, J., and P. Alford. "The Dark Consequences of Marital Rape." *American Journal of Nursing,* July 1989, 946–49.

DeMaris, Alfred, and Jann K. Jackson. "Batterers' Reports of Recidivism after Counseling." *Social Casework: The Journal of Contemporary Social Work,* October 1987, 458–65.

Family Violence Bulletin. The University of Texas at Tyler.

Gelles, Richard J. *The Violent Home.* Newbury Park, CA: Sage Publications, 1987.

———— and Murray A. Straus. *Domestic Violence.* New York: Simon and Schuster, 1988.

Journal of Family Violence.

McNeely, R. L., and Gloria Robinson-Simpson. "The Truth about Domestic Violence: A Falsely Framed Issue." *Social Work,* November–December 1987, 485–90.

Straus, Murray A. "Family Violence." In *2001: Preparing Families for the Future,* edited by David H. Olson and Meredith Kilmer Hanson. Minneapolis: National Council on Family Relations, 1990, 26–27.

Williams, K., and R. Hawkins. "The Meaning of Arrest for Wife Assault." *Criminology,* January 1989, 163–81.

Chapter
14

Parent-Child Interaction

Insanity is hereditary. You get it from your children.

Lillian Holstein

During the long period that *Homo sapiens* has been on earth, one might think that parents would have discovered the best way to raise children. Obviously, however, this is not the case. Children are as difficult today as they ever were. Indeed, when conduct problems and delinquency rates are considered, it seems that our child-rearing procedures are less effective than formerly, although the use of other criteria might lead to a more optimistic conclusion. Nevertheless, the inexorable fact remains that children's desires and aims are often a far cry from those of adults, and it may be that this conflict of interests will never be resolved completely.

While the problems of child rearing remain great, the present era has seen the rise of two interrelated phenomena that are new in every sense of the word. The first of these is the popularization of the belief that childhood experiences are the crucial determinants of adult personality. The formative years, as they are called, have come to be regarded as a personality mold. Psychiatrists and child guidance centers have reported an almost limitless number of case histories attesting to the needs and need deprivations of children. On the basis of these case histories as well as derivative child-centered theories of personality formation, thousands of books, pamphlets, and articles have been published, read, and widely discussed. As a result of this "parent education program," children's needs and problems, as well as techniques for the solution of these problems, have become an established part of the American ethos.

The second development has been the widespread and sustained interest in the study of children on the part of academicians. Anthropologists have surveyed child-rearing practices in other societies; sociologists have studied relationships between childhood experiences and delinquency, crime, alcoholism, and mental illness; psychologists have conducted empirical surveys on intelligence testing, rewards and punishments and motivation, as well as on the personality manifestations stemming from specific child-raising techniques. Courses in child psychology and in the sociology of child development, based largely on the implications of these studies, have come to be offered in many of our colleges.

Public and professional interest in child study shows no sign of waning. On the contrary, interest in the subject seems to be increasing. As students of the family, therefore, let us examine the phenomenon of childhood, which has so fascinated our culture.

HISTORICAL BACKGROUND

In view of the current interest in child study, it is difficult to realize that childhood was not considered a very important phase of life throughout most of human history. Medieval painters, for example, made no attempt to portray childhood. If a scene called for children, the artist simply painted adult men and women on a reduced scale. This miniaturizing of adults was due not to the artist's incompetence, but to the fact that childhood had no place in the medieval world.

By the seventeenth and eighteenth centuries, the philosophy of treating children as little adults had long since passed. Children were recognized as children. The problem was how to prepare them for adulthood. To this end, child rearing was geared to obedience, industriousness, and dependability. In reading letters and documents of the colonial period, one is struck by the repeated use of terms like "obedient," "faithful," "hard-working," "humble," "earnest," and "God-fearing."

Colonial parents demanded much from their children and socialized them according to the demands of an agricultural, primary-group society. When the children were too young for hard labor, they were required to study and help their parents around the house.[1] Parents in colonial times needed their children and wanted them to stay close to home. Children's labor was needed, as was their assistance in old age. The discipline and

---

[1]John F. Walzer, "A Period of Ambivalence: Eighteenth-Century American Childhood: in Lloyd de Mause, ed., *The History of Childhood* (New York: Peter Vedrick Books, 1988), 357.

obedience that parents imposed served to establish close ties and lasting interdependence.

In the eighteenth century, according to Walzer, the idea that children should have a life of their own came into being.[2] This view conflicted with the traditional demands of family interdependence and children's deference to their parents. Over the years, it seems that this ambivalence has been replaced with the pursuit of individual happiness. Today demands on children are not so great. Parents do not expect their children to live nearby, to work for the extended household, or even to provide them with security in old age.

As conditions changed and as the urban rather than the rural way of life came to dominate the American scene, child-rearing patterns also changed. Families became smaller, formal education increased in importance, the patriarchal nature of the family group changed, and discipline and respect for authority came to be something less than cornerstones of the good life. During the nineteenth century such changes came slowly. As late as World War I the adage "Children should be seen and not heard" was still fairly common, even though fewer and fewer children seemed to abide by it.

After World War II, however, child-rearing practices changed rapidly—for the better, according to some; for the worse, according to others. But for better or for worse, the results of the change were to be felt for many decades. This change in the philosophy of child training was not caused by any single event or by any single person; yet if one person were to be selected as having the most lasting influence that individual probably would be Sigmund Freud.

THE FREUDIAN IMPACT

More than any of his predecessors, Freud emphasized the importance of infancy and childhood as determinants of adult personality. Working with his own patients, Freud was convinced not only that neuroses were rooted in sexual conflicts, but also that the roots of these conflicts developed very early in life. In the first stage, said Freud, the infant achieves sexual pleasure from the exploration of the erogenous zones (oral, anal, genital) of his or her body—hence the term "autoeroticism." By the age of five these explorations become localized in the genital region. During the first stage the infant also acquires pleasure from being nursed by the mother, and Freud held that this, too, is a sexual gratification; in fact, he believed that this physical and emotional contact developed into a love attachment for the mother. Such an attachment, however, is prohibited by a strong societal taboo against incest. Further, because the father loves the mother, the child

---

[2]Ibid., 374.

In the latency stage of child development, the son comes to identify with his father. (*Lea, Omni-Photo Communications*)

is confronted with a rival; hence the emergence of the Oedipus complex, in which the male child loves his mother and hates his father.

By the age of six or so, society's dictates having won out, the Oedipal phase gives way to a second stage, one of so-called latency. During this period between infancy and puberty, the child's love attachment for the mother is severed. The male child comes to identify himself with his father, and spends much of his time with companions of his own sex. The onset of adolescence marks the beginning of the third stage, a period when sexual interest reemerges and is directed toward members of the opposite sex.

Freud contended that both sexes normally pass through these three stages, but that in individual cases the normal process may not occur; that is, a person may fixate on the second stage and may develop a degree of homosexuality or a boy who is rejected by his playmates may regress to the comforting relationship he once had with his mother (first stage) and later on in life may have serious difficulty in adjusting to girls. Freud was open about the fact that his theories were based on sex, although in some of his writings sex was defined in general as well as specific terms.

As might be expected, Freud's beliefs shocked both laypeople and scien-

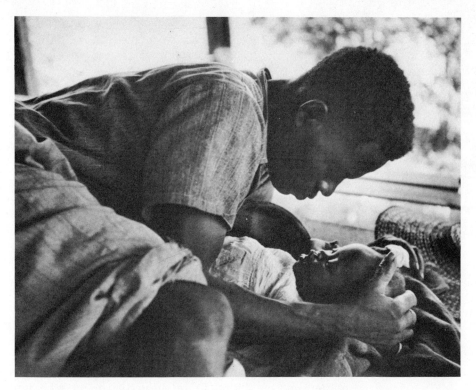

In the Freudian scheme the child's personality is being molded in infancy. (*George Silk, Life Magazine,* © *1951 Time Inc.*)

tists. Reared in the Victorian tradition, neither group at first could accept the view that infants and children had a sexual nature. Nevertheless, because of the heated controversy engendered by Freudian theory, the entire concept of childhood—particularly childhood sexuality—was subjected to much closer examination.

One of the cornerstones of Freudian theory is the reality of the unconscious, a powerful force that constitutes the mainspring of so many human actions. Between the conscious and the unconscious there is likely to be strife. The following case history, for example, seems to illustrate the Freudian point of view:

> Albert T., a young man of 26, was under intensive psychiatric treatment, having complained of a number of disturbing symptoms. Among the latter were recurrent nightmares, excessive perspiring, and the compulsion to wash his hands 15 or 20 times a day. When asked why he washed his hands so often, he replied that the city air contained poisonous microbes.
>
> Psychoanalysis revealed that when Albert was 15 years old his father had caught him masturbating in the bedroom. Overcome with shame and embarrassment, he had succeeded in "forgetting" the incident. Not long after-

ward, however, his hands began to appear dirty to him, and he took to washing them at frequent intervals. About the same time he began to have nightmares, and for no apparent reason would perspire heavily during the day.

The psychoanalyst was successful in his treatment of Albert. After a series of psychoanalytic sessions, the masturbatory incident which had been pushed back to the unconscious was brought to light, and with the recall of the traumatic boyhood scene with his father, the above-mentioned symptoms disappeared.

In cases such as this, Freud and his followers routinely subjected the patient to a lengthy and intensive soul-searching, or psychoanalysis. The purpose was to bring the unconsciously rejected event, usually sexual, back to conscious experience, thereby bridging the gap in the divided personality. Thus in Albert's case the disturbing symptoms disappeared with the recall of the precipitating experience. Generally speaking, Freudians contend that a person is abnormal, or neurotic, to the extent that his or her unconscious mind controls the conscious mind. The task of the psychoanalyst is to help rid the patient of this unconscious control.

The importance of infancy and childhood in the Freudian scheme of things now becomes clear. During these formative years sexual conflicts tend to arise, acceptance or rejection by parents is felt most keenly, and the child's personality is molded in almost a literal sense. This being the case, Freud warned implicitly against the overuse of punishment with children.

Aware of the possible effects of so-called traumatic experiences during infancy and childhood, Freud argued in many of his writings that parental love was a vital ingredient in the child's personality development. And although Freud certainly cautioned that there was a distinct danger in loving one's children excessively, his writings led to a concern over too little love rather than too much. Some of Freud's more ardent followers, in fact, tended to reject the notion of discipline altogether and to maintain that there was no such thing as loving a child too much.

In passing, it should be mentioned that Freudian teaching received unexpected support from the doctrines of John B. Watson and John Dewey, exponents of behaviorism and progressive education, respectively. Dewey's philosophy led to many of the modern concepts of education, with emphasis on personality development and training of the "whole child" rather than on discipline, drill, and the inculcation of the three R's. Watson's behaviorism focused sociopsychological attention on the conditioning process, which hitherto had been the province of Pavlov and his followers. In *Behaviorism,* Watson made the following claim:

> Give me a dozen healthy infants, well-formed, and my own specified world to bring them up in and I'll guarantee to take any one at random and train him to become any type of specialist I might select—doctor, lawyer, artist, merchant-chief, and yes, even beggarman and thief, regardless of his talents, penchants, tendencies, abilities, vocations, and race of his ancestors.[3]

---

[3]John B. Watson. *Behaviorism* (New York: W. W. Norton, 1924), 82.

Yet many of Dewey's and Watson's ideas have failed to stand the test of time, whereas Freudian doctrine is still in vogue and, however debatable, continues to exert a powerful influence on American thought.

RESEARCH FINDINGS ON FREUDIAN THEORY

It was predictable that such a revolutionary theory as Freud's would be sharply challenged. Taken collectively, Freudian contentions regarding the unconscious, the Oedipus complex, latency periods, dream analysis, the primacy of sexual factors, the etiology of mental illness, and the importance of infancy in personality development gave rise to unparalleled intellectual cries of anguish. Long and bitter academic arguments ensued—and the end is not in sight. The Freudian controversy, however, will be solved not by rhetorical arguments but by research, and in this area there is factual information to report.

If Freudian theory is valid, it follows that infants raised by Freudian precepts—breast-feeding, gradual weaning, "mothering," and late toilet training—will manifest superior personality traits as they grow older as compared with children reared by non-Freudian methods. Yet many studies now have been carried out—studies that involve the comparison of children reared by Freudian and by non-Freudian methods—and the results have failed rather consistently to support Freudian precepts.

The researchers, in this instance, admittedly have a difficult task. Parents often are inconsistent in their child-rearing practices; that is, they may use permissiveness in some situations and restrictiveness in others. Also, personality is not easy to measure. Children who show one type of result when tested at one stage of development may evidence different results when tested at a later stage. For these and other reasons, research on the subject continues.

Thus far, in spite of the case history–based claims of his followers, Freud's child-rearing theories have not stood up under empirical investigation, and no amount of talk can change this fact. On the other hand, anti-Freudians are wrong when they claim that Freudian theory has been disproved. Difficult as it seems for experts to take a neutral stand on the matter, the fact is that Freudian theory has not been disproved. It simply has not been proved.

Parents who wish to follow Freudian precepts have a perfect right to do so, in spite of the lack of empirical validation. Virtually all of our behavioral philosophy is based on faith rather than on science, and there is no reason to make an exception of child training. In fact, many clinicians who deal with problem children continue to make effective use of Freudian theory, at least as reported in individual case histories.

One could argue that over and above the validity or nonvalidity of his theories, Freud performed a service in focusing attention on the formative years of childhood. Yet if the formative years are not so important in personality formation, psychiatrists and social scientists have spent an unwarranted amount of time in studying childhood at the expense of other areas, such as the role of adolescence and young adulthood in personality development.

There have been few more original thinkers than Sigmund Freud, and ultimately many of his theoretical constructs may be vindicated. It is unfortunate for all concerned that his theories tended to split the intelligentsia into two opposing camps, with claims and counterclaims far outweighing objective analyses. The behavioral sciences are still in their infancy; theoretical contributions are needed badly, as are the concomitant empirical checks. There is no place in the present scheme of things for factional strife of the kind that catches the public in the middle.

THE CHILD-REARING "PENDULUM"

In the absence of a validated system of child rearing, American practices seem to operate according to fads and cycles. For example, in 1914 the government published the first edition of *Infant Care,* a book that has gone through many editions and has sold tens of millions of copies. As the various editions have been published, however, the advice given to mothers has changed remarkably.

In the 1920s, thumb sucking and masturbation were regarded as dangerous impulses that must be curbed. As late as 1938 the book showed a stiff cuff that would stop the baby from bending its arm, thus preventing thumb sucking. Yet in 1942, readers were told that masturbation and thumb sucking were harmless. In 1951, the caution was voiced that too much pampering might result in the child's becoming a "tyrant." At the present time, *Infant Care* takes remarkably permissive attitudes toward such subjects as weaning, toilet training, masturbation, feeding, and discipline of preschool children.[4]

Professional advice may change even before most parents have had a chance to consider it. Parental behavior moves at its own pace, sometimes in contradiction to current advice. For example, most experts advise parents not to spank their children because corporal punishment seems to be an ineffective method of teaching children how to behave. This message, though, either has not reached most parents, or else parents refuse to accept the experts' advice. Perhaps they are wary of the ebbs and flows of professional advice; parents tend to rely on child-rearing techniques passed down by the previous generation.

Reasons for the Pendulum

The reason that child-rearing advice varies—both from one period to another and from one magazine or book to another—is that a comprehensive and valid body of knowledge about children has failed to materialize. Much research

---

[4]Penelope Leach, *Your Baby and Child* (New York: Alfred A. Knopf, 1989), 463.

Child-rearing techniques that might be effective for one child might have totally different effects on another. (*T. Hopper, Woodfin Camp*)

has been conducted—the bimonthly *Child Development Abstracts* summarizes more than 1000 studies a year—and it is almost certain that the quantity will increase. Yet the researcher is faced with some formidable obstacles:

1. Obviously, all children are different. They differ not only in temperament, aptitude, and intelligence but also in their rates of physical and mental maturation. Child-rearing techniques that might be effective for one child might have a totally different effect on another.

2. In parallel fashion, parents also differ from one another; methods employed successfully by some parents might be ineffective when used by others. Statistical studies often tend to gloss over such differences.

3. It is often difficult to experiment with children. Researchers hardly can expect parents to lend their children for certain experimental purposes. In studies dealing with the effect of rewards and punishments, for example, is it reasonable to ask parents to let their children take part in an experiment (especially as part of the "punishment" group) that conceivably might have some effect on the youngster's personality?

4. Certain kinds of child study can be carried on best in the home or in a normal family setting; in fact, some investigators believe that one should not attempt to study the child without also studying the larger family group. Yet two difficulties are involved: (1) how to gain access to families that, let us say, were selected by random sampling methods; and (2) if access is gained, how does the researcher conduct the investigation or observation without disrupting the very thing that is supposed to be observed? This dilemma has not been resolved.

5. In the final analysis what criteria should be used in evaluating the results of specific child-rearing techniques? Shouldn't group welfare be considered as well as the child's own? Certain permissive techniques might well be conducive to need gratification on the part of the individual involved, yet might play havoc with overall group welfare. This particular problem has been noted by sociologists, but in all likelihood it will be some time before consensus is reached.

The above difficulties have been mentioned simply to give the reader an idea of the kinds of problems involved in child-training research. The list is by no means exhaustive. In view of the depth and the extent of the problems, however, one might expect that published advice on "how to raise your child" would be scarce and would be treated with skepticism by the public. Paradoxically, however, just the opposite is true. Popular writing on Your Child has reached flood proportions, and all the signs suggest that the public is eager for more.

PARENT EDUCATION

Parent education—the attempt to influence parental behavior through the spoken or written word—is hardly new. The first parents' meeting dates from 1815, in Portland, Maine; *Mother's Magazine* was first published in 1832. The first White House Conference on Child Welfare was held in 1909, and the Children's Bureau was founded in 1912.[5] In the ensuing decades, child-rearing information has been channeled through newspaper articles and columns, magazines, books, monographs and pamphlets, radio and television programs, study groups, child guidance centers, medical and nursing personnel, lectures, filmstrips, school offerings, and other educational programs.

It is easy to demonstrate that large volumes of child-rearing material are beamed regularly at a very large number of parents. The key question is this: "Does it have any value?" The issue has been debated intensively.

On the negative side, it is argued that parent education cannot be effec-

---

[5]James Croake and Kenneth Glover, "A History and Evaluation of Parent Education," *The Family Coordinator*, April 1977, 151–58.

tive in the absence of a scientific body of knowledge about child rearing. It is also argued that much so-called parent education stems not from researchers but from persons who lack awareness about current research.

On the positive side, it is argued that in spite of the paucity of factual information, the tremendous flow of educational material has served to focus attention on a most vital area. In this respect, the public has become acquainted with at least some of the research that has been conducted in the child-rearing field.

Parents also have had an opportunity to hear what some of the leading scholars are saying with respect to controversial child-study areas. This opportunity, in turn, probably encourages parents to discuss their child-training programs with one another and thus perhaps to gain a measure of self-confidence.

It is also likely that some of the written or spoken advice has helped certain parents by giving them insights that they might not have attained otherwise. Many parents who read newspaper or magazine articles dealing with child training adopt the "if the shoe fits, wear it" philosophy. In addition, it is not writers or counselors but *parents* who raise children. No one forces the parents to accept written or spoken advice; if they do so, they act of their own free will.

Arguments aside, the research findings on the effectiveness of parent education are moderately encouraging, but many questions about child rearing remain. Furthermore, much advice given to parents remains intuitive rather than scientific. "The pendulum of social change perhaps will swing once more in response to new ideas and feelings about what children need to learn and what parents need to know in caring for them."[6]

All things considered, there is room for guarded optimism with respect to the parent education movement. Admittedly, our fund of knowledge about child rearing has not grown as fast as parent educators would have liked. At the same time, if the public had to wait until a scientific body of child-rearing knowledge appeared, they would face a long wait indeed. In the meantime, it seems reasonable to familiarize parents with the results of the research that is being undertaken. Viewed in this light, most of today's child-rearing information probably would compare favorably with the advice offered in a variety of other behavioral areas.

CHILD ABUSE

One of the problems that could be reduced through more and better parent education is child abuse. Each year more than two million children are reported to authorities by teachers, neighbors, relatives, health professionals,

---

[6]Jerry J. Bigner, *Parent-Child Relations: an Introduction to Parenting,* 2d ed (New York: Macmillan, 1985), 438.

and others who suspect that a child has been abused physically or sexually.[7] Although only 40 percent of the reported cases are confirmed, other incidents go unreported. Regardless of how we interpret the statistics, the overall problem of child abuse remains formidable.

This problem has deep historical roots, but whether maltreatment is greater today than in the past is debatable. Furthermore, societal definitions of maltreatment have changed; what is considered abuse today might have been viewed in the past as necessary punishment. Our views of children also have changed. We no longer expect youngsters to toil in the fields or in factories. At one time, child labor was glorified and stiff discipline was enforced according to the dictum "Spare the rod and spoil the child." On balance, it seems that children are treated much better today than in earlier times.[8]

One reason for the perpetuation of maltreatment in modern times is the difficulty of breaking the cycle of violence transmitted from generation to generation.[9] Parents who were abused as children tend to repeat that aggression in dealing with their own children. Among many abusing parents, corporal punishment is more or less expected behavior. Teaching such individuals the dangers of their violence might do much to break the cycle of violence.

Another reason for maltreatment of children may be the inadequacy of state laws. Historically, beating children was not considered a crime. From Roman times through the early American colonial period parents actually had a legal right to execute their children for serious disobedience. Although such rights no longer exist, severe corporal punishment remained a legally acceptable form of child punishment.

Today most states have enacted criminal statutes that specifically prohibit "cruel treatment or intentional or willful infliction of actual or potential harm."[10] Violators of these statutes can be prosecuted and even jailed. Not all states, however, have enacted child-protection statutes. Even those that have done so generally do not go far enough in trying to bring the culpable parties to justice.

Arguing that our children need more protection, Hudson proposed a uniform statute to be considered for enactment by all states. This statute reads as follows:[11]

---

[7]Katherine M. Jamieson and Timothy J. Flanagan, eds., *Sourcebook of Criminal Justice Statistics—1988*. U.S. Department of Justice, Bureau of Justice Statistics (Washington, DC: Government Printing Office, 1989), 324.

[8]Anthony Synnott, "Little Angels, Little Devils," in Gerald Handel, ed., *Childhood Socialization* (New York: de Gruyter, 1988), 25–43.

[9]Joan McCord, "Parental Behavior in the Cycle of Aggression," *Psychiatry,* January 1988, 14–23. See also Philip G. Ney, "Transgenerational Child Abuse," *Child Psychiatry and Human Development,* Spring 1988, 151–68.

[10]Susan Smith Hudson, "The Broadening Scope of Liability in Child Abuse Cases," *Journal of Family Law* 27(3), 1989, 700–11.

[11]Ibid., 712–13.

Abuse of children. Any parent or other person who has the permanent or temporary care, custody or control of a child under the age of eighteen years who causes abuse to such minor child shall be guilty of a felony.

Liability of nonperpetrator of abuse. Any parent or other person who has the permanent or temporary care, custody, or control of a child under the age of eighteen years who has knowledge or reason to know that the minor child is being abused by another person but who takes no action to protect the child from the foreseeable risk of harm shall be guilty of a felony of the same class as the principal perpetrator.

Legal solutions cannot solve all of our child abuse problems. Explanations for the occurrence of child abuse are still under investigation. Social scientists have long known that severity of child abuse is associated with such factors as social isolation, mental health problems, lower income, and father's unemployment.[12] These factors may be critical when it comes to understanding child abuse and in planning for its reduction.

THE PERMISSIVE VERSUS THE RESTRICTIVE PHILOSOPHY

Although child abuse is a serious matter, it is unlikely that many college students will find themselves *personally affected* by the problem. College students, as future parents, are much more likely to be involved with the problem of how much freedom to grant their children and how much discipline is necessary. This is an extremely pertinent area; one wishes that definitive research evidence were available to be used as a guide. In the absence of such evidence, parents must rely largely on their own experience and common sense, plus such assistance from the authorities as is deemed reasonable. The following brief account is presented for the purpose of describing the problem rather than of solving it.

The Permissive School

Proponents of the permissive school of thought lean toward the view that the formative years are crucial for personality development. They believe that the child has certain needs or "rights," such as the need to be attended, to be loved, and to be accorded freedom of self-expression. Particular stress is placed on the child's need to feel secure; it is held that this feeling is best engendered through fondling, caressing, and ample physical contact with the mother. Physical punishment is to be avoided at all stages of child growth. Dr. Benjamin Spock writes as follows:

In the olden days, most children were spanked, on the assumption that this was necessary to make them behave. In the twentieth century, as parents and

---

[12]James A. Rosenthal, "Patterns of Reported Child Abuse and Neglect," *Child Abuse and Neglect* 12, 1988, 263.

professionals have studied, children can be well-behaved, cooperative, and polite without ever having been punished physically—or in other ways. I have known hundreds of such children myself, and there are countries in the world where physical punishment is unknown.[13]

Proponents of the permissive school do not reject all discipline, but they emphasize love, affection, understanding, and the satisfaction of the child's needs rather than the inculcation of respect for authority.

On the basis of common observation, most American parents seem to be rather permissive in child-raising practices. Whether this permissiveness reflects the bias of the "experts" or whether—as some writers have contended—Americans simply are soft-hearted is a matter of debate.

If Americans are indeed soft-hearted, they are not alone in the world. It may come as a surprise to learn that in many ways the Russians are quite permissive in their child care. It is not unusual for a Russian mother to spoon-feed her child until the latter is four or five years old!

Sweden took what many considered to be an extremely permissive step in 1979, when it passed a law prohibiting parents from spanking or cuffing their children or otherwise causing pain as a method of punishment. In the same year, a government committee proposed a law that under certain circumstances would permit children to divorce their parents!

The Restrictive School

Those who believe in a nonpermissive, or restrictive, philosophy of child rearing hold that such practices as extensive fondling, mothering, and caressing tend to result in a spoiled child. They believe that permissiveness, by definition, encourages a lack of respect for the rights of others and hence in the long run is detrimental to the best interests of society. Proponents of the restrictive school believe in furthering the child's personality development, but they feel strongly that personality formation hinges not so much on physical affection and freedom of self-expression as on the development of character and self-respect. The latter traits, it is held, can be developed most successfully through the cultivation of discipline, respect for authority, awareness of property rights, and other aspects of group order. Restrictive parents thus would be less reluctant to impose physical punishment than would permissive parents.

Advocates of the restrictive approach do not reject parental affection as an insignificant factor—any more than the permissive school rejects discipline—but in regard to *emphasis* it is held that discipline and respect warrant more consideration than do the physical manifestations of parental feeling. Restrictive parents, in other words, would be inclined to express love

---

[13]Benjamin Spock and Michael B. Bothenberg, *Dr. Spock's Baby and Child Care* (New York: Pocket Books, 1985), 408.

for their children by imbuing them with an awareness of responsibility and order rather than by catering to immediate needs. Some extremists reject entirely any display of physical affection or open manifestation of love, and instead try to "force" their children through the various stages of development, but this position is not typical of restrictive philosophy.

In the last generation or so, the restrictive approach to child rearing has not been much in evidence. Yet in the past few years—as juvenile crime has increased and youthful conduct has drawn more and more criticism— some calls have been made for a more restrictive approach. For example, in *Toughlove* the authors discourage permissiveness in dealing with misbehaving children. They offer sociological and cultural solutions for discipline problems, in opposition to the almost exclusively psychological orientation of the last generation. They justify the change in emphasis this way:

> All too often attempts at psychological solutions actually help feed and maintain the problem. Most psychological solutions rely on open, honest, and cooperative communication. Dependence on such modes of interaction enables insincere, manipulative people to continue their destructive behavior while they appear to be making changes. . . .
>
> First the family, with the support of others, must stop the destructive behavior by making a stand and precipitating a crisis for that young person. . . . Taking a stand and sticking to it is what makes *toughlove* tough for parents to do. It's scary and new. It's what makes *toughlove* controversial, but it's what makes *toughlove* work.[14]

An Assessment

Readers may ask, "Is it really necessary for parents to follow one school of thought or another? Why not combine the best of both philosophies?" In practice, it is likely that many parents do, or try to do, just that. The real danger in child rearing lies not in the choice of philosophy but in the application of extreme measures of either school of thought.

The child who is not only loved but is pampered and coddled, whose need satisfactions become the dominant element of parental action, and whose misdeeds remain consistently unpunished—this child may well become *persona non grata* to both children and adults. Such a child has received little in the way of preparation for responsible adulthood, however much love was bestowed by the parents. Childhood needs are important, but such needs are not the center of the universe, and the child who does not learn this fact at home is likely to suffer some hard knocks later on. Character, responsibility, respect for the feelings of others—all of these elements are necessary ingredients of personality. Parents whose permissive-

---

[14]Phyllis and David York, and Ted Wachtel, *Toughlove* (Toronto: Bantam Books, 1983), 85–86.

Of all the social roles, it would be difficult to contend that any are more important than the role of the parent. (*Tartsanyi, EKM, Nepenthe*)

ness allows them to disregard these factors would seem to be doing their children a disservice.

On the other hand, a child who has been reared in an atmosphere where obedience, discipline, and respect for the rights of others are stressed at the *expense* of physical love and demonstrated affection also may find himself or herself handicapped in a society where emotional warmth, expressiveness, and love are cherished values. Children who have been disciplined too severely and from whom physical displays of love and attention have been withheld are not likely as adults to look back with fondness on their childhood memories. If, as the Freudians maintain, emotional security depends largely on the physical love and affection received in childhood, the withholding of such love certainly would have adverse effects on adult personality structure.

In terms of the permissive-restrictive controversy—a debate that perhaps has aroused social scientists more than parents—no one can say with certainty just where the emphasis, if any, should fall. In the absence of more research information, perhaps the safest course for parents to follow is the middle of the road.

SEX EDUCATION

It is ironic that as birth rates outside of marriage are increasing among young teenagers, and as the number of Americans with AIDS may soon exceed 350,000 a year,[15] resistance to sex education remains strong in so

---

[15]John W. Wright, *The Universal Almanac 1990* (Kansas City: Universal Press Syndicate Company, 1989), 222.

many areas. Even those individuals who agree on the desirability of such programs are likely to disagree on the content.

Historically speaking, neither the church nor the school has shown much enthusiasm for the subject of sex education. In theory, at least, instruction in sexual and reproductive matters was the province of the home. Although no explicit policy was involved, children presumably were instructed in the "facts of life" by their parents.

It was evident, however, that in practice one of two things happened: (1) by the time the parents felt that the children were old enough, the latter already had received a variety of sexual information from dubious sources; or (2) because of embarrassment or the lack of an adequate vocabulary, parents simply ignored the topic of sex education altogether, trusting that the children would somehow acquire the necessary information from books, biology classes, or other competent sources.

Research evidence has confirmed this picture. Many surveys—from the 1940s to the 1990s—have revealed that American youth are ill-informed on topics of sex and reproduction. As the present writers can attest, this inadequacy extends to the college as well as to the noncollege population.

It appears that a large proportion of American youths are not only poorly informed on sexual matters, but also that much so-called sex education is of the "informal" variety. In brief, sex "education" comes too often from the street and involves the use of obscene language. As a result, the whole concept of sex in America has acquired lewd connotations—as evidenced by the hush-hush attitude in the home, pornographic inscriptions in public places, the snickering attitude toward nude art forms, and the endless supply of "dirty" jokes.

Deploring this state of affairs, many educators have advocated a fairly comprehensive sex education program, starting in the lower grades and continuing through high school. Some schools already conduct programs that include such topics as human reproduction, menstrual cycles, sexual anatomy, and childbirth. The major Protestant denominations also have instituted a fairly elaborate sex education program. Additionally, in most sections of the country illustrated booklets and pamphlets are now available to parents, giving answers to sex questions that young people are likely to ask. But whether the advocated sex education program is offered in the home, the church, or the school, the goal is the same: to take sex out of the gutter and to frame it in such a way as to promote healthier and more wholesome attitudes.

Basic to this philosophy is the belief that when a child is old enough to ask a meaningful question, a meaningful answer should be provided. Thus when a child asks, "Where do babies come from?" (often at age four or five), the recommended answer is "From the mother's body." To the question "How did it get there?" an acceptable reply is "The father planted the seed." More involved questions can be answered effectively with the aid of published diagrams and pictures.

Educators probably are correct in maintaining that when a child asks a relatively simple question such as "Where do babies come from?" it is not necessary to involve the child in an elaborate discussion of the sexual and reproductive processes. Detailed explanations, supplemented by pictures and anatomical diagrams, should be reserved for a somewhat later age. It is contended, however, that by junior high school young people should possess (1) the basic facts concerning sex and reproduction, (2) a vocabulary large enough to converse and read intelligently on sexual topics, and (3) an attitude toward sex that is wholesome enough to permit reading or discussion of the subject without embarrassment or shame.

Considerations

Although there is nothing intrinsically wrong with a sex education program such as that outlined above, certain considerations are involved, and these should be examined before any conclusion is reached. For instance, do the available books, pamphlets, and filmstrips, while they present sexual material straightforwardly, also point out the community's prevalent attitude toward sex? Are today's teachers really qualified to impart sexual information to young children? Are sex education programs being offered at the expense of basic courses in English, science, and mathematics?

As might be imagined, the community at large often is divided on precisely these issues. It must be kept in mind that the entire boy-girl relationship has changed; it is no longer the formal, standoffish arrangement of yesteryear. Our culture, in effect, now encourages the sexes to associate at a very young age. Therefore, because of this free association and day-to-day contact, some parents have questioned the implementation of certain sex education programs.

Sociologically speaking, a balanced program of sex education, in which individual learning privileges are made to mesh with community goals, might well prove advantageous to all concerned. A shortsighted program, in which the interests of one group are stressed at the expense of others, might prove less effective in the long run than no program at all. Much would depend on the way the undertaking was designed and administered. Therefore, before a specific sex education program is adopted, it would seem only reasonable to determine whether all interests—the children's, the parents', and the community's—are represented adequately.

SUMMARY

Of all the social roles, none is more important than that of the parents. It is they who have the major responsibility of preparing children for adulthood. Parents inculcate values and teach basic skills without which the child would face insurmountable difficulties.

We have shown in this chapter that a controversy still exists in our society over what constitutes the proper parental role. On the one hand, we find parents who border on extreme permissiveness; on the other, those who believe in the old adage "spare the rod and spoil the child." The majority of parents, though, try to find some middle ground where they can provide guidance, discourage delinquent behavior, and at the same time avoid physical or emotional abuse of their children. Most sociologists would agree that appropriate child-rearing practices fall within the middle range.

QUESTIONS

1. "In the short space of a generation or two we have become a child-centered society, and there is little indication that the situation will change." Discuss the reasons and the rationale behind this statement.

2. How did the concept of childhood in the Middle Ages differ from (a) that of the colonial period and (b) that of modern times?

3. Speaking generally, what was the Freudian conception of infancy and childhood? Why was the so-called Freudian impact so great?

4. What have been the results of empirical research designed to test the validity of Freudian child-rearing theory? Have the results tended to prove Freudian precepts, to disprove them, or neither? What are the practical implications of this type of research?

5. What is meant by the child-rearing "pendulum"? What are the reasons for the pendulum? What would be needed, in your opinion, to stop the motion of the pendulum?

6. What is meant by the term *parent education*? What do the various surveys show regarding the effectiveness of parent education? What can be said about the quality of these surveys?

7. Think about the nature and extent of child abuse in the United States. Sociologically speaking, what do you suggest as a solution to this problem?

8. What are the basic sociophilosophical differences between the permissive and the restrictive schools of thought on child rearing? Which side do you lean toward? Why?

9. *Sex education* is a term that seems constantly to be in the headlines. What does the term actually mean? Why does the subject give rise to divided opinion in so many communities?

10. What are the advantages of a school-based sex education program? What are the drawbacks of such a program? After weighing the pros and cons, which side do you find yourself on? Defend your position.

SELECTED READINGS

de Mause, Lloyd. *The History of Childhood.* New York: Peter Bedrick Books, 1988.

Deyoung, Mary. "Disclosing Sexual Abuse: The Impact of Developmental Variables." *Child Welfare,* June 1987, 217–23.

Elkin, David. "The Child Yesterday, Today and Tomorrow." *Young Children,* May 1987, 6–11.

Fehrmann, Paul G., Tomothy Z. Keith, and Thomas M. Reimers. "Home Influence on School Learning: Direct and Indirect Effects of Parental Involvement on High Shcool Grades." *Journal of Educational Research,* August 1987, 330–37.

Felson, Richard B., and Natalie Russo. "Parental Punishment and Sibling Aggression." *Social Psychology Quarterly,* 51(1), 1988, 11–18.

Finkelhor, David, and Jill Korbin. "Child Abuse as an International Issue." *Child Abuse and Neglect,* 12, 1988, 3–23.

Handel, Gerald. *Childhood Socialization.* New York: de Gruyter, 1988.

Hoffeth, Sandra L. "Updating Children's Life Course." *Family Relations,* February 1985, 93–115.

Jackson, Robert Max. "The Reproduction of Parenting." *American Sociological Review,* April 1989, 215–32.

Kraizer, Sherryll Kerns, George E. Fryer, and Marilyn Miller. "Programming for preventing Sexual Abuse and Abduction: What Does It Mean When It Works?" *Child Welfare,* February 1988, 69–78.

Newcomer, Susan F., and Richard J. Undry. "Mothers' Influence on Sexual Behavior of Their Teenage Children." *Journal of Marriage and the Family,* May 1984, 477–85.

Peters, John F. "Adolescents as Socialization Agents to Parents." *Adolescence,* Winter 1985, 921–33.

Pittman, Joe F. "Predicting Parenting Difficulty." *Journal of Family Issues,* June 1989, 267–86.

Reilly, Thomas W., Doris R. Entwisle, and Susan G. Doering. "Socialization into Parenthood: A Longitudinal Study of the Development of Self-Evaluation." *Journal of Marriage and the Family,* May 1987, 295–308.

Rosenfeld, Alvin, and Dorothy Levine. "Discipline and Permissiveness." *Pediatrics in Review,* January 1987, 209–15.

Russell, Graeme, and Alan Russell. "Mother-Child and Father-Child Relationships in Middle Childhood." *Child Development* 58, 1987, 1573–85.

Seagull, Elizabeth A. W. "Social Support and Child Maltreatment: A Review of the Literature." *Child Abuse and Neglect* 11, 1987, 41–52.

Trickett, Penelope K., and Elizabeth J. Susman. "Parental Perceptions of Child-Rearing Practices in Physically Abusive and Nonabusive Families." *Developmental Psychology* 24 (F2), 1988, 270–76.

Wells, Edward L., and Joseph H. Rankin. "Direct Parental Controls and Delinquency." *Criminology* 26(2), 1988.

Wilson, Harriett. "Parental Supervision Reexamined." *British Journal of Criminology,* Summer 1987, 275–301.

Zuravin, Susan J., and Ronald Taylor. "The Ecology of Child Maltreatment: Identifying and Characterizing High-Risk Neighborhoods." *Child Welfare,* December 1987, 497–506.

Chapter 15

Divorce and Remarriage

Divorce is one of the most difficult topics the sociologist has to deal with. Like crime and poverty and other social problems, divorce—it seems—is always with us. And like most other social problems, divorce elicits different responses from different people, sociologists included.

As sociologists and lawyers are well aware, the controversy over divorce has been a long one—and it continues today. On the one hand, it is argued, couples surely have the right to end an unhappy marriage—without being subjected to a variety of legal shenanigans. On the other hand, it is argued that the state has a vital stake in preserving a strong marriage system, so that divorce regulations are not only proper but necessary.

In the research sphere, a moderate fund of information about divorce has now been established, although significant gaps remain. Material in this chapter should give the reader some idea of "knowns and the unknowns" and of the "controversial and noncontroversial."

DIVORCE IN THE UNITED STATES: AN OVERVIEW

The Divorce Rate

Up to the time of the Civil War, divorce was so infrequent that it was not considered a problem. As divorce laws became somewhat liberalized in the

Table 15.1   UNITED STATES DIVORCE RATE FOR SELECTED YEARS

Year	Number of divorces	Divorces per 1000 population
1867	9,937	0.3
1887	27,919	0.5
1900	55,751	0.7
1910	83,045	0.9
1920	170,505	1.6
1930	195,961	1.6
1940	264,000	2.0
1950	385,144	2.6
1960	393,000	2.2
1970	715,000	3.5
1975	1,026,000	4.8
1980	1,189,000	5.2
1985	1,187,000	5.0
1986	1,159,000	4.8
1987	1,157,000	4.8
1988	1,183,000	4.8

Source: See the monthly vital statistics reports issued by the National Center for Health Statistics.

mid-1800s, various groups, fearful that family values were being undermined, demanded the national divorce figures be tabulated. The U.S. Census Bureau published the initial tabulations in the year 1867. The total number of divorces in that year was 9937. The numbers and rates of divorce for selected years since then are shown in Table 15.1. This table indicates that by 1975 the number of divorces had surpassed one million per year. In recent years there has been one divorce for each two new marriages.[1]

On the basis of the latest figures provided by the National Center for Health Statistics, we estimate that about 40 percent of today's marriages will end in divorce. Price, in a recent report to the National Council on Family Relations, predicts that about two-thirds of new marriages may end in divorce.[2] The question is, will these high forecasts become a reality? Will the rates remain at current level, or will the rates even begin to decline?

On the one hand, the "transmission hypothesis" supports the argument

[1]John W. Right, *The Universal Almanac 1990* (Kansas City: Universal Press Syndicate Company, 1989), 239.

[2]Sharon J. Price, "Divorce," in David H. Olson and Meredith Kilmer Hanson, eds. (Minneapolis, MN: National Council on Family Relations, 1990), 30.

for the continued increase in the rate of divorce.[3] That is, children of divorced parents are more likely to experience divorce than are children from intact homes. If this is so, then the marital dissolution rates forecast by Price could become a reality sometime in the 1990s.

Looking at the long-range trend, Glick points to some counter forces that could inhibit the divorce rate or even reverse the trend.[4] He observed that the crude divorce rate peaked at 5.3 per 1000 population in 1979. Since then the rates stabilized slightly below 5.0 divorces per 1000 population. The forces that may continue to keep them there include "a relative scarcity of eligible women for marriage—frequently referred to as a 'marriage squeeze.'" Historically, this condition tends to promote marital stability.

Vital statistics show that the duration of marriage and rates of divorce depend in part on the age of brides and grooms. Those who marry under age thirty are more likely to divorce, but their marriages last longer. Those who marry after age thirty have fewer divorces, but they do not wait as long to divorce. For example, half of the divorces for women marrying before age thirty are granted by about seven and a half years of marriage. About half of the divorces to women who marry after that age are granted by six years of marriage.[5] It is true that some couples get divorced even after twenty-five or thirty years of marriage, but such cases are few.

Geographic Variations

Recent divorce statistics show wide discrepancies in divorce rates among states. Some people find it surprising, for example, that on the average, divorce rates are lowest in large, urbanized, northern states and that they are highest in more rural, southern, and western states. As shown in Table 15.2, divorce rates range from 2.9 per 1000 population in Massachusetts, 3.2 in Connecticut, and 3.3 in Pennsylvania to highs of 7.0 in Arkansas, 7.1 in Arizona and Oklahoma, and 14.1 in Nevada.

There are a number of explanations for this regional differential. For one thing, a "frontier" area is generally less conformist than the longer-established sections of the country. Differences in the ethnic, racial, and religious composition of an area also affect the rates. For example, one reason for the lower rates in Massachusetts and Louisiana is the large Catholic population. It must be admitted, though, that all the reasons for the regional divorce differentials are not known. If they were, we would be in a much better position to understand the problem of divorce causation.

---

[3]Norval D. Glenn, The Marriages and Divorces of the Children of Divorce. Series 9, Papers (The University of Texas at Austin, Population Research Center, 1987).

[4]Paul C. Glick and Sung-Ling Lin, "Recent Changes in Divorce and Remarriage," *Journal of Marriage and the Family,* November 1986, 745.

[5]Arthur J. Norton, "Current Trends in Marriage and Divorce among American Women," *Journal of Marriage and the Family,* February 1987, 9.

Table 15.2   SELECTED STATES WITH THE LOWEST AND THE
HIGHEST DIVORCE RATES IN 1988
(Rates are per 1000 Population)

State	Highest rates	State	Lowest rates
Nevada	14.1	South Dakota	3.7
Oklahoma	7.1	North Dakota	3.6
Arizona	7.1	Maryland	3.6
Arkansas	7.0	New York	3.6
Alaska	6.9	New Jersey	3.5
Wyoming	6.9	Wisconsin	3.5
Tennessee	6.5	Minnesota	3.5
Florida	6.3	Pennsylvania	3.3
Kansas	6.2	Connecticut	3.2
Idaho	6.0	Massachusetts	2.9

Source: National Center for Health Statistics, "Annual Summary of Births, Marriages, Divorces, and Deaths: United States, 1988." *Monthly Vital Statistics Report,* July 1989, 12.

Migratory Divorce

It is often thought that geographic differences in divorce rates are due to the easy residence requirements in certain states, but this is not so. True, Nevada has a divorce rate almost three times the national average, but that state grants fewer than 15,000 divorces per year, or slightly more than 1 percent of the total.

While Nevada is not the only "quickie" divorce state, the number of migratory divorces is perhaps no more than 1 or 2 percent of all American divorces. After all, divorce laws have become much more liberal, so that the necessity to "migrate" for a divorce is reduced. Also, the legal entanglement of an out-of-state divorce continues to act as a deterrent.

THE FAULT SYSTEM OF DIVORCE

This system has deep roots. It is based on the age-old guilt and innocence concept. It is also based on the theory of *contest;* that is, the belief that justice can best be attained by having each party present his own side of the case—through his attorney—to the best of his ability. However, any resemblance between a divorce "contest" and a genuine lawsuit is illusory.

Under the fault system, one of the spouses—usually the wife—sues for divorce on the legal ground that is most applicable, the "applicability" often being determined by the plaintiff's attorney. In court, the plaintiff assumes the role of the innocent and good spouse, while the partner is painted various shades of evil. Witnesses are seldom called, and rarely does the court delve into the realities of the situation. And, perhaps most important, the defendant usually is not in court to defend himself. He has been notified of the hearing, but he generally does not bother to attend. Since he is not in court to refute the allegations made by the wife, the court assumes him to be guilty and the divorce is granted.

Occasionally the divorce suit is a real contest, with both spouses represented by their lawyers. But in at least 90 percent of fault cases, the spouses have more or less agreed beforehand which party will be the plaintiff, what the grounds will be, and that the defendant will not contest the suit—despite the fact that such an agreement is prohibited by law.

The following is an example of court dialogue:

LAWYER: And as a result of this [cruelty] . . . how did you feel?

PLAINTIFF: I felt bad. It didn't bother my husband any, though.

LAWYER: I mean, how did it affect you physically? Did it affect your health?

PLAINTIFF: Oh, yes! My health got to be very bad.

LAWYER: Were you able to eat properly?

PLAINTIFF: No, I lost my appetite. *He* ate like a cannibal.

LAWYER: Were you able to get the proper amount of sleep at night?

PLAINTIFF: Not usually. Often I would toss and turn the whole night.

LAWYER: Did you lose any weight?

PLAINTIFF: Oh, yes, a great deal.

LAWYER: About how much did you weigh when you were married?

PLAINTIFF: About 125.

LAWYER: And what did you weigh when you were separated?

PLAINTIFF: Less than 105.

LAWYER: As a result of all this . . . did you experience any nervousness?

PLAINTIFF: Yes. I was jumpy all the time. I used to get headaches and crying spells.

LAWYER: Prior to your marriage did you ever have spells like this?

PLAINTIFF: No, never.

COURT: Actually how serious was the state of your health as a result of your husband's actions?

PLAINTIFF: Well, toward the end I had to go to my family doctor almost every week, my nerves were so bad.

COURT: Who is your family doctor?

PLAINTIFF: Dr. Ralph Peterman, on Goren Street.

COURT: What did Dr. Peterman say to you?

PLAINTIFF: He said I shouldn't live with my husband any more; that I should leave him before I was a total wreck.

Note that the lawyer in this instance is merely trying to establish that his client's life "has been made intolerable" insofar as the legal meaning of the term is concerned, and, of course, this process entails the plaintiff's cooperation. Note, also, that while the court inquired into the doctor's opinion, no attempt was made to have him put on the witness stand and actually testify. What it all amounts to is that throughout the entire range of American law, fault-divorce litigation is the only instance where the defendant does not try to keep the plaintiff from succeeding!

As might be imagined, fault divorce has come in for heavy criticism over the years. Sociologists, social workers, reporters, screenwriters—almost everyone, it seems, has castigated the "system." Especially heavy criticism has come from within the legal profession itself, the feeling being that the fault procedure—with its obvious hypocrisy—breeds disrespect for the law. Also, it is no secret that the divorce lawyer has had a rather low status within the legal profession, even though the status ascription may seem unwarranted. Nevertheless, most of the top lawyers in this country have traditionally shunned divorce cases. One result is that in many cities a large share of all divorce suits are handled by a small group of lawyers.

THE NO-FAULT SYSTEM

As conceived by its designers, the purpose of no-fault divorce was quite clear: to eliminate the adversary aspects, the hypocrisy, and the legal folderol that had characterized the typical divorce suit. Accordingly, California—the first state to act on the matter—coined the phrase "irremediable breakdown" to apply to those marriages that could be legally severed under the no-fault concept. If the matrimonial ties were irremediably broken, as affirmed by the spouses, then the court was obligated to dissolve the marriage.

No longer would it be necessary for one spouse to accuse the other of a real or imagined wrongdoing. No longer would it be necessary to attend protracted court hearings to answer inane questions. Even the pleadings were changed from the former *"Helen Brown v. George Brown"* to *"In re the marriage of George and Helen Brown."* As a matter of fact, the California legislators went so far as to abolish the term "divorce" entirely, substituting instead the term "dissolution of marriage." (Technically, at least, there is no divorce in California!)

In 1979, California liberalized its divorce law still further. As of January of that year, couples who had been married less than two years—and who had no children and little property—were able to procure a divorce without a lawyer, and without going to court. The only fee was a court cost of $50.

Following the pioneer efforts of California, most of the other states adopted no-fault provisions. Sometimes the phraseology was different: "irremediable breakdown," "irreconcilable differences," "irretrievable breakdown," "no reasonable likelihood" of preserving the marriage, and so on, but it looked as though (finally) the fault concept of divorce was on its way out in the United States.

Before long, however, certain cracks began to appear in the no-fault edifice—or at least so it seemed to the critics. For one thing, the divorce rate in states like California increased noticeably. It was charged that many persons were getting divorced for trivial reasons, and since most divorces involved minor children, the best interests of youngsters were being disregarded. There were also complaints about alimony and property settlements.

One of the chief criticisms of the no-fault system pertains to the matter of definition. Exactly what do terms like "irremediable breakdown" and "irreconcilable differences" mean? It is one thing when the couple *agree* that the differences have become insurmountable, but what happens when they *disagree*? According to California law, the general principle has been that, if one party wants the divorce, he or she is entitled to it—despite any objections by the other party.

Because of trepidations about the above points, many jurisdictions have a divorce system that embodies both fault and no-fault concepts.

CAUSES OF DIVORCE

In view of the billions of words that have been written about separation and divorce, can anything be said regarding causation? What, specifically, is the cause of so much marital breakup? Sociologists are asked this question almost as often as they are asked, "What causes crime?" Neither query, however, is likely to elicit much enthusiasm, for the social scientist does not think in terms of unilateral causation. From the sociological perspective, causes are generally thought of as interrelated links in a sequential chain of events, rather than as single factors. Thus, while the lawyer may state that sexual maladjustment is the chief cause of divorce, and while the social worker may blame juvenile crime on poor housing, the sociologist is quite skeptical of such pat explanations.

If divorce is really caused by sexual maladjustment, why is it that the divorce rate has increased as sex education programs have expanded? And if juvenile delinquency is caused by poor housing, how is it that delinquency has increased as housing conditions have improved? It does not take much deep thinking to realize that phenomena like crime and divorce cannot be explained by simple, isolated causes.

For the sake of convenience, let us examine divorce causation from two points of view, in keeping with the framework of the present volume—namely, the societal and the individual. Societal refers to those conditions associated with social and institutional structure such as economic conditions, technological change, religion, and so on. Individual factors would include the various physical, intellectual, and personality components that come into play whenever two or more people interact.

Societal Factors

Change must be explained by a variation rather than by a constant; or, to put it somewhat differently, one variation must always be explained in

Sociologists generally think of divorce as the result of interrelated links in a sequential chain of events. (© *1981, Hopker, Woodfin Camp*)

terms of another variation. And since divorce and separation rates seem to have risen not only in the United States but in the civilized world at large, it behooves us to list some of the widespread social changes that might be involved.

1. *Changing family functions.* As was explained in Chapter 1, whereas the economic, medical, educational, protective, religious, and recreational functions were once a built-in part of family life, over the years such functions have largely been taken over by outside agencies. The family, as a result, is less of a functional unit than formerly; hence, the reasons for keeping marriages intact are not so compelling as they once were.

2. *Casual marriages.* Parents no longer have the control over mate selection that they used to have. Marriages based on romantic love are more or less taken for granted. Hasty marriages are not infrequent, and youthful marriages are quite common. Some writers feel that this combination of changes has been reflected in a rising rate of marital dissolution.

3. *Jobs for women.* In an age when women were unfairly barred from jobs—and as a consequence were dependent on their husbands for economic support—the prospect of a divorce must have been a

rather grim one for wives. With the entrance of large numbers of women into the labor market, an important barrier to divorce was removed.

4. *Decline in moral and religious sanctions.* While the Catholic church still does not recognize divorce, most of the Protestant denominations have taken a more liberal view of the matter. Also, community opinion no longer represents the barrier of yesteryear. The stigma attached to divorce has largely, if not entirely, disappeared.

5. *The philosophy of happiness.* Whereas marriages were formerly held in place, so to speak, by functional and institutional bonds, modern couples have come to think of happiness as the principal matrimonial goal. If happiness fails to materialize to the degree anticipated, divorce or separation is often resorted to. Whether or not marital happiness is more widespread today than formerly remains a moot question. However, it is reasonable to suppose that young people today are more concerned with happiness and that, when their aspirations are not achieved, marital breakup is a more likely consequence than it was a century ago.

6. *More permissive divorce laws.* Prior to the Revolutionary War, many of the colonies had little or no provision for divorce. Even during the nineteenth century, divorce was presumed to be granted only for "grave and serious reasons." During the twentieth century, however, more and more new grounds were added, and in recent years some form of no-fault divorce has been adopted by most states. As the legal concept of marital dissolution has changed from "grave and serious reasons" to "divorce on demand," increasing numbers of people availed themselves of the opportunity.

Individual Factors

Insofar as individual factors are concerned, the list seems to be interminable: sexual incompatibility, personality problems, infidelity, excessive drinking, financial difficulties, in-law relationships, and so on. One or more studies, for example, indicate that the following are associated with divorce.[6]

1. Poor marital preparation
2. Early age at marriage
3. Prior divorce

---

[6]Scott J. South and Glenna Spitze, "Determinants of Divorce over the Marital Life Course," *American Sociological Review,* August 1986, 583–90. See also Ruth B. Dixon and Lenore J. Wietzman, "When Husbands File for Divorce," *Journal of Marriage and the Family,* February 1982, 108. Sharon Price-Bonham and Jack O. Balswick, "The Noninstitutions: Divorce, Desertion, and Remarriage," *Journal of Marriage and the Family,* November 1980, 960–61.

4. Husband-wife discrepancy in educational attainment
5. Premarital pregnancy
6. Being raised in a broken home (the "transmission hypothesis")

There is some indication that men and women may divorce for different reasons.[7] There is also evidence to suggest that the types of complaint heard in lower-class divorce cases are different from those voiced in the middle and upper classes.[8] The latter classes, for instance, seem to have more "personality conflicts," while lower-class grievances often include drunkenness and physical abuse.

Historically such marital problems were used to ascertain guilt or innocence of each spouse during the divorce proceedings. In recent years the question has repeatedly been asked: Cannot society's interests be served without recourse to the "guilt and innocence" concept of divorce? At times it seemed that no two legislatures could agree on an answer, and even today each state has its own particular divorce code. Starting with California in 1970, however, the "no-fault" concept—wherein the whole idea of blame or guilt is eliminated—caught on rapidly, and at present most states have such provisions. A few states still utilize the fault system, and, to repeat, many states have both fault and no-fault provisions. In reality, therefore, we are operating under a dual system of divorce.

GROUNDS FOR DIVORCE

It is difficult to appreciate the jumble of divorce laws in the United States until one checks the statutes of the individual states. Several states have but a single ground (irretrievable breakdown), but just as many have a dozen or more grounds. Although the wording of the various statutes makes it difficult to arrive at a precise figure, there appear to be close to fifty legal grounds in the various states and territories:

Abandonment

Adjudication of mental
  incompetence

Adultery

Any cause rendering the marriage
  void

Application following decree of
  divorce from bed and board

Attempt to corrupt son or prostitute
  daughter

Attempt to murder spouse

Bigamy

---

[7]Margaret Guminski Cleek and T. Allan Pearson, "Perceived Causes of Divorce: An Analysis of Interrelations," *Journal of Marriage and the Family*, February 1985, 183. See also Linda Thompson and Graham B. Spanier, "The End of Marriage and Acceptance of Marital Termination," *Journal of Marriage and the Family,* February 1983, 112.

[8]William A. Vega, George J. Warheit, and Kenneth Meinhardt, "Marital Disruption and the Prevalence of Depressive Symptomatology among Anglos and Mexican Americans," *Journal of Marriage and the Family,* November 1984, 822.

Consanguinity

Conviction of a felony

Crime against nature

Cruel and inhuman treatment

Desertion

Deviant sexual conduct

Drug addiction

Force, menace, or duress in
obtaining the marriage

Fraud

Gross misbehavior and wickedness

Habitual drunkenness

Idiocy

Impotence

Imprisonment

Incapability of procreation at time of
marriage

Incest

Incompatibility

Incurable physical incapacity

Indignities

Infection of spouse with
communicable venereal disease

Insanity

Intolerable severity

Irremediable breakdown of marriage

Membership in sect believing
cohabitation is unlawful

Mental cruelty

Mental incapacity at time of
marriage

No reasonable likelihood of marriage
being preserved

Nonsupport

Physical incompetence at time of
marriage

Proposal to prostitute wife

Refusal by wife to move with
husband to this state

Seven years' absence, absent party
not being heard from

Sodomy or buggery

Treatment seriously injuring health
or endangering reason

Unnatural sexual intercourse with
person of the same sex or of a
different sex or a beast

Vagrancy by husband

Voluntary separation

Wife being pregnant by another
man at time of marriage without
knowledge of husband

Wife being prostitute prior to
marriage without knowledge of
husband

Willful neglect

Interestingly enough, in spite of the wide array of available grounds in the United States, the large majority of them are seldom used. Adultery, for example, is probably used in less than 1 percent of all divorce suits, widespread publicity to the contrary. Three grounds—incompatibility or "irreconcilable differences," cruelty (variously defined), and separation or desertion—would account for perhaps 90 percent of all divorce cases in this country.

CHILDREN AND DIVORCE

One of the most important—and most publicized—aspects of divorce is the effect on children. Sociologists have also been interested in the reverse problem: the effect of children on divorce. That is, does the very presence of children tend to militate against divorce? Family researchers have given a good deal of thought to both of these problems.

"Irrenconcilable differences" between spouses is a vague but commonly stated reason for divorce. (*Andrew Brilliant, Picture Cube*)

In days gone by, a substantial majority of divorces did not involve children. Today, divorces involve over one million children per year.[9]

What about the effect of divorce on these children? It is reasonable to expect that in some cases divorce will free both the children and their parents from conflict, violence, and abuse. Researchers report that "ongoing high levels of conflict, whether in intact or divorced homes, produce lower self-esteem, increased anxiety and a loss of self-control."[10] Parental separation in such cases may be more beneficial for children than continued conflict. The children may actually feel a sense of relief that it's finally over.[11]

While the benefits of divorce do occur, Weitzman reported in an award-winning research project that "divorce today spells financial disaster for too many women and for the minor children in their custody."[12] This sociologist emphasizes that economic changes in the life of the family have a "drastic psychological effect on the children of divorce." Mothers must spend too many hours earning money at the very time that their children need them the most.

---

[9]Ibid., S. J. Price, 1990, 30.

[10]David H. Demo and Alan C. Acock, "The Impact of Divorce on Children," *Journal of Marriage and the Family,* August 1988, 642.

[11]Constance Ahrons, "Waiting to Divorce Can Be Disservice to Children," *Marriage and Divorce Today,* October 20, 1986, 2.

[12]Lenore J. Weitzman, *The Divorce Revolution* (New York: The Free Press, 1985), 400. See also Penny L. Devillier and Craig J. Forsyth, "The Downward Mobility of Divorced Women with Dependent Children: A Research Note," *Sociological Spectrum,* 1988, 295–302.

Divorce today spells financial disaster for too many women and for the minor children in their custody.

The answer to problems of divorce is not to force couples to stay in unworkable marriages but to improve the legal responsibility of the father. It is he who is generally better off financially after the divorce.[13] An even more basic approach is to seek help through marital counseling. Certainly some couples could find happiness together if they utilized professional assistance in resolving their difficulties.

Perhaps the most effective and yet the least tried preventive method deals with improving mate-selection procedures. The seeds of many unhappy marriages seem to be present at the time of marriage. Careful screening, using some of the mate-selection techniques described earlier, might improve the quality of marriage in many cases.

REMARRIAGE AFTER DIVORCE

As divorce rates have increased, remarriage rates have increased proportionately. Data in Table 15.3 show that during 1970 some 31 percent of all marriages involved a previously married bride or groom. By 1986 this percentage had increased to about 46 percent. At some point during the

---

[13]Ibid., Weitzman, 400.

Table 15.3   PERCENT OF MARRIAGES WITH PREVIOUSLY MARRIED
BRIDES AND GROOMS, 1970–1986

Year	All remarriages	First marriage of bride, remarriage of groom	Remarriage of bride, first marriage of groom	Remarriage of bride and groom
1970	31.2	7.6	7.3	16.3
1971	31.8	7.9	7.3	16.6
1972	32.9	8.2	7.4	17.3
1973	35.2	8.7	7.8	18.7
1974	36.9	9.2	8.1	19.6
1975	39.5	9.9	8.5	21.1
1976	41.1	10.7	8.8	21.6
1977	42.2	10.8	9.1	22.3
1978	42.7	10.7	9.3	22.7
1979	43.3	11.2	9.5	22.6
1980	43.5	11.2	9.8	22.5
1981	45.1	11.8	10.1	23.2
1982	44.9	11.7	10.3	22.9
1983	45.2	11.6	10.5	23.1
1984	45.0	11.5	10.7	22.8
1985	45.3	11.4	10.9	23.0
1986	45.6	11.3	11.2	23.1

Source: National Center for Health Statistics, "Advance Report of Final Marriage Statistics, 1986." *Monthly Vital Statistics Report,* 38 (3), 1989, 12.

1990s the number of remarriages may well equal the number of first marriages.

Vital statistics show that 76 percent of divorced women and 85 percent of divorced men will eventually remarry.[14] Most do not wait long. In 1986, 27 percent of remarrying brides and 31 percent of remarrying grooms married within one year after divorce. About half of the divorced women remarry within 3.7 years, and most men remarry within 3.4 years.

Remarriage brings new hopes and happier lives for many. It also presents new challenges. Even when children from previous marriages are not present, remarriages differ from first marriages in at least four ways:[15] (1) In remarriage, there is a possibility of interacting with the previous spouse.

---

[14]Statistical information that follows is reported in National Center for Health Statistics. Advance Report of Final Marriage Statistics, 1986. *Monthly Vital Statistics Report,* 38 (3), (Hyattsville, MD: Public Health Service, 1989), 5.

[15]Marilyn Ihinger-Tallman and Kay Pasley, *Remarriage* (Newbury Park, CA: Sage Publications, 1987), 18.

(2) The first marriage provides a baseline to judge the second marriage. (3) There may be a change in the individual's level of maturity from first to second marriage. (4) Social expectations at the time of first marriage may be different from those at the time of the second marriage.

For example, a person marrying in the 1980s and remarrying in the 1990s might have to adjust to different social and economic circumstances. In the 1990s, there is a greater awareness of fairness in marriage, and the "me first" philosophy of life is losing its popularity. The 1990s have already been referred to as "the we decade."

STEPFAMILIES

In addition to problems involved with the choice of a second spouse, remarriage may suffer from difficulties arising from various types of stepparent-stepchild relationships. Unlike traditional families, stepfamilies face a whole series of complicated interpersonal relationships and living arrangements.

By way of illustration, let us consider the type of stepfamily that is most like the traditional nuclear family: one or both spouses are remarried, one or both have children from their previous marriages, neither has children in their current marriage.

Even in this relatively simple case, numerous questions inevitably arise: How congenial are the relationships likely to be between the children? Between the children and their parents? Between the children and their stepparents? Does the couple desire to have children of their own, and how does this desire—or lack of it—affect their marriage? If they do have children of their own, does not a new set of problems arise? To what extent do stepparents cooperate with parents in maintaining contact with the children?

Custody of Children After Divorce

It should be noted that in the above illustration no mention was made as to whether the remarried couple did or did not have custody of the children. But clearly, the custodial factor adds yet another dimension to an already-crowded problem area.

The fact of the matter is that divorced parents often have difficulty in finding a mutually satisfactory arrangement with regard to child custody. The problem is complicated by the fact that decisions about custody are made at the time of divorce, when the facts relating to subsequent remarriage are generally not known. It is at the time of divorce, also, that the animosity between parents is often at its peak, a fact which further aggravates the custodial issue. All things considered, it is little wonder that court decisions which make the most sense at the time of divorce sometimes prove to be ineffectual in the long run.

Admittedly, if the parents cooperate with one another custodial problems may be minimal, yet cooperative parents are the ones who are least

Remarriage may become a factor in deciding on custodial issues such as visitation and living arrangements for children.

likely to get a divorce in the first place. In any case, custodial issues such as living arrangements, who will be responsible for financial support, and who will have legal responsibility are matters usually left to the discretion of the court.

In practice, court decisions are more varied than one might think. The Silvers, who have studied the way custody issues are usually resolved, found the following to be among the most common court-imposed arrangements.[16]

1. *Sole custody.* In sole custody all of the rights, duties, and obligations for the physical, emotional, and psychological well-being of an offspring are vested in one parent. The court may award visitation to the other parent.

2. *Split custody.* In this arrangement, each parent is given sole custody of one or more of the children. Traditionally, girls go with the mother, boys with the father.

3. *Divided (alternating) custody.* Here, the time spent with each parent is divided into finite blocks. The custodial parent exercises ex-

---

[16]Gerald A. Silver and Myrna Silver, *Weekend Fathers*, New York: Berkley Books, 1986, 59–62.

clusive control whenever the children are with that parent. The other parent has visitor status.

4. *Joint legal custody.* In joint legal custody, legal responsibility is shared by both parents, while physical custody is given to one parent.

5. *Joint physical custody.* In this instance, both parents share equally the physical control of the child, while legal control is vested in only one parent. The child may spend several weeks, or months, with one parent and then go to the other. But only one parent has full legal custody.

Whichever way the court rules, decisions tend to be controversial. The most commonly heard complaint is that judges almost always grant sole custody to mothers. The Silvers argue that co-parenting is a more ideal relationship, since children need both parents. Judges, however, must consider postdivorce conflicts as well as the circumstances that led to the divorce. In the light of our present knowledge, about all that can be said is that both parents and judges should have enough flexibility to find the custodial arrangement that best suits the long-range interest of the child.

SUMMARY

In this chapter we have discussed divorce, remarriage, and stepfamilies. We pointed out that the family after remarriage can be exceedingly complex, both as an object of study and as a problem for the participants. Furthermore, social scientists have not reached the stage where definitive statements can be made about such phenomena as marital selection following divorce, prognosis for remarriage, and the most effective custodial arrangements for children. We have, however, raised a number of pertinent questions. It is hoped that students will ask even more.

Meanwhile, it is clear that most people do adjust to change: they overcome problems and maintain family ties even after divorce. After all, whether divorce occurs or not, most people enter their middle and later years as somebody's spouse, parent, or grandparent. This stage of family life will be examined in the next chapter.

QUESTIONS

1. What has been the trend of the divorce rate in the United States? If you were to make a prediction, what would you predict about the future trend? Why?

2. Vital statistics gathered over many years show that divorce rates vary from state to state. How would you account for this?

3. Are the causes of divorce the same as the grounds for divorce? Explain.

4. "Causes of divorce are perceived differently by different categories of people." What does this statement mean? Explain, using specific illustrations.

5. What is the fault system of divorce, and what have been the chief criticisms leveled against it?

6. What is the no-fault system of divorce, and what have been the criticisms leveled against it?

7. In the United States there appear to be some fifty different grounds for divorce. What accounts for this "jumble of divorce laws"?

8. Divorce causation is discussed in terms of societal and individual factors. How do these two sets of factors differ from one another? Can you think of any additional "societal" factors?

9. Explain in a few paragraphs why the presence of children in marriage is no longer a significant deterrent to divorce.

10. What major question needs to be answered before the effect of divorce on children can be ascertained with greater certainty? Propose a research project to answer that question.

11. What advice would you give to a divorced person contemplating remarriage? Be specific and justify your answer.

12. What have been some of the major findings with regard to remarriage? In your opinion, what areas are most in need of further research? Why?

SELECTED READINGS

Ahrons, Constance R., and Roy H. Rodgers. *Divorced Families*. New York: W. W. Norton, 1987.

Ambert, Ann-Marie. "Relationships between Ex-Spouses: Individual and Dyadic Perspectives." *Journal of Social and Personal Relationships,* 5, 1988, 327–346.

Buehler, Cheryl. "Divorce-Related Stressors: Occurrence, Disruptiveness, and Area of Life Chance." *Journal of Divorce,* Fall 1987, 25–50.

Dahl, Ann Sale, Kathryn Markhus Cowgill, and Rigmor Asmundsson. "Life in Remarriage Families." *Social Work,* January–February, 1987.

Demo, David H., and Alan C. Acock. "The Impact of Divorce on Children." *Journal of Marriage and the Family,* August 1988, 619–648.

Devillier, Penny L., and Craig Forsyth. "The Downward Mobility of Divorced Women with Dependent Children: A Research Note." *Social Spectrum,* 8, 1988, 295–302.

Furstenberg, Frank F., Jr., S. Philip Morgan, and Paul D. Allison. "Parental Participation and Children's Well-Being after Marital Dissolution." *American Sociological Review,* October 1987, 695–701.

Ganong, Lawrence H., and Marylin Coleman. "Do Mutual Children Cement Bonds in Stepfamilies?" *Journal of Marriage and the Family,* August 1988, 687–698.

Garfinkel, Irwin, and Donald Oellerich. "Noncustodial Fathers' Ability to Pay Child Support." *Demography,* May 1989, 219–233.

Glenn, Norval D., and Kathryn B. Kramer. "The Marriages and Divorces of the Children of Divorce." *Journal of Marriage and the Family,* November 1987, 811–825.

Goldfarb, Sally F. "Child Support Guidelines: A Model for Fair Allocation of Child Care, Medical, and Educational Expenses." *Family Law Quarterly,* Fall 1987, 325–349.

Grestel, Naomi. "Divorce and Stigma." *Social Problems,* April 1987, 172–186.

Hobart, Charles. "The Family System in Remarriage: An Exploratory Study." *Journal of Marriage and the Family,* August 1988, 649–661.

Ihinger-Tallman, Marilyn, and Kay Pasley. *Remarriage.* Newbury Park, CA: Sage Publications, 1987.

Isaacs, Marla Beth, and George H. Leon. "Social Networks, Divorce, and Adjustment: A Tale of Three Generations." *Journal of Divorce,* Summer 1986, 1–16.

———, "The Visitation Schedule and Child Adjustment: A Three Year Study." *Family Process,* June 1988, 251–256.

Johnson, Colleen Leary. "Postdivorce Reorganization of Relationships between Divorcing Children and Their Parents." *Journal of Marriage and the Family,* February 1988, 221–231.

———, Linea Klee, Catherine Schmidt. "Conceptions of Parentage and Kinship among Children of Divorce." *American Anthropologist,* 90, 1988, 136–144.

———, and George H. Leon, "Remarriage and Its Alternatives Following Divorce: Mother and Child Adjustment." *Journal of Marital and Family Therapy,* 14 (2), 1988, 163–173.

Keith, Verna M., and Barbara Finley. "The Impact of Parental Divorce on Children's Educational Attainment, Marital Timing, and Likelihood of Divorce." *Journal of Marriage and the Family,* August 1988, 797–809.

Kiecolt, Jill K., and Alan C. Acock. "The Long-Term Effects of Family Structure on Gender-Role Attitudes." *Journal of Marriage and the Family,* August 1988, 709–717.

Lesser, Elena K., and Joel J. Comet. "Help and Hindrance: Parents of Divorcing Children." *Journal of Marital and Family Therapy,* 13 (2), 1987, 197–202.

Martin, Teresa Castro, and Larry L. Bumpass. "Recent Trends in Marital Disruption." *Demography,* February 1989, 37–51.

McCombs, Amanda, Rex Forehand, and Gene H. Brody. "Early Adolescent Functioning Following Divorce: The Relationship to Parenting and Non-parenting Ex-Spousal Interactions." *Child Study,* 17 (4), 1987, 301–310.

McLinton, James B. "Separate but Unequal: The Economic Disaster of Divorce for Women and Children." *Family Law Quarterly,* Fall 1987, 351–409.

Morgan, Leslie A. "Outcomes of Marital Separation: A Longitudinal Test of Predictors." *Journal of Marriage and the Family,* May 1988, 493–498.

O'Flaherty, Kathleen M., and Laura Workman Eells. "Courtship Behavior of the Remarried." *Journal of Marriage and the Family,* May 1988, 499–506.

Peek, Charles W., Nancy J. Bell, Terry Waldren, and Gwedolyn T. Sorrell. "Patterns of Functioning in Families of Remarried and First-Married Couples." *Journal of Marriage and the Family,* August 1988, 699–708.

Seltzer, Judith A. "Children's Contact with Absent Parents." *Journal of Marriage and the Family,* August 1988, 663–677.

Stolberg, Arnold L., Christopher Camplair, Kathlyn Currier, and Mary J. Wells. "Individual, Familial and Environmental Determinants of Children's Post-Divorce Adjustment and Maladjustment." *Journal of Divorce,* Fall 1987, 51–68.

Trent, Katherine, and Scott J. South. "Structural Determinants of the Divorce Rate: A Cross-societal Analysis." *Journal of Marriage and the Family,* May 1989, 391–404.

Weitzman, Lenore J. *The Divorce Revolution: The Unexpected Social and Economic Consequences for Women and Children of America.* New York: The Free Press, 1985. (Winner of the 1986 Book Award from the American Sociological Association.)

Chapter
16

The Middle and Later Years

Everyone desires to live long, but no one would be old.

SWIFT

*A*phorisms aside, why include a chapter on aging in a text on marriage and the family? The answer, of course, depends on the student's age. For younger students it may be rewarding to look down the road a bit to see what's ahead. For older students, the topic may have more immediate relevance. But, regardless of age, there are three sound *sociological* reasons to include a chapter on middle and later years.

Aging Society   In the first place, ours is an aging society. As early as 1900, life expectancy in the United States was around 50 years.[1] By 1970, the figure had jumped to roughly seventy-five for women and sixty-seven for men. Today it is closer to 71 for men and 78 for women.

In 1900, about one person in twenty-five was over the age of 65. As Table 16.1 shows, presently one out of eight people are over that age. Even more remarkable, the number of people who are over eighty-five years old

---

[1]*Information Please Almanac 1990.* (Boston: Houghton Mifflin, 1990), 818.

Table 16.1 POPULATION SIXTY-FIVE
YEARS AND OVER AS A
PERCENT OF TOTAL: UNITED
STATES, 1900–2050

Year	Number	Percent
1900	3,084,000	4.0
1910	3,950,000	4.3
1920	4,933,000	4.7
1930	6,634,000	5.4
1940	9,019,000	6.8
1950	12,270,000	8.1
1960	16,560,000	9.2
1970	19,980,000	9.8
1980	25,544,000	11.3
1985	28,605,000	12.0
1990	31,697,000	12.7
2000	34,921,000	13.0
2030	64,580,000	21.2
2050	67,412,000	21.8

Sources: From 1900 through 1980, Cynthia M. Taeuber, *America in Transition: An Aging Society,* Current Population Reports, series P-23, no. 128 (Washington, DC: Bureau of the Census, 1983), 3. For years since 1980, Gregory Spencer, *Projections of the Population of the United States by Age, Sex, and Race: 1983 to 2080.* Current Population Reports, Series P-25, no. 952 (Washington, DC: Bureau of the Census, 1986) 7–8.

increased from less than one million in 1960 to well over two million in 1990.[2]

It should be pointed out, in this connection, that most generalities about aging do not apply equally to men and women. Consider, for example, the following facts about the over-65 group:[3]

	Percent women	Percent men
80 years and over	3.5	1.7
Living with spouse	39.2	74.9
College graduates	7.9	12.8
Employed	7.2	15.9

[2]Ibid., 794.

[3]U.S. Bureau of the Census, *Statistical Abstract of the United States, 1989* (Washington, DC: Government Printing Office, 1989), 37.

Social Conscience   The second reason for including a discussion of aging pertains to social conscience. Recent decades have seen an increasing awareness of the elderly as people and not just as age cohorts. Mandatory retirement has come under attack, and the view of older people as capable, productive members of the society has become widely accepted.

Better Understanding through Research   A final reason for age inclusion—and one that is related to both of the preceding points—is that social scientists are spending an enormous amount of time on the subject. Sociologists, psychologists, gerontologists, home economists, social workers, and a variety of family specialists all have contributed to a better understanding of the middle and later years.

Many scholarly journals now include one or more articles on some aspect of aging in almost every issue. Family texts also are devoting an increasing amount of space to the subject. All in all, it is easy to demonstrate that an examination of middle and later years is an appropriate subject for college study.

MARRIAGE AS DEVELOPMENT

Basic to any discussion of the middle and later years is the concept of *developmental marriage*. Nelson Foote, the first sociologist to elaborate on the idea, wrote as follows:

> To expect a marriage to last indefinitely under modern conditions is to expect lot. Certainly marriage counselors report many cases of mates who disclose no specific cause of dissatisfaction, yet complain that they have lost interest in their marriage. Successful marriage may thus come to be defined, both by married people and by students of marriage, in terms of its potential for continued development, rather than in terms of momentary assessments of adjustment.[4]

In line with these developmental aspects, there are four possible patterns. Couple A, after a comparatively happy beginning, may go steadily downhill. Couple B, after an initial period of maladjustment, may reconcile their problems to the point where their marriage becomes more rewarding with the passing of time. Couple C may experience an up-and-down pattern over the years. Couple D may report no significant changes.

Of the four patterns, which is the most typical? Earlier studies reported that marital satisfaction declined with the passing of time. A number of methodological problems remained to be worked out, however, and more

---

[4]Nelson Foote, "Matching of Husband and Wife in Phases of Development" (Paper presented to the Third World Congress of Sociology, Amsterdam, 1956).

recent studies show that the decline in satisfaction may level off in middle age and then begin to improve.[5]

The authors' personal observations—based on a fair number of students' marriages over a period of several decades—tend to support the U-curve hypothesis. The first few years seem to be the most difficult. But once the initial hardships and obstacles are overcome, the marital-satisfaction line seems to head upward. Obviously, there are exceptions. As couples age, health factors often disrupt the marital equilibrium. Nevertheless, all things considered, marriage in the later years apparently has a great deal to offer.

THE EMPTY NEST

During the *life course*[6] of a married couple comes a time when the children begin to leave the home. That period of time, called the "launching stage," can be very short if there is only one child. When there are more children, the launching stage begins when the first child leaves the home, and it ends when the last child leaves. The period after the last child leaves home is called "the empty nest."

This concept has lost much of its meaning in recent years. High divorce and remarriage rates, postponement of marriage, and having "last chance children" have altered the relationship between parents and their children. For example, postponement of marriage in recent years seems to have changed a long-standing tradition in America. That tradition meant that most children left the home to get married and form a new family. Other reasons for leaving the home included being temporarily away in college or serving in the military.[7]

Today, on the other hand, as children postpone marriage, the timing of the launching stage may become a source of intergenerational conflict. Parents and children may disagree on whether the children should establish premarital residential independence. Because this is a relatively recent phenomenon, "much more research needs to be directed to uncovering the basis of generational consensus and conflict over the patterns of premarital residential independence."[8]

---

[5]Laurence Steinberg and Susan B. Silverberg, "Influences on Marital Satisfaction during the Middle States of the Family Life Cycle," *Journal of Marriage and the Family,* November 1987, 751–760. See also Gary R. Lee, "Marital Satisfaction in Later Life: The Effects of Nonmarital Roles," *Journal of Marriage and the Family,* 1988, 775–783.

[6]The phrase "life course" is synonymous with the phrase "life cycle." "Life course" is probably more accurate if we perceive the life events to be sequential rather than cyclical.

[7]Calvin Goldscheider and Francis K. Goldscheider. "Family Structure and Conflict: Nest-leaving Expectations of Young Adults and Their Parents," *Journal of Marriage and the Family,* February 1989, 87.

[8]Ibid., 96.

Finally, the postponement of marriage, coupled with the recent trend of postponement of childbearing among middle-class Americans, has also given a new meaning to the "empty nest." The traditional notion that the empty nest begins in middle age does not apply to mothers who have their first child after age thirty-five. It is ironic that women in this age group were considerably more likely to become mothers in 1970 than in the late 1980s,[9] yet the phrase "last chance children" appeared only recently.

The impact on parents upon entering the empty nest stage is not easy to predict. For one thing, numerous studies show that children do not improve the quality of marriage. If that is the case, their moving away from home could hardly constitute a crisis. Yet there are many parents who deeply miss their association with the children. Which parents will experience relief and which will suffer emptiness remains to be discovered.

The longer people live, the greater the risk of isolation and loneliness. The problem is particularly acute among women, because wives outlive their husbands. Most men age with a companion by their side, while the large majority of women age alone. The majority of women live to more than seventy-five years, yet after that age only about 22 percent of them will still live with their husbands.[10]

The majority of older people age in rather good health. Table 16.2 shows that most people are able to function well into old age. Note, for example, that while women live longer, they are more likely then men to have physical difficulties after age 65. Women also have more trouble doing housework, preparing meals, and shopping.

The data in Table 16.2 show that while the majority of elderly people can perform daily tasks on their own, managing a house is a real problem for a substantial number. The most frequently impaired activity is walking. While well over 20 million people over 65 can walk without difficulty, almost five million cannot.[11]

Having a physical impairment, however, does not mean that the person is incapacitated. The number of persons over 65 with a functional limitation is about 2.5 million. This is the group most likely to face institutionalization, loss of independence, and curtailment of active living. If the family and society provide the necessary support, however, most of the other elderly can continue living an active and satisfying life.

---

[9]National Center for Health Statistics, Advance Report of Final Natality Statistics, 1987. *Monthly Vital Statistics Report,* 38 (3), 1989, 18.

[10]Abraham Monk, "Aging, Loneliness and Communications," *American Behavioral Scientist,* June 1988, 532–563. See also Gary R. Lee and Masako-Ishii Kuntz, "Social Interaction, Loneliness, and Emotional Well-Being among the Elderly," *Research on Aging,* December 1987, 459–482.

[11]Deborah Dawson, Gerry Hendershot, and John Fulton, "Aging in the Eighties—Functional Limitations of Individuals Age 65 Years and Over," *Advance Data from Vital and Health Statistics of the National Center for Health Statistics,* No. 133, June 10, 1987, 5.

Table 16.2 PERCENT OF MEN AND WOMEN OVER 65 WHO HAVE
DIFFICULTIES PERFORMING SELECTED TASKS

Age	Eating	Walking	Bathing	Shopping	Cooking	Light housework
			Women			
65–69	0.9	12.9	5.1	6.4	4.2	4.0
70–74	1.0	17.8	9.1	9.4	5.5	6.2
75–79	3.3	22.2	11.1	14.5	8.3	8.4
80–84	3.4	31.4	19.2	24.7	14.0	14.0
85 +	4.4	43.3	30.1	41.6	29.5	27.4
			Men			
65–69	1.7	11.5	5.3	4.1	2.6	3.5
70–74	1.4	14.9	6.1	5.3	3.6	3.4
75–79	2.3	15.6	7.8	7.6	5.1	5.2
80–84	3.0	24.2	12.3	13.9	7.8	8.2
85 +	4.3	32.2	23.1	26.8	18.5	15.2

Source: Deborah Dawson, Gerry Hendershot, and John Fulton, "Aging in the Eighties: Functional Limitations of Individuals Age 65 Years and Over," *Advance Data from Vital and Health Statistics,* no. 133, June 10, 1987, 3,4.

ROLE DIFFICULTIES IN THE LATER YEARS

If we define the later years as those that begin, say, at age sixty-five, then it appears that not all societies accord the same status to this age group. In some societies the aged are looked upon as repositories of wisdom and/or wealth, and are accorded high status. In others—for example, hunting and gathering societies—the aged may be looked upon as economic burdens.

It also appears that the status of the aged varies from time to time within the same society. A good example is our own society. Social historians have often written about the respect and veneration afforded to older people in our colonial period.[12] But a broader historical scrutiny of colonial New England indicates that the honor and respect shown to the elder may have had more to do with their economic status and prominence in the community than with the fact that they were old. The indigent, regardless of age, were likely to be left to their own resources if they did not have relatives to take care of them.[13] Findings such as these have made sociologists much more

[12]John Demos, "Old Age in Early New England," in Michael Gordon, ed., *The American Family in Social-Historical Perspective* (New York: St. Martin's Press, 1983), 293.

[13]John B. Williamson, "Old-Age Relief Policies in the New Land, 1650–1900," in Beth B. Hess and Elizabeth W. Markson, eds., *Growing Old in America* (New Brunswick: Transaction Books, 1985), 59.

Most older people desire to live in their own homes. (*Ken Heyman*)

cautious in making historical generalizations relative to the aged. There is no doubt that the elderly face a number of age-related problems: retirement, dependency, ill health, social isolation, loss of a spouse, lack of mobility, reduced income, inability to take care of house and yard—the list is long, and all too familiar. One would expect, therefore, that—by this time—programs would have been developed to prepare people for "the road ahead." As of now, however, such programs have been slow in coming.

SOCIAL SUPPORT NETWORKS FOR THE ELDERLY

Kinship Networks

Despite the desire of older people to live in their own homes, research indicates clearly that a majority live near their children and that mutual visitation—and mutual help—is quite commonplace.[14] The majority of aging parents and their children often need and support each other, whether they live together or apart. In America, two, three, and sometimes four generations of families keep in touch with each other and remain ready to help each other regardless of their residence. Income permitting, distance is not a barrier to periodic contacts. Note, for example, the enormous increase in airline traffic before Thanksgiving and Christmas as relatives travel to be with their family.

Peer Group Networks

The problems of old age—ill health, loneliness, fear of crime—are reduced among those elders whose social networks include their peers. In part this happens because peers and kin have different functions. Heinemann puts it this way:

> While emotional needs of the individual are met by both family and friends alike, kin and peer ties are not interchangeable because each meet different emotional needs for the individual. . . . For example, children become socioemotional insurance policies for parents and important sources of identity, especially for an elderly mother. These one-sided relationships transcend differences and function to ensure solidarity and a sense of security. In contrast, relationships with friends are characterized by symmetry and equality; they provide not only mutual gratification, but also a sense of integrity and self-worth. They confirm identity rather than function as a source of it.[15]

Drawing on a variety of research studies, Aizenberg and Treas conclude that for the elderly, having friends contributes to having a more fulfilled life.

> Although no conclusive evidence exists on the relationship between the morale of older people and their family involvements, a number of studies show that life satisfaction or happiness is positively associated with interaction with friends . . . As friends most often are chosen from among people at the same

---

[14]Statistics on aging in this section are provided by Donald G. Fowles, *A Profile of Older Americans: 1987* (Long Beach, CA: American Association of Retired Persons, 1987). For an extensive review of this topic, see Jay A. Mancini and Rosemary Blieszner, "Aging Parents and Adult Children: Research Themes in Intergenerational Relations," *Journal of Marriage and the Family,* May 1989, 275–290.

[15]Warren A. Peterson and Jill Quadagno, *Social Bonds in Later Life* (Beverly Hills, CA: Sage Publications, 1985), 170.

The problems of old age are reduced among those elders who have the benefit of peer companions. (*Ruohomaa, Black Star*)

stage of the life cycle and with similar characteristics, they often serve as confidants and act as important buffers against trauma in coping with the role transitions that accompany late life.[16]

Because of such findings, housing projects for the elderly are often age-segregated. The rationale is that concentrating the aging population in one area will increase opportunities for contact and improve chances for developing lasting peer networks. In such an atmosphere, there should be higher morale and greater life-satisfaction.

The Voluntaristic Model

Social Security, Medicare, and Medicaid help to free the elderly from a strict material dependence on their offspring. Also, as their educational level improves, the elderly should be better equipped to relate to their family. In

---

[16]Rhonda Aizenberg and Judith Treas, "The Family in Late Life: Psychological and Demographic Consideration," in James E. Birren and K. Warner Schaie, eds., *Handbook of the Psychology of Aging* (New York: Van Nostrand Reinhold Co., 1985), 180.

For the elderly, having friends contributes to a more fulfilling life.

brief, intergenerational relationships may come to be effectively voluntaristic rather than obligatory.

This voluntaristic model, proposed by Hess and Waring in 1978,[17]
seems to have developed as predicted. The emphasis among aging people
in America, just as it is in younger age groups, is on being independent.
"Parents are concerned that they be not only financially but also emotionally
self-sufficient."[18]

SEX AND THE AGED

As aging people become healthier and more independent, their quality of
life becomes an important issue. As we have shown above, relating to their
children, having friends, and being independent are some of many determi-

---

[17]Beth Hess and Joan Waring, "Changing Patterns of Aging and Family Bonds in Later Life,"
The Family Coordinator, October 1978, 311–12.

[18]Joan Aldous, "New Views on the Family Life of the Elderly and the Near-Elderly," *Journal
of Marriage and the Family,* May 1987, 233.

nants of the quality of life. But when asked about their concerns, most people approaching old age mention their worry about their ability to have a satisfactory sex life.[19]

Their worries and fears of losing sexual ability stem from the portrayal of older people in our society as being asexual. And unfortunately, some of them readily accept that image. The truth is that most older people can enjoy sexual life for as long as they remain healthy. But, as with other important matters dealing with aging, the differences between sexes are substantial. Women seem to have the biological ability to participate as sexual partners longer and at higher frequencies than men.

Men are disadvantaged because the incidence of physiologically caused impotence increases with age. Since women do not have similar problems, they are often able to carry on uninterrupted sexual activity well into old age. The good news for men is that most physiological problems today are treatable, if the impotence is diagnosed correctly. Physicians, however, lament the fact that popular advice sometimes results in psychological treatment before a medical diagnosis is even attempted. As a result, some physicians feel that many men are not receiving the help they really need.

Some men fear to approach physicians because of their belief that a medical diagnosis of impotence usually means the end of sex. While this fear was real in the past, today many cases of chronic or irreversible impotence can be remedied using penis implants. These are devices that produce erection at will and without sacrifice of sensation.

But it is neither physiological nor psychological problems that are a major obstacle for having a fulfilling sex life in older ages. The major problem is a sexual incompatibility between marriage partners. Furthermore, the disadvantages of incompatibility are not shared equally by both sexes. The research findings, according to Botwinick's review of the literature, seems to be conclusive on this point.

> It is paradoxical that men seem more sexually active than women, and yet, it is they who are the limiting factor in women's sexual gratification in marriage. Decline in sexuality starts later in life among women than men, and is of a lesser magnitude. All this makes for a diminution of woman's sexual fulfillment later in life.[20]

One "remedy" for this problem could come from a greater awareness of the mate-selection process. Women marrying equal-age or older men should anticipate the earlier waning of the sexual desire of their husbands.

It would be foolish, of course, to expect that sex life can remain unchanged indefinitely for men or for women. After all, sex is a biological process that does produce biosexual changes in both men and women. For men, ejaculatory fluid is reduced—which means there is less need to ejaculate—and the intensity and duration of orgasm lessens. For women, there

---

[19]Jack Botwinick, *Aging and Behavior* (New York: Springer, 1984), 113.

[20]Ibid., 102.

Most older couples can enjoy a sexual life together as long as they remain healthy. (© 1984, Hopker, Woodfin Camp)

is reduced vaginal lubrication, the intensity of orgasm may be lowered, and a certain amount of elasticity may be lost.

It would be equally foolish, certainly, for healthy people regardless of their age to terminate sexual activity simply because they fear the normal biological changes. Yet many of the elderly do disengage from sex years before significant disabilities occur. Fortunately, as more enlightened attitudes have come to prevail, the percentage of such cases has apparently declined.

ELDER ABUSE

Despite the overall positive interaction between parents and their middle-aged children, occasionally there is a darker side. Over the last ten years, research has surfaced to indicate that some elderly people are being physically abused by their children. The prevalence of such abuse can be ascertained only from local studies. A recent survey in the Boston area, for instance, revealed the following prevalence rates:[21]

Type of abuse	Rate per 1000 persons over 65 years old*
All types	32
Physical violence	20
Chronic verbal aggression	11
Neglect	4

*The rates do not add to 32 because some couples reported more than one type of abuse.

In this sample, the rates were no higher for minorities than for whites, and no significant differences were found by religious, economic, or educational background.

Most elders are not victimized by their children, but by spouses, who perpetrated over three-fourths of all abuses. When children were perpetrators, victims were more likely to be mothers than fathers.[22]

Physical violence among family members varies from low-level violence such as a push, a slap, throwing something at someone without hitting them, to more severe levels such as hitting with a fist, biting, and kicking. This most severe category was reported to occur in 5 percent of the cases. Out of that, the number of cases per year is considerably less because some people over sixty-five may experience such unpleasantness only once in their life. However, because the total population of people over sixty-five is large and growing, even small rates may translate into thousands of cases across the nation.[23]

WIDOWHOOD

Widowhood (the term is used here to apply to males as well as to females) is a problem of many dimensions: social, emotional, financial. The numbers alone are staggering: over eight million women over sixty-five and 1.55 mil-

---

[21]Karl Pillemer and David Finkelhor, "The Prevalence of Elder Abuse: A Random Sample Survey," *The Gerontologist,* 28 (1), 1988, 53.

[22]Ibid., 54.

[23]Jordan I. Kosberg, "Preventing Elder Abuse: Identification of High Risk Factors Prior to Placement Decisions," *The Gerontologist,* 28 (1), 1988, 45.

lion men are widowed.[24] In fact, more than half of all American women over sixty-five are widowed.[25] With figures such as these, it is easy to see why widowhood is a societal as well as an individual problem.

To begin with, widows suffer from the lack of preparation for dealing with bereavement or for adjusting to society as a single person. Additionally, death of a spouse often presents financial difficulties. Life insurance does not carry with it common benefits that are commonly assumed. Although women are beneficiaries in a large number of cases, the stereotype of the rich widow is largely false. The benefits, furthermore, are often consumed by doctors' bills and funeral arrangements.

Financial difficulties aside, there is also the deep emotional shock and the sense of personal loss. And, of course, there is the loneliness and necessity for making new living arrangements—and a new social life.

The widow may move in with her grown children—and thus become a part of the so-called three-generation household—or she may try to "go it alone." Each choice presents a number of unavoidable problems. Widowhood itself is a long-term rather than a short-term proposition. Solie and Fielder report that, on the average, the period of widowhood lasts eighteen years.[26]

What is the answer to this very real problem of widowhood? Alas, there is none—at least, not at present. Women live substantially longer than men. Also, at the normal marrying ages women tend to be somewhat younger than the men they marry. Barring some advances in biomedical research, therefore, and in the absence of a change in our age-at-marriage pattern—both of which are problematical at best—widowhood will continue to be a fact of life.

SUMMARY

Society is becoming more aware that the quality of life at older ages has its roots in the decisions people make in their youth. We stressed in this chapter that as long as the younger generation emphasizes youth and beauty for women more than for men, status and prestige will increase with age for men and decrease for women. Consequently, most divorced and widowed men can remarry considerably younger women, leaving millions of women to face old age alone. Also, men who fail to form families earlier in life tend to fare poorly in old age.

While statistics tell this story well, it is the poets from Shakespeare on

---

[24]Donald G. Fowles, 1987, 3.

[25]Ibid., 3.

[26]Linda J. Solie and Lois J. Fielder, "The Relationship between Sex Role Identity and a Widow's Adjustment to the Loss of a Spouse," *Omega,* 18 (1), 1987–88, 33.

who captured the idea eloquently. One of the most eloquent statements was penned by Joseph Addison (1672–1719), English poet, essayist, and statesman:

> He who would pass his declining years with honor and comfort, should, when young, consider that he may one day become old, and remember when old, that he has once been young.

QUESTIONS

1. There are a number of sociological reasons for including a chapter on aging in a text designed for college students. What are these sociological reasons? Can you think of any other ones?

2. What is meant by the concept of development marriage, and what do the research studies show regarding the outcome?

3. The so-called empty-nest period stretches for a longer period of time than ever before. Why? Have the research surveys discovered any trauma associated with the empty nest?

4. What are some of the determinants of the respect afforded to the older people in our society? Do you expect that the treatment of aging people varies by their social class? Explain.

5. The question of "what to do with the aging people who cannot take care of themselves" has been a problem throughout American history. What do you think should be some solutions? Do the solutions lie with the American people's conscience or do they lie elsewhere?

6. What kind of social networks do you think are the most important in the lives of older people? Explain why some networks are more important than others.

7. Explain what is meant by "the voluntaristic model" in later life relationships.

8. Few generalities about aging apply equally to both sexes. Discuss how this statement applies to biosocial determinants of sex life in later years.

9. What are some of the problems facing widows in our society? Are the problems facing widowers more or less formidable than those facing widows?

10. What social changes would be required to reduce sex inequality in older ages?

SELECTED READINGS

Adams, Rebecca G. "Patterns of Network Change: A Longitudinal Study of Friendships of Elderly Women." *The Gerontologist,* 27 (2), 1987, 222–227.

Aldous, Joan. "New Views on the Family Life of the Elderly and the Near-Elderly." *Journal of Marriage and the Family,* May 1987, 227–234.

Bretschneider, Judy G., and Norma L. McCoy. "Sexual Interest and Behavior in Healthy 80 to 102-Year-Olds." *Archives of Sexual Behavior,* 17 (2), 1988, 109.

Brody, Jacob A., Dwight B. Brock, and T. Franklin Williams. "Trends in the Health of the Elderly Population," *American Review of Public Health,* 8, 1987, 211–34.

Climo, Jacob J. "Visits of Distant-Living Adult Children and Elderly Parents." *Journal of Aging Studies,* 2 (1), 1988, 57–69.

Datan, Nancy, Dean Rodeheaver, and Fergus Hughes. "Adult Development and Aging." *Annual Review of Psychology,* 38, 1987, 153–80.

DeViney, Stanley, and Angela M. O'Rand. "Gender-Cohort Succession and Retirement among Older Men and Women, 1951–1984." *The Sociological Quarterly,* 29 (4), 1988, 525–540.

Essex, Marilyn, and Sunghee Nam. "Marital Status and Loneliness among Older Women: The Differential Importance of Close Family and Friends." *Journal of Marriage and the Family,* February 1987, 93–106.

Evans, Linda. "Old Age Dependency in Historical Perspective." *International Journal of Aging and Human Development,* 27 (2), 1988, 75–80.

Finley, Nancy J. "Theories of Family Labor as Applied to Gender Differences in Caregiving for Elderly Parents." *Journal of Marriage and the Family,* February 1989, 79–86.

————, M. Diane Roberts, and Benjamin F. Banahan. "Motivators and Inhibitors of Attitudes of Filial Obligation toward Aging Parents." *The Gerontologist,* February 1988, 73–78.

Gentry, Margaret, and Arthur D. Shulman. "Remarriage as a Coping Response for Widowhood." *Psychology and Aging,* 3 (2), 1988, 191–196.

Goldscheider, Frances K., and Calvin Goldscheider. "Family Structure and Conflict: Nest-Leaving Expectations of Young Adults and Their Parents." *Journal of Marriage and the Family,* February 1989, 87–97.

————, and Linda J. Waite. "Nest-Leaving Patterns and the Transition to Marriage for Young Men and Women." *Journal of Marriage and the Family,* August 1987, 507–516.

Heaton, Tim B., and Caroline Hoppe. "Widowed and Married: Comparative Change in Living Arrangements." *Social Science History,* Fall 1987, 261–280.

Johnson, Colleen Leary. "Relationships among Family Members and Friends in Later Life." In *Families and Social Networks,* edited by Robert M. Milardo, Newbury Park, CA: Sage Publications, 1988, 168–189.

Kenny, Maureen E. "Family Ties and Leaving Home for College: Recent Findings and Implications." *Journal of College Student Personnel,* September 1987, 438–442.

Kuntz, Masako-Ishii, and Gary R. Lee. "Status of the Elderly: An Extension of the Theory." *Journal of Marriage and the Family,* May 1987, 413–420.

Lee, Gary R. "Marital Satisfaction in Later Life: The Effects of Nonmarital Roles." *Journal of Marriage and the Family,* 1988, 775–783.

————, and Lee B. Whitbeck. "Residential Location and Social Relations among Older Persons." *Rural Sociology,* 52 (1), 1987, 89–97.

Litwack, Eugene, and Stephen Kulis. "Technology, Proximity, and Measures of Kin Support." *Journal of Marriage and the Family,* August 1987, 649–661.

Mancini, Jay A., and Rosemary Blieszner. "Aging Parents and Adult Children: Research Themes in Intergenerational Relations." *Journal of Marriage and the Family,* May 1989, 275–290.

Morganti, John B., Milton F. Nehrke, Irene M. Hulicka, Jerry F. Cataldo. "Life-span Differences in Life Satisfaction, Self-Concept, and Locus of Control." *International Journal of Aging and Human Development,* 26 (1), 1988, 45–56.

Morris, Monica. *Last-Chance Children: Growing Up with Older Parents.* New York: Columbia University Press, 1988.

Pillemer, Karl, and David Finkelhor. "The Prevalence of Elder Abuse: A Random Sample Survey." *The Gerontologist,* 28 (1), 1988, 51–57.

Rook, Karen S. "Reciprocity of Social Exchange and Social Satisfaction among Older Women." *Journal of Personality and Social Psychology,* 52 (1), 1987, 145–154.

Solie, Linda J., and Lois J. Fielder. "The Relationship between Sex Role Identity and a Widow's Adjustment to the Loss of a Spouse." *Omega,* 18 (1), 1987–88, 33–40.

Steinberg, Laurence, and Susan B. Silverberg. "Influences on Marital Satisfaction during the Middle Stages of the Family Life Cycle." *Journal of Marriage and the Family,* November 1987, 751–760.

Stull, Donald E. "A Dyadic Approach to Predicting Well-Being in Later Life." *Research on Aging,* March 1988, 81–101.

Weizman, R., and J. Hart. "Sexual Behavior in Healthy Married Elderly Men." *Archives of Sexual Research,* 16 (1), 1987, 39–44.

White, Lynn K. "Gender Differences in Awareness of Aging among Married Adults Ages 20 to 60." *The Sociological Quarterly,* 29 (4), 1988, 487–502.

FIVE

The Family and Social Change

Chapter

17

The Changing Status of Women: Women's Rights and Women's Liberation

*T*he struggle for equality between men and women both in America and abroad has had limited success. Regardless of the political or economic system involved, inequality continues. The vitality of various movements to reduce sex inequality in America attests to the resolve of men and women to try to solve this problem. Nevertheless, the persistence of inequality, despite the best of intentions, may mean that the root causes have not been clearly identified.

Still, there has been progress in the area of women's rights, particularly in the educational and occupational spheres. This progress has been the result of long and hard struggle—and the struggle is far from over. The story of the various changes—culminating in the current women's liberation movement—is the focus of the present chapter.

CHANGES IN COURTSHIP

In the colonial period, matrimony was looked upon as an economic necessity. Marriages often were influenced by the wishes of the respective families, while the importance of romantic love was played down. Courtship itself was not regarded as an integral part of young people's lives, and much of it was highly formalized. Parental approval was necessary before a dating relationship could begin.

The twin processes of urbanization and industrialization, however, altered the existing social structure. When the first census was taken in 1790, for example, there were only thirty-three cities in the United States, none of which had a population as large as 100,000. Today hundreds of cities have populations of more than 100,000.

In any case, certain changes were already discernible by the first half of the nineteenth century. The use of dowries, never as prevalent in America as in Europe, soon ceased altogether. Parental permission to begin courtship was no longer a strict necessity, and the custom of precontract became extinct. Although parents still had a fair measure of control over their sons' and daughters' marriages, love matches were growing in favor. Furthermore, a rapidly increasing urban population meant that young people had more leeway in the choice of mates. It was no longer necessary to marry the boy or girl on a nearby farm simply because of the shortage of available partners. Indeed, it became customary for a girl to have more than one suitor.

Although dating was becoming more liberal, it should not be thought that the nineteenth century was an age of amatory laxness and premarital frivolity. On the contrary, courtship customs were fairly restrictive. Even though young people had a relatively free hand in choosing mates, the selection process itself followed a prescribed course.

The "Pedestal"

One of the characteristics of the period, especially among the propertied classes, was gallantry. Women were placed on a pedestal and, in true chivalric fashion, were presumed to be morally and spiritually superior to men. The fair sex was believed to be endowed with a sense of dignity and purity, and the function of the male was that of protection. Escorts were not only obliged to protect the good names of their ladies, but as late as the turn of the century a couple could not attend social events without the proper surveillance.

Barbara Welter puts it as follows:

> In a society where values changed frequently, one thing remained the same— a true woman was a true woman, wherever she was found. If anyone dared to tamper with the complex of virtues which made up True Womanhood, he was damned immediately as an enemy of God, of civilization, and of the Republic.[1]

---

[1]Barbara Welter, "The Cult of True Womanhood: 1820–1860," in Michael Gordon, ed., *The American Family in Social-Historical Perspective* (New York: St. Martin's Press, 1983), 372.

Social gatherings, as they were called, included church affairs, concerts, community dances, picnics, and home parties. Boys were not supposed to lay hands on the girls they escorted, and many a young lady supposedly remained unkissed except by her fiancé.

Naturally there were lapses, as there are under any social code. That kissing, hugging, and fondling did occur is suggested by the now-defunct expressions "sparking" and "spooning." But insofar as community attitudes were verbalized, and to the extent that such attitudes were expressed in the public media—newspapers, magazines, novels, speeches, and sermons—courtship in the last century was held to be a *prelude to marriage,* and as such was regarded with a seriousness worthy of the marital state.

On their part, ladies were exhorted to act like ladies. They were presumed to hold an exalted moral position, and their behavior was supposed to reflect that position. They were expected to act in a dignified manner, to be gracious in social situations, and never to be forward in their relations with men. It goes almost without saying that women were forbidden to smoke, drink, or use coarse language. Welter states that "it was a fearful obligation, a solemn responsibility, which the nineteenth-century American woman had—to uphold the pillars of the temple with her frail white hand."[2]

Women of the period were even loath to use realistic terms when referring to the human body. Thus, arms and legs were called "limbs." Frost reports that "American women described their bodies from head to waist as stomach, and from there to the foot as ankles. They refused to mention specific parts of the body even to doctors. . . . Some expectant mothers refused to have doctors attend them during childbirth, preferring to use midwives. And husbands were barred from the sight of a birth."[3]

As Schlesinger aptly points out, the shadow of Queen Victoria fell almost more heavily on America than on her native land:

> Mrs. Trollope was exasperated to discover that men and women could visit the art gallery in Philadelphia only in separate groups, lest exposure to classical statues cause embarrassment in mixed company. . . .
>
> Visiting a ladies' seminary, Captain Marryat was stunned to see a square piano with four limbs, each of which, to protect the pupils, had been dressed in little trousers with frills at the bottom.
>
> The sickness of prudery grew in the course of the century. By the 1880's the public library of Concord, Massachusetts, was banning the *Adventures of Huckleberry Finn* as a dirty book. . . .[4]

---

[2]Ibid.

[3]J. William Frost, *The Quaker Family in Colonial America* (New York: St. Martin's Press, 1973), 180.

[4]Arthur Schlesinger, Jr., "An Informal History of Love, U.S.A.," in James R. Barbour, ed., *Human Sexuality 79/80,* Annual Editions (Guilford, CT: The Dushkin Publishing Group, 1979), 6.

Feminine Attire

One of the hallmarks of the 1800s was the attire of the lady—modest to an extreme. One authority reports that

> she covered herself from top to toe with numerous layers of clothing and an abundance of fluff and ruffles. Her body was not only concealed, it was made almost impregnable: it was a fortress with outworks of crinoline and an inner citadel protected by a tightly laced corset through which ran strips of bone or steel. The perfect young lady was one who moved and dressed in a manner that would not reveal the existence of her body.[5]

The excessive use of body coverings was aimed at lessening the sexual appetite of the male. According to the rules of the game, women were permitted to attract men, but not by any such direct approach as revealing parts of their bodies. In fact, the reader may be surprised to learn that in the early days of our seashore resorts, men and women were not permitted to go swimming together. One beach was used by the gentlemen bathers, while a separate one was reserved for the ladies. As late as World War I, Atlantic City employed watchers (with tape measures!) to determine whether female exposure was excessive.

The "System"

How did the ladies attract the male animal? Because they were supposed to be passive and retiring in their relations with men, women attempted—theoretically, at least—to capitalize on these very qualities. They were gracious, dignified, and ladylike. They were supposed to exude goodness and respectability. Also, if we can believe the literature of the period, women were adept at the use of flattery and were skillful in the exploitation of their "helplessness." In brief, they were presumably able to appeal to the "gallant side" of man's nature.

The above portrayal represents a generalization, of course; one suspects that there were many exceptions. Any number of women must have resented the insipid role assigned to them.

The Modern Era

Following World War I it became obvious that courtship customs were changing, and by World War II the era of the dainty lady had become a distant memory. In spite of dire warnings by the older generation, young women began to smoke, drink, use male vocabulary, listen to risqué jokes, engage in athletic activities, and in general repudiate the retiring demeanor that had characterized their grandmothers.

---

[5]Clarence Leuba, *The Sexual Nature of Man* (New York: Doubleday and Company, 1954), 5.

This woman is dressed in typical nineteenth-century attire. The abundance of ruffles and heavy fabric makes the body seem impregnable. (*Brown Brothers*)

As the ladylike role was abandoned, it was almost inevitable that women's fashions would change. It was time for the modern woman to wear modern clothes. Little by little the layers of petticoats were pared away. Bustles disappeared and corsets were left off. As the armor was removed, feminine clothing took on a more functional look. Frills and ruffles were replaced by a simplicity of design. Dresses no longer contained yards of bulky material. Necklines became lower, sleeves and hemlines were shortened.

On the social front, dating often started at an extremely young age. And whereas in earlier generations, courtship was normally initiated with matrimonial aims, now it was often undertaken *as an end in itself*. Dating, in other words, was no more likely to be used as an instrument of mate selection than as a means of spending an enjoyable evening.

Parents had only moderate control over their daughters' dating behavior

In the nineteenth century, women were viewed by many as weak, helpless, and in need of protection by men. (*Culver Pictures, Inc.*)

and almost none at all over their sons'. It was often difficult for mothers and fathers to keep abreast of their children's social life. From time to time, boys and girls became engaged without their parents' knowledge; and in some cases they even married without their parents' permission. (Historically, the circle had come full turn—in reverse. Whereas it was once customary for parents to marry off their children without the latter's consent, it was now quite easy for children to marry without their parents' consent!)

What factors were responsible for these pronounced changes? Urbanization and industrialization have already been mentioned, but the movement from farm to city was accompanied by commercial amusements such as movies, athletic events, dance halls, and, of course, bars. Opportunities for meeting young people of the opposite sex increased rapidly, and dating came to denote activities of the solitary couple rather than group participation, as formerly.

Other factors also contributed to the change in courtship procedures; for want of a more precise term these elements are often referred to as a "decline in the authoritarian tradition." Between the two world wars, new child-rearing methods emerged, and the old philosophy of "spare the rod and spoil the child" was being reversed. Parents were told not to overdiscipline their children, and in the interests of personality development young people were given more and more freedom.

The church, too, seemed to have waned in influence. Attendance declined, and in some areas the clergy were discovering that their sermons were being heard largely by older people. Society in general was adopting a more permissive attitude toward youths of both sexes. For better or worse, behavior that once have been considered shocking was now commonplace. Boys and girls held hands and put their arms around one another in public. Terms like "flirting" and "spooning" gave way to "necking," "petting," and "making out." Kissing lost all matrimonial significance, and most people of dating age indulged in personal intimacies.

Most surprising of all—at least in the eyes of the older generation—was the fact that the new system of courtship actually seemed to work. Even though women were no longer exalted and placed on a pedestal, romantic love flourished as never before, and the marriage rate remained high. Indeed, one of the distinctive features of modern matrimonial selection is the priority accorded to romantic love. Financial obstacles, parental opposition, housing problems, religious or social-class differences—all could be worked out. The only indispensable prerequisite to marriage, presumably, is love.

CHANGES IN SEX MORES

Throughout the 1800s, sexual codes in the United States remained strict. It is true that the extreme penalties imposed by the colonists—flogging, the scarlet letter, the death sentence—were no longer in effect. But nineteenth-century America was in no mood to take sex lightly. Spiritually and morally, women had been placed on a pedestal, and woe betide the female who brought discredit to the fair name of womanhood. A girl who indulged in premarital coitus not only suffered loss of reputation but was often marked for life, especially if she had an illegitimate child (in which case the child was similarly stigmatized). It is little wonder that premarital coitus was sometimes referred to as "a fate worse than death."

Unmarried males, on the other hand, were allowed much more leeway, and the age-old double standard of "boys will be boys" prevailed; in fact, during the nineteenth and early twentieth centuries prostitution flourished in most large cities, and it was quite common for young men to avail themselves to this opportunity. Thus boys could "sow their wild oats" while preserving their respect for the purity of womanhood, because prostitutes were considered to be of lower-class origin or to be "fallen women."

Behavioral Changes

As the twentieth century dawned, however, the same forces that tended to liberalize courtship customs served to weaken the existing sexual mores; indeed, it is difficult to separate the two. The emancipation of women, accelerated urbanization, the decline in secular and religious controls, and a more permissive attitude on the part of the public—all were involved. Three additional factors should be mentioned in this connection: (1) the automobile, with its phenomenal growth after World War I; (2) the increased availability of contraceptive devices; and (3) a relatively quick and simple cure for venereal disease, which became generally available after World War II.

Although attitudinal and behavioral changes in sexual conduct emerged gradually, World War I seems to have been a major dividing line between the old and the new. As in the case of courtship patterns, the 1920s witnessed a break in the sexual dam. Necking and petting became widespread—and remain so today. Premarital coitus increased greatly, especially on the part of engaged or almost engaged couples. In the convenient privacy of the automobile, and with the ever-increasing availability of birth control measures, the issue often was not whether the girl should permit a goodnight kiss, but whether the couple should engage in sexual intercourse.

Organized prostitution, on the other hand, seems to have declined sharply—in part, no doubt, because of the general increase in sexual activity on the part of single women, and in part because of the association that prostitution came to have with civic corruption and crime.

Changes in Attitude

Although American sexual behavior has changed significantly during the past decades, equally important from the sociological view are the many changes in attitudes. Most of the changes have been gradual, and many appear to be unrelated. Yet they are related in the sense that they have all moved in the same direction—toward a more permissive set of regulations pertaining to sex. It might be added that our current attitudes seem quite natural to the younger generation; the contrast becomes apparent only when these views are compared with those of the nineteenth century.

The American woman of this earlier period, at least ideally, held a position of refinement and dignity. Sex was presumed to be abhorrent to her; even after marriage, myth had it that any sexual response on her part was unladylike. Admittedly, the ladylike role was rejected in some instances. In fact, Degler has presented some interesting evidence suggesting that attitudes toward female sexual response—and the response itself—were not as negative as most social historians contend.[6]

[6]Carl N. Degler, "The Emergence of the Modern Family," in Michael Gordon, *The American Family in Social-Historical Perspective* (New York: St. Martin's Press, 1983), 61–79.

In any case, as the emancipation movement gained headway, marital coitus came to be regarded by the public at large as an activity that was pleasurable for the wife as well as the husband. Terms like "sexual compatibility" and "sexual adjustment" began to be heard, and impotence on the part of the husband was incorporated as one of the grounds that the wife could use in a divorce suit. Today, of course, mutual pleasure in the sexual realm is held to be an important factor in overall marital happiness, and a variety of marriage manuals are available to instruct newlyweds in coital techniques.

While wives were becoming sexually emancipated, there was a gradual but steady increase in the number of words and phrases that were permissible in polite company. Whereas before World War I sex was a subject deemed unfit for feminine ears, the succeeding decades witnessed a "let's-bring-sex-out-in-the-open" philosophy. As a result, people in all walks of life—both males and females—came to have a better understanding of the subject.

THE WOMEN'S RIGHTS MOVEMENT

Although female emancipation was clearly evident in such areas as wearing apparel, courtship, and sexual behavior, there were more important changes on the horizon. It must be remembered that throughout the colonial period women had inferior status in virtually all walks of life. While they were protected by law from severe verbal and physical assaults, and while they were generally loved and respected by their husbands, colonial wives found themselves in a subordinate position—socially, legally, and economically. This condition persisted well into the nineteenth century.

Within the home, for example, the wife was subservient—a "helpmate," with all that term implies. Welter has written as follows:

> A wife should occupy herself only with domestic affairs: "wait till your husband confides to you things of high importance—and do not give your advice until he asks for it," advised the *Lady's Token*. At all times she should behave in a manner becoming a woman, who had "no arms other than gentleness." Thus, "if he is abusive, never retort."
>
> A *Young Lady's Guide* suggested that females should "become as little children" and "avoid a controversial spirit." *The Mother's Assistant and Young Lady's Friend* listed "Always Conciliate" as its first commandment in "Rules for Conjugal and Domestic Happiness." Small wonder that these same rules ended with the succinct maxim: "Do not expect too much."[7]

As late as 1850 a wife had no legal control over her own personal property; all her belongings were legally in the hands of her husband, to dispose of as he saw fit. Her services also belonged to him, and she had no legal

---

[7]Welter, *The Cult of Womanhood,* 378.

right even to the custody of her own children. Women were not permitted to vote, nor was their education taken very seriously. Female wage earners and career women were looked upon with suspicion and sometimes were excluded from social functions. In general, a woman had few alternatives to marrying and fulfilling her childbearing and homemaking "destiny."

The above inequalities, of course, are incompatible with democratic concepts, and it was inevitable that a protest movement, known as the women's rights movement, should arise. In 1848, the momentous first convention was held in Seneca Falls, New York, and a declaration of sentiments was adopted. The basic objectives were threefold: (1) to free the persons and property of married women from the absolute control of their husbands and to establish the wife as a legal personality, (2) to open the doors of higher education to all women, and (3) to procure full political rights for women.

The booming factory system also was instrumental in raising the status of women. Cheap labor was needed, and what better source than young farm girls? In spite of abominable conditions, it soon became apparent that the girls were excellent workers. It was also shown that women, given a chance, could support themselves. Once women were freed from their strict economic dependence, the cry for legal and educational equality grew louder. As might be expected, there was serious opposition to the women's rights movement from both press and pulpit. Many men denounced the whole idea; indeed, remnants of such opposition can still be found. Once the first gains had been made, however, the movement surged ahead on all fronts.

Legal and Political Gains

It would not be an exaggeration to say that throughout most of American history, women were veritable legal ciphers. The following cases provide examples:

> In 1863, a woman in Massachusetts slipped and fell on the ice. Being a woman, she was unable to sue for damages. Her husband, however, was awarded thirteen hundred dollars by the courts as compensation for his loss of her labor—money he could spend as he pleased—without consulting his wife.

> One man who failed in business was supported for years by his wife, who established a successful milliner's shop. Eventually he died, leaving her shop and her savings, legally his own, to somebody else. Had he died in debt, everything she had would have been sacrificed to pay off his creditors—although the law did allow her to keep her own clothes, a single table, six chairs, six plates, six knives and forks, one sugar bowl, and twelve spoons.[8]

---

[8]Olivia Coolidge, *Women's Rights: The Suffrage Movement in America* (New York: E. P. Dutton, 1976), 9–10.

It was not until 1920 that American women were accorded the right to vote by the nineteenth amendment to the Constitution.

Over the years, however, inequities of this type were removed as the various states amended their laws regarding married women's property. Today a wife remains legal owner of the property she possessed before marriage. She can negotiate contracts, operate her own business, and keep her earnings. Inheritance laws generally give husband and wife equal status, a principle that also applies to child custody and guardianship.

Politically, too, women have been granted equal rights, although it was not until 1920 that they were accorded the right to vote by the nineteenth amendment to the constitution. In future years women will probably become more influential, because there are more women than men in the population, an imbalance that is increasing.

In addition to their voting power, women in recent periods have held a wide variety of political and administrative offices, such as Treasurer of the United States, Secretary of Labor, Secretary of Health, Education, and Welfare, Director of the Passport Office, Director of the Mint, Head of the Interstate Commerce Commission, Assistant to the President for Consumer Affairs, Director of the Bureau of Public Assistance, and Supreme Court Justice. Several women have been elected to the post of state governor and lieutenant governor. Women also have run—albeit unsuccessfully—for the presidency of the United States. Currently twenty-nine women are serving in Congress.[9] At the local level, women have held virtually every elective and appointive office that men have held.

Educational Advancement

In the colonial period it was deemed neither practical nor prudent to expose young women to serious education. Even in the nineteenth century, anti-feminists protested stoutly against providing girls with "boys' education." Historical documents reveal a variety of bizarre reasons for this position. It was held, for example, that education would affect the female's health, make her nervous, encourage her to be dissatisfied, to run away from home, or to be treacherous. Perhaps the chief objection was that formal education would weaken her role as homemaker.

In spite of varied protests, the nineteenth century saw the admission of girls into elementary schools and eventually into secondary schools. In 1883, feminine education scored a victory when Oberlin College admitted women as well as men. In 1837, Mount Holyoke Seminary for Girls was established in Massachusetts, thanks to the pioneering efforts of Mary Lyon. Vassar College opened its doors in 1865, followed by Smith in 1871, Wellesley in 1877, and Bryn Mawr in 1880. The University of Michigan meanwhile had admitted women in 1870, and by the turn of the century coeducational colleges and universities were becoming commonplace. To-day the great majority of the more than 2000 institutions of higher learning in the United States are coeducational, including practically all professional schools.

Indeed, as we enter the 1990s, overall educational figures show no sex discrimination. Once relegated to summer school, girls now are more likely than boys to graduate from high school. In 1950, women received about 24 percent of the undergraduate degrees granted. Currently the figure has grown to around 52 percent.[10]

Economic Improvement

Unless they were employed as servants, colonial women had little occupational opportunity. Even during the early 1800s, after certain types of jobs had been opened to women, female wage earners continued to be stigmatized by inferior social status.

The first large-scale influx of female workers took place in the New England factories. Most of the workers were unmarried farm girls, some

---

[9]*Information Please Almanac, 1990* (Boston: Houghton Mifflin, 1990), 39.

[10]*Information Please Almanac 1990,* 843.

hardly more than children. They were welcomed, nevertheless, because they not only were conscientious employees but would work for low wages.

During the Civil War an increasing number of occupations were opened to women, a phenomenon that was to be repeated in the First and Second World Wars. During World War II, women were employed as welders, mechanics, machinists, taxi drivers, and streetcar operators; in fact, with the exception of heavy-duty laboring jobs, females could be found in virtually every branch of industry. Also, because of their excellent record, women were made a permanent part of the armed forces.

Today there are more than 52 million women in the work force.[11] Of those not in the labor force, the great majority are retired or have home responsibilities. From the sociological perspective it is important to note that currently even mothers with small children are likely to be employed outside the home. "Regardless of marital status or the presence of young children, labor force participation has become the norm for women."[12] Since 1986, more than half of all women with children under three years of age have been in the labor force.

Over and above their widespread employment in factories, women can be found increasingly in white-collar, managerial, and professional occupations. They now serve as business executives, bank presidents, scientists, editors and publishers, physicians, college professors, lawyers and judges, engineers, and clergy. The role of women in literary, artistic, and entertainment fields is well known, and they hold a superior position in fashion and design. In brief, women have entered practically all employment fields, including those that in an earlier period were reserved "for men only."

SOCIOLOGICAL ASPECTS OF WOMEN'S LIBERATION

It is difficult to pinpoint the exact beginning of the modern women's liberation movement, but certainly the 1963 publication of Betty Friedan's *The Feminine Mystique* played an important part. In her travels across America and her interviews with housewives from every social stratum, Friedan detected a shadowy unrest. Despite obvious material comforts and often a relatively high standard of living, wives were experiencing a sense of purposelessness and discontent. In the first chapter, Friedan begins as follows:

> The problem lay buried, unspoken, for many years in the minds of American women. It was a strange stirring, a sense of dissatisfaction, a yearning that women suffered in the middle of the twentieth century in the United States. As she made the beds, shopped for groceries, matched slipcover material, ate peanut butter sandwiches with her children, chauffeured Cub Scouts and

---

[11]Sara E. Rix, *The American Woman, 1988–89* (New York: W. W. Norton, 1988), 366, 370.

[12]Ibid., 341.

Women have entered practically all employment fields, including those that in an earlier period were reserved "for men only."

Brownies, lay beside her husband at night, she was afraid to ask even of herself the silent question: "Is this all?"[13]

Although Friedan's "platform" was greeted with derision in some quarters, many people—particularly in the younger age groups—agreed with her position. Slowly at first, then more and more rapidly, women's liberation groups made their voices heard. They made demands for more and better jobs, equal social and athletic facilities, child-care centers, legalized abortions, and equal educational opportunities—especially at the graduate and professional level. In brief, whether the issue was economic, political, social, or sexual, the demand was loud and clear: down with the double standard.

[13]Betty Friedan, *The Feminine Mystique,* 4th ed. (New York: W. W. Norton, 1983).

It soon became apparent, furthermore, that women's liberation was more than a slogan, more than a fad. It was demonstrably an idea whose time had come.

Although women have not yet reached parity with men, most of the signs seem encouraging. Title VII of the Civil Rights Act prohibits discrimination in employment based on sex as well as on race and religion. The Federal Minimum Wage and Hour Law applies equally to males and to females. The Equal Pay Act requires equal pay for equal work.

At the college level, as stated earlier, women have made giant strides. The trend in graduate and professional training is also encouraging. Women's enrollment in recent years has doubled or tripled in fields such as business, medicine, law, pharmacy, and veterinary medicine.

EFFECT OF THE WOMEN'S MOVEMENT ON MARRIAGE

It is reasonable to suppose that the women's rights movement and women's liberation have had an effect on marriage and the family. After all, some 65 percent of women with children under eighteen and more than 73 percent with children between the ages of six and seventeen are in the labor force.[14]

Certainly the women's movement has affected marriage, but how has that effect been manifested? One manifestation is postponement of marriage. Another is the increase in divorce rates. Marital postponement may be due to the fact that women now have viable alternatives to matrimony, alternatives that formerly were closed to them. For example, since job opportunities have become increasingly available, the rise in the divorce rate probably is related to the fact that fewer women have to remain trapped in an unhappy marriage.

In other respects, however, the women's movement probably has strengthened marriage. Education, for instance, certainly has established an additional bond between husband and wife. It is no longer necessary for husbands to be condescending or for wives to feel inferior. Also, women's improved occupational status has strengthened marriage in an economic sense: wives often have reinforced or even preserved marriages through their financial contributions.

Opinion polls show that even though husbands do not contribute as much to household upkeep and child rearing as do their employed wives, increasing numbers of women prefer to combine marriage, motherhood, and a career. Here is the trend as reported by Gallup and by a *New York Times* survey.[15]

---

[14]*Information Please Almanac*, 1990, 61.

[15]Through 1985 the results are found in George H. Gallup, *The Gallup Poll* (Wilmington, DE: Scholarly Resources, 1986), 105–7. For 1989 see *The New York Times*, August 10, 1989, A1,A26.

PERCENTAGES OF WOMEN WHO
PREFER MARRIAGE, CHILDREN, AND
FULL-TIME JOB OR CAREER

Year	Age	Percentage
1989	18–44	55
	45+	40
1985	18+	38
1980	18+	33
1975	18+	32

The response of female college students confirms the national findings. When women in our classes were asked, more than 80 percent reported that they intended to combine marriage and a career. One respondent epitomized the feelings of most of our students when she wrote:

> The old days are gone forever. Today, if a girl wants a career—well, everybody respects her for it. And I'm one of those girls. I've nothing against marriage. Actually, I plan to combine both marriage and a career. But right now, career comes first. Of course, I can always change my mind.

This last statement drives home a very pertinent point. The recent women's liberation movement *has* provided women in all walks of life with a choice. Those who wish to do so still can select the "marriage only" option. But for others, the temper of the times now makes it possible to explore career possibilities without sacrificing a rewarding matrimonial relationship.

SUMMARY

Although women have not yet reached parity with men, times are changing in favor of equality between the sexes. Nowhere is this change more evident then in women's rights. Courtship, marriage, sexual behavior, education, the job market—virtually every traditional sphere has been liberalized. And although the results have proved beneficial to all concerned, the struggle for equal rights continues.

QUESTIONS

1. What is meant by the "pedestal" concept of women, as exemplified in nineteenth-century America? Do traces of this concept remain today?
2. How did feminine attire in the nineteenth century relate to the pedestal concept?
3. Describe the changes that took place—in courtship, feminine attire, the "pedestal," and so forth—during the modern era.

4. Describe the changes that took place during the same period in (a) sexual attitudes and (b) sexual behavior.

5. Specifically, what was the women's rights movement? What were its goals? What were its accomplishments? Explain.

6. Do you see women's liberation as a continuation of woman's rights—or are the two movements qualitatively different? Defend your viewpoint.

7. Betty Friedan's *The Feminine Mystique,* published in 1963, played an important part in the women's liberation movement. What specific points or recommendations did Friedan make? By and large, have these recommendations been accepted?

8. Do you feel that the women's movement has run its course, or do you believe that it is here to stay—as a continuing process? What are your reasons?

9. In your opinion, what have been the effects of the woman's rights movement and women's liberation on marriage and the family?

10. What, if anything, do you think should be on the agenda of the women's movement? Explain.

SELECTED READINGS

Bokemeier, Janet L., and William B. Lacy. "Job Values, Rewards, and Work Conditions as Factors in Job Satisfaction among Men and Women." *The Sociological Quarterly,* 28 (2), 1987, 189–204.

Buechler, Steven M. "Elizabeth Boynton Harbart and the Woman Suffrage Movement, 1870–1896." *Signs: Journal of Women in Culture and Society,* 13 (1) 1987, 78–97.

England, Paula, George Farkas, Barbara Stanek Kilbourne, and Thomas Dou. "Explaining Occupational Sex Segregation and Wages: Findings from a Model with Fixed Effects." *American Sociological Review,* August 1988, 544–58.

Fiorentine, Robert. "Men, Women, and the Premed Persistence Gap: A Normative Alternatives Approach." *American Journal of Sociology,* March 1987, 1118–39.

Fox, Bonnie J. "Conceptualizing 'Patriarchy'." *Review of Canadian Sociology and Anthropology,* 25 (2), 1988, 163–181.

Grint, Keith. "Women and Equality: The Acquisition of Equal Pay in the Post Office: 1870–1961." *Sociology,* February 1988, 87–108.

Jaffee, David. "Gender Inequality in Workplace Autonomy and Authority." *Social Science Quarterly,* June 1989, 375–390.

Jameson, Elizabeth. "Toward a Multicultural History of Women in the Western United States." *Signs: Journal of Women in Culture and Society.* 13 (4), 1988, 761–91.

Katz, David. "Sex Discrimination in Hiring: The Influence of Organized Climate and Need for Approval on Decision Making Behavior." *Psychology of Women Quarterly,* 11, 1987, 11–20.

Kingston, Paul W., and Steven E. Finkel. "Is There a Marriage Gap in Politics?" *Journal of Marriage and the Family,* February 1987, 57–64.

Kirkcaldy, Bruce. "Sex and Personality Differences in Occupational Interests." *Personal and Individual Differences,* 9 (1), 1988, 7–13.

Leonardo, Micaela. "The Female World of Cards and Holidays: Women, Families, and the Work of Kinship." *Signs: Journal of Women in Culture and Society,* 12 (3), 1987, 440–453.

Lorence, Jon. "Gender Differences in Occupational Labor Market Structure." *Work and Occupations,* February 1987, 23–61.

Ratcliff, Kathryn Strother, and Janet Bogdan. "Unemployed Women: When 'Social Support' Is Not Supportive." *Social Problems,* February 1988, 54–63.

Reid, Pamela Trotman. "Perceptions of Sex Discrimination among Female University Faculty and Staff." *Psychology of Women Quarterly,* 11, 1987, 123–28.

Ryan, Barbara. "Ideological Purity and Feminism: The U.S. Women's Movement from 1966–1975." *Gender and Society,* June 1989, 239–257.

Schneider, Beth. "Political Generations and the Contemporary Woman's Movement." *Sociological Inquiry,* Winter, 1988, 4–21.

Sorensen, Glorian. "Women, Work, and Health." *American Review of Public Health,* 8, 1987, 235–51.

Sugarman, David B., and Murray A. Straus. "Indicators of Gender Equality for American States and Regions." *Social Indicators Research,* 20, 1988, 229–270.

Swerdlow, Marian. "Men's Accommodations to Women Entering a Nontraditional Occupation." *Gender and Society,* September 1989, 373–87.

Tickamyer, Ann R., and Janet L. Bokemeier. "Individual and Structural Explanations of Nonmetropolitan Women and Men's Labor Force Experience." *Research in Rural Sociology and Development,* 4, 1989, 153–170.

Weeks, O'Neal M., and Darla R. Botkin. "A Longitudinal Study of the Marriage Role Expectations of College Women: 1961–1984." *Sex Roles,* 17 (1/2), 1987, 49–58.

Zimmer, Lynn. "Tokenism and Women in the Workplace: The Limits of Gender-Neutral Theory." *Social Problems,* February 1988, 64–77.

Chapter
18

Some Alternatives to Family Living

*N*ot too long ago the future of the monogamous, two-parent family in America seemed to be in doubt. After all, it is no longer considered strange or deviant to cohabit, to remain single, or to choose some other alternative to monogamous family living. As it turns out, however, despite greater tolerance for different lifestyles, traditional values still dominate in our culture. A recent Gallup poll found "virtually unanimous public support for traditional family ties (94 percent)."[1] Unlike the situation during the 1960s, the alternatives to marriage and the family have lost some of their appeal.

Nevertheless, there are a number of alternative lifestyles. Some, like group marriage, have never attracted a following. Others, such as cohabitation and staying single, involved a substantial number of people. Swinging and communal living also are viable lifestyles among a small but persistent segment of the population.

---

[1]George Gallup. *The Gallup Poll: Public Opinion 1988* (Wilmington, DE: Scholarly Resources Inc., 1989), 181.

This chapter examines some of the more publicized lifestyles, together with their implications for the future.

STAYING SINGLE

In the past, the prospect of life without marriage was rather dismal for most people. Although this is still true to a certain extent, American folklore is full of stories that portray singlehood as an ideal way of life. As Pollner wryly observes,

> legendary heroes are rarely married. When they are, their marriages are often referred to as a "fate worse than death." Rip Van Winkle slept 20 years and awakened happily to find his wife dead. Jesse James, in one ballad, is killed while drudging as a henpecked husband, while other traditions state that he was shot while hanging the picture of his 'doggone wife' on the wall. Paul Bunyan wanted nothing to do with women and felt that 'even as memories and fancies they are nuisances.[2]

The most provocative description of single living comes from the media portrayal of "the good life." Singlehood on television is often associated with excitement, glamour, freedom, and sexual fulfillment. In any role on television—from the ubiquitous detective to lawyers, teachers, and doctors—the richest, most exciting people are very often single. The contrasts between married and single life, as portrayed on television, tend to be sharp and easy to observe: it almost seems as though single people are having all the fun. . . .

In view of the buildup that singlehood receives in the media, one could argue that more people should prefer single life. In reality, however, the large majority of American men and women desire to marry and be a part of a close family relationship. Millions of unmarried people in our society are either temporarily single or do not have the opportunity to marry. Nevertheless, some men and women deliberately choose singlehood as a permanent way of life.

Whether unmarried by choice or by chance, single people are joining "singles" organizations in unprecedented numbers. Singles clubs and various special-purpose singles groups have become commonplace. Major churches have initiated special ministries for singles. Some churches even hold annual conventions that are attended by thousands of single men and women.

Most singles groups, secular or not, provide entertainment and an opportunity for social interaction in pleasant surroundings. In large cities the choice of groups and activities is large enough to keep an unmarried person socially active every day of the year! In Los Angeles County, for example, a

---

[2]Mildred Pollner, "Better Dead Than Wed," *Social Policy*, Summer 1982, 28.

Single couples are increasingly forming groups and clubs where singles' activities are planned for every day of the year. (© 1983, Watriss/Baldwin, Woodfin Camp)

single person can choose in any one week from dozens of activities, such as these advertised in a publication called the *Singles Register:*[3]

Community Education lecture: "Looking for Love in All the Right Places."

A Touch of Class. Complimentary dinner buffet and Southland's most danceable music highlights . . . Black tie/cocktail dress recommended.

---

[3]*Singles Register,* September 22, 1989, 8.

Lecture, "Making Romance Work."

Singles Scene, featuring representatives from major singles' organizations, lectures, dance.

Social hour, free refreshments, lecture, "Self-esteem for Singles."

In addition, there are singles cruises, night clubs, photo safaris, and activities ranging from church socials to swinging parties. Singles organizations offer something for every taste and for every day of the year!

What accounts for this lifestyle? For one thing, women are about as likely as men to delay marriage in order to graduate from college. A better education means a better job, and more and more women have been making names for themselves in business and industry. Understandably, some women are reluctant to give up their careers and their independence in favor of matrimony.

Not surprisingly, our knowledge of the never-married group has grown in recent years. There is a suggestion, for example, that this group is somewhat unusual. Cockrum and White report that

> Never-married adults are more likely to define singlehood as a permanent lifestyle than are divorced individuals. Marriage rates are higher for divorced singles in comparison to never-married singles in every age group. Therefore, the single experience is probably more gratifying and less problematic for never-married adults.[4]

It should also be mentioned that at one time a stigma was attached to both the never-married and the divorced, but this is no longer true. Today a young woman who prefers a career to marriage is not stigmatized but may even be envied, especially if she is successful.

An obvious advantage for singles living alone is the lack of conflict that often arises between married persons. In addition, singles do not have to account to anyone for how they spend their time and their money. On the other hand, as illustrated in Chapter 1, when two people share their living expenses, they can save money. That is one reason why so many college students cohabit or live with a roommate of the same sex.

Costs notwithstanding, it seems that staying single has become an acceptable way of life for many Americans. As Cornish notes: "Already, singles are changing the tone of economic, educational, and even religious events."[5] Whether the percentage of singles will increase in the future—and if so, what the consequences will be—is something that college students may wish to think about.

---

[4]Janet Cockrum and Priscilla White, "Influences on the Life Satisfaction of Never-Married Men and Women," *Family Relations,* October 1985, 555–56.

[5]Edward Cornish, "The Coming of the Singles Society," *The Futurist,* July/August, 1987, 58.

Staying single has become an acceptable way of life for many Americans.

COHABITATION

Along with singlehood, cohabitation has also emerged. Cohabitation is sometimes thought to be a kind of trial marriage, but the two terms have different connotations. Trial marriage is a relationship wherein the partners live together for a certain period of time while deciding whether to make the arrangement permanent. Cohabitation, according to the dictionary, is simply "living together in a sexual relationship when not legally married."

Although cohabitation occurs in all walks of life—and among all age groups—in recent years it has often come to be associated with the college population. As practiced today on college campuses, cohabitation seems to have different meanings for different people. In one study, most cohabitors who married after cohabitation looked back on their experience as a preparation for marriage.[6] A recent review of the literature, however, shows that no more than 20 to 30 percent of cohabiting couples marry each other.[7]

---

[6]Mark Kotkin, "To Marry or Live Together?" *Lifestyles: A Journal of Changing Patterns,* Spring 1985, 160.

[7]Michael D. Newcomb, "Cohabitation and Marriage: A Quest for Independence and Relatedness," in Stuart Oskamp, ed., *Family Processes and Problems* (Newbury Park, CA: Sage Publications, 1987), 129.

Further, those who do marry are considerably more likely to divorce than those who never cohabited before marriage.[8] In fact, research findings during recent years have tended to disprove the hypothesis that cohabitation is a way of improving the quality of mate selection through trial marriage.

The Extent of Cohabitation

It is difficult to estimate the extent of cohabitation among students in the United States because different researchers define the term in different ways. Some define cohabitation simply as a nonmarital "living together relationship with a member of the opposite sex." Others include a time element; for example, "living together for a period of three or more months." Nevertheless, at the beginning of the 1980s, various studies showed that approximately 25 percent of American college students had cohabited.[9] Since that time the cohabitation rates in the general population have increased,[10] and it may be that the proportion of cohabiting college students has also increased.

Using a single figure may give the impression that all cohabitation relationships are the same, but in reality, such relationships differ in both motivation and commitment. Researchers have identified at least six distinct types of cohabitation. Macklin lists them as follows:[11]

1. Temporary convenience or mutual benefit.
2. Affectionate relationship but open to other simultaneous relationships.
3. Affectionate, monogamous relationship.
4. Trial marriage or a conscious testing of a relationship.
5. Temporary alternative to marriage (e.g., while awaiting divorce settlement or graduation).
6. Permanent alternative to marriage.

Figures for each type of cohabitation are not available, but some characteristics of those who have "lived with a heterosexual partner for at least three months without marriage" have been noted.

Characteristics of Cohabitors

Do people who cohabit differ in some ways from those who do not? As a group, noncohabitors are more religious than cohabitors; there is no

---

[8]Neil G. Bennett, Ann K. Blanc, and David E. Bloom, "Commitment and the Modern Union: Assessing the Link between Premarital Cohabitation and Subsequent Marital Stability," *American Sociological Review,* February 1988, 137.

[9]Barbara J. Risman et al., "Living Together in College: Implications for Courtship," *Journal of Marriage and the Family,* February 1981, 77.

[10]Newcomb, 1987, 129.

[11]Eleanor D. Macklin, "Cohabitation in the United States," In J. Gipson Wells, ed., *Current Issues in Marriage and the Family* (New York: Macmillan, 1983), 65–66.

disagreement on this point. Aside from this generalization, however, research has revealed much about women cohabitors but little about the men. A recent national survey of unmarried women revealed that most cohabiting women but only 24 percent of noncohabiting women were living in broken families by age fifteen.[12] Other distinguishing characteristics of cohabiting women included a more liberal attitude toward abortion and a greater likelihood of becoming pregnant and of having had a child.

Other studies also showed that cohabitors, both males and females, are more likely to use drugs. "Cohabitors reported significantly greater use of all drugs except nonprescribed medication."[13]

Findings regarding the sociodemographic characteristics of cohabitors tend to be inconclusive, although most cohabitors live in metropolitan areas.[14] Some earlier research seemed to show that cohabitors were better educated and more likely to be employed. Tanfer's study of a national sample of women showed just the opposite, however. In that study, it was found that "cohabitors have lower educational attainment and are less likely to be employed than noncohabitors . . . one fourth of the current cohabitors reported that they were 'keeping house' in contrast to only 10% of women who have never cohabited."[15]

In view of the present state of research, it is difficult to assess the true characteristics of the cohabiting population, especially the men. In addition, recent research has focused more on psychological and sexual dimensions rather than on the couples' role arrangements. (Research in the 1970s and early 1980s showed little difference between role arrangements among cohabiting and married couples. In both types of relationships, women were more likely than men to be responsible for household tasks. Not much has changed since then among married couples; it is not known whether the same is true among cohabitors.)

In recent years we have learned more about the sex life of cohabiting couples. Several studies reveal that cohabiting couples have intercourse more frequently than married couples of similar age and duration of marriage.[16] Yet the subjective appraisal of sexual satisfaction does not seem to differ from that of married couples.[17]

---

[12]Koray Tanfer, "Patterns of Premarital Cohabitation among Never Married Women in the United States," *Journal of Marriage and the Family,* 1987, 487.

[13]Michael D. Newcomb, "Cohabitation, Marriage and Divorce among Adolescents and Young Adults," *Journal of Social and Personal Relationships,* 3, 1986, 480.

[14]Tanfer, 1987, 486.

[15]Ibid., 486.

[16]E. Sandra Byers and Larry Heinlein, "Predicting Initiations and Refusals of Sexual Activities in Married and Cohabiting Heterosexual Couples," *The Journal of Sex Research,* May 1989, 219.

[17]Ibid., 220–221.

Individual and Societal Implications

There is no doubt that cohabitation is more prevalent now than it was a generation ago, and the reasons are not hard to find: a more permissive societal attitude toward sex in general, and premarital sex in particular; the women's movement, with its challenge to the sexual double standard; improved methods and availability of birth control.

With regard to the college scene, several additional factors are involved. The 1960s saw the emergence of the youth counterculture, centered in many instances on college campuses. Colleges and universities themselves grew in size and complexity, affording students of both sexes an anonymity not previously possible. Most important, perhaps, was the erosion of the university position of *in loco parentis*. Deans and administrators, faced with a growing and vociferous student body—and a sprawling physical plant—soon desisted in their attempts to "legislate morality." As a result, curfews were lifted, students were permitted to live in off-campus housing, and coed dorms came into being.

What have been the individual and societal effects of cohabitation, and what will the future bring? Difficult questions, surely, and it is little wonder that there is some disagreement among authorities. On the one hand, Tanfer feels that cohabitation is not a challenge to marriage, that it is not taking the place of marriage now nor will it in the future. Virtually all cohabitants go on to marriage at some point in their lives. Instead, it is believed that cohabitation is becoming institutionalized and accepted as part of the marriage system. This process is much the same as that by which casual and steady dating were invented and accepted in the past.[18]

> In many cases, I suspect that, rather than providing a good test for compatibility in marriage, living together constitutes an immature version of "playing house" for which students are seeking adult approval. . . . Family life educators should view students' interpretations of living together critically. So far as I know, for example, there is no persuasive evidence that living together helps to avoid divorce. In fact, there is no evidence at all.

> Students may unknowingly be creating a self-fulfilling prophecy. They enter relationships partly to see if they will last and, by keeping the possibility of discontinuing the relationship in mind, they actually help to cause the breakup, . . . Living together, viewed thus, becomes a way for substantial numbers of young people to avoid responsibility.[19]

In our opinion, cohabitation in the United States is here to stay—with future trends uncertain. Regardless of trends, however, the likelihood of any significant effect on the marriage rate is slight.

---

[18]Tanfer, 1987, 494.

[19]Gerald Leslie, "Personal Values, Professional Ideologies, and Family Specialists: A New Look," *The Family Coordinator*, April 1979, 159.

A common word in the swinging vocabulary is discretion. (*Philip Jon Bailey*)

SWINGING

In essence, swinging is a voluntary and temporary swapping of mates for sexual purposes. The swapping generally involves two or more couples, although occasionally an unattached person—usually a female—is included. But whatever the combinations, the sexual exchange takes place with the full consent of all parties concerned. Swinging thus differs from adultery, since the latter ordinarily occurs without spousal agreement.

Swinging usually takes one of two forms. In the first, two couples simply spend a quiet evening together, in the course of which an exchange of mates takes place for sexual purposes. In the second, a number of couples have a party—at which time a whole series of sexual exchanges occurs. Many swingers reportedly begin with the two-couple arrangement, later "graduating" to the group conclave.

After their initial encounter with swinging, some couples never repeat the experience. Others adopt it as a lifestyle. Today swingers are organized through a national network of local organizations and clubs that actively promote swinging as a way of life.

The Extent of Swinging

Estimates of the number of swingers in the United States range from thousands to millions, depending on who does the estimating. Understandably, those who indulge or who are sympathetic to the idea see swinging as a popular way of life. Others consider swinging to be little more than a fad, with extremely limited acceptance. Regardless of its popularity in the past, however, swinging continues to fascinate some married couples.

One indication of interest in swinging is the number of swing clubs listed in the North American Swing Club Directory. According to the editors of the directory, "Through the growth of swing clubs and publications . . . activist swing clubs and a few swing personalities, a social network has developed on local, national, and international levels."[20] Counting the clubs in 1988, there were 192 such clubs listed in 40 states and the District of Columbia. In 1990, the directory contained 175 clubs in 38 states!

Swingers can find each other in a variety of ways. Personal advertisements in dozens of swingers' magazines, newspapers, newsletters, and tabloids bring interested couples together. As shown in the *International Directory of Swing Clubs and Publications*, there were 94 publishers of such materials in 1990.

In the near future, computers might compete with the printed word in swingers' circles. In 1990, the North American Swing Clubs Association included for the first time a listing titled "Computer Swinging." A couple with a personal computer at home or at the office can express their desires for swinging in the manner described in Chapter 10 ("Modes of Mate Selection"). As in ordinary dating, a swinger is looking for a way to contact others with similar interests.

Characteristics of Swingers

Who are the swingers? Do they have any distinguishing characteristics? Why do they embark on such an unusual way of life? Surveys show that swingers "tend to come from the middle to the upper classes, to be above average in education, to be predominantly white, and to have a wide range of ages, but fall mainly in the thirty-five-year-old to forty-five-year-old bracket.[21]

Whatever their characteristics, it seems certain that husbands are more likely than wives to initiate swinging. In Murstein, Case, and Gunn's study, for example, forty-four out of sixty-two couples with swinging experience

---

[20]*International Directory of Swing Clubs and Publications* (Buena Park, CA: North American Swing Club Association, 1990), 1.

[21]Richard J. Jenks, "A Comparative Study of Swingers and Nonswingers: Attitudes and Behavior," *Lifestyles: A Journal of Changing Patterns,* Fall 1985, 5–6.

reported that the husband initiated the idea, five reported that the wife initiated it, and thirteen decided mutually.[22]

In the same study it was also found that swingers have "weak ties to parents, religion, and social conventions."[23]

Researchers disagree about swingers' mental and emotional characteristics. On the one hand we read the following findings:

> These data do not support the conclusion that the swingers . . . were "terribly disturbed" individuals with marginal adjustment to society. It would be more accurate to say that they vary from societal norms . . . and possess an unusually high interest in sex. Given this high interest in sex and the relatively weak ties to parents, religion, and societal conventions, it is not surprising that otherwise reasonably adequately functioning individuals, having concluded that their sexual needs could not be satisfied solely through marital sex, might seek to satisfy them through unconventional sexual encounters.[24]

On the other hand, Duckworth and Levitt found that most swingers are not well adjusted. Instead, "some swingers may be emotionally disturbed to varying degrees, some may have sexual problems, and others could be substance abusers."[25] Although the sample in this study was small and geographically restricted, there is much literature to show that swinging is sometimes accompanied by guilt, loss of self-esteem, fear of rejection by other couples, emotional weariness in the never-ending search for new partners, and threat of venereal disease.

The Outlook

What is the overall assessment of swinging, and what is the outlook for its future? Thus far, the research findings seem clear enough. Those who embark on swinging and who are emotionally suited report many personal and marital benefits. Many, however, seem to experience negative effects and drop-out. Because relatively few couples are inclined to try the activity in the first place, it is difficult to see much future for swinging. After a rather widely publicized beginning, the practice seems to have tapered off.

COMMUNES

Although communes have existed in the United States since the colonial era, there were two peak periods. The first extended roughly from 1800 to the Civil War and included such well-known groups as Brook Farm, Har-

[22]Bernard I. Murstein, David Case, and Steven P. Gunn, "Personality Correlates of Ex-Swingers," *Lifestyles: A Journal of Changing Patterns,* Fall 1985, 43.

[23]Ibid., 33.

[24]Ibid.

[25]Jane Duckworth and Eugene Levitt, "Personality Analysis of a Swinger's Club," *Lifestyles: A Journal of Changing Patterns,* Fall 1985, 43.

mony, Oneida, Amana, Zoar, and Bethel. After the Civil War, however, the movement declined, and by 1900 only a handful of communes were left.

In the late 1960s there was a resurgence that caught both sociologists and the general public by surprise. Communes of all shapes and sizes seemed to spring up overnight: sacred and secular, urban and rural, structured and unstructured. Exactly how many communes were formed in the 1960s and 1970s is unknown, but the number probably ran into the thousands. The rate of failure was also high, however; it became obvious that although communal living had certain advantages, the problems often proved insurmountable. Let us examine both sides of the subject.

Difficulties Involved

People join communes for any number of reasons, but in most cases the underlying factor relates to a general dissatisfaction with society. Commune members contend that their own way of life is superior to the "cutthroat" methods employed on the outside. Therefore, to avoid materialistic contamination, communes tend to become separatist—and the most practicable way to do this is to locate in a rural area.

The catch is that most commune members were reared in an urban or suburban environment. As a consequence, they lack agricultural skills. There is also a scarcity of equipment, for farm machinery is expensive. Land itself is scarce, for good farm acreage is also expensive. Inadequate plumbing, lack of indoor toilets, poor cooking facilities, insufficient heat—such things tend to aggravate the problem. Everything costs money, and in the culture of the commune the unalterable reality is that money is scarce.

There are urban communes, of course, but they also have economic problems. On the one hand, if members do not work and contribute money the group cannot survive. But, if they do work, they often feel entrapped by the very system they set out to avoid. Heat, light, rent, taxes, maintenance, repairs, food, clothing. Everything costs money. . . .

Other problems facing the modern commune include a weakness in social organization and a lack of commitment. Many groups appear to be at loose ends. Goals are often ill-defined, and group loyalties are tenuous.

Leadership presents a special problem in communal living, because the "gurus" themselves often have no real authority. Lacking both enforcement powers and personal experience, they are nevertheless expected to serve as both guide and beacon. And since social organization in the modern commune is often weak, the leader is expected to take up the slack—a most difficult task.

Rewards

In spite of the various problems faced by communal members, the rewards can also be great for those who seek relief from competitive lifestyles. In our study of a contemporary commune, a number of respondents voiced satisfaction with this style of life. For many, life on the outside had been a smothering experience, and now—for the first time—they felt an inner peace. For others, the commune proved to be a haven, where one could meet people with the same outlook on life. Most respondents enjoyed the sociability, fellowship, and the security involved. Nearly all appreciated the opportunity to vent their dissatisfaction with society—without adverse repercussions.

The Balance Sheet

What has been America's reaction to the modern communal movement? What does the future hold? Like many social innovations, communes initially provoked mixed reaction, although there is no doubt that they were roundly criticized in the press. Communes were accused of fostering disrespect for authority, of encouraging licentious living, of providing a haven for the shiftless, and of accepting the community's services without a corresponding payment of taxes.

Defenders, on the other hand, pointed out that communes (1) provided an alternative way of living for those who wanted it, (2) served as therapy for certain personality types, (3) helped society by absorbing some of the more dissatisfied elements, and (4) created a better understanding of the larger community among those who became disillusioned with group living.

Objectively, both supporters and critics seem to have been wrong. Despite dire predictions, communes have undermined neither the family nor the larger social system. Except in isolated instances, they have not even disrupted the local community. As for licentious living, most communes failed to develop along the free-sex lines that had been predicted. On the contrary, "the majority of former commune members have married, and most did so after leaving their communal group."[26]

Some observers feel that the communal movement passed its peak and that the end is just a matter of time. They feel that the movement grew out of the youthful unrest of the 1960s and early 1970s, and that, in effect, the motivation is gone.

From a sociohistorical perspective, however, we would disagree. It is true that most of the communes that sprung up in the sixties and seventies are now defunct. But some still remain. It is highly unlikely, furthermore, that the movement will die out. More likely, the number of communes will rise and fall depending on the social conditions.

It must be remembered that the basic reason for establishing a commune is a degree of dissatisfaction with society at large. The fact that these utopian ventures have been a recurrent part of the American scene for some

---

[26]Angela A. Aidala, "Communes and Changing Family Norms," *Journal of Family Issues*, September 1989, 333.

300 years suggests that the movement will continue—sometimes weak, sometimes strong.

SUMMARY

This chapter has examined some of the more widely publicized lifestyles, together with their implications for the future. Although America always has been a monogamous society, a number of "alternative" lifestyles are practiced today. Some, such as group marriage, never have attracted many followers. Others—such as remaining single, cohabitation, and communal living—have involved substantial numbers of men and women.

Nevertheless, the popularity of marriage in the total American population remains high. Conversely, the various alternative lifestyles, combined, have attracted considerably fewer people than was predicted a decade or two ago. In fact, some observers believe that an increase in traditional lifestyles may characterize the 1990s.

One thing seems certain. As long as men and women have primary-group needs, and as long as children require both emotional and economic support, the popularity of the two-parent family is likely to remain high.

QUESTIONS

1. What are some cultural sources of support for singlehood as an ideal way of life?
2. Describe the lifestyles of members of singles' groups. What are some advantages and some disadvantages of their lifestyles?
3. Staying single has both positive and negative features, and college students sometimes find themselves favoring one side or the other. If you were asked to choose either the positive or the negative side of remaining single, which would you choose? Defend your position.
4. How much cohabitation is there in the United States? Why is this so difficult to answer? What are some of the methodological problems involved?
5. Are cohabitors different from noncohabitors in personality, social background, religion, and so forth? What does the research show?
6. As far as the participants are concerned, what problems are involved in cohabitation? What are the rewards?
7. In your opinion, will cohabitation increase, decrease, or level off? Defend your answer.
8. Do swingers have any personal or social characteristics that set them apart from nonswingers? What do the research surveys show?
9. Make an assessment of swinging. Is it a growing phenomenon? What do you see as the outlook for the future?
10. One of the distinguishing characteristics of modern communes is that most of them are short-lived. What is the explanation?

11. Protagonists point out a number of rewards inherent in communal living. What are these rewards?

12. What has been the societal reaction to the modern communal movement? What, in your opinion, does the future hold?

13. Based on what you have heard and read, would you like to live permanently in a commune? On a temporary or trial basis? Why or why not?

SELECTED READINGS

Aidala, Angela A. "Communes and Changing Family Norms." *Journal of Family Issues*, September 1989, 311–338.

Allen, Katherine R. "Forgotten Streams in the Family Life Course: Utilization of Qualitative Retrospective Interviews in the Analysis of Lifelong Single Women's Family Careers." *Journal of Marriage and the Family*, August 1987, 517–526.

Bennett, Neil G., and Ann K. Blanc. "Commitment and the Modern Union: Assessing the Link between Premarital Cohabitation and Subsequent Marital Stability." *American Sociological Review*, February 1988, 127–138.

Bernikow, Louise. *Alone in America*. New York: Harper & Row, 1986.

Blumstein, Philip, and Pepper Schwartz. *American Couples*. New York: Pocket Books, 1985.

Byers, Sandra E., and Larry Heinlein. "Predicting Initiation and Refusals of Sexual Activities in Married and Cohabiting Heterosexual Couples." *The Journal of Sex Research*, May 1989, 21–231.

Cargan, Leonard. "Stereotypes of Singles: A Cross-Cultural Comparison." *International Journal of Comparative Sociology*, 27 (3,4), 1986 200–208.

Chapman, Audrey B. *Man Sharing: Dilemma or Choice*. New York: William Morrow, 1986.

Cockrum, Janet, and Priscilla White. "Influences on the Life Satisfaction of Never-Married Men and Women." *Family Relations*, October 1985, 551–56.

Cornfield, Noreen. "The Success of Urban Communes." *Journal of Marriage and the Family*, February 1984, 115–26.

Cornish, Edward. "The Coming of the Singles Society." *The Futurist*, July/August 1987, 6, 58.

Cunningham, John D., Harriet Braiker, and Harold H. Kelley. "Marital-Status and Sex Differences in Problems Reported by Married and Cohabiting Couples." *Psychology of Women Quarterly*, Summer 1982, 415–27.

DeMaris, Alfred, and Gerald R. Leslie. "Cohabitation with the Future Spouse: Its Influence upon Marital Satisfaction and Communication." *Journal of Marriage and the Family*, February 1984, 77–84.

Duckworth, Jane, and Eugene E. Levitt. "Personality Analysis of a Swinger's Club." *Lifestyles: A Journal of Changing Patterns*, Fall 1985, 35–45.

Feldman, Harold, and Margaret Feldman, eds. *Current Controversies in Marriage and Family*. Beverly Hills, CA: Sage Publications, 1985.

Glick, Paul C. "Marriage, Divorce, and Living Arrangements." *Journal of Family Living,* March 1984, 7–26.

Houseknecht, Sharon K., Suzan Vaughn, and Ann Statham. "The Impact of Single-hood on the Career Patterns of Professional Women." *Journal of Marriage and the Family,* May 1987, 353–366.

Jenks, Richard J. "Swinging: A Replication and Test of a Theory." *The Journal of Sex Research,* May 1985, 199–210.

———. "A Comparative Study of Swingers and Nonswingers." *Lifestyles: A Journal of Changing Patterns,* Fall 1985, 5–20.

Keith, Pat M. "Isolation of the Unmarried in Later Life." *Family Relations,* July 1986, 389–95.

Kephart, William M. *Extraordinary Groups.* New York: St. Martin's Press, 1987.

Kotkin, Mark. "To Marry or Live Together?" *Lifestyles: A Journal of Changing Patterns,* Spring 1985, 156–70.

Laur, Robert H., and Jeanette C. Laur. *The Spirit and the Flesh: Sex in Utopian Communities.* Metuchen, NJ: The Scarecrow Press, 1983.

Minturn, Leigh. "Sex-Role Differentiation in Contemporary Communes." *Sex Roles,* January 1984, 73–85.

Murstein, Bernard I., David Case, and Stephen P. Gunn. Personality Correlates of Ex-Swingers." *Lifestyles: A Journal of Changing Patterns,* Fall 1985, 21–34.

Newcomb, Michael D. "Cohabitation and Marriage: A Quest for Independence and Relatedness." in *Family Processes and Problems,* edited by Stuart Oskamp. Newbury Park, CA: Sage Publications, 1987, 128–156.

———, "Cohabitation, Marriage and Divorce among Adolescents and Young Adults," *Journal of Social and Personal Relationships,* 3, 1986, 473–494.

———, "Sexual Behavior of Cohabitors: A Comparison of Three Independent Samples." *The Journal of Sex Research,* November 1986, 492–513.

Smith, Harold Ivan. *Movers and Shapers: Singles Who Changed Their World.* Old Tappan, NJ: Fleming H. Revell Company, 1988.

———, *Single and Feeling Good.* Nashville: Abingdon Press, 1987.

Spakes, Patricia. "The Supreme Court, Family Policy and Alternative Family Life-styles: The Clash of Interests." *Lifestyles: A Journal of Changing Patterns,* Spring 1985, 171–86.

Tanfer, Koray. "Patterns of Premarital Cohabitation among Never-Married Women in the United States." *Journal of Marriage and the Family,* August 1987, 483–497.

Yamaguchi, Kazuo, and Denise B. Kandel. "Dynamic Relationships between Pre-marital Cohabitation and Illicit Drug Use: An Event-History Analysis of Role Selection and Role Socialization." *American Sociological Review,* August 1985, 530–46.

Chapter
19

Family-Strengthening Programs

W hether they are taken singly or collectively, the alternative lifestyles discussed in the previous chapter probably pose no real threat to the institution of marriage. At the same time, the very existence of these modern alternatives implies that the current American family may not be fulfilling the needs of at least some of its members. In any case, a fair number of "family-strengthening" programs have now made their appearance. The nature and the effectiveness of these programs—together with their implications for the future—are the subject of this final chapter.

THE FAMILY COURT MOVEMENT

In 1899, the first juvenile court was organized in Chicago. Less than half a century later, juvenile courts had been established in every state, and today these courts are part of American jurisprudence. In 1914, the first family court was established in Cincinnati; although a number of other cities followed suit, family courts have never received the widespread acceptance enjoyed by juvenile courts. Both types of court, however, have been simultaneously praised and criticized.

As they were set up originally in the various states, juvenile courts operated under the legal philosophy of *parens patriae*. The state, acting through the juvenile court, assumed the necessary responsibility for delinquent children, who presumably were being neglected by their real parents. Delinquent children thus received the same protection and guidance as neglected children, and their relationship with the state became that of parent and child rather than that of "Commonwealth v. _____ ."

One criticism of the *parens patriae* philosophy suggests that juvenile courts were accused of coddling and pampering youthful delinquents and of fostering an attitude of irresponsibility. Little wonder—so the argument went—that juvenile crime rates rose to such high levels.

In spite of this objection, the juvenile court system has not been abolished; indeed, no one has even suggested a return to the old system, wherein youthful delinquents received the same treatment as adult offenders. Instead, the procedures have changed, and the goals have been made more realistic.

The family court also has had its ups and downs. As originally conceived, the family court was to have been to the family what the juvenile court was to the child. Theoretically, at least, it was to be empowered to handle such problems as annulment, legal separation, divorce, alimony, desertion and nonsupport, child custody, adoption, and illegitimacy. Employing a wide range of personnel—probation officers, social workers, psychiatrists, nurses, investigators, and marriage counselors—the court was intended to resolve family difficulties to ameliorate interpersonal conflicts, to offer professional guidance, and in general to preserve family ties.

This was the theory, but in practice a number of difficulties arose. For one thing, personnel costs for social workers, counselors, and the like were high, and some communities were reluctant to pay the bill. Other communities were unwilling to grant the necessary jurisdictional power to a single court.

In states where family courts were set up, it was often difficult to procure adequate judges. Although both juvenile and family court judges should be mature individuals with keen insight into human nature, it is no secret that most judges do not relish such assignments. Finally, the existing family courts added to their own problems by neglecting to provide adequate information about the work they were doing. Most courts, for example, failed to build a solid, factual body of knowledge that might serve as an aid to understanding and solving the very problems for which the courts were created.

Positive Features

Although family courts have not fulfilled their original promise, they have many positive features. The economic argument, for example, is probably in their favor, for although a family court is certainly not cheap to operate, neither are the alternatives. In an integrated family court, all domestic cases are heard under one roof, with a resultant improvement in administrative and economic efficiency. In the alternative procedure—still in existence in many of our large cities—three or more different courts assume jurisdiction over family matters.

Another advantage of the family court is that it provides professional help for those who need it most. Domestic relations cases in our large cities are staggering in number, and most of our civil courts are not equipped to handle the daily flow. For this reason alone, some sort of family court arrangement is almost inevitable in today's urbanized society.

The research possibilities inherent in the family court system also should be mentioned. Solutions to problems such as divorce, desertion, and delinquency hinge on the isolation of the causes that produce these problems, and social scientists devote an immense amount of time to research. A family court, with a small statistical research unit, provides an ideal laboratory for the collection and analysis of information about family problems.

The fact that many of the existing family courts have not used research procedures is largely a budgetary matter. Faced with the choice of adding a statistical research unit or employing additional social workers, many courts have chosen the latter course, and that situation creates a vexing cycle. Lacking adequate budgetary provisions, family courts have not been able to fulfill their early promise. As a result, being unable to demonstrate their success, they cannot easily make demands for an improved financial base.

In spite of the drawbacks, however, no one has suggested a better method for handling the various family-related problems that arise in modern society. Overall, family courts have done much good, and it is hoped that they will improve their record in the future. To do so, they will need adequate financing—and this in turn means a higher level of public support than has existed in the past.

MARRIAGE COUNSELING

Although marriage counseling is often associated with the family court, the two movements have quite different histories. Marriage counseling in the United States was originally little more than an informal advisory service, performed in addition to the regular duties of the doctor, lawyer, social worker, or teacher. As the need grew, counseling services came to be an adjunct of family-welfare agencies and child-guidance clinics. Although the pattern had been set somewhat earlier in Europe, it was not until 1929 that the first formalized American marriage counseling agency was organized: the Marriage Consultation Center in New York City, founded by Drs. Abraham and Hannah Stone. A year later Paul Popenoe organized the American Institute of Family Relations in Los Angeles. In 1932, Emily Mudd opened the Marriage Council of Philadelphia. The two latter organizations are still in business, and they are still performing valuable community services.

In the following decades, scores of marriage counseling agencies were organized in various parts of the United States. Although not all of them have survived, the counseling movement as a whole has increased in scope. In 1942, the American Association for Marriage and Family Therapy (AAMFT) was organized. With emphasis on upgrading professional standards, exchanging counseling methods, and otherwise improving services, the association has achieved an excellent reputation.

The AAMFT now has some 7000 members, plus a number of authorized training centers. Membership is drawn largely from other professions: medicine, social work, psychology, sociology, and the ministry. Understandably, these individuals often can devote only a portion of their time to marriage counseling.

Marriage counseling agencies themselves range from relatively large and complex organizations to one-person units. Some of the agencies operate through medical or religious sponsorship; others are under the auspices of civic or educational institutions. Private agencies, however—those operated for profit—are few and far between. Most marriage counselors are far from able to support themselves solely through clients.

Criticisms of Marriage Counseling

A number of criticisms—implicit or explicit—have been directed against marriage counseling. The most frequently heard allegations include the following:

1. There are no real qualifying standards for marriage counselors. Practically anyone can become a marriage counselor. This charge is both true and false. As far as the AAMFT is concerned, standards are certainly high. The catch is that one does not have to belong to the AAMFT to be a practicing marriage counselor. Only a handful of states have licensing procedures for the practice of marriage and family counseling. As a result, incompetent or unprincipled persons occasionally have become counselors—with grievous results. From time to time other states have considered procedures for licensing or certification, but so far progress has been slow. Ironically, therefore, one of the major criticisms against marriage counseling is one over which qualified counselors themselves have little control.

2. Research in marriage counseling has lagged. This charge appears to be largely true. After all, marriage counseling is an applied area, and the counselors consider themselves to be practitioners rather than researchers. There is some indication that research is improving, although the improvement has been moderate thus far. Other types of advisory service—educational, vocational, financial—also have lagged in research, however, and it would be less than fair to single out marriage counselors for special criticism.

3. Because there is no established body of knowledge to draw on,

marriage counseling is largely intuitive—more art than science. This charge also may be true, but the obvious rebuttal is that there are ways of helping people—and marriages—other than through the application of scientific principles.

But if marriage counseling is much closer to art than to science, are the agencies justified in charging for their service? The answer must be affirmative. Any number of services in our society—legal, economic, and psychiatric—charge regularly for their advice, and there is no reason why that prerogative should be denied to marriage counselors. In fact, marriage counseling agencies generally are organized as nonprofit institutions, and the fees are relatively modest.

4. Marriage counselors themselves do not agree on their goals. The recent charge is largely false. Counseling is a helping profession, and the goal of counselors is to help those with marital problems. Confusion arises from the fact that in an earlier period the counselors' objective—above all else—was to "save the marriage." Currently, however, most counselors will not hesitate to recommend a divorce if the marriage seems to be beyond repair.

Marriage counseling agencies routinely handle premarital problems. Some agencies—particularly those located near college campuses—report that a fair proportion of their clients are either engaged or soon-to-be-married couples.

Assessment of Marriage Counseling

There is little doubt that the field of marriage counseling has failed to develop a verified body of knowledge. As a result, different counselors are likely to use different approaches in handling marital and familial problems, such as psychoanalytic, transactional, behavior modification, eclectic, and conjoint family therapy.

Nevertheless, in spite of some formidable obstacles, the field of marriage counseling has made definite progress. The AAMFT is a vigorous organization, always ready for self-improvement. The number of meaningful articles and books dealing with counseling has increased, and the advent of no-fault divorce procedures has made the public more aware of counseling facilities.

Furthermore, marriage counselors as a group are intelligent, hardworking individuals who believe in the efficacy of their work. There is also reason to believe that these counselors' personalities are more in tune than most people's with the philosophy of "helping." They are certainly experienced men and women who persevere at a most difficult and trying task. In brief, it would be quite unlikely that dedicated, qualified persons such as these could fail to improve the well-being of the community.

Empirical results seem to bear out this assumption. A number of follow-up studies—designed to ascertain the effectiveness of marriage counseling—have been undertaken, and for the most part the results have been positive.

Finally, the marriage counselor affords couples with problems an opportunity to present their case to a professionally trained, objectively oriented person. If the marriage counselor did not exist, where would the couple go for help? Most probably to a friend or relative or to the family doctor—or to nobody. Well-intentioned though they may be, friends and relatives are likely to have neither the competence nor the objectivity to deal with marital conflict. And, medical doctors, qualifications aside, are extremely busy people, with a limited amount of time to devote to marital problems.

All things considered, marriage counseling appears to be a necessary and significant component of modern society. Because there is nothing on the horizon to suggest that society will become less complex or that marital problems will decline, it seems likely that the importance of marriage and family counseling will increase in the years to come.

MARRIAGE-ENRICHMENT PROGRAMS

Although there is some overlap, marriage-enrichment programs are basically different from marriage counseling. Marriage-enrichment methods involve persons with apparently satisfactory marriages who use professional services to learn more about marriage and the family. The goals of marriage enrichment are to anticipate marital problems, to discover possible patterns that could lead to marital difficulties, and to prevent serious marital trouble from developing.

Marriage-enrichment programs are relatively new. The practice started in the early 1960s, but the term "marital enrichment" was not coined until 1971.[1] In 1973, the Association for Couples in Marriage Enrichment (ACME) was formed, and it caters to different types of couples. As a current brochure of the association states: "A.C.M.E. activities are for couples of all ages and in every stage of their marriage. Events are planned for pre-marrieds, newly-weds, remarrieds, long-term marriages, two career couples, middle-aged couples, and retirees. Marriage enrichment is for all couples who want growth in their marriage relationship."[2]

How the Programs Function

Although they are called by different names—Marriage Encounter, Pairing Enrichment, Marriage Diagnosis—marriage-enrichment programs operate

---

[1]David Mace, "Three Ways of Helping Couples," *Journal of Marital and Family Therapy*, April 1987, 183.

[2]*Marriage Enrichment* (Winston-Salem, NC: The Association for Couples in Marriage Enrichment, undated).

Toughlove group. Hundreds of thousands of couples have already participated in one of the marriage-enrichment or parent-education programs. (*Olitsky, Toughlove*)

under a common assumption: that although the nature of marriage has changed a great deal, many spouses have not kept pace with the change and therefore are not realizing the full benefits of their own marriage.

The basic goal of marriage enrichment is to enhance the relationship between husband and wife. This improvement, in turn, is believed to hinge on improved communication. Although no two enrichment programs are exactly alike, most involve small groups of married couples convening for a series of weekend meetings. The meetings themselves—usually held in a church or school building, or in a private residence—are conducted by a qualified professional person interested in the family, such as a member of the clergy, an educator, a sociologist, or a marriage counselor. The fees are nominal, though lodging and meals tend to add to the costs.

During the meetings a number of topics are covered and various pedagogical techniques are used—lectures, filmstrips, reading materials, and question-and-answer sessions. Yet because the emphasis is on improving communication between spouses, the enrichment program includes certain concepts not normally found in the classroom. One is the concept of "team couples," couples who already have been through the enrichment program.

In addition to using the team couple, marriage-enrichment programs employ a variety of other concepts: self-awareness, disclosure, dialogue, reciprocity, and esteem building. The number and the kind depend on the orientation of the person in charge.

The Balance Sheet

Marriage enrichment suffers from some of the same deficiencies as marriage counseling, such as occasional inadequacy of personnel and a general scarcity of research information. Nevertheless, the program holds genuine promise. Many couples have participated, and there are indications that many have been helped.[3]

The reason is basically simple. By stressing positive rather than therapeutic processes, the program aims at stopping marital discord before it starts. By emphasizing improved communication between spouses, the marriage-enrichment approach—theoretically, at least—gives the couple the means of at least partially controlling their own marital destiny.

FAMILY-LIFE EDUCATION

Thus far the "preservation" programs discussed here, such as marriage counseling and marriage enrichment, have dealt largely with married couples. One of the oldest and largest programs, however—generally referred to as family-life education—involves high school and college students.

High School Courses

Because early records were not always kept, it is difficult to pinpoint the origin of family-life courses in American high schools. One of the first courses was offered in Tulsa in 1918, but the major impetus for such courses did not come until after World War II, when family-life offerings were added to the curriculum in response to public demand. Today, high school enrollment in such courses probably runs well over a million.

There is significant variation in the content of famiy-life courses. Some offer instruction in nutrition and family meals, infant training, textiles and clothing, home management, and similar subjects. Others center on such topics as dating and courtship, sex education, etiquette, and social relationships. Both types are likely to be under the jurisdiction of the home economics department, although the specific names of the courses (Life Adjustment, Social Relations, Personal Relationships, Family Problems) show some variation.

For the most part, family-life courses have been well received, as judged by the response of both the students and their parents. A well-taught family-life course can mean a great deal to persons of high school age, beset as they are by a growing awareness of social and sexual relationships. It is little wonder that the number of family-life courses has grown over the years.

On the other hand, the courses have not escaped criticism. From time to time there have been headline-capturing statements that family-life offer-

---

[3]Mace, "Three Ways of Helping Couples," 182–184.

ings are merely frills—snap courses with little academic or utilitarian value. Generally, however, the courses have outlasted their critics. As far as we know, they have become a permanent part of the educational curriculum.

College Courses

College courses dealing with family are generally of two kinds: institutional and functional. The former are concerned with the family as a social institution and normally include such topics as the history of the family, marital customs in other societies, legal aspects, theories and research on mate selection, marital adjustment and maladjustment, and various aspects of sexual behavior. Although there is some overlap, functional family courses concern themselves more with premarriage and marriage, and generally cover such areas as dating, engagement, sex education, relationships with in-laws, budgeting and insurance, and bringing up children.

Institutional courses in the family were offered in American universities before the turn of the century, and shortly after World War I the first functional courses were introduced. The latter courses proved to be quite popular with students, and in a relatively short time, functional courses—often titled "Preparation for Marriage"—had been adopted at hundreds of colleges. At present the number of such courses may equal or surpass the number of institutional courses.

In an attempt to measure the effectiveness of functional marriage courses, a number of studies have been undertaken wherein (1) students' attitudes are measured before and after they take the course or (2) attitudes of students who have been exposed to a course are compared with attitudes of a control group who have not been so exposed. No matter what evaluation method is used, functional marriage courses have been found consistently to have positive value.[4]

Institutional courses in the family also have been exceptionally well received by students, and today a great majority of American colleges and universities offer either one course or the other. In fact, family courses are among the most widely offered of all sociology courses.

OTHER PROGRAMS

In addition to the programs described above, a host of other agencies and services—both governmental and private—deal with the preservation of American Family Life. Governmental agencies include the Bureau of Fam-

---

[4]Richard Kerckhoff, Terry Hancock, and panel, "The Family Life Educator of the Future," *The Family Coordinator,* October 1971, 315–325; and Leland Axelson, "Promise or Illusion: The Future of Family Studies," *The Family Coordinator,* January 1975, 3–6. Finally, see Margaret Arcus, "A Framework for Life-Span Family Life Education," *Family Relations,* January 1987, 5–10.

ily Services, the Children's Bureau, the Social Security Administration, the Home Economics Education Service, the Public Housing Administration, and a variety of state and local agencies.

Among the private organizations concerned with the family are the National Council on Family Relations, the Groves Conference on Marriage and the Family, the National Congress of Parents and Teachers, the Family Service Association of America, the American Association of Marriage and Family Therapy, and many others.

We also should mention ongoing research. The family field is fortunate in having a large number of empirical investigators, as the footnotes and references in this volume attest. Moreover, modern research methods are expensive; when it is realized that the bulk of family research has involved relatively little money (as compared, say, with the financial outlay for the physical sciences), the record becomes noteworthy indeed.

Research findings and statistics relating to the family also are published by certain government agencies such as the Bureau of the Census, the National Vital Statistics System, the Women's Bureau, and the Department of Labor. Yet most family-related research has been—and doubtless will continue to be—undertaken by university researchers. At present, most of the work is being done by sociologists, although psychologists, anthropologists, and home economists also have made valuable contributions.

Some idea of the scope of family interests can be obtained from a partial listing of the professional journals in the field:

Adolescence

The American Family

American Journal of Family Therapy

Child Welfare

Family Advocate

Family Law Quarterly

Family Perspective

Family Process

Family Relations

Family Service Highlights

Gender and Society

International Journal of Sociology of the Family

Journal of Comparative Family Studies

Journal of Divorce

Journal of Family History

Journal of Family Issues

Journal of Family Welfare

Journal of Marriage and the Family

Journal of Marriage and Family Therapy

Journal of Sex and Marital Therapy

Journal of Sex Research

Journal of Youth and Adolescence

Lifestyles: A Journal of Changing Patterns

Marriage and Family Living

Marriage and Family Review

Sage Family Studies Abstracts

Sex Roles

THE FUTURE

Nineteen chapters ago, we pointed out that the American family shows signs of both weakness and strength. In the intervening pages, the pros and cons have been spelled out.

On the one hand, certain traditional family functions have been taken over by agencies other than marriage. Sexual gratification, once considered the exclusive province of the husband and wife, is condoned increasingly outside marriage.

Wife abuse and child abuse have been publicized increasingly. Non-marital pregnancy has climbed sharply. Divorce rates, as most Americans know by now, have headed skyward. And as the institution of marriage has weakened—at least, so the argument goes—a number of alternative life-styles have developed, several of which were discussed in the previous pages.

On the other hand, common observation suggests that our family system is not falling apart. Most Americans not only marry, but—in spite of severe pressures—manage to stay married. Children are still cherished, and from all indications family life seems to be a genuinely rewarding experience. And although it is true that in recent years a number of alternative lifestyles have emerged, they do not seem to have weakened the dominant family system. Indeed, public and professional interest in the family—as evidenced by marriage counseling, family-life education, marriage-enrichment programs, and the like—remains high. In other words, we are still a family-centered society—or so the counterargument goes.

The final question, then, is this: In which direction is the American family heading—up or down?

Most Americans still cherish their children, and from all indications, family life seems to be a genuinely rewarding experience.

We are inclined to be moderately optimistic. Most people seem to be strongly concerned with their own families. The kin family network continues to show a pervasive vitality. There is no grassroots movement to overthrow the "system." The same is true at the professional level. In fact, despite certain acknowledged weaknesses, all the family-strengthening programs discussed in the previous pages are substantially stronger today than they were a decade or so ago.

It is true that the divorce rate has risen, but although this must be considered a negative trend, there is one rebuttal: no-fault procedures may act as a safety valve. Because discordant couples find it much easier now to procure a divorce, those marriages which remain intact may well represent a stronger, more solidified marital base than in the past. The same principle can be applied to alternative lifestyles. Since these provide people in all walks of life with a genuine alternative to marriage, couples who choose matrimony probably constitute a better-adjusted, more satisfied group than in previous times.

Finally, we are optimistic because of our gratifying experience with the thousands of college students who have taken our courses in the family. As a group, they have been quick to grasp the institutional significance of the family and the importance of striking a balance between individual and societal needs. They are also aware that their own premarital and marital roles must be evaluated from both perspectives. Although students do not necessarily agree with the instructor or with each other on what constitutes the optimal point of balance, they are in general accord with the framework in which debate should be held. As long as the family, the society, and the individual can be viewed reciprocally—as interdependent parts of the whole—there is cause for optimism.

QUESTIONS

1. What are the similarities between the family court and the juvenile court? What are the differences?

2. As in so many areas of social action, family courts have both positive and negative features. What are these contrasting features?

3. Despite the negative features involved, it is often said that no better method exists for handling family problems than the family court. Do you agree with this contention? Why or why not?

4. What are the origins of marriage and family counseling in the United States?

5. What criticisms have been made with respect to marriage counseling? What are the refutations to these criticisms?

6. How would you assess the effectiveness of the marriage counseling movement?

7. What is the basic difference between marriage counseling and marriage enrichment?

8. How do marriage-enrichment programs function?

9. "College courses dealing with the family are generally of two kinds: institutional and functional." How do these two kinds differ from one another? Can you visualize a family course embodying both institutional and functional elements? Explain.

10. Some observers feel that the American family is on the downgrade, with a rather dismal future. Others believe that in spite of some demonstrable weaknesses, the family not only will survive but actually will be strengthened in the years ahead. What is your personal view? Defend your position.

APPENDIX

The Physiological Basis of Marriage

Although most family courses are taught by sociologists, the family itself has any number of dimensions, for example, religious, historical, legal—and physiological. Ideally, it would be better if family sociologists restricted their teaching to the sociological aspects, leaving the historical parts to historians, the physiological areas to physiologists, and so on. Usually, however, there is but one course in the family available to undergraduates, and for this reason most family texts are necessarily eclectic in their approach.

As a consequence, this appendix has been included, its purpose being to provide the student with a basic description of the physiological aspects of marriage. Such a description should fit the needs of those taking the family course. As a minimum, students should know the names and functions of the various organs involved in sexual behavior and reproduction. It is hoped, also, that a knowledge of the genital differences between male and female will help the reader understand the problem of marital sex adjustment discussed in Chapter 13.

MALE SEXUAL ANATOMY

The genital and reproductive apparatus of the human male constitutes a centralized and highly dynamic sexual system. The system is also rather complex, and for present purposes it will be necessary to limit our discussion to the following organs: testes, vas deferens, prostate gland and seminal vesicles, epididymis, and penis.

The testes take their name from the Latin root of the word for "witness" or "testify," recalling an ancient custom whereby the man solemnly placed his hands on his genitals when taking an oath.[1] Also known as male gonads, or sex glands, the testes have a primary function of manufacturing sperm and a secondary function of secreting male sex hormones. Because abdominal temperature is too high to permit sperm manufacture, the testes are normally carried on the outside of the body, in a skin pouch called the scrotum. In about 85 percent of all males, the left testis is lower than the right.

Within the testes are hundreds of *seminiferous tubules,* the organs that actually produce the sperm. (The aggregate length of these tubules in both testes is about one mile!) Beginning at puberty, the tubules start to manufacture immense quantities of *spermatozoa,* the structures that contain all the hereditary material—in the form of chromosomes and genes—that is transmissible to the offspring. The process of sperm manufacture (spermatogenesis) continues for many years, in some cases throughout the entire life span of the male; at least, there are authentic records of 80- and 90-year-old men who have become fathers. In most cases, however, sperm manufacture apparently slows down in later years, although not a great deal is known about this phase of human reproduction.

Scattered among the seminiferous tubules are groups of *interstitial cells,* which release the sex hormones—the androgens and the estrogens. These hormones are responsible for such secondary sex traits as pitch of voice, body and facial hair, and musculature. While both men and women produce both types of sex hormone, males produce a much greater quantity of androgen, females a much greater quantity of estrogen.

Along the side of each testis lies an *epididymis,* a coiled, tube-like organ that serves as the storage place for the ripened or nearly ripened spermatozoa. From the epididymis, spermatozoa pass into the *vas deferens,* a tube that carries the sperm to the penis, whence they are expelled through the urethra.

While most people are aware that the human sperm is an actively moving or motile organism, it is not so well known that, for all its whiplike capacity, the sperm is largely inactive until it mixes with the fluids secreted by the prostate glands and the seminal vesicles. It is the secretions from these glands, plus the spermatozoa, that make up the substance commonly referred to as seminal fluid, or semen.

The sudden physical release or expulsion of semen through the urethra is known as the male ejaculation, and the subjective sensation accompanying ejaculation is called orgasm. In the case of preadolescent males, orgasm may occur without ejaculation, a situation which also applies to adult males who are afflicted with ejaculatory impotence. So far as is known, however, no male can experience ejaculation without also experiencing orgasm.

It might also be mentioned that there is no necessary relationship between *virility* and *fertility,* even though these terms are sometimes used interchangeably. Fertility, in this connection, refers primarily to the male sperm count. Males with a

---

[1]Herant Katchadourian, *Human Sexuality,* San Francisco: W. H. Freeman and Company, 1974, 2.

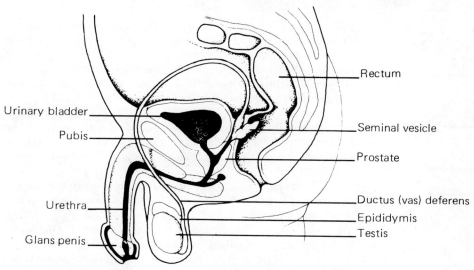

Urinary bladder

Pubis

Urethra

Glans penis

Rectum

Seminal vesicle

Prostate

Ductus (vas) deferens

Epididymis

Testis

The male reproductive system.

The male reproductive system.

deficient sperm count, of course, cannot become fathers. These same men, however, may be quite virile; that is, they may be masculine or manly and evince a normal sex drive with complete coital powers. It must be kept in mind that the testes have a dual function: the manufacture of spermatozoa and the release of male sex hormones. Apparently there is no one-to-one relationship between these two functions.

The male sex organ, the *penis*, is the instrument of seminal implantation, and as such it must have the capacity for erection. This is brought about through a rather intricate combination of physical and psychological factors. Physiologically, the penis not only contains an elaborate network of spongy tissue, but also includes constricting bands of muscles and a rich supply of blood vessels. In addition, the external surface is covered with a special set of sensory nerve endings.

In times of sexual excitation—facilitated, as it were, by the size and location of the penis—nerve impulses flow to the muscle fibers. The blood vessels thereupon become engorged, the erectile tissue enlarges, and the entire sex organ becomes extended and takes the form usually referred to as erection. This erectile process is sometimes called *tumescence,* and the reverse process—which sets in after ejaculation has occurred or after sexual excitation as passed—is known as *detumescence*.

Erectile capacity in the male probably hinges as much on psychological as physiological factors. If they lack any other kind of sexual outlet, for instance, most males experience nocturnal sex dreams, replete with ejaculation and orgasm. While such experiences are infrequent among older men, teen-age boys report these "wet dreams" to be monthly or even weekly occurrences.

FEMALE SEXUAL ANATOMY

Unlike the male, the female's sex organs are for the most part internal rather than external. The *labia majora* and *labia minora* (the outer and inner lips of the female genitalia) are external, although the labia majora contributes little to the sexual response of most females. The labia minora is a highly sensitive area, as is the *clitoris,* which is the counterpart of the male penis. The labia majora, the labia minora, and the clitoris together make up the *vulva.*

The clitoris is a small organ—a fraction of an inch long—whose function is sexual rather than reproductive. Although it is partly imbedded in tissue, the clitoris, like the penis, is richly endowed with nerve endings and blood supply. During sexual excitation, the organ enlarges somewhat and becomes engorged with blood. However, unlike the penis, there is no such thing as a clitoral erection.

The female organ of copulation is the *vagina,* a muscular, cylindrical tube extending into the body at an upward angle. Normally in a collapsed state, the vagina is only three to four inches long; however, the tubular walls are highly distensible—as indeed they must be to meet the exigencies of childbirth. It should be mentioned, in this connection, that the vagina is largely devoid of nerve endings.

When a girl is born, her vaginal opening is bordered by a membrane, the *hymen,* which partially closes the entrance to the vagina. The hymen is usually ruptured during the initial sexual intercourse, although for other reasons it may be broken earlier. Interestingly enough, the hymen has no known sexual or reproductive function and may simply be a vestigial organ. In some lower animals, for example, the vaginal opening is covered by a membrane except during the rutting period.

The female sex glands—corresponding to the male testes—are the *ovaries,* which, like the male gonads, have a dual function: (1) the production of ova (eggs), and (2) the manufacture of the female sex hormones. This latter process is more complicated than the corresponding testicular activity, since in addition to estrogen (responsible for the female secondary sex traits) *progesterone* is also secreted. Progesterone is the hormone that facilitates the prenatal development of the child and the subsequent parturition (childbearing) process.

The ovaries—rounded structures about an inch in diameter, located on each side of the pelvis—are functionless until puberty (roughly 11 to 14 years of age), at which time *menarche,* or first menstruation, occurs. This is generally an indication that ova are being produced, a cyclic function that will continue until menopause sets in some three decades later.

About as big as a dot, the human egg is just large enough to be seen with the naked eye, and hence is many times larger than the sperm. All the transmissible hereditary traits of the mother are carried in the ovum. Normally, an egg is released every 28 days, one ovary functioning one month, the other ovary the next month, and so on. Following ovulation, the egg is usually, though not always, "captured" in the Fallopian tube, or oviduct, the upper end of which contains a fingerlike expansion designed to receive ripened ova. (There is no direct connection between ovary and oviduct.) The egg has no power of self-locomotion but is pushed through the oviduct by ciliary action and wavelike muscular constrictions.

If the egg has been fertilized (in which case it is known as a zygote), it is carried through the oviduct to the uterus, a pear-shaped structure approximately three inches in length. The zygote eventually affixes itself to the uterine wall, an area richly supplied with blood vessels, and the process of prenatal development

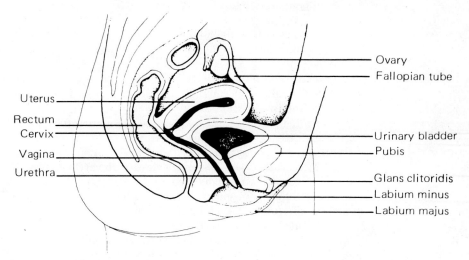

Uterus

Rectum

Cervix

Vagina

Urethra

Ovary

Fallopian tube

Urinary bladder

Pubis

Glans clitoridis

Labium minus

Labium majus

The female reproductive system.

The female reproductive system.

begins. Approximately nine months after conception this developmental process is completed, whereupon the uterine muscles contract and parturition commences.

If the egg has not been fertilized, it disintegrates and is sloughed off, together with the unused uterine lining. This, of course, is the process known as menstruation.

THE MENSTRUAL CYCLE

Like all female mammals, the human female is so constituted that her reproductive process is cyclic in nature. An egg is ovulated, it passes through the oviduct, it is eliminated. Another egg ripens in the other ovary, it is ovulated, and so on. This recurrent process is known as the menstrual cycle and corresponds to the estrous cycle of lower animals, although there are differences.

Over the years, there has been much misunderstanding about the human reproductive cycle, both on the part of primitive groups and among civilized societies. Some primitive peoples regard the female as unclean during menstruation and impose strict taboos against associating with her during this period. Civilized societies, while generally recognizing menstruation as a normal biological function, have not always understood the relation between ovarian phases and fertility. Although not all of the details are known, research has uncovered the basic physiological principles governing the cycle of reproduction, and these facts should be understood by students of the family.

One of the keys to an understanding of the human menstrual cycle is the realization that *nature intended the egg to be fertilized*. During the process of ovulation, the ovarian follicle secretes certain hormones (estrogen and, later, progesterone), which act upon the lining of the uterus. A cellular growth takes place and the mucous membrane that lines the uterus is expanded. Concurrently the uterine blood supply is increased, and the lining is structurally changed in preparation for the zygote, or fertilized egg. If the egg is not fertilized, these uterine changes have been for nought. Consequently, the newly prepared lining breaks down and peels off from the wall of the uterus. The subsequent discharging of the unused lining and the "ready" blood supply, plus the sloughing off of the unfertilized (and now disintegrated) egg, constitutes menstruation. In a very real sense, therefore, the direct cause of menstruation is the nonfertilization of the ovum.

Menstruation lasts for several days, with varying degrees of discomfort experienced. Most women evidence emotional variations—crankiness, irritability, or depressions—that correspond to certain phases of the menstrual cycle and about which, unfortunately, nothing much can be done.

Women have also recognized that fluctuations in sexual desire occur during various phases of the menstrual cycle. Most often mentioned as being the peak periods of sexual receptivity are the days immediately preceding and following menstruation. However, some knowledgeable writers have reported that the peak period tends to correspond with the time of ovulation. About all that can be said with certainty is that there is much variation among women.

The Cultural Interpretation

Most treatises on sex education take pains to point out that menstruation is a normal biological process, experienced by women the world over. This is an involved point, however, and whether menstruation is indeed a "natural" process is a matter of interpretation. Menstruation does occur among women everywhere and is a natural consequence of nonfertilization. On the other hand, it can be demonstrated that menstruation is, in one sense, a *cultural* phenomenon!

Among lower animals, where there are no cultural restrictions, whenever an egg is produced, it is normally fertilized. Exceptions would occur in areas where there is an extreme shortage or absence of males, or in the case of captive or domesticated animals where the sexes are purposely separated. If *Homo sapiens* lived as a creature of the wild, it is quite likely that fertilization would generally follow ovulation. Humans do not live like animals, however; they have developed a family system and a complex culture, and in all societies there are cultural restrictions that preclude indiscriminate coitus.

In primitive groups there are rules prescribing mating behavior, and taboos relative to sexual intercourse. And in civilized societies there are severe restrictions on sexual matters. Within our own culture, premarital coitus is limited and premarital pregnancy is frowned upon. Furthermore, most American couples practice some sort of birth control. Both phenomena—premarital restrictions and the utilization of birth control—are culturally determined.

Menstruation does not occur in other species, and in the absence of cultural regulations it might well be considered "unnatural" by the human animal. One could almost say—if it weren't for the play on words—that "menstruation is natural but it is cultural"; that is, it is natural, given the present cultural setting.

Fertility Period

Although the average length of the menstrual cycle is about 28 days, individual women have reported cycles as short as 20 and as long as 60 days. In the normal 28-day cycle, the period of maximal fertility is roughly the midpoint of the cycle; in fact, it is not generally realized that conception must occur within a narrow period of time. The human egg starts to disintegrate shortly after it leaves the follicle, and sperm mobility is reduced in a matter of hours, although in both instances exact figures are hard to come by. Most authorities doubt whether the egg can be fertilized more than 12 to 24 hours after it leaves the follicle. Human sperm apparently lose their penetrating power after 48 hours.

Menopause

Just as menarche, or first menstruation, denotes the beginning of a woman's fertile period, menopause marks the end. Like other aspects of the female's reproductive process, menopause shows some individual variation. After age 40, as the climacteric approaches, most women evidence irregular menstrual periods. At some time between the ages of 40 and 50, menstruation stops altogether, though exceptions do occur. Reported pregnancies after age 47 are rare, however, and after 50 they can be considered freaks of nature. There are authenticated cases, nevertheless, in which individual women have given birth at the age of 57!

It should be pointed out that menopause does not necessarily denote the cessation or diminution of sexual desire. Some women do find themselves less desirous of coitus after menopause has been reached, but just as many or more seem to notice no significant change. Some women even experience an increase in sexual desire following menopause, presumably because the fear of pregnancy has been removed.

Whether human males undergo any experience comparable to the female menopause is still being debated. There is no male menopause in the sense of sperm production ceasing abruptly at a given age. As they get older, most males do experience some decline in virility, and perhaps in fertility, although the diminution is evidently more gradual than it is for females.

CONCEPTION

Fertilization is a function of the gametes, the name applied to the egg or sperm. A great many more human gametes are produced than are actually used, especially in the case of the male—a phenomenon that is quite common throughout the animal world. The ovaries of a human female contain thousands of ova, but they are in an immature state, the normal process being for one egg to ripen each menstrual cycle from puberty to menopause. Precisely which ovum ripens—out of the large supply available—is apparently a matter of chance.

By comparison, the number of male spermatozoa dwarfs the female supply, for in the course of his life the human male produces *billions* of mature gametes. As a matter of fact, there are more than enough sperm in a single human ejaculate to produce a population twice the size of the United States! And in a month or so, one human male produces sufficient numbers of spermatozoa to populate the earth

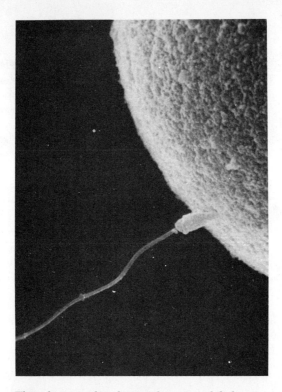

This photograph, taken with a powerful electron microscope, shows the moment of conception, as the sperm makes contact with the egg. (*D. W. Fawcett and E. Anderson*)

at its present density. All of these gametes, incidentally, could fit in a space about the size of a needle. Out of this prodigious supply, exactly which sperm, if any, fertilizes the egg is again presumably a matter of chance.

Students have sometimes raised the question "What difference does it make which sperm fertilizes which egg?" The answer is that it makes a great deal of difference. All the gametes—male and female—differ in their genetic content, and the child's physical features, native intelligence, and the presence or absence of hereditary defects all hinge on the crucial meeting of particular sperm and particular egg.

Other questions have also been raised: How do the spermatozoa locate the egg at exactly the right spot? Why isn't the egg fertilized in the ovary rather than the oviduct? Why is only *one* egg ovulated at a time, and why does only a *single* sperm penetrate the egg? And if only one ovary and oviduct function at a time, what would prevent the spermatozoa from heading toward the "wrong" ovary?

To take these questions singly, conception normally takes place in the upper portion of the oviduct. It cannot take place below this point—in the uterus or vagina, for example—because the ovum would have disintegrated. Conception can take place *above* the oviduct (i.e., in the space between ovary and oviduct). Fertilization in this area is infrequent, however, for among other things the spermatozoa are likely to lose their mobility (striking power) before this point is reached. Even if the egg is fertilized above the oviduct, the chances are that it will descend in normal fashion and implant itself in the uterine wall. Very occasionally, however, an egg fertilized above the oviduct escapes into the abdomen, with an abdominal pregnancy resulting.

Once the spermatozoa are deposited in the vaginal tract, they head in all directions. Some never leave the vagina, and some do not get past the uterus. On a probability basis, one-half of the remainder would be expected to move toward the wrong (inoperative) ovary since, so far as is known, there is no chemical attraction between sperm and egg. (Under a slide, a sperm will swim past an egg, although admittedly this situation would not necessarily obtain under natural conditions.) In any event, that conception occurs at all is due to the fact that the number of ejaculated spermatozoa is so large. In all likelihood, relatively few male gametes survive to reach the upper portion—the fertilization area—of the oviduct. And even here, the diameter of the oviduct is relatively large compared with the size of the gametes, and it is probable that some spermatozoa by-pass the egg.

As to why only *one* sperm fertilizes an egg, the answer seems to hinge on the chromosomal allotment of the species. Every species has its own number of cellular chromosomes (the diploid count), the human number being 46. However, the gametes produced in the ovaries and testes have only 23 chromosomes, the haploid count. When sperm and egg meet, the 23 chromosomes from each gamete unite to form the zygote, so that each of us starts life as a single cell with a full complement of 46 chromosomes.

If more than one sperm penetrated an egg, the "extra" chromosomes would either be unusable or, possibly, would complicate the diploid count, perhaps with dire consequences to the offspring. Therefore, as soon as one sperm enters the egg a protective membrane or coating is formed, thus preventing further penetration.

Multiple Pregnancies

Human conception normally involves one egg and one sperm, with subsequent development inside a single placental sac in the uterus. Occasionally, plural ovulation takes place—more than one egg is ovulated from the same ovary or from different ovaries—in which case multiple conception may occur. The resultant offspring are usually termed fraternal or two-egg twins. Fraternal twins may or may not be of the same sex, they develop in separate placentae, and are no more alike genetically than siblings. Identical twins, on the other hand, are the product of one sperm and egg with the original zygote splitting and ultimately forming two separate individuals. Identical twins are always of the same sex, usually share common fetal membranes, and are genetically indistinguishable. Fraternal twins, incidentally, occur about twice as often as identicals.

In recent years, modern drugs have tended to cloud the statistical picture. On the one hand, birth control pills serve to depress the figures, while fertility pills—those which *stimulate* ovulation—tend to increase the incidence of twins. Many of the "supertwins" of recent years—the triplets, quintuplets, and septulets—have been born to mothers who had been taking fertility pills.

Unfortunately, there is a high mortality rate among twins and supertwins. Among the smaller animals there is little danger, for the uterus is designed to hold

Fraternal twins. (*Christa Armstrong/Photo Researchers*)

large numbers. The tiny field mouse, for instance, has six or more litters a year, each one containing a dozen or so offspring. But in the larger animals, including humans, the uterus is geared for a single embryo, and when there are two—or four or six— prenatal conditions become somewhat "crowded." In the case of sextuplets or octuplets, for example, it is most unlikely that all the offspring will be born alive and live to adulthood.

Fetal Development

Returning now to the subject of normal conception, the subsequent development of the zygote is a truly remarkable process. At the end of the first month the embryo is approximately one-quarter of an inch in length, having increased its original weight several thousand times. Even at this early stage of development, close examination will reveal the beginnings of body, head, arms, and legs. At the end of three months the fetus has grown to some three inches in length: bones and teeth have begun to develop, sex can be determined, and spontaneous movements are occasionally made. By the fifth month the fetus is nearly a foot long and weighs about one pound. Fingernails and toenails are well developed and head hair has begun to grow.

By the seventh month the weight has increased to about three pounds, and fetal movements can easily be felt by the mother. Should birth occur at this time the child would have a chance for survival. By the ninth month—the full term—the weight is in the area of seven pounds and the length some 20 inches. From the moment of conception until full-term birth, the fetus increases in size and weight several million times!

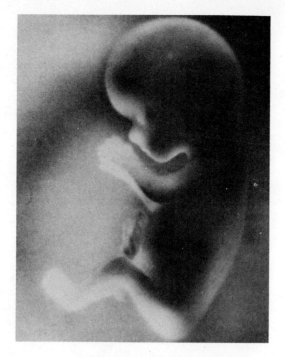

Fetus at three months. (*Wide World Photos*)

To provide for this tremendous increase, the uterus also increases to many times its original size and weight. Within the placenta, nourishment and oxygen pass from mother to offspring by a process of membranous absorption (osmosis). Note, however, that there is no direct connection between the two blood streams. The body makes its own blood and does not, as is sometimes believed, receive its supply from the mother. Nor is there a neural connection between mother and offspring. The common superstition that a prenatal experience on the part of the mother—a so-called "maternal impression"—can in some way affect the unborn child is simply a superstition. There is no known method by which such impressions can be conveyed to the fetus. The dietary condition and general physical and emotional well-being of the mother, however, may play an important part in the overall sequence of prenatal development.

It might be mentioned that, whereas the average pregnancy lasts 9 months, or approximately 273 days, there is a remarkable range of variation among human females. Some successful pregnancies have lasted less than 6 months, while others have exceeded 13!

Among the lower animals the pregnancy, or gestation, range is truly prodigious. At one mammalian extreme is the opposum—a mere 10 to 13 days. At the other is the elephant, with a gestation period of nearly 2 years. Generally speaking, the larger the animal, the longer the gestation. None of the largest animals normally have plural offspring.

Name Index

Abbott, Pamela, 168
Abramowitz, S. I., 16
Acock, Alan C., 236, 292, 298, 299
Adams, Bert, 247, 248
Adams, Rebecca G., 315
Agresti, Barbara Finlay, 142
Ahrons, Constance R., 292, 298
Aidala, Angela A., 351, 353
Aizenberg, Rhonda, 308, 309
Aldous, Joan, 310, 315
Alford, P., 259
Allen, Katherine R., 353
Allen, Michael Patrick, 168
Allison, Paul D., 298
Alvirez, David, 131
Alwin, Duane F., 168
Ambert, Ann-Marie, 298
Amick, Angelynne E., 219
Amin, Ruhul, 149
Amman, Jacob, 105, 107, 108, 109, 115
Anderson, Carrie, 220, 259
Arcus, Margaret, 363
Ariès, Philippe, 38, 55
Armstrong, Penny, 131
Asmundsson, Rigmor, 298
Astor (moneyed class), 152
Atkinson, Clarissa W., 55
Atkinson, Jean, 258
Atkinson, Maxine P., 73, 187
Auletta, Ken, 168
Axelson, Leland, 363

Bach, Robert L., 126
Bachrach, Christine A., 209

Bahr, Howard M., 121
Bailey, Wilford C., 147
Baker, David P., 15
Balswick, Jack O., 289
Barnes, Annie S., 148, 149
Barnes, M., 187
Barrett, Paul T., 175
Barth, Richard P., 227, 235
Basavarajappa, K. G., 187
Bausano, Mary, 104
Bean, Frank D., 131
Beck, Rubye W., 149
Beck, Scott H., 149
Beeghley, Leonard, 157, 168
Bejin, A., 55
Bell, Nancy J., 299
Bell, Susan Groag, 55
Beller, Andrea H., 16, 237
Bengtson, V. L., 16
Bennett, Judith M., 55
Bennett, Neil G., 344, 353
Bennett, William J., 9, 15
Berger, Bennett M., 103
Berger, Eugenia H., 15
Bernard, Russell H., 34, 120, 131
Bernikow, Louise, 353
Biddle (moneyed class), 152, 153
Bigner, Jerry J., 271
Billy, John O. G., 231
Bingham, Raymond, 220
Birrn, James E., 309
Blackburn, George, 149
Blackwell, James E., 149
Blanc, Ann K., 344, 353
Blankenship, Virginia, 252

381

Subject Index